Advance praise for James Risen's

THE LAST HONEST MAN

"James Risen is one of our country's greatest investigative reporters, and Frank Church, the senator at the heart of this book, is an American icon — a man of supreme confidence, integrity, and wisdom. The dark truths he exposed about America's spy agencies are shocking even by today's standards. A gripping book, *The Last Honest Man* is a spectacular piece of reporting that reads like a spy novel with the eloquence of great history."   — **Ken Burns**

"*The Last Honest Man* is a vitally important, timely story about how our elected politicians — few of them perfect — can protect us from tyranny by insisting that presidents, spies, and generals follow the law. It is also a ripping good read: a Washington thriller that reliably sorts fact from myth about the Mafia, JFK, and the CIA, while re-investigating improbable episodes of a tumultuous era."

— **Steve Coll, Pulitzer Prize–winning author of**
Ghost Wars: The Secret History of the CIA, Afghanistan,
and Bin Laden, from the Soviet Invasion to September
10, 2001 **and** *Directorate S: The C.I.A. and America's*
Secret Wars in Afghanistan and Pakistan

"*The Last Honest Man* is an urgent reminder about the power of telling the truth in a world increasingly filled with lies. We have never needed Frank Church — or James Risen — more."

— **Nicholas Pileggi,** *New York Times*
bestselling author of *Wiseguy* **and** *Casino*

"James Risen's engrossing book is more than a biography of a hugely significant senator, more than the resurrection of one of the most influential congressional committees of the 20th century, and more than a colorful tour of the CIA's assassination plots, mafia ties, and outrageous mind control experiments. It's a vivid reminder that American democracy is always fragile."

— **Jonathan Alter,** *New York Times* **bestselling**
author of *The Defining Moment: FDR's Hundred Days and*
the Triumph of Hope **and** *His Very Best: Jimmy Carter, a Life*

"In a time when our entire American legislative apparatus has been swallowed whole into a gaping maw of partisan venality and metastasizing ignorance, it is astonishing to encounter a narrative in which a United States senator uses actual oversight of an actual, fundamental problem to make us a better nation. But once upon a time, Frank Church did precisely that. In *The Last Honest Man*, James Risen tells the tale with precision and insight."

— **David Simon, creator of *The Wire***

"This new biography of one of the Senate's most principled and effectual bulwarks against America's warfare state, by one of America's greatest investigative reporters, couldn't be more engrossing. And as we finally come up for air after a generation of disastrous war, it couldn't be more important."

— **Rick Perlstein, *New York Times* bestselling author of *Nixonland: The Rise of a President and the Fracturing of America*, *The Invisible Bridge: The Fall of Nixon and the Rise of Reagan*, and *Reaganland: America's Right Turn 1976–1980***

"A timely and long overdue reassessment of perhaps the most important congressional investigation of the last century, *The Last Honest Man* resurrects Frank Church and reveals his quest to expose and remedy the overreach of US intelligence agencies before 1975. This book should be required reading for any elected official seeking to pick up where Church & Co. left off nearly fifty years ago."

— **Tom O'Neill, author of *Chaos: Charles Manson, the CIA, and the Secret History of the Sixties***

"With *The Last Honest Man*, James Risen has proven himself to be not just one of America's greatest investigative reporters but also a great modern historian. And his cast of characters in this page-turner could not be any richer: from its protagonist, Senator Frank Church, one of the most consequential lawmakers of the 20th century, to Kennedy, Nixon, and J. Edgar Hoover and from Martin Luther King Jr. to mobster Sam Giancana to the CIA's notorious 'poisoner in chief,' the sinister Dr. Sidney Gottlieb. Above all else, Risen documents the outrageous abuses of government power that the Church

Committee exposed, especially at the CIA and FBI — crimes, and disclosures, that continue to shape our world today."

— Philip Shenon, New York Times bestselling
author of A Cruel and Shocking Act: The Secret
History of the Kennedy Assassination

"James Risen has at last brought us the richly reported biography that Frank Church, one of the most consequential senators of the 20th century, deserves. At a time when so many lawmakers are predictably partisan and deferential to the executive branch, Risen reminds us of another era: when a liberal could represent Idaho, a Democrat could challenge his own party's presidents, and a senator could assert Congress's role in national security."

— Jonathan Martin, New York Times bestselling
co-author of This Will Not Pass: Trump, Biden,
and the Battle For America's Future

THE LAST HONEST MAN

THE CIA, THE FBI, THE MAFIA, AND THE KENNEDYS — AND ONE SENATOR'S FIGHT TO SAVE DEMOCRACY

BY
JAMES RISEN

WITH
THOMAS RISEN

LITTLE, BROWN AND COMPANY
NEW YORK   BOSTON   LONDON

To Penny and Amanda

Little, Brown and Company
Hachette Book Group
1290 Avenue of the Americas, New York, NY 10104
littlebrown.com

First Edition: May 2023

Little, Brown and Company is a division of Hachette Book Group, Inc.
The Little, Brown name and logo are trademarks of Hachette Book Group, Inc.

The publisher is not responsible for websites (or their content)
that are not owned by the publisher.

The Hachette Speakers Bureau provides a wide range of authors for speaking events. To find out more, go to hachettespeakersbureau.com or email HachetteSpeakers@hbgusa.com.

ISBN 9780316565134
Library of Congress Control Number: 2022952283

Printing 1, 2023

LSC-C

Printed in the United States of America

Contents

A Note on Sources   *xi*

PROLOGUE: *"Senator Cathedral"*   3

PART ONE   "If I make no mark elsewhere" (1924–1975)

1	*"Happier times"*	17
2	*"The finest diction in the Army"*	29
3	*"If you don't run you will never get there"*	41
4	*"Persona non grata"*	54
5	*"A betrayal"*	65
6	*"War prolonged and unending"*	85
7	*"We stand up now"*	103
8	*"An enormous hue and cry"*	118
9	*"As long as the KGB does it"*	130
10	*"We have stood watch"*	143
11	*"This will cost you the presidency"*	156

CONTENTS

PART TWO "We doubt that any other country would have the courage" (1975)

12 *"A delicate balance"* 171

13 *"The dirty facts"* 180

14 *"Like what?" "Like assassinations."* 195

15 *"I had been asked by my government to solicit his cooperation"* 204

16 *"Who will rid me of this man?"* 218

17 *"The White House, can I help you?"* 229

18 *"We met your man in the Congo"* 247

19 *"What the president wanted to happen"* 265

20 *"The abyss from which there is no return"* 270

21 *"Under a double shadow"* 284

22 *"The man who made a police state out of America"* 297

23 *"No holds were barred"* 306

PART THREE "A volcano cannot be capped" (1975–1984)

24 *"Vindicated and pleased"* 327

25 *"As dangerous as any stimulant"* 335

26 *"One more service to render"* 346

27 *"I see you have a presidential haircut"* 358

28 *"And then it was over"* 368

29 *"I've got to do it"* 382

EPILOGUE *"They did great damage"* 400

CONTENTS

Acknowledgments 408

Illustration credits 409

Bibliography 413

Notes 423

Index 449

A Note on Sources

THE LAST HONEST MAN is the product of hundreds of interviews with former Church Committee members and staffers, former intelligence officials, Church family members and friends, and many others knowledgeable about Frank Church and the Church Committee. The book also relies on thousands of pages of recently declassified documents, unpublished personal letters, notes and memoirs, as well as other materials, including some quite sensitive that have never before been reviewed by authors or other outsiders, all of which shed light on Frank Church and the Church Committee.

THE LAST HONEST MAN

Prologue

"Senator Cathedral"

"HAVE YOU BROUGHT with you some of those devices which would have enabled the CIA to use this poison for killing people?" Senator Frank Church, dressed in a dark brown suit with a color-splashed designer tie, stares out into the Senate Caucus Room and, employing the precise diction that is his trademark, questions William Colby, the director of the Central Intelligence Agency.

It is September 16, 1975, and the first public hearing of the Church Committee has just begun. The history-drenched Senate Caucus Room in the Russell Senate Office Building, where the Senate Watergate Committee had previously held its hearings and where John Kennedy and Robert Kennedy had both announced their presidential campaigns, is buzzing. Committee staffers crowd into seats just behind the senators sitting along the long dais at one end of the room, while reporters covering the hearing huddle together at a press table within arm's length of Colby and the witness table. The television lights are so bright that some committee staffers and reporters are wearing sunglasses.

The subject of the hearing is an investigation into why the CIA secretly stored a cache of lethal shellfish toxin for use in assassinations despite a presidential order to destroy it. Church has just asked Colby to show him what kind of weapon a CIA assassin would use to fire the toxin at a victim.

"We have indeed," replies Colby, staring unsmilingly right back at Church from behind his glasses, carefully combed hair, and light tailored suit. Colby sits up straight at the witness table, looking unbearably WASPish while trying to ignore the reporters and photographers crowding around him.

Mitchell Rogovin, a dark-haired, left-leaning civil liberties lawyer hired by Colby to be a special counsel to the CIA specifically to deal with the Democratic-controlled Church Committee, takes out a strangely designed, battery-operated pistol, shaped like a .45 handgun with a large sight attached atop its barrel. He walks up to the dais and lays the gun in front of Church.

"Don't point it at me," Church jokes to Rogovin.

Church reaches across the wide table for it, but can't quite get it. "I wonder if…" Church asks, his voice trailing off.

F. A. O. "Fritz" Schwarz, the Church Committee's chief counsel, wearing a gray-green suit and sitting to the right of Church, realizes Church wants him to get the gun, and quietly asks Rogovin to push it his way. "Mitch, could you roll it over a little bit?" Rogovin slides the pistol across the table to Schwarz, along with the dart that is fired by the gun. Schwarz then picks up the gun and dart and hands them to Church.

Senator Frank Church holds up a CIA dart gun at the beginning of the Church Committee's first public hearing in September 1975. Beside Church is Senator John Tower of Texas, the top Republican on the Church Committee.

Church holds up the gun in his left hand, pointing it toward the ceiling, his finger off the trigger. John Tower, the committee's ranking Republican, sitting on Church's left, stares at the gun as Church holds it aloft. News photographers, kneeling just in front of the committee dais, quickly go to work, taking shot after shot of Church holding up the dart gun.

The next day, the photograph of Frank Church holding up the dart gun is splashed across the front pages of newspapers throughout the United States. The photo becomes the iconic image of the Church Committee. It is the image of Frank Church that history remembers.

* * *

In September 1975, Frank Church was taking his star turn.

After months of intense investigative legwork, closed hearings, fights with the White House, internal committee politicking, and overwhelming press attention — all on a $2.25 million budget — the Church Committee was finally going public. Over three days in mid-September, the Church Committee, which was conducting the first major congressional investigation into decades of abuses committed by the CIA, the Federal Bureau of Investigation, the National Security Agency, and the rest of the United States intelligence community, was holding its first public hearings, in between two assassination attempts on President Ford, the arrest of Patricia Hearst, and the premiere of *Three Days of the Condor,* a dark Robert Redford movie featuring rogue hit men inside the CIA.

The hearings showcased the two sides of Frank Church: the ambitious, publicity-seeking politician yearning for acceptance in Washington — the Frank Church who knew that holding up the dart gun would generate buzz and headlines — and the radicalized outsider who hated the Washington establishment, the Frank Church who despised the American imperialism represented by a spy agency prepared to kill foreign leaders with toxin-filled darts. Days before the public hearings began, Church offered a preview with a jeremiad against the rise of American militarism, which he believed had enabled the intelligence community's abuses that he was investigating, and which he now was convinced threatened to lead to dictatorship.

"I think perhaps our addiction to war in the last thirty years has had something to do with [CIA abuses]," Church said in an appearance before the Women's National Democratic Club on September 8, 1975. "We've engaged in more active warfare than any other nation in the world, and that has a certain brutalizing effect."

Yet despite Church's deeply felt need to overturn the status quo in Washington's national security establishment, his hunger for acceptance and headlines was never far away. After the first public hearing, Church privately told his aide Loch Johnson how pleased he was with the publicity garnered by the dart gun. Church thought that "displaying the exotic weapon provided a bit of drama that the committee needed to focus attention on the need for intelligence reform," recalled Johnson.

Before the hearing, by contrast, CIA director Colby had recognized that the dart gun could be a potential public relations disaster for the Agency, and had resisted Church's demands that he bring it with him when he testified. Church Committee staffer Paul Michel was assigned to force the CIA to bring it. Michel told Sayre Stevens, a top Colby aide, that "we wanted the dart gun at the hearing," Michel recalled in an interview. "Stephens and the other officials at the CIA were not happy about that at all. I told them that when director Colby comes [to the committee hearing], the gun comes too. The gun will be subpoenaed if you don't."

Colby relented. He later credited Rogovin for grabbing the dart gun and passing it to Church, so that "I, as the director of the CIA, wasn't photographed holding the weapon."

The press covering the Church Committee saw only this publicity-seeking side of Frank Church. They never recognized his radical side — probably because most reporters didn't listen or pay attention to what he actually said during his speeches and other public remarks. That helped create a media narrative that sought to dismiss the Church Committee's public hearings as nothing more than a platform for Frank Church's long-rumored presidential bid.

Yet gradually, as the public hearings continued from September until they finished in December, the scale of the illegal activities and abuses of the intelligence community came into greater focus, even as the questions about the political purposes behind the Church Committee never really went away.

The public hearings forced officials from the CIA — and from the FBI, the NSA, and other agencies — to go on the record about past abuses in ways they never had before. In the process, the hearings provided an unprecedented forum for a national debate on the proper limits of the power of the government's dark side, which for decades had undergone uncontrolled growth with little outside scrutiny. The hearings would also prove to be the high-water mark of Frank Church's career.

* * *

The year 1975 brought America the first summer movie blockbuster, *Jaws;* the disappearance of Jimmy Hoffa, the former Teamsters leader who had crossed the Mafia; and the release of Bruce Springsteen's breakthrough album, *Born to Run.* Saigon fell to the North Vietnamese at the end of April, disco was heating up, and in America it felt like the 1960s were finally over.

It was also the year of Frank Church.

During 1975, Frank Church, like an American Cicero, offered the United States a brief glimpse of what it would be like to turn away from its imperialistic ambitions, which had darkly surfaced during the Cold War, and return to its roots as a republic.

Church had briefly gained fame before; the Democratic senator from Idaho had led the congressional opposition to the long and grinding war in Vietnam. But 1975 was the moment he became a cultural icon.

In 1975, Frank Church was the chairman of what was officially known as the Senate Select Committee to Study Governmental Operations with Respect to Intelligence Activities — but what is known to history as the Church Committee. At a critical, progressive moment in the mid-1970s, Frank Church led the Church Committee's unprecedented effort to unearth decades of abusive and illegal acts secretly committed by the United States government, then sought to curb the government's power ever to commit such illegal acts again.

By 1975, Frank Church had come to believe that the future of American democracy was threatened by the rise of a permanent and largely unaccountable national security state, and he sensed that at the heart of that secret government was a lawless intelligence community. In order to save the nation, Church was convinced, America's spy agencies would have to be reined in.

To a great degree, he succeeded. By disclosing a series of shocking abuses of power and spearheading wide-ranging reforms, Frank Church created the rules of the road for the intelligence community that largely remain in place today. More than anyone else in American history, Frank Church is responsible for bringing the CIA, the FBI, the NSA, and the rest of the government's intelligence apparatus under the rule of law for the first time.

This is the story of that remarkable moment — and of the man who seized it.

* * *

During 1975, Frank Church came to be seen by the public as America's chief investigator, the man who was revealing the nation's darkest secrets — secrets that, in turn, could help explain how the nation had lost its way in the decades since World War II. Frank Church became a symbolic figure standing at the crossroads between national security and civil liberties. Depending on how they viewed the proper balance between the two, Americans grew to either love him or hate him.

Throughout that year, network television and newspapers were filled with stories about Frank Church and his investigations. Not only was the Church Committee launching its landmark inquiries of the CIA, FBI, and NSA, but another committee led by Church was making headlines with its investigations of corporate bribes of foreign leaders by some of America's biggest companies. Stories about Frank Church's many investigations vied for space on the front page of the *New York Times*. Reporters were constantly on Church's heels, seeking his comments not only about his own investigations but also about the constant stream of stories about the CIA and FBI being published by many of the nation's top investigative reporters, who themselves struggled to keep up with the rapid-fire disclosures coming out of the Church Committee.

Frank Church wasn't president, but for a brief moment in 1975, he was something close to it.

His whole life had been leading up to this moment, and 1975 brought out Frank Church's best — as well as his worst.

Frank Church had many flaws. He suffered from political ambition that was sometimes blinding. He was a publicity hound with a careful, studied speaking style that could make him seem pretentious and arrogant; he earned the nickname "Senator Cathedral."

Senator Frank Church

Other senators often didn't trust that he would fulfill his private promises, suspecting that he would instead find legalistic ways out of his commitments. But he was an honest man at heart. And his integrity would drive his life's work: trying to save the American republic from what he feared most, its transformation into a dangerous, militaristic empire.

Frank Church refused to conform to the Washington establishment's confident belief in American interventionism. Instead he was convinced that the nation had lost its way in the decades after World War II through the creation of an unaccountable national security state that pushed the United States into endless wars abroad and threatened democracy by stifling dissent and suppressing civil liberties at home. His core belief that America had strayed from its republican roots animated Church's politics, but that belief went so far beyond the bounds of accepted establishment thinking in the mid-20th century that most of his critics in Washington ignored what Church actually said about it. Instead, they sought to diminish him by focusing on his overly precise diction and his naked presidential ambition. As a result, they missed the man.

* * *

Church's iconoclastic thinking, as well as his signal achievements, were shaped by his life leading up to his walk into history in 1975.

He was shaped by Idaho, where he grew up; by China, where he served in World War II; by Bethine Clark, the politically savvy daughter of the governor of Idaho who became his wife; by cancer, which he barely survived as a young man; and by the Senate. But mostly, he was changed by the Vietnam War.

He was born in one of the most isolated places in an isolationist America in the 1920s, a country with few international commitments and no significant, permanent national security establishment. But his life, and the country, would be radically altered two decades later, when Church came of age as an Army intelligence officer serving half a world away in China during World War II, just as the United States was suddenly being transformed into a global superpower.

During the final days of World War II, Church first began to express his fears over what he saw as America's new imperial ambitions. He was unnerved by the elation other Americans serving with him in the Army in China exhibited after the dropping of the atomic bombs on Hiroshima and Nagasaki. He personally witnessed the Japanese surrender in China, and was disgusted that the United States had so closely allied itself with a corrupt warlord like Chinese nationalist leader Chiang Kai-shek.

He won his first Senate race in 1956 when he was just 32, and when he arrived in Washington he was viewed by the political elite as little more than a boy, in over his head. Lyndon Johnson, the Texas Democrat who was then the Senate Majority Leader, mercilessly schooled Church.

In his first few years in the Senate, Frank Church consciously positioned himself in the mainstream of the Democratic Party of the 1950s, liberal with a tinge of Cold War hawkishness, styling himself after his friend, the senator and later president John F. Kennedy.

But during the 1960s and the early 1970s, the Vietnam War revived Church's skepticism about American imperial overreach. For Church, Vietnam brought back memories of China, of American support for a corrupt regime, and he turned against the war long before almost any other major American political figure. Church emerged as an early advocate for congressional hearings on U.S. policy in Vietnam at a time when official Washington still considered any questioning of the war disloyal heresy. In the process, he helped change the national debate about the war and gave mainstream legitimacy to the anti-war movement.

As the war ground on and American casualties mounted, Church experienced a more fundamental political transformation: he lost his belief that the United States was always a force for good in the world, and he came to see the Vietnam War as a symptom of the uncontrolled power of a national security state that had grown beyond recognition.

By the 1970s, Church had become a radical in the Senate. He wanted to overthrow the status quo in American national security policy, despite the obvious political risks for a senator from one of the most conservative and rural states in the nation.

Church finally helped to stop the Vietnam War by repeatedly pushing Congress to use its power of the purse to threaten to cut off funding for the conflict. The growing popularity of Church's legislative solution to end the war helped force President Richard Nixon to negotiate a peace agreement.

But unlike so many others in Washington, Church wasn't willing to return to the status quo after Vietnam. He began to investigate the sources of economic and political power that he believed had led the nation into Vietnam, and which he believed were still perverting U.S. foreign policy. He launched a landmark investigation into the rising global power of America's corporate giants, and the trail he followed ultimately led him to a much broader investigation of the CIA.

*　　*　　*

Until he began to investigate the Agency, Frank Church knew little about the shape, scope, and power of the modern CIA. His own experience in Army intelligence in World War II offered him no insight into the comprehensive transformation the CIA had undergone in the decades since its postwar founding. In fact, few in Congress at the time knew much about the CIA, since there was virtually no congressional oversight of the spy agency or of the rest of the intelligence community.

When the Church Committee began to investigate the CIA, FBI, NSA, and other agencies, it marked the first time there had been any serious congressional inquiry into the national security state. As a result, the Church Committee's hearings became something like a constitutional convention, airing basic questions about the proper balance between liberty and security.

It was a watershed moment in American history. By bringing the intelligence community under the rule of law and imposing congressional oversight for the first time, Frank Church made sure there was no permanent "Deep State" — a hidden and unaccountable national security hierarchy — within the American government. The Deep State remains a myth, a right-wing conspiracy theory, precisely because Frank Church brought the intelligence community fully into the American system of government. Ever since the Church Committee completed its work, histories of the CIA, the FBI, and the NSA have been divided between what they managed to get away with before the Church Committee and what they have been allowed to do since.

Church's historic achievement — bringing the intelligence community under the rule of law — did not come easily. Three Church Committee witnesses were murdered, including one before he could testify. No one has ever been able to determine whether any of them were killed because they talked — or were planning to talk — to the committee. But the coincidences kept piling up, and the killings brought an unnerving sense of danger to the Church Committee.

Church's achievement was also not inevitable. Many others in Congress had tried and failed to rein in the intelligence community before him, going back to the days right after the CIA was founded in the wake of World War II. Those earlier failures had led to decades without any independent oversight or meaningful legal controls on the intelligence community's behavior. Lax controls allowed the CIA in particular to be turned into a dangerous weapon, one often wielded by presidents in ways that the American people didn't approve — or even know about.

Without oversight, the CIA and the rest of the intelligence community had grown into a secret government-within-a-government. That growth had rapidly accelerated in the 1950s under President Dwight D. Eisenhower, who came to view global covert operations conducted by the CIA as an essential substitute for all-out war. He wanted to challenge the Soviet Union in the Cold War without a direct military confrontation, and the CIA became his primary tool for doing so.

Eisenhower set the pattern for the CIA's dark future by directing the Agency to help stage coups in Iran and Guatemala, while also trying to overthrow foreign leaders in countries from the Congo to

Cuba. In return for these risky, high-stakes covert actions, Eisenhower had given the CIA enormous freedom to act, and Allen Dulles, his CIA director, took full advantage of Eisenhower's loose supervision. That led the CIA to commit other horrific abuses with little presidential oversight, notably surreal mind-control programs that relied on the drugging of countless unwitting American citizens.

Like Eisenhower, his successors found the CIA a tempting secret weapon, and presidents from Kennedy to Nixon continued to use the Agency's covert-action arm whenever diplomacy became too difficult or too awkward. And, just like Eisenhower, none of them ever imposed much scrutiny on any of the Agency's operations, except when something went spectacularly and publicly wrong, like the Bay of Pigs fiasco in Cuba or the downing of a U-2 spy plane by the Soviets.

For decades as a result, the CIA's operations faced only glancing scrutiny from the White House, and virtually none from Congress. True oversight would have to wait until 1975 — and the arrival on the national stage of a senator from Idaho named Frank Church.

PART ONE

"If I make no mark elsewhere"

1924–1975

CHAPTER 1

"Happier Times"

THE EDITOR AT the *Boise Capital News* had to double-check the name on the letter he had just read. It was April 1939, and the letter, which had recently arrived at the newspaper offices, was a well-crafted, deeply informed defense of the isolationism of Idaho's Senator William Borah—an argument for why the United States should stay out of another war as storm clouds gathered over Europe.

Could this really have been written by a 14-year-old?

The editor checked and discovered to his amazement that the letter really had been written by an eighth grader at North Junior High School, a boy by the name of Frank Church. Impressed, the editor published Church's letter on the newspaper's front page.

The newspaper soon received several letters from readers who couldn't believe the front-page letter had been written by a boy in junior high school, so the Boise paper ran a follow-up letter from Church's social studies teacher confirming that he was indeed the author. "I remember my father reading it and coming out of his chair, demanding to know what impudence led me to believe I had the right to publish a letter in the newspaper without first consulting him," Church later recalled.

But Church's father, a tradition-bound Catholic shopkeeper, would never be able to rein in his son's ambitions, which would soon range far beyond Boise and the Mountain West.

*　*　*

Frank Forrester Church III was always considered special.

He was always the smartest kid in school; he was so affable that he attracted friends easily, and he spoke and wrote more clearly than most adults. Frank Church always stood out, especially in a state that was then so empty it had far more sheep than people.

He was born on July 25, 1924, in Boise, which was then a small city — really not much more than a small town — of just 20,000 in one of the most remote regions of the United States. Boise was the capital of Idaho, a state that itself was something of an afterthought in the Anglo-American settlement of the West in the 19th century, and one of the only states settled from the West as well as the East.

Long before modern irrigation techniques transformed it into an agricultural center, much of southern Idaho was a desert, to be crossed as quickly as possible by people following the Oregon Trail to the West Coast. Settlers finally stopped ignoring Idaho and came flooding back from California and the rest of the country when gold was discovered in the territory in 1860, and again in 1883. Gold attracted an odd assortment; the early settlers included Mormons coming north from Utah, as well as a large cohort of defeated Southern Confederates looking for quick riches and a place as far away from the influence of the victorious Union as possible. Booming lead, silver, and gold mining in northern Idaho brought an influx of miners, including many immigrants from Ireland and elsewhere, while oppressive practices by mine owners led to strikes, violence, and union organizing. Many of the early Irish immigrant miners clashed with their English-immigrant supervisors; that gave an ugly English-Irish dynamic to some of the early minefield wars.

Idaho's politics became a volatile and toxic mix in the late 19th and early 20th centuries, an era that climaxed with the assassination of former governor Frank Steunenberg in 1905. The sensational trial that followed, in which prominent union leaders were accused of being complicit in the murder, was one of the most celebrated in American history; the trial was in effect a proxy fight for control over the minefields of the Mountain West between the forces of labor and management. The rise of a unionized workforce in the northern minefields — where lead and silver mining eventually came to dominate—gave Idaho's politics a raucous edge in the first decades of the 20th century, even as the state grew beyond the earlier minefield wars and became increasingly conservative.

Idaho had been a state for only 34 years by the time Frank Church was born, but he was already the third Frank Church to live there. His grandfather, also Frank Forrester Church, was lured by gold; he was enough of a risk-taker to leave his home in Maine for Idaho's goldfields in 1871. He left Idaho briefly to study mineralogy, but only so that he could return and advance on the technical side of the mining industry. He came back to the mining boomtown of Idaho City to work in the assay office, which handled the critical task of measuring the purity and content of the gold dug by miners. He also entered local Democratic Party politics, and in 1893 was rewarded by President Grover Cleveland, who appointed him assayer in charge of the U.S. Assay Office in Boise, a plum bit of political patronage.

Frank Forrester Church Jr.—Frank Church's father—was born in 1890; he was a short, balding, heavy-set Catholic with a shopkeeper's cautious personality, with none of his father's sense of adventure or political drive. In 1913 he married Laura Bilderback, who was more attractive and outgoing than her husband, and who also had a better sense of humor. By the 1920s, Frank Church owned his own sporting-goods store in Boise.

The genes seemed to have skipped a generation; Frank Forrester Church III was much more like his grandfather than his own father— with a touch of his mother's urbane personality mixed in. Apart from being Frank Church's foil—his conservative Republicanism seems to have helped drive his son in the opposite direction—his father had only a limited impact on Church's personality and growth.

Frank Church was the namesake of his father and grandfather even though he was the second son. His brother, Richard, was nearly nine years older—and, like their father, played only a limited role in Frank Church's early life. In fact, one of the remarkable aspects of Church's life is that it is difficult to identify ways in which he was shaped in his childhood and teenage years by his family. His mother certainly influenced his personality more than his father, but it was hard to discern where his intelligence and early interest in the wider world came from. It was one reason why he was considered so remarkable at such a young age: no one really knew what to make of his unique attributes.

A young Frank Church (right) with his mother,
Laura, and his older brother, Richard.

Frank was sick during much of his childhood, suffering frequent bouts of bronchitis and sinusitis. He started at a Catholic elementary school but was ill-suited to its narrow, strict parochial
teaching. Though Frank was naturally left-handed, the nuns at his
school tried to force him to do everything right-handed, and he
became ambidextrous as a result. His older brother's biggest impact
on Frank's life came when he persuaded their father to transfer
Frank to public school; Frank flourished in the more open environment. (Richard Church went on to a career as an officer in the
Marine Corps.)

The Church family generally enjoyed a comfortable middle-
class life, but when Frank was growing up in the midst of the
Depression of the 1930s, they were forced to cut corners by renting
out the upstairs floor of their home. By the time he was a teenager
and the Depression was easing, the Church family often spent summers at a cabin on Warm Lake, Idaho, about 100 miles north of
Boise. His father's sporting-goods store sold fireworks, and on the

Fourth of July his father would take Frank and his friends to shoot off all of the unsold fireworks in a spectacular display.

Frank's father was not much of a hunter and didn't teach his son — a notable failing in early-20th-century Idaho. Frank learned to hunt and fish mostly from the father of one of his childhood friends, but never really took to it. He had almost no athletic ability, and showed little interest in sports, apart from occasionally playing tennis. Frank Church was an oddity — a city kid at heart who just happened to have been born in the Mountain West. "He was not a great hiker or camper," observed his son, Chase Church.

While he was an indifferent outdoorsman, he excelled at school, once he got away from the nuns. No one else in his school even came close. It was the world of the mind and of words and language that attracted Church. "He seemed to be a star from the moment he started school," LeRoy Ashby, coauthor of a well-crafted 1994 biography of Church, said in an interview. "Teachers looked to him as a model."

Inevitably, some of the other kids resented Church for being a teacher's pet who was constantly showing off his smarts; they believed he could get away with things that they could not. In middle school, for example, he poked a girl sitting in front of him in the rear end with a pen, and she turned around and hit him. Yet she was the one suspended from school; the teacher simply couldn't believe that Frank Church would have done anything to provoke her.

Frank Church may have been a teacher's pet, but his brains were undeniable. His teachers realized that he was unique, and eventually most of his classmates saw that his intelligence demanded respect. He had a good sense of humor, inherited from his mother, and by high school was at the center of a large circle of friends who hung out in downtown Boise, and he was easily elected student body president. "Frank took after her (Laura Church) personality-wise," recalled Stan Burns, a boyhood friend.

Church's father was politically conservative and deeply religious, but as he grew, Frank Church turned away from both the Republican Party and the Catholic Church. It was as if he was rejecting his father and the confined life his father symbolized for him.

Frank Church later liked to tell the story that his father's Republicanism had inadvertently led him to the Democratic Party. His father enjoyed debating politics with his son, and to keep up, Frank would often go to the local library to do research so that he could argue the Democratic point of view, supporting Franklin Roosevelt and the New Deal, against his father's Republicanism. Church later joked that the research stuck, and he became a lifelong Democrat in one of the most solidly Republican states in the nation.

"His father hated Roosevelt with a passion," recalled Carl Burke, Church's best friend growing up in Boise. "Those were bitter debates."

"He liked to argue, he was good at it...his father would delight in taking him on," recalled Stan Burns. "You could see Frank's intellectual superiority...he had this really magnetic personality."

*   *   *

He was so serious about politics and intellectual pursuits as a young boy that Frank Church's role model was not a football player or a Hollywood star, but William Borah, the senator whom he had stoutly defended in his remarkable letter to the *Boise Capital News*. Not only was Borah the first public figure to have an impact on Church's life, but he would shadow Church throughout his career.

Borah was an iconic figure who dominated Idaho politics for a generation, yet he was still an odd choice as a role model for a teenager who was evolving into a Roosevelt Democrat. Borah was very complicated, both as a politician and as a man. He first gained fame as part of the prosecution team in the high-profile 1907 trial of the labor leaders accused of involvement in the Steunenberg assassination. Borah faced off against legendary defense attorney Clarence Darrow, who won the acquittals of the labor leaders; even though he lost, Borah's handling of the case attracted national headlines just as he began his long career in the Senate.

Borah went on to become Idaho's longest-serving senator; he was hailed as a progressive early in his career, when he pushed for the creation of the graduated income tax and the direct election of U.S. senators, who had previously been appointed by state legislatures. Yet he later became an isolationist, leading the fatal opposition to the League of Nations after World War I and the American turn inward in the 1920s and 1930s, which enabled the unimpeded rise of Hitler and fascism. The ugliest chapter in his career came in the early 1920s, when he joined forces with Southern Democrats to defeat federal legislation to outlaw lynching.

Borah also had an intense affair with Alice Roosevelt Longworth, the celebrity daughter of Teddy Roosevelt, while they were both married; her husband became Speaker of the House. Borah is believed to be the father of Alice Roosevelt Longworth's only child, whom she once cleverly called "Aurora Borah Alice."

In 1940, Church — a 15-year-old boy still unaware of his hero's flaws — went to the state capitol in Boise to pay homage after Borah died and was lying in state. Later, during his time in the Senate, Church would frequently and very publicly cite Borah as his role model, even keeping a portrait of Borah prominently displayed in his Senate office and arranging for another Borah portrait to hang in the offices of the Senate Foreign Relations Committee, which Borah had chaired.

But those close to him believe that by then, Church had long since outgrown his boyhood adulation of Borah, and that he continued to publicly embrace him while serving in the Senate simply because it was good politics in Idaho. "I always thought it made a good campaign [slogan]," said Stan Burns. "I never believed it...I think it served Frank's purpose politically to say that someday he hoped to be the equal of Senator Borah."

Early in his Senate career, in fact, Church privately learned some harsh facts that further tarnished his image of Borah. When Church went to pay his respects to Borah's widow, Mary McConnell Borah, at her Washington apartment, she enjoyed the attention and began to reveal how she had made ends meet after Borah's death. "She said that after the funeral, she didn't have any money, but then she found boxes of cash that he had hidden," recalled Bryce Nelson, an aide who went with Church to meet her. It became clear to Church that Borah had been corrupt, which seemed to confirm gossip he heard separately in the Senate. "That made Church think differently about Borah," Nelson remembered.

Church never publicly discussed what he had learned about Borah from his widow — who would live to be 105. A decade before her 1976 death, Church helped her move into a nursing home in Oregon; he sought to help Borah's widow again in 1969, when she was unable to pay her nursing-home bills.

*   *   *

It was in public speaking and debate that the young Frank Church most took after Borah, who was considered one of the great orators of his day. (Borah's two-hour speech against the League of Nations on the Senate floor on November 19, 1919, was long deemed one of the greatest speeches in Senate history, even if it advanced the ill-fated cause of isolationism.) Like Borah, Church loved to play with words; in high school, he would often practice public speaking alone in front of his mirror at home. His speech teacher called him a natural, and with Church leading the way, the Boise High School debate team won the state championship. Soon, his debating skills would give Church his first opportunity to see the world beyond the Mountain West.

In April 1941, Church boarded an outbound train at the Union Pacific station in downtown Boise, and traveled south and east on his way to Charleston, South Carolina, where he was to compete in a national public-speaking contest for high-school students, sponsored by the American Legion. By this point, Church was fast growing into a man. He was a tall, handsome 16-year-old with dark-set eyes, dark hair, and full lips, and a frame so thin that he looked gaunt. In marked contrast to his reedy appearance, he had developed a deep, stentorian voice. But Church's speaking style was perhaps most notable for his clipped and precise diction, which suggested he was far more cosmo-politan than a teenager from Boise had any right to sound.

As Church crossed the country, he was shadowed by the threat that America might soon be dragged into World War II. Things had changed dramatically in the two years since he wrote his pro-Borah letter to the newspaper, in which he had urged America to heed the isolationist senator from Idaho and stay out of world affairs.

War was now raging in Europe, and Germany looked unstoppa-ble. France had fallen the year before, along with most of Western Europe, and now London was being bombed by the Luftwaffe. President Roosevelt had persuaded Congress to approve his Lend-Lease program to provide embattled Britain with warships, while also embarking on a major rearmament program to modernize the mor-ibund American military.

But Roosevelt knew that the American public was still reluctant to go further and enter the war on the side of the Allies. Borah con-tinued to steadfastly oppose any American involvement in the war up until his death in 1940, and Charles Lindbergh—the greatest living American hero thanks to his 1927 solo flight across the Atlantic—was helping to lead the opposition to U.S. intervention in the European war, speaking at massive rallies of the America First Committee. A poisonous brew of isolationism, anti-Semitism, and proto-fascism lingered in the political climate in the United States, despite the growing menace posed by Hitler. American politics teetered on a knife-edge.

Still just a junior at Boise High, Church had easily won the state and regional debate playoffs. Now he was one of four finalists from across the country facing off for the national championship on the campus of The Citadel, the old military college in downtown Charleston.

For the contest's championship round, Church decided to use his speech to give voice to a new generation of Americans who might have to fight a war. No longer an isolationist, he now urged a muscular American role in the world. In his first-ever public address outside Idaho, Frank Church was going to break with the political tradition of William Borah.

Church didn't want to play it safe in his speech, and so decided to take on some of the most volatile political issues roiling the nation that spring. He argued that America had to remain true to its values of democracy, civil liberties, and the rule of law in the face of unprecedented threats.

In a remarkably nuanced and thoughtful address for a 16-year-old high school junior, Church laid out a set of beliefs that would guide him for the rest of his life. His speech clearly mirrored the famous "Four Freedoms" speech that Franklin Roosevelt had delivered a few months earlier.

"During the past year, the American people have witnessed with apprehension the destruction of democracy in all parts of the world," Church began. "We have witnessed this conquest at the hands of a brutal, alien philosophy of life and we have determined, in unanimity, that the fate of France, the fate of Norway, of Belgium, and of Poland shall not be the fate of America."

In the face of this danger, Church called for a vigorous defense of "the American Way," which he defined as having three pillars: social, economic, and political freedoms.

America's social freedom, he said, stemmed from a society that was "free, classless and equal," unlike Europe's "society of privilege." But that social freedom would be worthless "in an economy where all industrial policy is decided and directed from above, and where every position, every advancement is dependent upon the whims of a political bureaucrat." Only with economic freedom could the "natural ambition to succeed" flourish in America.

Social and economic freedom would not survive, however, without political freedom, which had to be protected "against any kind of limitation."

But for all his praise for the advantages of the "American Way" over the fascist models then ascendant in Germany, Italy, and Japan, Church warned of the American system's flaws as well—particularly those that allowed elites to gain greater power, and which trampled the rights of minorities and the dispossessed.

The American system's greatest weakness, Church said, was economic concentration in the hands of a few powerful industrialists: "Monopoly alone can destroy all its advantages and inevitably results in shocking abuse of power." Only the federal government, he argued, could break the power of the monopolist, and "it must use this authority. It must wage a constant fight against abuse of power and favor justice for the common man."

Indeed, the true threat to political freedom in America came from within, Church warned, rather than from Germany or other foreign enemies. "Even at this moment an insidiously inspired propaganda campaign is causing that confusion. This campaign is being waged, not against social freedom, not against economic freedom, but against the third principle of the American way—political freedom. If this principle fails, the others shall perish; if it endures, the others will endure. The incomparable privilege of political freedom is more than majority rule or representative government. It is protection for the minority. It is the freedom granted to every individual to speak, to read, and to think as he pleases... We must respect the political freedom of every citizen and every sincere minority, for only in that manner can we protect democracy."

If America upheld its civil liberties and protected the rule of law in its Constitution, Church vowed, the United States would emerge from the coming war victorious. "If, during the crisis that confronts us, today and tomorrow, we defend social, economic and political freedom, guided by the precepts of Christian faith, we shall have maintained the American Way. Preserve, protect and defend these three principles and, no matter how dark the future may be, a united

America will move forward with unshakable courage and irresistible power toward unlimited democracy and happier times."

When he finished, Church was met by thunderous applause from an audience shocked by the eloquence of the 16-year-old from the mountains. He easily won the championship and its accompanying college scholarship, and returned to Boise a local hero. The money and stature he gained from his win would allow him to attend Stanford University.

The American Legion speech changed Frank Church's life; he was now moving quickly toward a wider world beyond Boise, beyond his father, Borah, and the narrow impulses of his state.

*　*　*

Back in Boise in his senior year of high school, Church was elected student-body president, and his political ambition began to tell. "I knew he was going to get into politics when he was president of Boise High School," Carl Burke observed.

But Church also had a mischievous side, which sometimes led him to pull elaborate pranks. After seeing a hypnotist perform, Church decided to pretend to hypnotize one of his friends, a boy named Orville Poorit. Church and his friends staged an assembly at Boise High where Church appeared to place Poorit in a trance and then stuck pins in him; the cooperative Poorit didn't flinch. So convincing was the performance that an alarmed teacher scolded Church, insisting "this evil must be stopped before it goes further." Undeterred, Church kept the ruse going for days: he arranged for Poorit to stand up in a class in a trancelike state and announce to the teacher that "Frank Church wants to see me"; moments later, Carl Burke came to the classroom to tell the teacher that "Frank Church wants to see Orville Poorit."

In another high-school incident, Church was jailed for a few hours for angrily complaining to a local sheriff about the lack of due process in the arrest of other boys who had been fighting after a Boise High basketball game.

Church's life was altered forever when he met a girl. Not just any girl—the daughter of the governor of Idaho. Bethine Clark was a pretty, broad-shouldered brunette with a big smile. Not only was she the daughter of Idaho's Democratic governor, Chase Clark, but she belonged to the most influential family in Democratic Party politics in the state. Bethine's grandfather had been the first mayor of Idaho Falls, her uncle had served as governor a few years before her father, and her cousin was a U.S. senator. Rivals in the Democratic Party in Idaho nicknamed the family the "Clark machine."

They first met when Bethine was still living in Idaho Falls, in eastern Idaho, where her father was a lawyer; Frank and Bethine both attended a statewide student-government convention. When her father was elected governor in 1940, Bethine and her family moved to Boise and she transferred to Boise High, quickly joining Frank Church's circle of high-school friends. She was as bright and as interested in ideas and politics as Church, but Bethine was far more extroverted and gregarious — a natural politician.

To a remarkable degree for teenagers, Frank and Bethine were attracted to each other on an intellectual level; they shared a thirst for knowledge and an interest in history, current events, and politics that shaped their friendship long before they began to date. "Frank Church was the only high school student I knew who had read *Mein Kampf*," Bethine recalled in her memoir. "He was the first person I ever knew who always related things to Jefferson or Washington or the Constitution. I mean he absorbed all of that."

They eventually became classic mid-century high-school sweethearts, with a healthy dose of literate romance. While still in high school, Frank loved to recite the poems of A. E. Housman to Bethine, including one of his favorites, "To an Athlete Dying Young."

"This was depressing stuff for courtship," Bethine would later write, "but it worked for a romantic like me. I never knew anyone who loved language as much as Frank did."

But in their final year in high school, Frank and Bethine were not yet ready to commit to each other; she later characterized their "courtship" at the time as "both affectionate and distant."

Their relationship would be tested by war.

CHAPTER 2

"The finest diction in the Army"

FRANK CHURCH AND Carl Burke had gone out for ice cream in downtown Boise and were driving around on a lazy Sunday when they turned on the car radio and heard that Pearl Harbor had just been attacked by the Japanese. It was December 7, 1941, and the United States was suddenly at war.

Frank Church was in the middle of his senior year in high school when America was plunged into World War II, and he immediately began to think about joining the military. "We all knew in high school that it was just a question of when you were going to go," recalled Burke. "You were going to go. There was no denying that fact and there was no dissent."

Still, Church decided to wait rather than rush headlong into military service. He stayed in high school, graduated in 1942, then stuck to his plan to attend Stanford University in the fall. Church was ambitious enough to see himself as an officer, and he was clever enough to realize that getting at least a start on college would help make that happen. So he didn't join the millions of other American boys who lined up to enlist in the feverish first days after Pearl Harbor.*

---

* During that same period in the immediate aftermath of Pearl Harbor, Bethine's father—Idaho governor Chase Clark—was leaving behind a racist legacy in connection with one of the worst acts of injustice in modern American history:

While Frank went to Stanford, Bethine left for the University of Michigan, and the distance between Palo Alto and Ann Arbor began to strain the couple's relationship. When it came to both the war and Bethine Clark, Frank Church remained in limbo.

* * *

Church didn't stay at Stanford for long: he left for the Army in the spring of his freshman year. The military quickly recognized his brains, and he was sent for specialized training before he was even made an officer. In the summer of 1943, he was briefly sent to Lafayette College in Pennsylvania for training as a Spanish linguist, but his orders were soon changed and Church was secretly sent to Camp Ritchie, Maryland, for intelligence training.

In the years leading up to World War II, the United States government only had a small intelligence apparatus, the vestiges of a much bigger program that had been allowed to atrophy after budget cuts led to the closing of the famous "Black Chamber" in the late 1920s. The Black Chamber had been a highly successful, decade-long secret operation run jointly by the Army and the State Department in which analysts read and decrypted the cable traffic of foreign embassies in Washington. Secretary of State Henry Stimson later defended his decision to shut down the Black Chamber with a remark that became infamous in intelligence history: he said that "gentlemen do not read each other's mail."

But with World War II raging, there was a sudden and obvious demand for better intelligence, and the Office of Strategic Services

---

the U.S. government's internment of thousands of Japanese Americans. President Roosevelt ordered Japanese Americans living on the West Coast to be interned in 10 camps, including one in Idaho. When the Army announced in April 1942 that it planned to build an internment camp in Idaho, Governor Clark opposed the idea—but only because he didn't want any Japanese-American internees in the state. "I realize we've got to put them some place, but I don't trust any of them," Clark said. A month later, he said in a speech that Japanese "act like rats" and said they should all be sent "back to Japan, then sink the island." Clark finally agreed to the construction of a camp, but only after Idaho's powerful agricultural interests convinced him they needed the cheap farm labor the internees could provide. The Minidoka internment camp near Twin Falls, in southern Idaho, eventually held about 13,000 Japanese Americans. After Chase Clark lost his bid for reelection in 1942, Roosevelt named him a federal judge.

was created to be the nation's wartime spy agency. Founded and led by William "Wild Bill" Donovan, a lawyer who had been a highly decorated Army officer during World War I, the OSS handled espionage, sabotage, and paramilitary operations behind enemy lines. Donovan brought an adventurous romanticism to the OSS, and he recruited its agents largely from the American elite: among them was poet Archibald MacLeish; Paul Mellon, of the wealthy Mellon banking family; and even Julia Child, long before she became famous as a television chef.

The OSS became the stuff of legend, but its impact was minor in comparison with the war-winning work of the British and American code-breaking units that deciphered German and Japanese codes. The OSS's biggest legacy was that it served as the precursor to the CIA, and was the training ground for future CIA directors Allen Dulles, Richard Helms, and William Colby; all three would figure prominently in the Church Committee's investigation of the CIA.

But Frank Church didn't go to Camp Ritchie to join the OSS or become a spy. Instead, he trained to become an Army intelligence analyst. For even with the creation of the OSS, the Army still needed traditional battlefield intelligence—commanders had to know about the enemy right in front of their forces. The Army needed its own analysts who could combine all the available information collected from photoreconnaissance aircraft, radio intercepts, prisoner interrogations, and other sources to determine the enemy's strength and location, as well as the identities of its units and their leaders.

To meet the demand for analysts, smart young soldiers like Frank Church were grabbed from other parts of the Army and trained at Camp Ritchie, a covert base hidden away in the mountains of Maryland along the Pennsylvania border, near where Camp David, the presidential retreat, is today.

While Church was there being trained as an analyst, Camp Ritchie was also the secret training center for a unique group of immigrants and Jewish refugees whom the Army had selected for intelligence work against the Nazis. Now famous as "the Ritchie Boys," they used their native fluency in the language and culture of Germany to interrogate prisoners and defectors, as well as to conduct other spy missions. Some landed with the U.S. Army on D-Day and spread out across Normandy, then spent the rest of the war gathering some of the most valuable battlefield intelligence against the Germans that American commanders in Europe ever received.

Meanwhile, Bethine Clark was mystified. Despite her continued ambivalence about Frank Church, despite the fact that she was dating other men while she was at the University of Michigan and Frank was in the Army, she was still regularly writing to Church and closely tracking his progress in the Army. She was puzzled when he suddenly disappeared from his language-training program at Lafayette College. No one would tell her where he had gone or what had happened to him.

Too stubborn to take no for an answer, Bethine went to Washington to see Virgil Clark, the wife of her cousin, Senator D. Worth Clark of Idaho. Even as a college student, Bethine knew how to wield political influence.

Virgil Clark readily agreed to help Bethine, and after pulling rank as a senator's wife with officials at the Pentagon, she discovered that Church was secretly training at Camp Ritchie. Army officers at the secret base were mortified when Bethine Clark later called up looking for a 19-year-old trainee named Frank Church: "Young lady, if you'll tell me how the hell you found him...I'll call him, dammit, to the phone!" She had blown Camp Ritchie's cover.

After finishing intelligence training, Church still had to go through Officer Candidate School, but he was so weak and out of shape that he almost washed out. His Selective Service card from 1949 states that Church was six feet tall but weighed only 140 pounds; his weight was certainly much less than that when he first joined the Army years earlier during the war. "He just wasn't a good strong kid in those days," recalled Burke. "When he took the TB (tuberculosis) test, he always tested positive. He had a hell of a time at Fort Benning," where Church went through the officer training program. "Benning damn near killed him, he was so skinny."

* * *

Church finally went to war in early 1945, when as a 20-year-old officer he shipped out for India and then traveled with his small intelligence unit over the Burma Road to China. He was assigned as an intelligence officer to the U.S. Army's Chinese Combat Command, which was supporting the Chinese Nationalist Army of Chiang Kai-shek in its bitter fight against the Japanese.

Frank Church and his older brother, Richard, both in uniform during World War II.

Church wrote frequently to Bethine, and the letters show that their relationship remained ambiguous, stuck somewhere between friendship and love. The letters suggest that they had a sexual relationship, but that Frank was unwilling to commit to her, even though he knew she had started getting serious about another man she met at Michigan. The letters reveal a running argument between Bethine and Frank over whether their relationship was going anywhere or not—an argument that continued throughout the last year of World War II.

"I didn't come to Michigan for a cheap good time," Frank wrote to Bethine from New Delhi in April 1945, in a letter obviously referring to a time they had sex in Ann Arbor while he was on leave. "And what I found wasn't cheap. You should know that. If I was looking for common pleasures, I could find them easy enough. And I would find them elsewhere, not in Michigan."

Almost every letter Frank and Bethine wrote to each other showed signs of their struggle, as neither one seemed willing to fully commit. Frank wrote in one letter that "you challenged me for an answer, and I have none...Bethy, I don't mean to hurt you. I'd do anything to make you happy…only a selfish, thick-headed good-for-nothing would act as I have acted."

In June 1945, Church wrote to her from Kunming, China, in a letter that recognized that she was now seeing other men, including a cadet at West Point. He wrote that he envied "the lucky characters at Michigan and elsewhere who can, by virtue of location alone, date you at your pleasure."

She wrote him a letter that same month that must have left Church confused. Bethine wrote that the "West Point scourge has gone and I think I still remain heart free and fancy flying."

* * *

As an intelligence officer in China, Church was almost always at headquarters far behind the front lines, but he had at least one brush with action. In 1945, he was leading his small unit down a remote road in China when he heard a commotion that convinced him that Japanese troops were nearby. Night was falling, so Church ordered his soldiers to move to the opposite side of a nearby stream and dig defensive positions. He was about to join them when he realized his rifle was jammed. In the fading light, he crawled under a truck to clean his rifle by the light of a flashlight, which he hid under a blanket.

By the time he was finished cleaning his rifle, it was too late for him to join his troops, who might mistake him in the dark for a Japanese soldier. Church spent the entire night lying underneath the truck, staying awake in case of a Japanese assault.

The next morning, Church and his team reunited, only to find that there were no Japanese troops nearby; the din that had put them on alert had been caused instead by a group of drunken Chinese soldiers. But Church's lonely nighttime vigil still impressed the men of his unit.

Church's intelligence job was as an "order of battle" analyst, charged with identifying individual Japanese military units facing the Americans and the Chinese. Church took it upon himself to memorize the names of the Japanese officers commanding those units. That knowledge paid off when the officer in charge of providing intelligence briefings for General Robert McClure, the chief of the Chinese Combat Command, was out. McClure's staff scrambled to find someone else who could provide that day's briefing, and they asked around headquarters for anyone who knew enough to identify the Japanese front-line units and explain their locations and commanders. Church said he could do it.

Church's well-honed oratorical skills and his remarkable ability to analyze intelligence reports impressed General McClure. He made Church, still just 20, his main briefer, and from that moment on, Church was frequently by McClure's side. But Church privately began to chafe at McClure's excessive attention. During a lavish dinner at which he was the only lieutenant among a group of senior officers, McClure "introduced me as the man with the finest diction in the Army, and during the course of the evening asked me to read aloud one of his favorite stories." He wrote to Bethine that the luxurious dinner had made him feel like McClure's "court jester."

McClure liked Church so much that he chose him to join the small American delegation to witness the formal surrender of Japanese forces in China in Nanking in September 1945. "It is strange to find oneself, after all these years of war, in the midst of the Japanese Army," Church wrote to Bethine. It was "a great day for China. And it was amazingly good fortune for me to have been able to witness the event. Someday if I make no mark elsewhere, some Chinese historian will run across my name on the memorial roster, buried among those of the other guests who were invited to attend. I felt like a member of the chorus, high upon the platform backstage, in one of the final acts of history."

McClure also made sure that Church was awarded a Bronze Star for his intelligence work, with a citation that made it clear that McLure believed Church had done much better than the intelligence officer he had replaced. Church's intelligence reports had provided "highly accurate" order-of-battle reports, Church's Bronze Star citation read, that "materially expanded upon and improved reports and studies produced by the G2 section prior to his arrival." The citation also commended Church for the special studies he had written on the Japanese Army in China, which were so well prepared "that intelligence agencies made requests for additional copies and language personnel in the field used the special studies as chief guides during interrogations" of Japanese prisoners.

But reading the complete citation for Church's Bronze Star, it is hard not to conclude that McClure gave Church the award as a favor, mainly because he loved listening to him talk. "First Lt. Church gave daily presentations to the combined staff sections, which were so unanimously acclaimed that the commanding general personally commended him," his citation read. So why not reward the officer with the best diction in the Army?

Despite the plaudits from McClure, the war left Church depressed and with a sense of dread. "I am fearful that the United States is about to launch itself into a program of unprecedented imperialism," Church wrote Bethine after the Japanese surrendered.

"With few exceptions indeed, people I meet over here speak elatedly of the atomic bomb," he wrote in another letter to her. "There are those who tell me, with the expression of the most revealing astonishment and with incredulous enthusiasm, that our discovery is as yet so imperfect that only one tenth of one percent of its total explosive energy has thus far been realized. Apparently it is not enough to have at last developed the instrument of our own self-destruction. We even applaud approaching doom! And in a way, Bethy, it is fitting retribution."

Despite his growing fears that America was on the verge of turning into a cold, imperial superpower, Church had done so well as an intelligence analyst that the Army wanted to keep him. In December 1945, Church received a letter from the Army saying that he had been recommended for a position in a newly expanded, postwar Army intelligence service. In January 1946, Church wrote a letter back declining the offer, saying that "I very much appreciate being included in the list of prospective candidates, but I must advise you that it is my intention to return to civilian life."

If Church had accepted the offer to make intelligence his postwar career, there is a good chance he would have ended up in the CIA when it was created in 1947, thus becoming part of the spy agency — and perhaps complicit in its abuses — rather than leading an investigation of it. In hindsight, his decision to reject the Army's offer was a critical choice that fundamentally altered his life.

*　*　*

Church left the Army in 1946, and by then Bethine was engaged to Milt Chamberlain, the West Point cadet she had met at Michigan. But when Church got back to Boise, Stan Burns convinced him that Bethine wasn't happy about her engagement, and that she obviously still cared for Church. His friend told Church that "if he had any interest in Bethine that he must pursue that because the flame was still flickering," Burns recalled. Church went to her house, took her for a drive, and immediately asked her to marry him.

Bethine said yes, but demanded that Frank wait until after he went back to Stanford to finish college, to make sure that he really meant it. Angry that she had so suddenly broken off her previous engagement, Bethine's father kicked Frank Church out of his house. (The two men eventually reconciled.)

After he left the Army, Church went through a jarring experience that many others of his generation were encountering at the same time—he returned to college as an undergraduate after serving as an Army officer halfway around the world. He was no longer the boy from Idaho who had arrived at Stanford in 1942.

Church emerged from World War II much more liberal in his political thinking than he had been when he joined the Army. His experience in China had left him disgusted with the corruption and exploitation of Chiang Kai-shek's regime, while the sudden expansion of America's global power left him fearful that imperialism would alter the nation's character. In the years immediately after the war, he was even briefly attracted to the left-wing politics of Henry Wallace, Franklin Roosevelt's former vice president, who ran for president on the Progressive Party ticket in 1948. "Yesterday Bay, Carl and I managed to get seats at the San Francisco Opera House for the great rally in honor of Henry Wallace," Church wrote to Bethine in 1947. "The hall was crowded with over 4,000 people, while a cheering throng of about equal size milled about outside the building. Wallace received a standing ovation from the audience. I liked him. I liked his fighting spirit, his frankness and his great sincerity. It was an exciting affair."

Church joined the Stanford debate team and was asked to give a series of public speeches, thanks not only to his growing reputation as an orator but also to his military service in China; convulsed by a civil war between the Nationalists and Communists, China was constantly in the headlines at the time.

"I have been anxious to strike out at Chiang's China for a long time," Church wrote Bethine. In an hour-long speech at an auditorium on Stanford's campus, he got his chance, attacking the corruption and incompetence of Chiang's Nationalist Chinese government. "If I were to give substantially the same talk to a large, representative group in Boise," he wrote to his fiancée, "[the Boise newspaper] would roar in righteous anger for days."

After growing up in overwhelmingly white Idaho (Idaho's population of 524,873 in the 1940 census included 519,292 whites and only 595 Blacks), Church was also starting to struggle to better understand racial discrimination. During a Stanford debate against the University of California, he defended labor unions, citing their efforts to organize Black workers. "Unions are the most active of all our institutions in their attempt to correct racial discrimination," Church wrote Bethine, describing his argument during the debate. "I mentioned a Negro Congress I had attended in San Francisco, and pointed out that there were no representatives of the Chamber of Commerce there, that management had not so much as sent an office boy, but that three very prominent labor union presidents were there, officiating on the platform."

After Church graduated Phi Beta Kappa from Stanford, he and Bethine were married at the Clark family mountain ranch in Idaho on June 21, 1947, followed by a six-week honeymoon driving an old DeSoto convertible through Mexico. Their marriage, already fueled by a mixture of love and politics, would prove to be sustained by both: Bethine would become Frank Church's most important political adviser and confidante throughout his career. (The fact that, back in the 1890s, William Borah had also married the daughter of an Idaho governor, Mary McConnell Borah, may not have gone unnoticed by Frank Church.)

In the fall of 1947, Church started at Harvard Law School. But he and his wife struggled with life in Cambridge, especially after she became pregnant and he began to suffer severe back pains that his doctors didn't understand. Church also had no interest in following his classmates onto the traditional Harvard Law career path that led to an elite Eastern law firm. He was eager to return to the West.

He transferred back to Stanford's Law School, and in 1948 his son, Frank Forrester Church IV, was born in Palo Alto. But the return to California did not ease his back pain.

Months of serious back pains gave way to groin pains, and in 1949 an operation finally revealed that Church had testicular cancer. "When I was wheeled into the recovery room, the doctors told [Bethine] it was cancer and that it was very, very serious," Church

Frank and Bethine Church at their wedding on June 21, 1947.

later wrote in a first-person account of his bout with cancer in *Good Housekeeping* magazine. "They'd removed a tumor, together with the lymph nodes and glands on my left side all the way up to my kidney. They didn't think further surgery would be of any use. They told Bethine to prepare for the worst — that I probably had no more than six months to live."

Church got better news a week later. Doctors at Stanford Medical School discovered that he had seminoma, a less-extreme form of testicular cancer that could be treated through the use of radiation. Frank Church had a chance to survive, but his treatment was still limited by the medical knowledge and technology available in the late 1940s.

For seven weeks he underwent deep X-ray therapy, exposing him to brutal levels of radiation designed to kill any remaining cancer cells. The radiation worked, but at a terrible cost: "The X ray slowly burned my flesh purple," he would later recall, "and left me feeling terribly nauseated." Bethine was barely able to help him keep down fluids and food in between fits of vomiting; through trial and error, they discovered that his system could handle lamb chops, baked potatoes, and root beer. "I was able to drink root beer and more root beer and keep it down. I had a glass of it in front of me all the time," he wrote. Still, by the end of the treatments he weighed just 90 pounds.

Church became deeply depressed when there was a brief fear that his cancer had spread. "It was the lowest I'd ever been in my life," he wrote. But it was a false alarm; his treatments worked, and Church soon began to recover.

Surviving cancer convinced Church that he didn't have time to wait. "I think having cancer made it harder on him in some ways and maybe it made it easier on him in some ways," Bethine Church said later. "I think Frank was never as willing to take a risk as I have been, [but] I think having cancer made him much more willing to take a risk." In fact, Church later said that his brush with death from cancer convinced him that he shouldn't accept gradual progress in his career. He told himself that he might not live long, and so he had to take risks, and right away, while he was still young. For Frank Church, that meant going back home to Idaho and gambling big in politics.

CHAPTER 3

"If you don't run you will never get there"

IN THE YEARS after World War II, Idaho was a Republican-leaning state, but it wasn't impossible for Democrats to win statewide elections. There were still strains of left-wing populism that dated back to the early days of labor unrest in the minefields of northern Idaho, and the New Deal had won over a generation of voters. Franklin Roosevelt won Idaho in every presidential election from 1932 through 1944, and Harry Truman carried it in 1948. In the 1950s, Republican president Dwight Eisenhower was overwhelmingly popular in Idaho, but ticket-splitting between candidates from opposing parties was relatively common and Democrats had some success.

Frank Church came home from California and took a government job to pay the bills while he dived into politics in Boise. He won a leadership role in the Boise-area Democratic Party, which was weak at the time, and in 1952 gave the keynote speech at the party's state convention and ran for the state legislature. He lost the race, but not his taste for politics.

He also became head of the Idaho branch of Crusade for Freedom, a campaign established in the 1950s ostensibly to help raise funds for Radio Free Europe. Church did so well with the fundraising drive that he was invited, along with other leading volunteers, to travel to West Berlin.

But the truth was that Crusade for Freedom was nothing more

Frank Church speaks on behalf of Crusade for Freedom
in the 1950s, before his election to the Senate.

than an anti-Communist propaganda campaign designed to hide
the fact that the CIA provided the funding for Radio Free Europe—
part of the CIA's larger efforts to influence media around the world.
Church would learn about the CIA's involvement only years later,
after he was in the Senate, and that revelation was just the first of
many that would make him question the spy agency's role in American society. "That was the beginning of my disillusionment," he
later said.

* * *

By early 1956, Frank Church decided he would skip any further
local political races. He was going to challenge Herman Welker for
a seat in the United States Senate.

Welker was a former Los Angeles lawyer who had returned to
his home state of Idaho to get into politics, and was first elected to
the Senate in 1950. That was the year Senator Joseph McCarthy, a
Republican from Wisconsin, launched his red-baiting witch hunt,
and Welker quickly began to model his fledgling political career
after him. Welker became so closely identified with McCarthy that
he earned the nickname "Little Joe from Idaho."

In February 1950, McCarthy burst out of the obscurity of the Senate's backbenches and onto the national stage with an infamous speech in Wheeling, West Virginia, claiming, with no evidence, that he had a list of 205 Communist Party members who worked in the State Department.

Within months, Welker, not yet elected to the Senate, was emulating McCarthy. On July 4, 1950, in a campaign speech in eastern Idaho, Welker announced darkly that he knew of "87 Communists in Idaho." It was a total fabrication, but the ploy worked, and Welker was elected that fall.

Once in the Senate, Welker continued to copy McCarthy, spending most of his time on red-baiting rather than on issues affecting Idaho. Photographs from his time in the Senate show that he even had the same kind of dark-circled eyes and menacing looks that were McCarthy's trademark.

Frank Church decided to run against Welker almost on impulse. He wanted to take a risk and try for a major office, and Welker's Senate seat was the next one up for grabs. "I'm not so sure that there was that much thought given to it, whether or not it was the right year for Frank to run," said Carl Burke, his longtime friend who served as his campaign manager in 1956 and in later races. "I remember in the early part of 1956, Frank began to talk about the possibility of running for Senate on the theory that if you don't run you will never get there."

At first, Church's family and friends were skeptical of his longshot bid. They thought Church was too young and too unknown, and not yet ready to take on a nasty Republican incumbent like Welker, who would likely resort to mudslinging and dirty tricks to stay in office. Church would also be going against a Republican national tide, since Eisenhower was running for reelection in 1956 and seemed headed for a landslide victory.

But Church believed in his own ability to persuade, and that his mastery of public speaking and his ability to clearly explain his views could win over people who might otherwise think he was too young or too liberal. He and his wife were willing to get in their four-door Kaiser sedan and drive up and down Idaho, talking to voters in every high-school gym in the state, if that's what it took.

Church first had to win the Democratic primary, and that meant emerging from a crowded field that featured former Senator

Frank and Bethine Church posing with Bethine's mother, Jean Clark, while campaigning for Frank's first Senate race in 1956.

Glen Taylor, a country-western singer and entertainer who had become a constant presence on the ballot in Idaho since he first ran for the Senate in 1940. Taylor had won a single term in the Senate in 1944, but Democratic leaders had come to consider him little more than a gadfly after he left the party in 1948 to be Henry Wallace's running mate on the left-wing Progressive Party ticket against President Harry Truman. When Taylor ran for reelection to the Senate in 1950, the Democratic establishment was determined to defeat him. Party leaders backed a primary challenge by former senator D. Worth Clark, Bethine Church's cousin (whose wife, Virgil, had helped Bethine track down Frank at Camp Ritchie during World War II). Clark used the Republican playbook against Taylor, attacking him as a Communist dupe, and defeated Taylor in the primary. Clark then lost to Welker in the general election.

Despite the party's opposition to Taylor, he was not going to be a pushover for Church. Taylor was a strong-willed liberal who was far ahead of his time; while running for vice president in 1948, he was arrested and roughed up in Birmingham, Alabama, for attempting to address an integrated campaign event. Taylor had a loyal base of liberal supporters, and with six candidates in the crowded primary in 1956, in which the centrist Democratic vote could be divided, he had a good chance of emerging as the party's nominee.

What's more, Taylor now detested the Democratic Party establishment just as much as they hated him, and he saw the young Frank Church as nothing more than a puppet of the most powerful Democratic family in the state. (On the campaign trail, Frank Church did not talk about his own brief flirtation with Henry Wallace in the 1940s.)

The Clarks had denied Taylor an election once before, and he was convinced they were trying to do so again — even if no one with the Clark family name was on the ballot. "The Clark political dynasty had run out of blood-line relatives to carry on their activities, so in this 1956 election they had to place their bets on Frank Church, a young attorney," Taylor later wrote in his memoir. "He became the dynasty's last hope by virtue of the fact that he was married to Chase Clark's daughter."

Herman Welker was eager to run against Taylor, who he thought would be easy to beat in the general election. In August, Welker predicted that Taylor would win the upcoming Democratic primary. "Glen Taylor will be nominated by the Democrats," Welker said in a newspaper interview. "And I hope so, because I look forward to defeating him in November."

Church and Taylor emerged as the two main contenders for the Democratic nomination, and the August primary was a seesaw battle. When the first results came in, Taylor was leading and seemed to have the election won. But a late surge helped Church, and he was declared the winner by 200 votes.

"Organization Democrats in Idaho are jubilant this week because they have finally dumped Glen Taylor," observed the *Spokesman-Review*, a Spokane Washington newspaper that was influential in nearby northern Idaho.

But Taylor was furious and deeply suspicious, especially after the state admitted a few days after the election that a typographical error in the official results had given 30 extra votes to Church, making the true margin of victory just 170 votes. Idaho officials said they could not order a recount because state law made no provision for one.

Taylor charged that Church and the Democratic establishment had stolen the primary, and began his own freelance voting-fraud investigation, focusing on the results in the town of Mountain

Home in southern Idaho, where he had received far fewer votes than he had in previous elections. Taylor went door-to-door in Mountain Home, asking people how they had voted. The police in Mountain Home pulled him in to meet the mayor, who told Taylor that he had to stop his canvassing because the mayor's office had received complaints that Taylor was bothering people. But the county attorney told Taylor he could continue, and he finished his count in one precinct of Mountain Home. Taylor claimed his count showed that more people had voted for him than had been officially recorded.

In September, Taylor went to the Democratic state convention to confront Church, hoping to get him to agree to a recount of six precincts in Mountain Home. But when Taylor arrived at the convention, he found that many of his own supporters now wanted him to drop his fight and back Church. He claimed that a group of "friends," acting as intermediaries, offered him $9,000 if he would drop his investigation in Mountain Home and give ten campaign speeches on behalf of Church.

"The offer, of course, was an attempt to bribe me," Taylor wrote in his 1979 memoir. "I was broke, in debt and had no idea what I would do to earn a living, much less how to pay off my debts."

Taylor claimed he rejected the offer, and Church repeatedly denied that any such offer had ever been made. Taylor went back to Mountain Home to get voters to sign affidavits. But the police and mayor kept trying to stop him, and Taylor finally dropped his fraud investigation.

* * *

Ignoring Taylor, Church focused instead on Welker, who now looked vulnerable. Welker had angered the Republican establishment in Washington by openly criticizing Eisenhower, and he had voted against key White House initiatives while targeting administration officials for red-baiting investigations.

Although there had been scant local press coverage of the worst scandal involving Welker—a scandal that the Church campaign knew about—his reputation had still started to sink in Idaho. He had largely ignored the state for six years while pursuing his McCarthy-style witch-hunts, and as a result had little support among Idaho's Republican leaders. Welker had attracted four challengers in the Republican primary, managing to win with fewer than half the votes.

Meanwhile, rumors about Welker's drinking and erratic behavior were becoming widespread in Boise. Welker "was subject to fits of melancholia and violent outbursts of temper," Taylor recalled in his memoir. "He had become paranoid, was carrying a gun."

At this point, Church's allies were prepared to use the dirt they had quietly gathered on Welker—much of which was readily available from the national press. The opposition-research pamphlet they wrote—*The Shameful Record of Herman Welker!*—put all the dirt they had collected on Welker together in one place.

Among many other things, the pamphlet referred to his role in a blackmail scheme that led to the suicide of a Democratic senator, and also included a reprint of a *New York Daily News* story about a mysterious dockside meeting between Welker and a group of New York mobsters in 1955, topped by a question in large red letters: "Are headlines like these a credit to the state of Idaho?"

"What kind of a man is Herman Welker?" the pamphlet asked. "In his six short years in Washington, Welker has acquired a reputation as a domineering and arrogant person. Washington newspapermen covering the Senate have often expressed their disrespect for him. Welker has openly abused the president, his associates, and his program...committee hearings have seen Welker explode into violence, cursing and calling names."

Church's campaign staff and allies were planning to distribute the pamphlet throughout the state, hopefully torpedoing Welker's campaign just before the election.

But Frank Church said no.

When he first saw the pamphlet, "I looked at it in horror," he later remembered. "I told them to burn them." He ordered that all 50,000 copies of the pamphlet be set ablaze in the alley behind his campaign headquarters in downtown Boise, insisting that an aide "stand by the incinerator until every last one of them was turned to ash," recalled Church's son in his memoir.

Church told his staff that he wanted to focus on the issues and on Welker's record. He didn't want to win by getting down in the gutter with him. "I always had a feeling of relief," Church later recalled, "that I never circulated that kind of material about Herman Welker."

*   *   *

When Frank Church refused to use the pamphlet and ordered the copies burned, it was one of the defining moments of his life. It set the stage for a political career in which he sought to battle on the issues, rather than through mudslinging.

But the truth was that when he ran for reelection in 1956, Herman Welker had plenty to answer for, most notably the blackmail scheme that led to the suicide of another senator — one of the ugliest episodes in the history of the United States Senate.

Two years before the 1956 campaign, at 8:30 a.m. on June 19, 1954, Senator Lester Hunt of Wyoming had walked into the Senate's office building. It was a Saturday morning, and the building's hallways were nearly empty. Under his coat, Hunt carried a .22 caliber rifle.

Elevator operator Ronald Maurice took Hunt up to the third floor. Hunt entered his personal office, closed the door, and shot himself. An affable first-term Democrat, a former governor, dentist, and one-time semipro baseball player, Hunt was 61.

Mike Manatos, a Hunt aide, soon arrived and found Hunt in his office. The Wyoming senator was pronounced dead at 12:32 p.m. at Casualty Hospital on Capitol Hill.

Nationally syndicated columnist Drew Pearson soon broke the explosive story behind Hunt's suicide. For months, Pearson revealed, Hunt had been the victim of a blackmail scheme by two fellow senators: Herman Welker of Idaho and Senator Styles Bridges of New Hampshire.

Their scheme was a poisonous product of McCarthyism. A year earlier, in June 1953, Hunt's son, Lester Jr., had been arrested in Lafayette Park near the White House for soliciting an undercover Washington police officer. At the time, police in Washington and other major cities often ran undercover sting operations to ambush and arrest homosexuals. Hunt's son was not prosecuted, and the case was quietly dropped. The matter seemed closed until Welker and Bridges heard about the case and realized they could use it as a weapon against one of their Senate enemies. Both Bridges and Welker — but particularly Welker — were ardent McCarthy disciples, and the persecution of homosexuals was an ugly element of McCarthyism.

Lester Hunt became a target of Welker and Bridges because he was one of Joe McCarthy's most scathing critics in the Senate, and was one of the first senators to try to stop him. He had an early glimpse of McCarthy's demagoguery when he served on a Senate panel investigating accusations that the U.S. Army had mistreated German prisoners of war who had been involved in a massacre of American soldiers who had surrendered during the Battle of the Bulge in World War II. Although McCarthy was not on the committee, he intervened in order to defend the Germans and attack the U.S. Army. Before he discovered anti-Communism as his cause, McCarthy turned the 1949 hearings into his own vehicle for publicity as a boorish ally of the SS officers who had slaughtered American prisoners. He viciously berated U.S. Army officers who testified before the committee.

When McCarthy launched his red-baiting campaign the following year, Hunt saw through him, and in response introduced legislation to eliminate the legal immunity extended to speeches in the Senate. McCarthy was using his Senate immunity to libel and slander government officials, and Hunt believed that McCarthy wouldn't continue if his immunity was lifted.

In a speech on the Senate floor in support of his legislation in December 1950, Hunt complained that, unless the law was changed and immunity removed, senators with "deep seated and malicious hatred of any person" could stand up on the Senate floor and lie about them with impunity. They could accuse their enemies of "evil, vile and contemptible crimes," including treason. Senators who did so faced no consequences "for the destruction of our enemy's character, the loss of a good reputation...or for any unfair, unjust, evil consequence which may follow."

Hunt didn't mention McCarthy by name in his speech, but everyone knew who he was talking about. The anti-immunity legislation failed, but Hunt gained quiet plaudits from other senators who were also getting fed up with McCarthy.

Hunt also found McCarthy appalling on a personal level. Hunt's son later recalled that his father considered McCarthy to be "an opportunist and liar and drunk." The two men had to share a hotel room once when their plane was forced down in Pittsburgh, and Hunt's son recalled that his father "felt unclean about having associated with that person. He really had a strong dislike for him personally."

But his opposition to Joe McCarthy brought Hunt dangerous enemies, especially Herman Welker, McCarthy's hatchet man. So when he heard about the arrest of Hunt's son, Welker saw his chance for revenge.

To make their blackmail scheme work against Hunt, Welker and Bridges got down in the weeds of the solicitation case against his son. They met with local Washington, D.C., police officers and began pressuring them to reopen the case and seek Lester Hunt Jr.'s prosecution.

Meanwhile, Welker contacted an intermediary in order to pass a threatening message to Senator Hunt. He called Glenn "Red" Jacoby, the athletic director at the University of Wyoming, who knew Hunt well from Hunt's time as Wyoming governor. Jacoby had also known Welker as a child growing up in Idaho. Welker called him and told Jacoby to tell Hunt, who was up for reelection in 1954, that unless he quit the Senate, his son would face prosecution, and the story of his son's case and accusations of his homosexuality would be publicized all over Wyoming.

Either through Jacoby or other go-betweens, the threat got back to Hunt. Hunt refused to back down, or to give in to the blackmail.

But Welker and Bridges kept up the pressure, and the case against Hunt's son was revived. He was charged and convicted in a brief trial in October 1953. For his "crime," he paid a $100 fine.

Over the following months, Hunt continued to fight the threats from Welker and Bridges to publicize the case in Wyoming. But finally the strain became too great, and Lester Hunt shot himself.

Hunt had confided in Drew Pearson about the blackmail plot against him in December 1953, but Pearson did not report on it until after Hunt's death. Because he had known about the blackmail plot for so long, Pearson was able to publish a column about it almost immediately after Hunt's suicide, naming Welker and Bridges as the culprits. "The incident was one of the lowest types of political pressure this writer has seen in many years," Pearson wrote.

"Lester Hunt, a much more sensitive soul than his colleagues realized, just could not bear the thought of having his son's misfortunes become the subject of whispers in his re-election campaign," Pearson wrote. "Those must have been some of the worries that troubled Senator Hunt as he left his home early the other morning, a .22 rifle half-hidden under his coat."

Drew Pearson's column was so shocking that many other journalists in Washington shied away from following up on the story, especially after Welker and Bridges denied the blackmail charge and threatened to take legal action against Pearson. Welker and

Bridges persuaded a Washington police officer to sign an affidavit denying some of the story's details—without really disputing the fact that the two senators had pressured the police to prosecute Hunt's son. Welker even made a point of participating in a eulogy for Hunt at a Senate memorial service.

The Senate took no action against Welker or Bridges, and never conducted any investigation into the circumstances surrounding Hunt's death. Welker never expressed any remorse.

Herman Welker seemed to have emerged largely unscathed from his role in the blackmail scheme against the tragic Lester Hunt, and, as he began to gear up for reelection in early 1956, there was still no sign that anyone back in Idaho could beat him.

He had not expected Frank Church.

* * *

Even without slinging mud, Church was confident by late October that he had Welker on the run. Welker was refusing to debate him, and wouldn't "come out and fight," Church said. In an October 29, 1956 story in the *Times-News* of Twin Falls, Idaho, Church noted wryly that he had traveled to Burley, Idaho for a scheduled debate with Welker, but when he arrived, he found that Welker had not come in person, "substituting in his place a phonograph record in which he hurled peevish charges at me. I have never before been called upon to conduct a debate with a phonograph record." The next day, Welker told the Burley newspaper that it was a "regrettable snafu" that he hadn't appeared in person.

Church hammered away on a key issue—that Welker had been a frequent critic of the popular Eisenhower, and had often voted against Eisenhower's programs in the Senate. It may have seemed like an odd tactic for a Democrat to criticize a Republican for not being Republican enough. But it was Church's way of convincing voters who planned to vote for Eisenhower in 1956 that they should split their ticket and also vote for Church.

To counter Church, Welker received only tepid support from the Republican Party; his battles with the Eisenhower White House were now coming back to haunt him. Eisenhower did not come to Idaho to campaign for Welker, instead sending only a bland letter of endorsement. "Of course, you and I have differed on certain issues over the past three and a half years, and I have been informed that these differences have been exploited in this campaign," Eisenhower's letter stated. "Unfortunately, little recognition has been given to the many times you have whole-heartedly supported the Administration in advancing key parts of its program." Welker featured the letter in a newspaper campaign ad, but it only served to underline Eisenhower's lack of enthusiasm.

But just as it seemed that Church was cruising to victory, Glen Taylor resurfaced, announcing he was running as a write-in independent. Taylor splashed an ad across local newspapers in Idaho, explaining that he was reentering the race to save voters from having to choose between a "McCarthyite and a front man for a corrupt machine." In his ad, Taylor went public with his allegation that "Church and his machine" tried to pay him $9,000 "to forget a recount and campaign for Church."

"Why are you so desperately afraid of a recount, Mr. Church?" asked the Taylor advertisement.

Taylor's belated reentry threatened to divide the Democratic vote and hand the election to Welker. State Democratic chairman John Glasby angrily told reporters that Welker and Taylor had formed an "unholy alliance" to defeat Church.

Many years later, Taylor admitted that Glasby was right: his write-in campaign was bankrolled by Welker, Taylor wrote in his memoir. When he decided to launch his write-in campaign, Taylor revealed, he went to Welker for money, and Welker gave him $35,000. "Welker was the darling of the most reactionary elements in the nation, as well as in the state," Taylor wrote. "Those eastern and Texas reactionary McCarthyites! That's where the real dough was, and Welker would have plenty...Welker's campaign was going badly. His only hope—if indeed he had any hope—was my write-in campaign...I could shake Welker down."

But Taylor's last-minute write-in campaign fizzled.

Church won the Senate election with more than 56 percent of the vote, nearly matching Eisenhower's 61 percent margin in Idaho in the presidential election. Taylor received only 13,415 write-in votes, and was not a factor in the election.

Frank Church, newly elected United States Senator, was just 32 years old. He had just helped vanquish McCarthyism.

Herman Welker died of a brain tumor in October 1957, two years before the publication of *Advise and Consent*, Allen Drury's best-selling fictionalized account of the Hunt suicide and blackmail plot. After Welker's death, Frank Church and others in Idaho and Washington wondered whether an undiagnosed brain tumor could explain at least some of Welker's erratic behavior, including rumors about his drinking.

In January 1958, a full year after Frank Church had been sworn into office as a United States Senator from Idaho, Glen Taylor sent Church a letter asking him to take a polygraph test about the voting results in the 1956 primary.

Church ignored the letter.

CHAPTER 4

"Persona non grata"

ON HIS VERY first day in the Senate in 1957, Frank Church—who looked so young that tourists walking through the U.S. Capitol sometimes mistakenly thought he was a Senate page—received his first rough political lesson from Senate Majority Leader Lyndon Baines Johnson, the Texas Machiavellian who, one aide said, ran the Senate "just like an orchestra leader."

After being sworn into office by Vice President Richard Nixon, Church was walking from the well of the Senate to his new seat in the back of the chamber, glancing up proudly at his wife, Bethine, in the visitor's gallery, when he suddenly felt his arm being grabbed. Lyndon Johnson, from his front-row seat, pulled Church to a stop. The powerful majority leader was literally strong-arming Church. He had a lecture to give him.

"I had no sooner taken the oath and stepped down and started to walk up the central aisle to my seat in the rear of the chamber," Church later recalled, "when I encountered this long arm of Lyndon Johnson reaching out and grabbing me as I passed and pulling me in to his desk there, front and center." Johnson was trying to line up support for an arcane procedural motion that was crucial to his complex strategy to pass civil rights legislation in 1957, and he wasted no time applying his special brand of suffocating pressure. He brought Church in close—then took him to school.

"Now Frank, you are the youngest member of this Senate, and

you have a great future," Church recalled Johnson saying. "There's a lot going for you. But the first thing you ought to learn is that in Congress you get along by going along."

"He said, 'Now, we've got a motion here that Clinton Anderson [a Democratic Senator from New Mexico] offered and it relates to a matter that is not important to your state. People of your state don't care how you vote on this, one way or the other, but the leadership cares. It means a lot to me. So I just point this up to you. Your first vote is coming up, and I hope you'll keep it in mind, because I like you, and I see big things in your future, and I want for you to get off on the right foot in the Senate.'"

Church was noncommittal — at least he thought he was — and ultimately voted against Johnson on the procedural issue, an early skirmish in what would turn out to be a long and bitter battle in the Senate over civil rights legislation in 1957.

As soon as he voted against Johnson, Church realized he had made a rookie political mistake. "Apparently I had left the impression with Senator Johnson that I was leaning toward him or would certainly vote with him, and he never came back to me a second time and never checked with me before the vote." When Church voted against Johnson, "he picked up his pen and threw it down on his desk. And I didn't see him pick it up again. I knew then that I was in deep trouble with the Majority Leader.

"For the next six months he never spoke to me, which was a part of his famous treatment," Church added. "He said nothing to me that was insulting; he just simply ignored me. When I was present with other senators, he talked to other senators. It was clear to me, and made perfectly clear, that I was a persona non grata with Lyndon Johnson."

Church had joined the Senate's liberals in voting against Johnson on the procedural issue. Northern liberals in the Senate had been pushing for civil rights legislation for years, but had been repeatedly blocked by the power of Southern Democrats to use the Senate's arcane rules to kill the legislation. The liberals now feared that Johnson was using this latest procedural vote to once again stop civil rights legislation, rather than smooth its passage.

What the liberals failed to see was that Johnson was playing a long and complicated game, and was trying to appease Southern Democrats on procedural issues while he gradually used his legendary powers of persuasion to convince them not to block civil rights legislation from coming to a vote on the Senate floor. If the legislation actually got to a vote before the full Senate, Johnson knew it would pass. But he also knew that the aggressive, head-on approach of the Senate's northern liberals would only solidify Southern opposition, so it was doomed to fail. This fight over the power of senior Southern Senators to use the filibuster and other Senate procedures to block civil rights legislation was the central battle in the Senate when Frank Church arrived in January 1957.

At the time, Church was still largely politically unformed. He was bright, an impressive public speaker, and had undergone the chastening experiences of war and cancer. After World War II, he had become unnerved by what he feared were America's imperial ambitions around the world, and had flirted with the leftist politics of Henry Wallace. But by the time he joined the Senate he had come to accept the hawkish tenets of the Cold War; thanks to the tense nuclear standoff with the Soviet Union in the 1950s, Church's fears of an American empire had temporarily receded.

So he entered the Senate as a fairly conventional 1950s Democrat. He agreed with the Democratic criticism that the Eisenhower administration was guilty of complacency, but he was nonetheless a mainstream politician who had been elected in Idaho thanks to ticket splitters who voted for Eisenhower for president and Church for Senate. While he harbored a vague ambition to focus on foreign policy, he was still a traditional Cold Warrior, like most Democrats, and he arrived in the Senate with no radical foreign-policy ideas. He seemed to have temporarily forgotten about his postwar fear that America's new superpower status would turn the republic into an empire.

"When I first came to the Senate, I had a Cold War perspective," Church recalled in a 1979 interview. "The world was divided into Communists and Free World governments. It was our responsibility to contain Communism because of its monolithic character."

His views on domestic policy were also conventional, but mostly vague. And when it came to issues affecting Idaho, he favored large government infrastructure projects to spur the development of the state's immense natural resources, but didn't consider their environmental impact.

But Church was quickly tested, and the choices he made in his early years in the Senate gradually transformed him from a conventional Democrat into a progressive force. Three battles that he began to fight in his first decade in the Senate—over civil rights legislation, a dam in Hells Canyon, Idaho, and the Vietnam War—helped prepare him to take on the CIA, the FBI, and the national security state in a way that no one in American politics had ever done.

*   *   *

The fight over civil rights legislation in the Senate in early 1957 came at a time when the nation was finally taking its first halting steps in the long march to address racial injustice after nearly a century of Jim Crow and legalized apartheid.

The 1954 Supreme Court decision in *Brown v. Board of Education*—that segregation in public schools was illegal—had helped the fledgling Civil Rights Movement gain momentum. Then, in December 1955, the arrest of Rosa Parks for refusing to surrender her seat to a white man on a bus in Montgomery, Alabama sparked the Montgomery bus boycott, which lasted 381 days. In November 1956, the Supreme Court ruled that segregated seating was unconstitutional, and the subsequent success of the Montgomery bus boycott helped set the stage for the rise of a national movement of nonviolent civil disobedience led by the young Rev. Martin Luther King Jr.

By early 1957, it was clear to Lyndon Johnson that the old Southern obstructionism in the Senate against civil rights could no longer hold. Eager to help Republicans win the support of Black voters in the North, the Eisenhower Administration had proposed civil rights legislation, and it had plenty of support in the House. The Democratic-controlled Senate would have to act or risk looking increasingly like the last bastion of Jim Crow in Washington.

Johnson also knew that as a Southerner, he could never achieve his ambition of winning the presidency if Northern voters saw him as the man who allowed Southern racism to prevail in the Senate. Johnson was determined to pass a civil rights bill in 1957, but the South still had enormous power in the Senate, so he had to maneuver in mystifying ways to do it.

Initially, Frank Church did not really understand the political dynamics at work in the Senate on civil rights. Church had long opposed segregation, but after growing up in virtually all-white Idaho, civil rights was largely an "intellectual" and not "a visceral thing" for him, recalled Ward Hower, Church's legislative aide at the time.

Church did not intend to take a major role in the debate over civil rights legislation. But he was now in the Senate's version of purgatory—frozen out by the Senate Majority Leader—so he wanted to find a way back into Johnson's good graces.

* * *

Despite his rocky start, Church soon began to settle into the Senate and Washington. He had to give up wearing blue suits so that he wasn't confused for being a Senate page because he looked so young. He installed his grandfather's brass name plate on his office door, showing his deep Idaho roots. The original Frank Forrester Church had nailed the brass plate to his own office door when he was named United States assayer in Boise.

Church's experimental radiation treatment for his testicular cancer had left him sterile, so in 1957 he and his wife adopted a baby boy; they named the child Chase, after Bethine's father. He was a younger brother for Forrest, who had been born in 1948 not long before his father began his cancer treatments.

The first of many of Washington's temptations also soon arrived, when Bobby Baker, Lyndon Johnson's fixer, tried to ingratiate himself with Church, posing an early test of Church's integrity. As soon as Bethine Church arrived in Washington following Church's election, Baker, doing Johnson's bidding, picked her up at her hotel in the Senate Majority Leader's limousine. Baker then drove Bethine around Washington, looking at "the houses of every Democratic congressman who had lost and was leaving town," she later wrote in her memoir. The implication of all this attention from Baker was that Frank and Bethine Church would get a special deal on a house—courtesy of Bobby Baker and Lyndon Johnson, thus leaving Frank Church vulnerable to Johnson's political demands. When Baker offered to show her more houses that afternoon, she begged off. Bethine got a real estate agent of her own and found a house to rent while she and Frank looked for something more permanent.

Frank and Bethine later settled on a well-designed but modest split-level, four-bedroom house on a cul-de-sac that backed up to an exclusive country club in the affluent Washington suburb of Bethesda, Maryland. Church and his family would live in the same

Frank Church with his family. On his right is his wife, Bethine, and on his left is his oldest son, Forrest. On Bethine's right is her mother, Jean Clark, and sitting is Bethine's father, former Idaho governor Chase Clark. Sitting next to him is Chase Church, Frank and Bethine's youngest son.

home, which sat on a third of an acre, for the rest of his Senate career. When they bought the house, for $43,500, Bobby Baker surfaced again, this time offering a sweetheart deal on a cheap mortgage. Church rejected the offer. "Church felt uncomfortable with the offer, and he didn't take it," recalls Peter Fenn, a family friend and later a Church staffer.

Before long, Frank and Bethine Church established themselves as frequent hosts of parties that brought together an eclectic mix of politicians, journalists, and Hollywood stars passing through Washington who were drawn to a new young liberal voice in Congress. Their parties had a classic late-50s to mid-60s cocktails-and-cigars style; Frank would smoke cigars while Theodore Beckel played guitar and led sing-alongs and Marlon Brando played pool in the basement. The Church children were usually included. "Marlon Brando sent me a book about raccoons, after I told him I liked raccoons," recalled Chase Church in an interview. Brando also gave ninth-grader Forrest Church some unusual advice before he went to his first high-school dance. "You aren't nervous, are you?" Brando asked the obviously nervous boy. The unusual advice he gave him was to gather people around him, start talking, and make big, grand gestures. "The secret to all success is gesticulation," Brando confided.

Political conversations consumed the Church household. "When I was really young," recalled Chase Church, "I didn't really identify with a lot going on. But generally speaking the dinner table was the time when people talked about current events; almost every night there was some talk of what was going on." Bethine Church, even more than Frank, was a political junkie; she couldn't get enough talk about politics. She was a striver, fixated on advancing her husband's career—which she saw as her own career as well. And she didn't care how much turbulence she kicked up while doing it. With her fierce protection of her husband's career and her intense political ambition, she was something of a mix of two future first ladies: Nancy Reagan and Hillary Clinton.

Washington insiders soon learned that understanding Bethine was the key to understanding Frank Church.

*　*　*

During dinner out at a restaurant with some friends one evening in Bethesda, Frank gave a toast to Bethine. "You are a hurricane. You are a volcano. You are a jewel."

The toast was a perfect description of Bethine, Carl Burke, Church's lifelong friend, once observed. "They work together as a team. They are truly in love. There are always fights."

What was already well-known in Idaho was also soon clear in Washington: Not only was Bethine a political junkie, but she was much more astute about politics than her husband. She had absorbed politics growing up as the daughter of a governor, and now that she was in Washington she refused to stick to the role of the traditional political wife. After Frank Church was first elected, Rosemary Smathers, the wife of Democratic senator George Smathers of Florida, took her out to lunch to warn her that she would hate Washington, because "the minute you get here, you're just a wife," Bethine wrote in her memoir. "The senator always has other things to do. There are people who want him around them, but they don't really care about whether you're there or not."

Bethine Church vowed never to let that happen to her. Instead, she was intensely involved in her husband's decision-making from the start of his Senate career. It wasn't long before she became known in Washington as "Idaho's third senator." Her granddaughter, Monica Church, later observed that "Bethine was kind of born at the wrong time; I think she wanted to be a senator." She would call the office every day to direct the staff, to remind them to make sure Church looked good, was meeting with the right people, and stayed on schedule. "If something bothered her, she would let you know," added family friend and Church staffer Peter Fenn. "She was in on everything." Whenever they returned to Idaho, it was Bethine who kept track of the details of politics, like never drinking in public — to avoid offending the state's large Mormon population. (Frank and Bethine would instead bring liquor in their suitcases from Washington, and have cocktails together in their bedroom at Bethine's mother's home in Boise.)

Church hired a secretary who, as one of her main tasks, was obliged to deal with Bethine and keep track of her daily orders and the political social life that Bethine engineered for Frank. "There was some friction between [my mother] and my dad's staff," observed Chase Church, "because they thought she was in the way. But he relied on her."

Bethine knew that she had a volatile temper, which often surfaced when she thought something — or someone — was getting in the way of her efforts to drive her husband to ever-greater political success. Frank Church was politically ambitious, but Bethine constantly pushed him to go further. Yet she was also self-aware enough to worry about the impact her sudden bursts of anger had on her relationship with her husband. "Once in a while I just blow sky high," she recalled in a moment of introspection in a 1979 interview.

> I have a really terrible temper and once in a while everything just gets too much for me and I just go off the deep end. Frank doesn't vent much venom or emotion about things. He's very even... But I think the fact that I have that

kind of disposition, I never hold a grudge more than twenty minutes and I can't be mad overnight, but I can just blow sky high and that I think almost helps relieve him. But I don't know. It's a very complex, it's a complex relationship but I think the one lucky thing I have is that having been his friend before I really fell in love with him, I think I have an ability to sort out what is our political life and what is our personal life. And I'm very different about our political life. I'm much more critical about decisions than I am about our personal life and this helps too...I'm a seat of your pants person and Frank is very cerebral about things.

Almost as soon as he arrived in Washington, Church hired another strong woman, Verda Barnes, who quickly became his political fixer in both Washington and Idaho. After Church hired her on to his Senate staff in 1957, she proved so valuable that within a few years he named Barnes his administrative assistant—then the Senate's term for chief of staff. She was one of the first female administrative assistants in the history of the Senate, and may have been one of the only people with a better feel for Idaho politics than Bethine Church.

Barnes had endured a hard, complicated life, and she used her hard-earned toughness like a weapon in defense of Frank Church. Born into a Mormon family in Idaho in 1907, she had married a grifter named Jack Barnes in 1930, but he disappeared while she was in the hospital giving birth to their daughter, leaving her with a mountain of unpaid bills. As a single mother in the 1930s, she plunged into Idaho politics, keeping her married name from her deadbeat husband.* She went to work for Glen Taylor after he was elected to the Senate in 1944, then followed him into the Progressive Party in 1948, when he was Henry Wallace's running mate;

---

* Verda Barnes received a shock when her long-lost husband reappeared, contacting her daughter, Valorie Taylor, at her home in Bethesda, Maryland. Carolyn Taylor, Verda Barnes's granddaughter, recalled in an interview for this book that Verda's ex-husband finally revealed that his real name was not Jack Barnes, but Jack Tierney. He had been a small-time con man who fabricated the Barnes name before marrying Verda and then skipping out on her and leaving her to pay his debts. When he showed up again, she wanted nothing to do with him, but Verda Barnes continued to use his fake last name.

she served as the chairman of the Progressive Party's Idaho state convention.

Barnes's ties to Glen Taylor nearly cost her the job with Frank Church. After Taylor's bitter accusations that Church had stolen the Democratic Senate primary from him in 1956, Bethine's father, Chase Clark, tried to stop Frank Church from hiring Barnes. But Church overruled his father-in-law.

Hiring Verda Barnes was one of the best decisions Church ever made. Her connections in both Idaho and Washington meant that she could take care of almost any political problem for Church with a few phone calls. She became not only Church's political minder, but the de facto chief political strategist for the Idaho Democratic Party. "Verda knew Idaho politics inside-out," observed Larry La-Rocco, a former Church staffer who was later elected to Congress from Idaho.

Verda Barnes was also Church's strongest connection to organized labor, a key Democratic constituency. Her strong labor ties were reinforced by her long-term affair with Andrew J. Biemiller, the AFL-CIO's chief lobbyist. "Everyone knew about it, it was common family knowledge, but you didn't speak about it," said her granddaughter, Carolyn Taylor, in an interview. "I remember him coming around, he had this sonorous voice," she added. It isn't clear whether Frank Church knew that his top aide was sleeping with labor's top lobbyist.

Verda Barnes and Bethine Church soon became the twin guardians of Frank Church's political career.

* * *

Despite his problems with Lyndon Johnson, Frank Church got plenty of positive publicity from the Washington press corps in his early days in the Senate; he offered a young, handsome contrast to the old, gray men who dominated the Senate in the 1950s. "In Frank Church [reporters] have found a refreshing and colorful new personality who has provided them with reams of copy in this abbreviated first week of the new congressional session," wrote a Washington correspondent for the *Salt Lake Tribune* in January 1957. Church basked in the new limelight, even as other senators soon began to call him a publicity hound behind his back.

Church also experienced a slightly embarrassing but humorous incident, when he inadvertently violated the Senate's stuffy and unwritten protocols. In his 1978 book *On Press*, the *New York Times* columnist Tom Wicker recalled an episode that occurred when both he and Frank Church had just arrived in Washington in 1957. "At a party for new senators, to which the press was invited, I fell into conversation with Frank Church, then thirty-two, the newly-arrived junior senator from Idaho, as green in Washington as I. When I asked how he'd been able to get elected at his age, Church joked that he'd been "in the middle between two nuts," a reference to his opponents (Welker and Taylor). During the same reception, Church and Wicker joined a larger group that included Senator Richard Russell, the tradition-bound and powerful Georgia Democrat who was the keeper of the Senate's rules. "I stole Church's thunder and told his story about being in the middle between two nuts," Wicker recalled. "No one laughed. Russell's face froze ominously; I could see Frank Church looking for a way to go through the floor. I had forgotten that both Herman Welker and Glen Taylor had been United States senators. No matter what their politics had been, they were not in Richard Russell's presence to be referred to as 'nuts' by a young whippersnapper from the press…or a junior senator from Idaho."

Church's brief, mortifying moment with Richard Russell was quickly forgotten, but it would take much more work for him to get back in the good graces of Lyndon Johnson.

CHAPTER 5

"A betrayal"

FRANK CHURCH KNEW he wasn't going anywhere in the Senate if he didn't get into the fight on civil rights, and by the middle of the summer of 1957, he finally had a chance to take the lead on that issue — and get out of Lyndon Johnson's doghouse in the process.

In July 1957, the civil rights bill was stuck in the Senate, its progress stymied over what became known as the jury-trial amendment. Searching for compromise legislation that could prevent Southern obstructionism and win Senate passage, Johnson was pushing a provision that would allow anyone charged with violating the new civil rights act the right to have a trial by jury, rather than just a judge. Southerners demanded the amendment, while liberals opposed it, knowing that all-white juries in the South — where jury duty was limited to registered voters, almost none of whom were Black — would never convict a white official for refusing to protect the civil rights of Blacks.

This time, Church broke with the Northern liberals, sided with Johnson, and voted for the jury-trial amendment. He viewed the jury-trial issue through the prism of the Mountain West, where union leaders had often had to fight both management and the courts during the early days of labor unrest in the minefields. But liberals were dismissive, saying the jury-trial requirement made the civil rights bill toothless.

Now fully engaged in the civil rights debate, Church spent his nights trying to find a solution to break the deadlock over the legislation. The answer Church came up with was elegant: the jury-trial amendment would be supplemented with yet another provision, requiring the desegregation of federal juries. If juries in federal courts in the South included Blacks, anyone who violated the new civil rights act suddenly stood a much greater chance of being convicted by a jury trial.

Church took his proposal to Johnson, who embraced it, and the new version of the legislation finally passed the Senate in August and was signed into law by President Eisenhower in September. Senator John F. Kennedy praised Church for finding a way to break the deadlock. Kennedy voted for Church's new approach, telling Bethine Church that her husband had been critical to passage of the legislation.

Church knew the bill was a compromise, but he saw it as the first step, and believed that the Senate had set an important precedent by passing the first civil rights legislation in a century. "I submit that our work in safeguarding civil rights cannot be accomplished in a single stroke," Church said on the Senate floor. "This law, in whatever form it may take, is but a single step . . . we will find it possible in the years to come to enlarge the scope of this civil rights bill to meet the needs of the coming times."

The Civil Rights Act of 1957 was an important step — the biggest since Reconstruction — toward expanding the rights of Black Americans. It helped pave the way for the landmark civil rights and voting rights legislation of the 1960s, which Church fought for as well. His experience in the battle over civil rights legislation in the 1950s and 1960s helped prepare him for the Church Committee's historic investigation in the 1970s of the FBI's racist record, especially the Bureau's harassment of the Rev. Martin Luther King Jr.

* * *

After having ignored Frank Church for months, Lyndon Johnson now showered him with praise and amply rewarded him for helping get the civil rights bill across the finish line. "After I had played a role in the passage of this legislation, Lyndon Johnson was warmly and massively grateful, so much so that I was almost stifled in his embrace," Church later recalled. "That was the way it was with

Lyndon Johnson...All at once I was in the Garden of Eden, and Lyndon Johnson could not be lavish enough in his praise of me."

Immediately after the bill's passage in August, Johnson appointed Church to be a delegate to an international conference in Argentina, his first overseas trip as a senator. It was quickly seen as a payoff. "Senator Church has now received his reward. He and Mrs. Church have departed for Rio de Janeiro, then on to Buenos Aires... all expenses paid," wrote columnist Drew Pearson. Johnson then gave Church a much bigger reward, naming him to the Foreign Relations Committee, a seat that he knew Church coveted.

Many observers, both at the time and later, believed that Johnson's victory on civil rights in 1957 could be credited to his ability to forge an alliance between Western and Southern senators that watered down the final legislation and made it more palatable to the South. In exchange for Western support for positions that tended to dilute the civil rights bill, critics accused Johnson of arranging for Southern senators to vote with Western Democrats in favor of one of the most important public projects in the West at the time: a huge government-funded dam at Hells Canyon on the Snake River, along the border of Idaho and Oregon. Johnson knew that the dam's construction had been a key issue in Frank Church's Senate campaign in 1956.

The Hells Canyon Dam was to be the second-largest dam in the world. It would cost $300 million to build—a huge sum in the 1950s. Johnson was suspected at the time of having engineered a quid pro quo between South and West, and historians later concluded the same thing.

Church always denied that he had participated in any explicit deal for his support for Johnson's compromise position on civil rights. "There was never any quid pro quo at all," Church later said. "And that really wasn't the way Lyndon Johnson worked, at least as far as my experience goes. He may have with other senators. He never did that with me."

But whether or not Church agreed to a quid pro quo, he benefited from Lyndon Johnson's efforts to broker an alliance between West and South: A bloc of Southern senators did help win Senate passage for the Hells Canyon public project in 1957.

The Hells Canyon vote provided a rare victory for Church in

what would turn out to be a marathon battle pitting advocates of a public dam against Idaho Power Company, the private utility that wanted to build three smaller dams of its own instead. The company's proposal had strong Republican backing in Idaho and in the Eisenhower Administration; Church and other Western Democrats, advocating for public rather than private hydroelectric power, were fighting an uphill battle.

More broadly, Hells Canyon was part of an emerging cultural battle in the West, as big businesses like Idaho Power were starting to successfully exploit public resentment against the federal government to win support for the private exploitation of natural resources.

The Hells Canyon debate has "divided the people of Idaho into hostile camps; it is regrettable that a determined and resourceful indoctrination campaign has been waged against this bill, and many in my state have been taught to believe that the Hells Canyon dam is a threat to Idaho," Church said in a 1957 Senate speech in support of funding for the public dam, a speech that predicted the rise of Reagan Republicanism and the so-called Sagebrush Rebellion of the 1970s and 1980s. "Some have been deluded to the point where they now assert that the future development of our great public rivers can safely be entrusted only to private interests."

Ultimately, Idaho Power won the Hells Canyon battle, with strong backing from the Eisenhower Administration. The public dam project, which had won a brief victory in the Senate in 1957, died in the House of Representatives, and Idaho Power went on to build its three private dams.

Critics believed that outcome was predictable, and that Johnson had thus won Western support for his compromise position on civil rights without giving the Westerners a substantive victory in return. The Senate vote in favor of the government-backed Hells Canyon dam had been largely symbolic.

Senator Paul Douglas, a leading liberal Democrat from Illinois and an outspoken critic of Johnson's civil rights legislation, which he thought was too weak, told Church that he had been tricked by Johnson. Douglas knew — as Johnson surely did too — that the Senate vote in favor of the Hells Canyon public dam would not stand for long.

Immediately after the Senate vote approving the Hells Canyon dam, Douglas turned to Church on the Senate floor and said

"Frank, I am afraid you Hells Canyon folk have been given some counterfeit money," Douglas recounted in his memoir. "I predicted that the private power boys would beat the bill in the House, either in committee or on the floor. That is precisely what happened."

While he lost to Idaho Power, the battle over Hells Canyon still had a lasting impact on Church. It played an important role in his gradual transformation from traditional advocate of large-scale infrastructure projects to conservationist and environmental pioneer. Ahead of his time, Church began to see that Idaho's greatest resource was its wild scenic beauty, which could attract a new kind of economic development — tourism.

Church's evolution on environmental issues began in 1958, as a result of what became known in Idaho as the "Oxbow Incident." Idaho Power had agreed to maintain salmon runs on the Snake River in order to win the right to build its dams. But in the fall of 1958, salmon seeking to run the river suffered a mass killing and population collapse as a result of Idaho Power's ineffective efforts to transport the salmon around the utility's Oxbow Dam construction site.

That environmental disaster helped change Church's thinking about Idaho's natural resources, transforming him from dam builder to conservationist. After the salmon catastrophe on the Snake River, in 1959 and 1960 he pushed legislation to prohibit dams on Idaho's Salmon River in order to prevent damage to its salmon-spawning grounds. Despite heavy opposition and several failures in Congress, Church persisted with the legislation, eventually winning passage after he broadened its scope beyond the Salmon River. The bill became the National Wild and Scenic Rivers Act of 1968, which today protects more than 13,000 miles of 226 rivers in 41 states from excessive development.

Long before other political leaders, Church "began to see the value of wild places and to believe that rivers offered more than power production opportunities and irrigation water," observed historian Sara Dant, in a study of Church's conservation record. And by the late 1960s, the public in Idaho was beginning to catch up to Church, showing increasing support for his focus on the environment. That gave Church the latitude he needed to mount one of the most ambitious campaigns of wilderness conservation in American history.

Church used federal legislation to preserve huge swaths of wilderness in his home state, and in the process almost single-handedly remade the map of Idaho. He was the political architect behind the creation of Idaho's 662,000-acre Hells Canyon National Recreation Area, 730,000-acre Sawtooth National Recreation Area, 205,000-acre Gospel Hump Wilderness, and 2.3 million-acre River of No Return Wilderness, the largest roadless area in the lower 48 states.

To fend off criticism and avoid the appearance of a conflict of interest, in 1971 Church and his wife sold their share in the Robinson Bar Ranch in Stanley, Idaho, a guest ranch near the proposed Sawtooth National Recreation Area. Bethine's family had owned the ranch for decades; she and Frank had been married there, so Bethine considered the sale a major personal sacrifice for the sake of her husband's political career. "Whatever the future may bring, we have concluded that we should not keep a business in these mountains to which anyone could point as a possible conflict of interest," Bethine Church said at the time. "We do not feel that we can retain the ownership of a guest ranch anywhere near the Sawtooths." The ranch was later bought by singer Carole King.

Wilderness conservation became one of Church's hallmarks, and he continued to push to expand protected areas even as a conservative backlash grew in the late 1970s. The legislation creating the River of No Return Wilderness, the crown jewel of Church's conservation efforts, would not be signed until 1980, when Church was running for reelection against a conservative acolyte of Ronald Reagan. The River of No Return preservation "was very tough," recalled LaRocco. "The mining industry was against it, the farm bureau was against it, and the Sagebrush rebels were sharpening their swords."

* * *

Frank Church was quickly emerging as a rising star in the Democratic Party, and the attention was giving him ambitions beyond Idaho and the Senate. He lobbied hard to be chosen to give the keynote address at the 1960 Democratic National Convention in Los Angeles — an early sign that he wanted to run for president. "He made it pretty clear right early in the game that he wanted [to give the keynote address]" John Carver, an early Church aide, later said. It was part of Church efforts at "getting a national reputation."

During the months leading up to the 1960 convention, none of the leading Democratic candidates had locked up the nomination, so Church decided not to publicly endorse any of them; he wanted to avoid alienating any party leader involved in selecting the key-note speaker. Privately, however, Church supported the front-runner, Senator John F. Kennedy. Lyndon Johnson, Kennedy's main rival, was furious when he finally realized that Church was not backing him, despite the fact that he had showered Church with benefits in the Senate.

But Church felt more kinship with Kennedy than with Johnson. The two men were both young veterans of World War II, were both interested in foreign policy, and were both becoming impatient for change in the Democratic Party and the wider postwar world. Above all, Church — like so many of his generation — fell for the Kennedy charisma.

The two first met when Kennedy came to Twin Falls, Idaho, to speak on Church's behalf during his first Senate campaign in 1956. Church didn't forget it. "Oh, I think it was definitely helpful," Church later said. "He was a national celebrity, and even though we failed to carry Twin Falls County in that election, Kennedy's appearance in such staunch Republican country was helpful to me." Johnson, by contrast, had not come to Idaho at all.

Senator Frank Church with John F. Kennedy — the only president that Church ever considered a friend.

Church also served with Kennedy on the McClellan racketeering committee in the late 1950s — work that Church found "distasteful," as an aide later put it. But it is where he first came into contact with Kennedy's younger brother Robert F. Kennedy, who was the committee's chief counsel, and who gained fame for his intense confrontations with Teamsters leader Jimmy Hoffa during the committee's hearings.

Knowing that Church was on their side, the Kennedy campaign quietly supported his selection to give the convention's keynote address. Church later said he believed they wanted him because Kennedy was concerned the Republicans would use his own youth and relative inexperience against him in the general election campaign against Vice President Richard Nixon. "So I think the reason the Kennedy people wanted me to be the keynoter... was because I was a senator who was even younger, conspicuously younger, than the candidate," Church recalled. "Being thirty-six at the time, I still looked to be about twenty-six, and Kennedy appeared to be in the vigor of his middle age by comparison." (After Kennedy finally wrapped up the nomination, the Massachusetts senator balanced the Democratic ticket by choosing Johnson, older and a Southerner, to be his vice-presidential running mate.)

Church realized that the keynote address would be his introduction to the nation, and so he worked on the speech for months. He carefully memorized his speech, but at the last minute, he was ambushed by the new technology in use at the convention for the first time — the teleprompter. "It was the first convention with the modern teleprompter, which Church had never used and did not need," Church's son Forrest recalled in his memoir. "He said to the convention manager that he did not want the teleprompter. This fell on deaf ears. The result was that throughout his speech, when he added a line or skipped a phrase, the operator would frantically roll the text backward and forward. The text on the teleprompter and the text in his mind were not the same. The operator, not knowing this, finally decided that the trouble must be position... [and] began rolling the [teleprompter] platform up a bit and then down a bit. The general effect... was a blur of moving words wherever he looked, and a grinding of gears as the platform moved."

Church was able to finish the speech, which in content, if not in form, was exactly what the Kennedy campaign had wanted.

Church's keynote reflected Kennedy's arguments on the campaign trail that the Eisenhower Administration — and by extension Richard Nixon, Eisenhower's vice president — had not been aggressive enough in pushing back against the Soviet Union.

"Two ways of life, Freedom and Communism, are locked in mortal competition," Church pronounced.

> The communists have seized a third of the world in 15 years! History does not record another conquest so large in so short a time. I submit to you that the fateful decisions taken in Washington today and tomorrow will determine whether our grandchildren shall be free. These are the grave stakes deeply involved in the coming national election, and the mission of the Democratic Party is to reawaken America to the mighty task before her. The hinge of the future swings on the United States. The maintenance of peace, the preservation of freedom, the fate of the world all ultimately depend upon American principle, American prestige, and American power.

Church's keynote address was little more than a stale rehashing of anti-Communist, Cold War–era dogma — and one of the worst major speeches of his career. John Carver, Church's aide, later said he thought it was a "lousy speech...it didn't go over." Eager to be part of Kennedy's circle at the height of Cold War tensions, Church's sense of outrage over the threat of American imperialism seemed to have vanished.

* * *

Frank Church campaigned intensely for Kennedy after the 1960 convention, and Church's old friend Carl Burke, who had run his 1956 Senate campaign, now helped run Kennedy's presidential campaign in Idaho.

When Kennedy beat Nixon in the general election that fall, Church was elated. He now had a friend in the White House — a young, vigorous leader of his own party, whom Church looked up to and was eager to follow. (Church's love-hate relationship with Lyndon Johnson was now on hold, since Johnson was now Kennedy's vice president and was largely sidelined by the Kennedy White House.)

Frank and Bethine Church fully bought into the Kennedy "Camelot" mystique, and soon found themselves caught up in the intoxicating swirl of the White House social circle. Bethine would look back on the early days of the Kennedy White House as "magical." Kennedy loved suddenly showing up at private parties around Washington, she later recalled: "I remember one in particular... Frank had to go to a different reception, with men from Idaho, so I was alone in a crowded room when the president came along to say hello. A woman simply dripping with diamonds shoved me aside to greet the president. Kennedy just leaned around her and said, 'Bethine, where's your fellow? Oh, I know, he's tending to business.' The diamond lady looked at me in bewilderment. In my date book I included one of my few commentaries on the day's schedule: 'Talked with JFK. Red Letter Day.'"

Church was easily reelected in 1962, making him the first Democrat ever to win reelection to the Senate from Idaho. Church benefited from his rising national prominence, a weak Republican candidate, and the fact that the election was held right after the Cuban Missile Crisis in October 1962 — arguably President Kennedy's biggest foreign-policy success.

But one of the biggest foreign-policy debacles in American history was already underway in Vietnam; the former French colony had been partitioned following France's defeat by Ho Chi Minh's insurgents in 1954, and Kennedy was quietly increasing American military support for South Vietnam in its war against both the Viet Cong and the communist government in North Vietnam. In the early 1960s under Kennedy, Americans were fighting and dying in Vietnam, even as they were officially listed only as "advisers" to the South Vietnamese army.

*　*　*

In December 1962, right after his reelection to a second Senate term, Church made his first visit to Vietnam, a trip with two other senators that led Church to begin to have doubts about the U.S. role in the war.

After arriving in Saigon, Church and the other senators were subjected to an intense public-relations blitz by American and South Vietnamese officials, who tried to convince them that the U.S.-backed counterinsurgency strategy was on the right track, and that the war was going well. Church was not fooled; he drew on his time as an Army intelligence officer in China during World War II, when he had seen the truth about the corruption of the Chinese nationalist regime of Chiang Kai-shek.

"I remember on that trip, I came away with my first strong misgivings about Vietnam and our policy over there," Church recalled later. "They took us on a typical cook's tour (old slang for a rushed and cursory visit) that was meant to impress. It was very unimpressive."

Church's visit included a tour of the so-called strategic hamlet program, where many of South Vietnam's rural citizens were forcibly relocated into villages little better than internment camps. It deepened his fears about Saigon's aloof leadership. "They took us out to a fortified village," Church recalled, "where we were supposed to be impressed with the fortifications...and I was simply impressed by the vast amount of jungle we flew over and the perfect cover it gave to guerrilla forces. And these fortified villages were pitiful little islands that meant nothing and could be easily surrounded and isolated. So it seemed to me that the whole military strategy showed a clear weakness of the South Vietnamese government among its own people."

Eventually, the Vietnam War would help define Church's political career and radicalize his views on American national security and foreign policy.

But not yet.

While Church raised questions about Vietnam with Kennedy Administration officials, he wasn't ready to become a vocal opponent of the war. During the Kennedy years, he aimed his criticism not at the White House but at the corrupt and abusive regime of South Vietnam's leader, Ngo Dinh Diem. In September 1963, Church cosponsored a Senate resolution calling for U.S. economic and military aid to be cut off "unless the government of South Vietnam abandons policies of repression against its people and makes a determined effort to regain their support." The White House was pleased; it gave Kennedy leverage in his talks with Diem. Kennedy's national security adviser, McGeorge Bundy, called Church and told him to "keep it up."

But the truth was that Church pulled his punches on Vietnam while Kennedy was president. Church was reluctant to tell Kennedy what he feared most: that his Vietnam policies were leading America into a senseless war. And years later, he was still willing to give Kennedy the benefit of the doubt, still willing to believe that Kennedy would never have made Lyndon Johnson's mistake of deepening American involvement in the war. "I like to believe that he would not have made the fatal error of committing American troops to another Asian war in pursuit of a policy that made no sense," Church later observed.

Frank Church had a blind spot when it came to John Kennedy; his willingness to believe the best of the only president whom Church ever considered a friend would lead to controversy years later, when the Church Committee uncovered the ugly truth about the CIA and the Kennedys.

* * *

On November 22, 1963, Frank Church was at the State Department, having lunch with Averell Harriman, the wise old man of Democratic politics who was then Undersecretary of State for Political Affairs in the Kennedy Administration, when he heard that President Kennedy had been shot in Dallas. Frank and Bethine Church walked through the next few days in shock; a black-bordered invitation came for a memorial service in the Capitol Rotunda, where Kennedy lay in state. There was a visit to the White House, where Kennedy's coffin again lay in state. And along with much of official Washington, the couple walked behind the hearse carrying Kennedy's coffin up to Arlington National Cemetery, where he was buried and an eternal candle was lit.

Their friend was dead, and now Lyndon Johnson, who had played such a powerful and volatile role in Frank Church's life when he was Senate Majority Leader before becoming vice president under Kennedy, was president. Frank Church would never have the kind of warm relationship with Johnson that he had enjoyed with Kennedy; Church would be much less willing to pull his punches to help Johnson, or provide political protection for him. In fact, their relationship, never stable to begin with, dramatically worsened after Johnson became president—because of Vietnam.

Church was much more open with his criticism of the war after Johnson became president. He began to make public comments that angered Johnson and were considered outside the hawkish mainstream of the Democratic Party at the time by both Johnson and other Democratic leaders. On March 15, 1964, Church told the *Washington Evening Star* that if North Vietnamese leader Ho Chi Minh "is regarded by most Vietnamese people, North and South, as the authentic architect of independence from the French, as the George Washington of Vietnam, so to speak, [then] it will be hard for us." During an executive session of the Senate Foreign Relations Committee on June 15, 1964, Church questioned Secretary of State Dean Rusk, who argued that the war in Vietnam was part of the international contest with communism. Church responded that the "great bulk of the revolutionaries are South Vietnamese" who viewed Ho Chi Minh as primarily a nationalist—and the war as "a continuation of the revolution that commenced much earlier, and did not end with the defeat of the French."

But Church was not yet ready to break fully with Johnson on Vietnam in 1964, fearing that the Republican presidential candidate Barry Goldwater, an extreme conservative who was even more hawkish on Vietnam than Johnson, would exploit Democratic divisions to win the White House in that fall's elections. That fear led Church to make what he later considered to be one of the biggest mistakes of his Senate career.

Senator Frank Church holds an intense conversation with President Lyndon Johnson in the White House Cabinet Room during the Vietnam War.

Eager for congressional authorization to escalate U.S. military involvement in Vietnam in 1964, Lyndon Johnson had his aides prepare a resolution that he could present to Congress when the time was right to give him a free hand to use force in Vietnam. In August 1964, Johnson found the excuse he was waiting for: a supposed North Vietnamese attack on U.S. Navy ships in the Gulf of Tonkin, off the coast of North Vietnam.

On the night of August 4, amid stormy seas, the USS *Maddox* and the USS *Turner Joy* reported that they had been attacked by North Vietnamese torpedo boats; the evidence subsequently showed almost certainly that no attack had taken place that night. Johnson seized on the supposed incident, fomented a crisis, and demanded that Congress swiftly pass a resolution granting him the power to wage unfettered war in Vietnam.

The Gulf of Tonkin Resolution passed the Senate with only two dissenting votes, and Church went along with the majority. "There is a time to question the route of the flag, and there is a time to rally around it, lest it be routed," Church stated in an August 6, 1964, press release explaining his vote for the resolution. "The attacks on our ships cannot be justified. It was an act of aggression on the high seas. When this country, or its ships, or its military personnel, are made targets of attack, then Congress will uphold whatever action the President takes in defense of American interests and American lives." The press release added that "Church said he believed President Johnson to be a man of peace who will do everything possible to keep the war from spreading in this seething and dangerous area of the world."

He voted for the resolution, "reasoning that the Democrats should stick together to help defeat Barry Goldwater," Forrest Church wrote in his memoir.

But "he regretted that vote to the end of his life."

*   *   *

Church intensified his opposition to the war after Johnson's landslide victory against Goldwater in the 1964 election. In December 1964, almost as soon as the election was over, Church gave a lengthy interview to *Ramparts* magazine, which was run by an old friend from Stanford, expressing deep concern over the expanding American role in the war. "The thing we must remember, is that there is no way for us to win their war for them," Church said. "It is a guerrilla war, at root an indigenous revolution against the existing government...I would hope we would recognize that it is not our country and never has been."

He also made clear that he didn't believe the regime in Saigon was worth the lives of American soldiers. The South Vietnamese government, he said, "must be viewed for what it is, a military despotism. Communist North Vietnam is also such a despotism, but this hardly gives the people of South Vietnam a clear-cut choice between free government and tyranny. Nor should we think of this war in terms of preserving a free economic system against the imposition of a socialist system, for the fact is that both the governments are committed to socialism."

Church's *Ramparts* interview was covered by the *New York Times*, and Church followed up with a major Senate speech in February 1965 that hit the same themes, calling for a political settlement in Vietnam.

Church's anger over Vietnam grew throughout 1965. Johnson had said during his reelection campaign the previous year that he didn't want to turn Vietnam into an American war, but in 1965 he introduced U.S. ground troops and began a rapid escalation of the conflict. Church believed that Johnson had broken a fundamental promise, and he was irate. "I supported Lyndon Johnson with enthusiasm [in 1964]," Church later said. "He said to the country, in words that everyone could understand, that American boys should not be sent to do the fighting that Asian boys should do themselves...No sooner had he become president...[than] he proceeded to convert the war in Vietnam into an American war. And that was a betrayal."

Church's views on Vietnam were heavily influenced by Hans Morgenthau, a prominent foreign-policy analyst who had been ousted from the Johnson Administration for publicly criticizing the war. Morgenthau viewed the conflict as a civil war and a sideshow that should not have become America's military focus. In early 1965, Church hosted a dinner bringing together Morgenthau and Senator J. William Fulbright, the Arkansas Democrat who was chairman of the Senate Foreign Relations Committee; the event was clearly part of Church's quiet efforts to move Fulbright to a position of more open opposition to the war.

By now, his views on Vietnam were also starting to influence his broader outlook on American foreign policy. He was no longer a Kennedy-style Cold Warrior. "The pendulum of our foreign policy can swing from one extreme to the other," Church said in his February speech in the Senate. "Once we thought that anything which happened abroad was none of our business; now we evidently think that everything which happens abroad has become our business. In the span of 30 years, an excess of isolationism has been transformed into an excess of interventionism.

"Why have we spread ourselves so thin?" he asked. "What compulsion draws us, ever deeper, into the internal affairs of so many countries in Africa and Asia, having so remote a connection with the vital interests of the United States?"

*   *   *

Church's increasingly public dissent on Vietnam worried Bethine Church, who feared that it would make him radioactive in Idaho. "Bethine early on told him don't go so far on Vietnam," recalled Peter Fenn. In fact, Church's growing opposition to the war was making Church a frequent target of Johnson's ire.

In March 1965, Church attended a White House briefing on Vietnam that President Johnson gave to a small group of senators. Johnson told the group that "there once was a senator who thought he knew more about war and peace than the president, and who predicted peace just before world war." It was a clear reference to William Borah, and it was designed as a slap at Church. "He said this looking straight at me," Church later recalled. At the end of the briefing, Johnson and Church stood alone, debating, while the other senators waited for them to finish. Senator Eugene McCarthy, the Minnesota Democrat who three years later would challenge Johnson for the presidency, quipped that "If Church had just surrendered, we could have gone home 30 minutes ago."

The Washington press corps ate up stories about the growing tension between Johnson and Church. There were reports in the press that during one conversation, Johnson had asked Church where he got his information on Vietnam. "Walter Lippmann," Church supposedly responded, referring to a legendary columnist.

Johnson allegedly replied, "Then the next time you want a dam, talk to Walter Lippmann."

The story was false, and had been leaked to the press by Johnson in an effort to make Church look bad. But Church would not back down.

Church also had a bitter private argument with Johnson about Vietnam when he flew with the president to San Francisco for the 20th anniversary of the United Nations in June 1965. During their flight, Johnson showed Church a new report about a bombing in Vietnam that had killed several American soldiers, then sneeringly said to Church, "I suppose you'd turn the other cheek."

Replied Church: "We're the ones that sent them out there. And we did so knowing the danger."

After that, Church later recalled, Johnson "whirled around in his chair and turned his back on me."

Church was now determined to move more openly and forcefully to oppose the war. In July 1965 he began to push for public hearings on Vietnam by the Senate Foreign Relations Committee, saying that the committee's closed-door meetings on Vietnam were having no impact. In an executive session of the committee, Church called for public hearings that would examine the "whole philosophical argument as it affects American foreign policy generally, which has led us into Vietnam."

But Fulbright, the committee's chairman, was not yet ready to follow Church and break so completely with the White House. Johnson was trying to stifle any significant congressional debate or criticism of his Vietnam policies, and in mid-1965 Democratic leaders like Fulbright were still willing to go along with him.

But Church kept pushing, and in November he wrote a widely read piece in the *New York Times Magazine* in which he argued that the United States had to recognize that it should no longer try to block nationalist revolutions in Vietnam and elsewhere around the world. The U.S. should "escape the trap of becoming so preoccupied with communism...that we dissipate our strength in a vain attempt to enforce a global guarantee against it."

Church also began to see signs that at least some people in Idaho shared his frustrations with the war. In early 1966, a sympathetic Idaho voter forwarded Church a letter he had received from a friend serving in Vietnam. "I've never been so disillusioned with our country as after my experiences here for the last five months or so," the soldier, then advising a South Vietnamese army unit, had

Senator Frank Church, with Senator J. William Fulbright, longtime chairman of the Senate Foreign Relations Committee, in the background. Fulbright and Church had a tense relationship, beginning when Church started pushing Fulbright to hold hearings on Vietnam; Fulbright never trusted Church.

written. "They said my battalion killed or captured 175 [Viet Cong] however I have only seen two bodies and 8 prisoners in all our actions...but these false paper reports satisfy Washington...They are living in a dream world. But I'm afraid they are only fooling themselves, and the American public."

In December 1965, President Johnson ordered a brief halt to the bombing of North Vietnam, but the pause failed to change anything. Frustrated, Fulbright was finally ready for public hearings, which were held in January and February of 1966. Church took a leading role in questioning high-profile witnesses, and in the process revealed his deepening opposition to the war.

During the hearings, Church kept his focus on the big picture about the war and American foreign policy, just as he had suggested the previous summer when he began to urge Fulbright and the committee to go public. He confronted Secretary of State Dean Rusk, the Johnson administration's main witness, by arguing that the United States was uselessly mired in a war that should be left to the Vietnamese, and that the White House was in denial about the true nature of the conflict:

"You can look at the war in Vietnam as a covert invasion of the South by the North or you can look at it as some other scholars do, as basically an indigenous war to which the North has given a growing measure of aid and abetment; but either way you look at it, it is a war between the Vietnamese to determine what the ultimate kind of government is going to be for Vietnam. When I went to school, that was a civil war. I am told these days it is not a civil war anymore."

Church also attacked the most fundamental argument used by Johnson to justify the war — that the United States had to fight in Vietnam to uphold the long-standing American policy of "containment" of the Soviet Union. Church argued that containment's original objective was to prevent Moscow from gaining control over Western Europe, and that Johnson was perverting its meaning by applying it to Vietnam. "Now it seems to me," Church said during the hearings, "that we have made no mistake so fundamental in American foreign policy than concluding that a design that was suitable for Europe would also be suitable for those regions of the world that have just thrust off European rule, and that we failed to take into account how very different the underlying situation was in Asia and in Africa, the ex-colonial regions of the world."

The nationally televised hearings were a much bigger hit than Church ever imagined when he began pushing for them; afterward, the committee was flooded with more than 20,000 letters and telegrams about the war. The public saw a restless Congress finally beginning to challenge the case for war, and that touched a nerve nationwide. The hearings — which became widely known as the Fulbright hearings — had a dramatic and lasting impact on American attitudes about Vietnam; they legitimized opposition to the Vietnam War for the American mainstream, and helped the antiwar movement expand beyond college campuses.

"Once it became apparent to the American people," Church

recalled later, "that there were members of this committee who...
disagreed with the war, the necessity of the war, and who strongly
opposed the widening of the war, then the general resistance to the
war and the debate itself over the war began to spread in the country."

Church's anti-war stance would be on trial in Idaho in both
1967 and 1968.

CHAPTER 6

"War prolonged and unending"

DURING HIS FIRST decade in the Senate, Frank Church had evolved from a conventional 1950s Democrat who accepted the hawkish tenets of the Cold War into a major liberal voice against the Vietnam War. He had pushed for the Fulbright hearings in 1966, which helped change the national debate over the war and gave mainstream legitimacy to the anti-war movement. He had become a thorn in the side of his one-time mentor, President Lyndon Johnson, because Church had gained too much stature to be easily dismissed like other early opponents of the war.

By 1967, at the start of his second decade in the Senate, Church began to move even further. Over the next few years, he came to see that the Vietnam War, seemingly unstoppable by Congress, was really a symptom of a much larger, structural problem in the way America dealt with the rest of the world, as well as with its own citizens. It was this decisive shift against the American status quo by Church, radical at the time, that would ultimately lead him to his greatest achievements.

While Lyndon Johnson was infuriated by Frank Church and other leading "doves" in Congress, he was even more enraged by the growing momentum behind the anti-war movement throughout the country. So under Johnson, the CIA began to spy on American anti-war activists, working with colleges, police, and other informants to identify the leaders of anti-war groups.

Church did not yet know about the CIA's secret efforts to spy on anti-war dissidents. In the mid-1960s, there was still no real congressional oversight of the CIA, and almost no one in Congress fully understood how the Agency had been transformed from its original purpose of providing objective intelligence analysis into a ruthless weapon that could be wielded both at home and abroad.

But Church had an instinctual sense that Vietnam was unleashing the power of the national security state that had been built in the wake of World War II, and that it was turning the United States into an imperial power rather than a democratic republic. Rather than becoming a force for peace, America was becoming a destroyer of it. Church's political outlook was now a heady mix of idealism and cynicism.

*　*　*

Frank Church, the mainstream politician from a conservative rural state, was quietly becoming a political radical. But that wasn't enough to satisfy his oldest son, Forrest Church, who as a student at Stanford had become deeply opposed to the war and increasingly rebellious against a father he now saw as an establishment sellout. Forrest Church's anger and frustration over the Vietnam War led him to become a pacifist — and to grow deeply depressed by American society.

Despite his father's opposition to the war, Forrest saw him as nothing more than a tool of the establishment. Forrest broke ties with his father, and their rift in the late 1960s became one of the most emotionally painful periods that Frank Church ever experienced. It served as a personal reminder for Frank Church and his family of the divisions that the Vietnam War was inflicting on the nation, and it led him to redouble his efforts to bring the war to an end.

Growing up, Forrest Church was his father's admiring son and his namesake — Frank Forrester Church IV. As a young boy, Forrest split time between Idaho and Washington, and attended schools in both, as his parents moved back and forth depending on the Senate calendar.

By the time he was in high school, Forrest stayed mostly in Washington; he went to Walt Whitman High School, an elite public high school in Bethesda, Maryland, often hanging out with Peter Fenn, his best friend — who practically lived with the Church family. Forrest Church shared many of his father's traits: he loved the life of the mind and showed little aptitude for sports. "Forrest was the kind of guy who loved to read Nabokov," recalled Fenn.

But his parents were often absent during Forrest's childhood and teenage years, as both his father and his mother made Frank Church's political career, rather than parental supervision, their top priority. When they were in Idaho, Forrest often stayed with his grandparents while Frank and Bethine tended to political business; in Washington they hired a live-in French-Canadian maid, who watched over Forrest and Chase when Frank and Bethine were at political or social events.

With lax supervision, Forrest grew independent. But in high school, he was still a conventional teenager, and readily enrolled at his father's alma mater, Stanford. He later admitted that he was probably accepted to Stanford because of his father; when Forrest arrived at Stanford in 1966, he even joined his father's old fraternity.

Before long, however, Forrest began drinking, partying, and experimenting with drugs, including LSD, and his mood darkened after a close college friend suddenly died while on a vacation. He grew depressed and anxious, just as his opposition to the war was also intensifying. As anti-war protests began to shake Stanford and other college campuses, Forrest Church was rebelling, moving inexorably away from his father.

"Much of our estrangement...had nothing to do with issues," Forrest Church later wrote in his memoir. "It had to do with my own emergent and inarticulate discovery of self, this at a time when my parents were fighting for political survival."

*　　*　　*

By 1967, just as his son was in turmoil, Frank Church's growing opposition to the war in Vietnam was running headlong into the changing politics of Idaho. A new force was emerging that was determined to challenge Idaho's political establishment—and Frank Church in particular—the Radical Right.

Ron Rankin was an angry ideologue searching for a place to build a right-wing paradise when he moved to Idaho in 1965. He wanted to bulldoze the local political landscape and remake the state into a sanctuary for like-minded zealots who thought Ronald Reagan was too liberal.

But first, he had to take on Frank Church.

Rankin had spent years on the political fringe of southern California, and was always impatient with moderation. Born in Oklahoma in 1929 and raised in California, Rankin was a committed activist who helped push the Republican Party in southern California far to the right in the early 1960s, just in time for the 1964 presidential campaign of Rankin's hero, Barry Goldwater. Goldwater's catchphrase — *Extremism in defense of liberty is no vice* — was a call to arms for an entire generation of committed young conservatives like Rankin.

When Goldwater was crushed that year in Lyndon Johnson's landslide victory, a disgusted Rankin gave up on California. Urban America was changing too fast. He left Orange County for Coeur d'Alene, in northern Idaho, after a calculated search for a small, rural state where he thought his hard-right politics could have an impact. Rankin "looked at the constitutions of the various states along the Rockies, from Idaho to New Mexico, and Idaho's constitution was so far backwards by contemporary comparison as to be, in our estimation, ahead of the others," he later explained.

By 1967, just two years after moving to the state, Rankin had found his new political cause — the defeat of Senator Frank Church, the state's liberal icon. Church stood in the way of Rankin's goal of remaking Idaho.

Rankin was outraged that Idaho had a liberal Democratic senator who was one of the leading voices in Washington against the war in Vietnam. Rankin was so angry with Church's anti-war stance that he wasn't willing to wait until 1968, when Church would be up for reelection. Instead, Rankin joined forces with a motley crew from Idaho's right-wing fringe, Gene Mileck, the dogcatcher of St. Maries, Idaho, and together they launched a recall campaign against Church. They were backed by a far-right California businessman whose sudden wealth came from what was later revealed to be a massive pyramid scheme. Their so-called Victory in Vietnam Committee began its recall effort against Church in March 1967, a year after the televised Fulbright hearings on the Vietnam War first brought national prominence to Church and his anti-war views. Rankin's group went after Church because, they said, he had "consistently opposed military measures which would help win the war in Viet Nam and save the lives of hundreds of Americans dying in Viet Nam each week the war continues."

Frank Church had to take Ron Rankin's recall campaign seriously, because it came at a dangerous time. Church's decision to become one of the first senators to openly oppose the Vietnam War had left him politically exposed at home. He had not faced the voters of Idaho since breaking with President Johnson on Vietnam, and he wasn't sure how they would respond to the fact that he had become a leading voice against the war.

What was worse, the recall came at a time when the Democratic Party in Idaho was badly divided. A bitter battle had erupted the year before between conservatives and liberals for control of the party, and Frank Church had sided with the liberals. That led to a rift between Church and the party's old guard, raising new questions about whether the party would unite to support him in the face of the recall attempt and his 1968 reelection bid.

In 1966, Cecil Andrus, who was then a young, ambitious, and liberal state senator, challenged Tom Boise, the longtime conservative boss of the state's Democratic Party machine. Andrus sought the Democratic nomination for governor against Boise's favored candidate, splitting the state Democratic Party into warring camps.

Beyond his own reelection campaigns, Frank Church rarely intervened in Idaho state politics. But by 1966, Church was chafing under Tom Boise's control over the state party machinery. Boise had been the state party's unrivaled leader since Franklin Roosevelt was president, but in the late 1950s and early 1960s he had angered Church by pushing controversial pro-gambling measures. Those proposals alienated the large Mormon population in southeastern Idaho, which Church assiduously courted each time he ran for reelection. While Church had depended on Tom Boise's machine in the past, he was also starting to see that the Idaho Democratic Party desperately needed a Kennedy-style generational change. So Church sided with Andrus, and arranged for Verda Barnes to fly in from Washington to help Andrus break the conservative grip on the party.

Andrus won the Democratic nomination — but only after Tom Boise's first choice for governor died in a plane crash. Andrus failed to unify the party, losing the general election to Republican Don Samuelson, in a race in which two independent candidates combined to take more than 20 percent of the vote. The Democrats also lost a House seat, and many Idaho conservatives fled the Democratic Party, never to return.

The 1966 Democratic Party civil war in Idaho led to recriminations against Church for his intervention. "Frank, yourself and Verda came to Idaho and engineered a political disaster for the Idaho Democratic Party," one longtime Idaho Democrat complained to Church. "Why did you do this to us?"

By intervening, "Church had reshaped the Idaho Democratic party into something closer to his own image—which terrified many Democrats," one journalist later wrote.

Days after the 1966 election, Carl Burke, Church's longtime friend and campaign manager, wrote Church a letter warning him that the party divisions posed a serious threat to Church's reelection bid in 1968. "The campaign wounds are still bleeding and the Democratic workers are looking for solace," Burke wrote. "We have a lot of things to do about the political situation in the state and how it should be run."

Burke later admitted that Church's decision to intervene in the state-party fight "wasn't necessarily the wisest political move. You usually make some political enemies any time you take sides in a primary you're not involved in yourself."

*　　*　　*

Ron Rankin's recall campaign began just months after the bitter Democratic split in 1966, and Frank Church knew he would have to work hard to mend fences throughout the state.

More broadly, national political observers saw the recall campaign as a sign of the political dangers facing liberal Democrats like Church who took strong stands against the Vietnam War. Far-right figures around the nation were thrilled by the proposed recall. "The darling of the doves and one of the chief advocates of a Viet Nam surrender policy may have to defend himself from the wrath of his constituents sooner than the 1968 general elections," wrote *The Eagle*, a right-wing weekly.

But Ron Rankin and the pundits didn't count on Church's ability to connect with Idaho voters. He had a knack for patiently and clearly explaining his positions and how he had reached them, earning the respect of many voters who didn't agree with his beliefs.

Political experts also failed to account for the fact that Idaho voters deeply resented outsiders, especially newcomers from California like Ron Rankin.

Rankin's recall effort was a bumbling disaster from the start. It wasn't long before the press discovered that the campaign's brochures were being printed in California, and that the group was backed by William Penn Patrick, a fringe figure in California politics who had unsuccessfully run against Ronald Reagan in the Republican primary for California governor in 1966. Patrick had made a fortune in the cosmetics business, and had dreams of using his money to unseat liberal Democratic senators across the nation.

In an interview published in the midst of the recall campaign against Church, Patrick told the *New York Times* that it would be followed by similar efforts targeting other liberal Democratic senators, including Fulbright and senator Wayne Morse of Oregon. "We're not going to sit idly and let some of these clowns elected to public office go their merry way," Patrick said. "We have to remind them. Even if you don't get the man recalled, you warn him. But we think we'll get Senator Church."

Patrick was an early pioneer in the kind of nationwide, right-wing campaign-finance strategy that would later become commonplace. But in the 1960s, outside money in politics still stoked controversy and resentment—especially in a small, insular state like Idaho.

Both Rankin and Patrick were widely viewed by Idaho voters of both parties as California carpetbaggers who didn't understand the state. What was worse, they were working with an irritating local gadfly, St. Maries dogcatcher Gene Mileck, who became the spokesman and public face of the recall campaign. Mileck, a small-town loner with a nasty streak, was known for feuding with members of his own family and for stubbornly waging petty court battles in which he represented himself. He didn't hide his bitter outlook from the press. He told the *New York Times* that "I sat around a long time, listening to the propaganda the John Birch Society and those deals put out. But then I got sick and tired of waiting for them to do something—other than write letters. So I decided to do something, and if you're going to do something, you've got to do it yourself."

Church responded by going on the offensive. He didn't try to hide his opposition to the war. Instead, he held public meetings and answered questions in every one of Idaho's 44 counties throughout 1967. "We would go to the county courthouses, and let people ask any questions they wanted," recalled Church aide Jerry Brady. "We would go into small towns, and go to a diner to eat. We had a little flask of bourbon, but we wouldn't drink in public."

Church repeatedly told the press that he wouldn't change his views on Vietnam just because of the recall campaign. "Should the day ever come when my conscience tells me to speak up in the Senate and I remain silent out of timidity or self-interest or fear of political reprisals, that day I will resign my office and there will be no need for a recall," Church — employing his typically formal language — told the *New York Times*.

Church also got some luck. His aide, Jerry Brady, ran into Ron Rankin at the Boise airport and struck up a conversation. Brady expressed enthusiasm for Rankin's recall campaign — without telling him that he worked for Church. Flattered by the attention, Rankin proceeded to explain his entire recall-campaign strategy. "I went up to him at the Boise airport and said I want to help you get rid of Church," Brady recalled in an interview. "We went to dinner, and then we talked at his motel, and that's how I found out what he was doing."

Church told the press everything they had discovered, then started to take public digs at the recall effort in speeches across the state. "Anybody who plays upon the war to catch votes, or waves a flag as a substitute for good hard analysis of the situation, these are the people I loathe most," Church told a meeting in Boise. He also frequently attacked Rankin and Patrick personally, saying, "I think that the people of Idaho have too much sense to be taken over politically and economically by carpetbaggers from California."

In the end, the recall campaign was a godsend for Frank Church. Most Idaho voters were angered by the recall effort, and it generated sympathy for Church throughout the state. "I don't like the way they're doing this thing," Fred Boynton, a Republican voter, told a reporter. "The people of Idaho voted him into office and the people of Idaho will vote him out of office when they damn well please."

Republican political leaders in Idaho had been staunchly opposed to the recall effort and had publicly asked Republican voters not to sign the recall petition. They feared that the recall campaign would spark a backlash and make it far more difficult to defeat Church in 1968. Idaho Republican chairman John McMurray told the *Idaho Statesman* that the recall campaign was "the most ridiculous, uncalled for, and most futile maneuver I have ever seen."

Herbert Snow, a Republican member of the Idaho House, said that "the time and the expense of this thing wouldn't be justified even if Church were an incompetent, which he isn't."

The recall effort quietly died in the summer of 1967, after Idaho attorney general Alan Shephard issued a legal opinion in June stating that a recall of a United States Senator was not constitutional.

Despite the recall effort in 1967 and the prospect of a difficult battle for reelection in 1968, Frank Church intensified his opposition to the Vietnam War. And in early 1968, Church went public with his new, dark fears that Vietnam could lead to a militaristic, imperial future for the United States. He did so in what was perhaps the greatest speech of his life.

*　　*　　*

Frank Church was a man who didn't really belong in his own time. He was decades ahead when he warned about the dangers that militaristic adventures like Vietnam posed for the health of the American republic. But he was also anachronistic, even old-fashioned, in his approach to explaining himself to voters and the nation. Unlike many other politicians of his day, Church still believed in long, formal, set-piece speeches, given on the Senate floor, to lay out his beliefs, just like William Borah. In some ways, Frank Church would have been more comfortable in the Senate of the 1920s.

His very formal speaking style, both in conversation and in his speeches, with precise diction and the steady rhythm of a monotone, was also increasingly out of place in a political landscape dominated by television. But he stuck with it.

That stylized manner had become second nature to Church, an outgrowth of the disciplined approach to oratory and debate that he had developed when he was a teenager. "He talked in paragraphs," one former aide said; he could sound as if he was giving a formal speech even during a casual conversation. His speaking style led critics, including some other senators, to dismiss Church as a pretentious blowhard; the "Senator Cathedral" nickname never left him.

But he never understood the criticism. His carefully curated use of language — he wrote his own speeches, or thoroughly rewrote drafts written by his staff — was a genuine reflection of his personality.

Church loved the entire process involved with public oratory; he relished writing, and crafting and practicing a proper delivery.

"In the morning he would get up and rehearse a speech while shaving or just standing in front of the mirror," Bethine later wrote. "He usually tried out a speech for a week or two. He loved the English language and worked his speeches over and over again until they felt good in his mouth. Only after he had practiced speaking his ideas would he make notes on yellow pads of paper. Most speeches, even very good ones, often sound better than they read. But everyone always said that Frank's speeches were different. He wrote like he spoke and spoke like he wrote.

"As a result of this prolonged speech-writing process, Frank was often talking to himself. The kids would come rushing in and say, 'The minibikes aren't working,' and he never told them he was too busy to help out. He would simply walk out the door, still speaking to himself, trying a phrase on his tongue."

On February 21, 1968, Church took to the floor of the Senate to deliver a formal speech to explain his views on Vietnam. He had been working on it for weeks, and he deployed all of the traditional rhetorical skills that had helped him win the American Legion oratorical award in high school nearly three decades before.

In a speech he entitled "The Torment in the Land," Church provided the context for his opposition to the war, and helped explain why America seemed to be spinning out of control.

Church spoke in the wake of the Tet Offensive, when North Vietnamese and Viet Cong forces launched a series of coordinated attacks throughout South Vietnam beginning on January 31, 1968, the first day of the Lunar New Year, a major Vietnamese holiday. The offensive caught the U.S. military by complete surprise, and it took weeks of some of the bloodiest fighting of the entire war for American forces to retake lost cities and towns around the country.

The Tet Offensive shocked Americans, who had been reassured by President Johnson and his advisers that the U.S. was winning the war and that the enemy was on the run. The greatest embarrassment for Johnson came in the onslaught's opening hours, when enemy troops attacked the U.S. embassy, the very symbol of

American power in Vietnam. Although the attack on the embassy failed, it — and the rest of the Tet Offensive — had a major political and psychological impact in the United States, dramatically shifting American public opinion on Vietnam and making early opponents of the war, like Frank Church, appear prescient.

The changed political climate after Tet gave Church greater confidence in his anti-war stance, and "The Torment in the Land" speech was Church's answer to political opponents who expected him to soften his opposition to the war to improve his reelection prospects. Instead, he used the speech to stake out a much more radical position than ever before. He stood on the Senate floor and said he believed that the Vietnam War was merely a symptom of the new brand of imperialism that had captured U.S. foreign policy since World War II — which, if left unchecked, threatened the very foundations of the republic.

"The war in Vietnam enters its fourth year since we commenced the bombing of the north, its fury intensified, and no end in sight," Church began.

> As though fascinated by the baited trap, we are poised to plunge still deeper into Asia, where vast populations wait to engulf us and legions of young Americans are being beckoned to their graves...The involvement of the United States in Vietnamese affairs, we should remember, began as just another foreign aid program. Our purpose was to help certain anti-Communist elements in South Vietnam strengthen themselves. But when we commenced to take over their fight in their country, converting their political struggle into an American war, I could no longer support the policy. As early as September, 1964, I began to speak out against it.
>
> In the intervening years, I have seen my worst fears confirmed. Step by step, we have been caught fast in a precarious Asian bog. Into its quicksands we can readily stray farther and sink deeper, but out of it there is no quick or easy path of extrication...

After laying out the wastefulness of the Vietnam War, Church expanded his lens, and warned that militarism now gripped the United States.

We bear the imprint of war prolonged and unending...violence begets violence, incessant warfare becomes, at last, the accepted companion of normalcy. Every night we watch on television the gory spectacle of the jungle war in Vietnam, the latest film in color flown to us directly from the battlefront. Year in, year out, the brutal drama penetrates every home, until burning villages, screaming children, and flowing blood become a routine part of the typical family scene.

Each morning our newspapers carry the latest body count of enemy dead, together with pictures of our own fighting men, bandaged and mangled. This brand of war pervades and brutalizes our culture...Today, we are much more a warfare than a welfare state...

If we could only overcome our obsessive preoccupation with other people's ideologies, we could start asking some practical questions. What, for instance, have we bought with armaments unlimited and foreign aid dished out on a global platter?

We have not bought security. After 20 years of the nuclear arms race, the Russian and American people are not the most secure, but the most imperiled people in the world. If the funeral pyre each government has set for the other is ever ignited, both peoples will be laid out upon it...no, we have not bought security.

If not security, have we bought peace? Again, the answer is no. Our policy of global intervention has meant war, not peace. During the past 25 years, the United States has engaged in more warfare than any other major power.

Then at least, have we not bought favor? Once more the honest answer is no. Our insistent involvement in the internal affairs of so many foreign countries meets with rising resentment and suspicion...

Fear blinds us; fear of communism which transcends faith in freedom; fear of a future that we cannot shape with our own hands; fear of sudden devastation hurling down from the skies. The nuclear monster we ourselves unleashed returns, like Frankenstein's, to haunt our lives...

In the face of all this, I wish I could express some confidence that, by an act of our own volition, we might soon commence to alter this country's foreign policy from one of general, to one of selective, involvement. But I have no such confidence. Like other nations before us that drank deeply from the cup of foreign adventure, we are too enamored with the nobility of our mission to disenthrall ourselves. Besides, powerful vested interests now encrust and sanctify the policy. Were we to wait for the hierarchy of either political party to advocate a change of course, I fear we would wait indefinitely.

As Church finished, other senators reacted in stunned silence.

After a moment, Senator Ernest Gruening, a Democrat from Alaska who had been one of the first in the Senate to turn against the war, rose up and spoke for Church's audience that day.

"This was one of the great speeches of all time," Gruening said. "I believe it ranks with the classics, with the addresses of Daniel Webster and other distinguished orators of the past. I cannot conceive of a more eloquent, searching and comprehensive analysis of our foreign policy."

Despite its power, Church's speech received little attention in the press, either in Washington or Idaho, because there was so much other news competing for attention. His speech was quickly overshadowed by Walter Cronkite's famous report from his trip to Vietnam, broadcast a week later, in which Cronkite called for negotiations to end the war. The fact that the *CBS News* anchor had turned against the war had an enormous impact on public opinion.

But Frank Church's speech stood the test of time. It clearly explained how America's global overreach was creating a national security state unaccountable to the American people. Seven years later, that would serve as the underlying theme of the Church Committee's investigative work.

* * *

Church still faced a reelection campaign in 1968, which was turning out to be one of the most politically chaotic years in modern American history, threatening the prospects for a liberal Democrat in Idaho. After a student-led counterculture movement, race riots in the streets of major cities, the bloody protests at the Democratic convention in Chicago, and the assassinations of Martin Luther King Jr. and Robert F. Kennedy, there was a sense among many middle-class and blue-collar voters in 1968 that the nation was lost. Republican politicians, from presidential candidate Richard Nixon on down, tried to exploit the anxiety among the people they started calling "the Silent Majority."

Church's opponent in 1968 was Republican congressman George Hansen, a loud and imposing figure. At six foot six, he matched his physical profile with a flamboyant persona and political pitchman style, drawn in part from his career as an insurance salesman.

A Mormon born in 1930 in Tetonia, Idaho, Hansen entered politics in 1961, when he won election as mayor of Alameda, Idaho, then merged that city with the larger Pocatello, and served as the city commissioner of Pocatello. In 1964 Hansen won one of Idaho's two congressional seats, bucking the national Democratic tide in a year when Lyndon Johnson was elected president in a landslide. Hansen ran on a platform as a staunch conservative against Johnson's Great Society social welfare and civil rights programs, and his victory turned Hansen into a rising star in the Republican Party as he warned against bureaucrats seeking to burden taxpayers and meddle in everyday life. He sharply criticized the growing environmental movement, attacking Church for sponsoring legislation to protect wilderness areas in Idaho. The League of Conservation Voters ranked Hansen among the "Dirty Dozen" House members who most regularly voted against environmental interests.

In 1968, Hansen gambled his safe House seat by running for Senate against Church, even though his aides thought it was a mistake. "I advised against it," said Richard Hendricks, who was then an aide to Hansen. "You're the boss. Whatever you say. You're signing the checks. But there is no way you can make it. Absolutely no way." But Hansen ignored the advice and took on Church, relentlessly assailing his opposition to the war in Vietnam. "He was a blustery big guy, very much anti-communist," recalls Church aide Brady. "But he didn't know much about foreign policy."

Hansen bludgeoned Church on other hot-button issues as well, often mischaracterizing Church's views in order to scare Republicans from crossing over to vote for the Democrat. Five years before the Supreme Court's 1973 decision in *Roe v. Wade* legalizing abortion, Hansen tried to attack Church for favoring legalized abortion (the phrase *pro-choice* was not yet in use), even though it was barely an issue at the time. Hansen distributed a pamphlet showing a fetus and called Church a "baby killer" — previewing the kind of Republican attacks on liberal Democrats that would become commonplace in the 1980s.

Hansen's red-meat tactics in 1968 deeply angered Bethine Church. At a political event years later, she refused to have anything to do with him, telling Hansen to his face that "after you called Frank a baby killer I never will shake your hand again."

Hansen replied, "Oh, Bethine — that's just politics."

"No, George," she responded. "That's just dirt."

*　*　*

In the midst of Church's bitter race against Hansen in the summer of 1968, Forrest Church, sporting a long beard and old clothes, arrived in Idaho from Stanford. Wanting nothing to do with his father or his campaign, he camped out in the basement of his grandparents' house in Boise.

The divide between Forrest Church and his father had now become a full-fledged family crisis, and it was becoming difficult to hide it from the outside world. Frank Church's campaign staff called Forrest a "ticking time bomb," and Hansen's campaign began to spread gossip about Church's "hippie son."

Forrest made things worse when he got drunk and drove wildly through the Idaho mountains, trashing a gas station and ramming through a blockade set up by U.S. Forest Service patrol officers trying to stop him. Once the officers discovered the driver was Frank Church's son, they decided not to arrest him. The officers agreed to let him go after a young Church campaign aide, who had been partying in the mountains with Forrest, told them who Forrest was and promised that he would take the car keys away from him. There is no evidence that Frank Church personally intervened with the Forest Service officers on his son's behalf, but the episode would have been damaging to Church's campaign if it had become public.

Forrest was acting out his rage — rage at the war, and rage at being Frank Church's son. He was torn between admiring his father and regarding him as a sellout who hadn't done enough to extricate the United States from Vietnam.

"My father and I were almost completely estranged during this period," Forrest Church later wrote in his memoir. "Everything that he had devoted his life to struck me as superficial...I had come to hate politics...as far as I could see it, everything my parents were involved in, belabored as it was with inevitable compromise, was a sham."

Peter Fenn, who joined his best friend Forrest in Boise that summer, recalled having to act as the "middleman" between Forrest and his father: "Frank didn't understand; he felt like his son was betraying him."

Hansen's campaign tried to exploit Church's family crisis by arranging for long-haired, scruffy-looking college-aged boys to hand out pro-Church pamphlets in Boise, claiming they were friends of Forrest Church.

But Hansen found that his personal attacks on Church backfired, because they reminded voters of the unpopular recall campaign from the year before. Hansen later said that during the campaign, he felt like he was "walking on eggshells... I walked onto a stage where any opposition [to Church] wasn't to be tolerated. I had to tread a careful line between exposing his voting record and not attacking him personally."

*　*　*

In the closing weeks of the campaign, Church's secret weapon was Verda Barnes. After she had helped Andrus in 1966, Church brought her back to Idaho in 1968 to take charge of his campaign. In order to guide Church's grass roots campaign efforts, Barnes put together a statewide voter identification program, which in 1968 was considered a campaign innovation.

"Church relied very heavily on Verda," recalled Cleve Corlett, a former press secretary for Church. "She was an old school politician, and knew how to use every advantage you had to get ahead." Barnes helped guide Church's strategy, framing his anti-war stance as a sign of his independence from the Johnson Administration. "I think he figured everybody knew he was against the war, so why try and change that," Corlett added. His campaign television and print advertisements — shot at the family ranch in Stanley, Idaho, before Church sold it to avoid accusations of a conflict of interest over wilderness preservation legislation — showed him walking alone through the countryside, a classic image of the independent Westerner.

Surprisingly, Church's strong opposition to the war worked in his favor in Idaho in 1968, since it made it impossible for Republicans to link Church to President Johnson, who was by then deeply unpopular in the state. By taking a stand against the Vietnam War, many Idaho voters saw that Church was taking a stand against the establishment. (Church distanced himself further from the national Democratic Party in 1968 by announcing that he would not attend the Democratic convention in Chicago. When the Chicago convention descended into violence and chaos, Church looked prescient.)

In November, Church was easily reelected with his largest margin of victory in any of his elections, even as Idaho went overwhelmingly for Richard Nixon in the presidential election.

Frank Church was now the undisputed leader of the liberal wing of the Idaho Democratic Party. He soon forged a liberal partnership with Cecil Andrus, who recovered from his 1966 defeat and was elected governor in 1970. Andrus would go on to win four elections for governor, and also served as Secretary of the Interior under

On a rafting trip in Idaho, Senator Frank Church talks to Cecil Andrus, Idaho's longtime Democratic governor.

President Jimmy Carter. Church and Andrus became the two most successful Democratic politicians in Idaho history. Their alliance was later sealed when Chase Church married Cecil Andrus's daughter.

Still, Frank Church was becoming increasingly frustrated as he continued searching for ways that a single senator from Idaho could bring the war in Vietnam to an end.

CHAPTER 7

"We stand up now"

AS THE 1970S began, Frank Church still dressed in navy-blue suits — seersucker when he was more daring — and still spoke with the precise diction and carefully rhythmic intonations of a university linguistics professor. Now in his mid-40s, he had gained some weight and was no longer frighteningly thin; filling out actually gave him a mature, darkly handsome look. In a slight nod to the fashion of the times, he had allowed his hair to grow thicker and ever-so-slightly longer since he had first arrived in the Senate, and his most daring possession was a yellow 1965 Ford Mustang convertible. But otherwise he looked as if the counterculture movement had passed him by.

Yet his throwback style hid the man. Deeply depressed and burning inside, Church had become a radical in senatorial clothing. He had always been a Western outsider who lusted to be an Eastern insider, but now his mental calculus was changing. He still longed to be accepted, still hosted dinner parties with his wife at their Bethesda home that mixed politicians and Hollywood celebrities, yet increasingly he was repulsed by Washington's establishment. He struggled with how to deal with the widening split in his identity. "He desperately wanted to be part of the establishment, but he was always the outsider," recalled former Church staffer Jerry Levinson.

Lyndon Johnson, Richard Nixon, and Vietnam had changed him. Mostly Vietnam. It was an endless war of attrition — fruitless, brutal, and corrosive. Frank Church was now convinced that it was a symptom of America's post–World War II transformation into a militaristic empire. He didn't understand why others in Washington's elite could not see the mortal danger to the republic.

"He became angrier and angrier at the establishment over the war," said Tom Dine, Church's top foreign-policy aide in the early 1970s. "He was undergoing a transformation, developing a strong anti-war mindset, and down deep I think he was becoming a pacifist."

Church had been against the war almost from the very beginning, at a time when virtually no other serious political leaders were willing to join him. Early on, his wife, ever the operator, had warned him that opposing the war was political suicide for a senator from a conservative state like Idaho. But after he beat a recall attempt in 1967, launched because of his opposition to the war, then won reelection in 1968, defeating a candidate who charged that he was too soft on Vietnam, Church now believed that he was on solid political ground in Idaho. Dine marveled that Church's "electoral genius" was to know how to be both a "national" senator and an Idaho senator. His knack for patiently explaining his positions on contentious national issues to Idaho voters had served him well on Vietnam. That success emboldened Church.

* * *

For years he had battled Lyndon Johnson over the war. Now, in the 1970s, Church had to fight Richard Nixon.

After his reelection in 1968, Church further intensified his opposition to the war, even as Nixon, the newly elected president, tried to win him over. In 1969, Church was invited to a private lunch with Henry Kissinger, Nixon's national security adviser, who made it clear to Church that the White House would open the world to him if only he would soften his stance on Vietnam.

"During his temptation, Frank was offered perks and a personal relationship with the president, as well as with Henry Kissinger," Bethine Church later wrote in her memoir. Church was merely amused by Kissinger's approach, and dismissed it.

In the early days of his administration in 1969, Nixon announced that his Vietnam policy would be based on "Vietnamization" — gradually reducing U.S. troop levels while building up the South Vietnamese Army to take the lead in combat. By cutting the number of American troops fighting and dying in combat, Nixon hoped to reduce the domestic opposition to the war. With the anti-war movement waning, Nixon would then have the political ability to wage war as long as it took to get the North Vietnamese to agree to his terms for a settlement.

Frank Church was one of the first to see the cynicism at the heart of Nixon's strategy, and he publicly called out Vietnamization as just another ploy to prolong the war. (In fact, more than 20,000 American soldiers were killed during the "Vietnamization" phase of the war, more than one-third the total death toll for the entire war.)

Church kept up the pressure. He remained consistent in his strong anti-war stance, year in and year out, even as troop levels decreased and other politicians began to move on to other issues. On October 15, 1969, during the "Moratorium to End the War in Vietnam"—a day set aside for a nationwide series of anti-war demonstrations and teach-ins—Church spoke to an audience packed into the Peace Corps offices in Washington, when many main-stream politicians were still reluctant to be seen as having direct connections to the anti-war movement. Church warned the crowd that "we can't go on with our money and our men fighting every-body else's wars all over the world; otherwise we'll end up with no money and no men." He found an appreciative audience: "So many turned up to listen to him denounce the 'spurious, jingoistic patriot-ism' of those criticizing the moratorium that [people] were literally hanging from the walls of the larger lecture hall, while others were desperately trying to hear what was being said in an overspill meet-ing in the corridors," wrote a reporter covering Church's speech for *The Guardian*, a British newspaper.

Church was just as vocal in his opposition to the war when he was speaking in Idaho as he was in Washington. In November 1969, Church told a crowd at Idaho State University in Pocatello that Viet-namization was "a policy for continued engagement in Vietnam, not disengagement." Church was now so confident about his political standing in Idaho that he wrote a lengthy explanation of his foreign-policy views for *Playboy* magazine, despite clucking from Idaho con-servatives. "It is rather a paradox to note how the so-called family-type politicians are getting articles published in *Playboy*," complained one letter to the editor of the *Idaho State Journal*.

But the conservatives who criticized Church for writing for

Playboy missed the fact that the article itself reflected Church's new radicalization. He wrote that, increasingly, he saw little difference between the brutal imperialism of the Soviet Union—which in 1968 had put down the "Prague Spring" democracy movement in Czechoslovakia—and the brutal imperialism of the United States, which was putting down an independence movement in Vietnam. "I believe that the Russians...suppressed the liberal government of Czechoslovakia because they feared the contagion of freedom for the rest of their empire, and ultimately for the Soviet Union itself," Church wrote. "Nor do I believe that, in suppressing revolutions in Latin America and in trying to suppress revolution in Vietnam, the United States is acting legitimately in its own self-defense. There are, God knows, profound differences between the internal orders of the United States and the Soviet Union...but in their foreign policies, the two superpowers have taken on a remarkable resemblance. Concerned primarily with the preservation of their own vast hegemonies, they have become, in their respective spheres, defenders of the status quo against the pressures of revolutionary upheaval in which each perceives little but the secret hand of the other."

Church's newly radicalized view of American foreign policy also made him more reluctant to spend his evenings with the experts at major foreign-policy think tanks and institutions, like the Council on Foreign Relations, which he now dismissed as cautious guardians of the establishment and the status quo. It certainly didn't help that the hawkish old guard at the Council on Foreign Relations tried to block Hans Morganthau, Church's anti-war ally, from receiving a fellowship from the institution. During the war, the Council on Foreign Relations—the most influential foreign-policy organization at the time—brooked no dissent, and virtually no debate, on Vietnam.

But even as he was speaking out more radically, Church was becoming increasingly frustrated that he was unable to have any real impact on Vietnam policy. He felt helpless as the casualty lists grew longer. Two presidents from different parties had waged unilateral war; the press was now calling the Nixon Administration "the Imperial Presidency."

But whose fault was that? Church believed that Congress was shirking its duties under the Constitution. In a 1969 article for the

Idaho Law Review, Church wrote that "the Roman Caesars did not spring full blown from the brow of Zeus. Subtly and insidiously, they stole their powers away from an unsuspecting Senate. They strangled the Republic with skillful hands...Senators of the United States...through our own neglect...have come to deal increasingly more with the form than with the substance of power."

By surrendering its power over issues of war and peace to the president, Church believed, Congress was enabling the creation of a dictatorship, allowing the United States to slide toward militarism and empire. Once Congress allowed a president to be the sole arbiter over matters of national security, he feared, the president could use that power to accuse political opponents of treason, shut down dissent, and thus end the nation's democracy. "Again and again, the Senate has acquiesced, while American Presidents have steadily drawn to themselves much of the power delegated to Congress by the Constitution," Church wrote in his law-review article. "In the process, especially in the field of foreign commitments and the crucial matter of our military involvement abroad, Congress as a whole — and the Senate in particular — has permitted a pervasive erosion of the bedrock principle on which our political system was founded, the separation of powers."

Church was convinced that it was time for Congress to try to stop the war — and he decided to sponsor legislation to do just that. As the 1960s ended and a new decade opened, Church turned from speaking out against the long war to trying to use legislation to bring it to a screeching halt.

*   *   *

In August 1969, Frank Church was listening to a Pentagon briefing to the Senate Foreign Relations Committee about Thailand. At the time, Church was wary that Nixon was planning to expand the Vietnam War into the rest of Southeast Asia, and he wanted answers about what contingency planning the White House had ordered the military to conduct. But the Defense Department officials giving the briefing refused to turn over their Thailand plans to Church and the rest of the committee, and only grudgingly said that the senators might be able to look at the plans if they came over to the Pentagon. Feeling insulted, Church angrily got up and walked out of the briefing.

"Presumably, this Republic is founded upon the sovereignty of the people," Church said in a scathing press release after the hearing. "But more and more, the Executive Branch of the government behaves as though it were the master — not the servant. The people have a right to know."

Church was fed up, and in December 1969 he took his first, incremental step toward using the congressional power of the purse to rein in Nixon's freedom to wage unilateral war. He sponsored legislation banning the funding for U.S. military forces in Laos and Thailand.

It was attached as an amendment to the bill that provided for the Pentagon's budget. His cosponsor was Senator John Sherman Cooper, a Kentucky Republican who had also turned against the war. Their proposal quickly became known as the first Cooper-Church Amendment.

The amendment was the start of a historic partnership between Church and Cooper. The two men — using a series of legislative vehicles that became known as Cooper-Church Amendments — would come to dominate the debate in Congress over Vietnam for the remainder of the war. Their bipartisan alliance would ultimately lead Congress to reassert its long-lapsed role over matters of war and peace.

John Cooper and Frank Church forged their partnership despite very different backgrounds. Born in 1901 in Somerset, Kentucky, Cooper was a generation older than Church, and unlike Church he had been born into wealth. But after he went to Yale, his father's fortune was wiped out, forcing Cooper to sell his family's mansion. Thanks to his family's stature in Kentucky, however, he became a judge, and later served as a military police officer during World War II. He came home to Kentucky after the war and dived straight into state politics.

As a Republican in what was then an overwhelmingly Democratic state, Cooper bounced in and out of the Senate in the decade after World War II. He was elected to the Senate in a special election in 1946, lost reelection in 1948, won another election to a vacated Senate seat in 1952, lost again in 1954, then won again in 1956. In between senatorial terms he served in a diplomatic post at the United Nations and later as ambassador to India during the Eisenhower Administration, becoming close friends with Indian prime minister Jawaharlal Nehru. His itinerant political career made Cooper an internationalist, willing to cross party lines on votes in the Senate.

With no end in sight to the war in Vietnam, Cooper was willing to join Church and rebel against a president of his own party. At Cooper's side was his young foreign-policy aide, Bill Miller, who so quickly impressed Church with his quiet organizational skills that he later hired him for a series of key posts, including staff director of the Church Committee.

For his part, Church relied on Tom Dine, his main foreign-policy aide, who had brought an aggressive new legislative approach to Church's office. "When I got into the office, the first thing I said was I'm going to the [Senate] floor," recalled Dine, to push legislation through final votes in the Senate. Until then, Church and his staff had never taken the lead in a major legislative fight with the national significance of the Cooper-Church Amendments. Church had a reputation among fellow senators as a speaker, not a major national legislator. The other Church staffers told Dine, "We don't go to the floor."

"The [Church] office was quite tame," recalled Dine. "I didn't know you did it any other way than fight on the floor."

Church and Cooper began with small steps. Their first bill — the Cooper-Church Amendment of 1969 — with its focus on Thailand and Laos, was designed only to block the spread of U.S. forces into other countries in Southeast Asia besides Vietnam.

Nixon did not object to the bill, denying that he had any plans for U.S. military operations in Laos or Thailand. (Although U.S. ground troops were not in either country, the CIA secretly conducted one of the largest covert-action operations in the Agency's history in Laos during the Vietnam War, while Thailand provided air bases used for the U.S. bombing campaign during the war.) This first Cooper-Church Amendment became law, and though it had no immediate impact, it set a precedent for the dramatic events of the following spring.

In April 1970, Nixon ordered a U.S. military invasion of Cambodia to destroy North Vietnamese military bases and supply centers in the country. Nixon's surprise invasion shocked the nation, triggering an explosion of outrage while intensifying the anti-war movement. College campuses were rocked by protests, and on May 4, National Guard troops shot and killed four people during protests at Kent State University in Ohio, further inflaming the nation. A photograph of a young woman kneeling and screaming over the body of one of the dead at Kent State became an iconic image of the anti-war movement, and Kent State inspired one of the great protest songs of the Vietnam War, "Ohio," by Crosby, Stills, Nash and Young.

On May 11, 1970, Church and Cooper introduced their second Cooper-Church Amendment, this time aimed at Cambodia. Their new legislation called for a ban on funding U.S. ground troops in Cambodia beyond July 1, 1970.

The Cooper-Church Amendment of 1970 arrived at the perfect cultural moment to become a touchstone for the millions of Americans opposed to the war in Vietnam. It was, in effect, the congressional response to Kent State. And while it only specifically dealt with Cambodia, *Cooper-Church* soon became popular shorthand for efforts to end the Vietnam War.

The Cooper-Church Amendment became the subject of seven weeks of debate on the Senate floor, focused on the constitutional balance of war-making powers between the president and Congress. "The real issue is to preserve the dignity and integrity of the constitutional role of Congress," Church said. "We stand up now or roll over and play dead."

Throughout the fight in the Senate, Cooper and Church became an iconic duo: Cooper, so quiet that listeners had to strain to hear him, with white hair that made him look like he came from central casting, and Church, finally given the national platform to display his remarkable abilities as an orator. Church spoke to the nation, with conviction. "Church's great magnetism...was that he really believed in these things," observed Bill Miller, the Cooper aide who later worked for Church.

Even as Cooper-Church dominated the news, Bethine Church, ever her husband's defender, bristled: "By right of seniority and majority, the amendments should have been called 'Church-Cooper,'" she later wrote. But despite Bethine's complaints, the Cooper-Church debate turned Frank Church into a political celebrity for the first time in his career. "With Cooper-Church," said Tom Dine, "Frank Church became a national figure."

Church was now constantly in the limelight, and he discovered that he loved everything about being famous. He couldn't get enough of it. Paul Newman became a Church supporter; even Liberace came to Church's house for dinner. (Liberace arrived by limousine with a male companion, which was then considered risqué in homophobic Washington. But it didn't bother the Church family. "He was very elegant," recalls Chase Church.)

The nightly images on network television news of death and destruction in Vietnam were now counterposed on Sundays by Frank Church on *Meet the Press* and other shows. Church got better and better on television, and was soon in high demand to give speeches to Democratic groups all over the country.

The fight over Cooper-Church "took a tremendous physical and emotional toll [on Cooper]," observed Miller. "Not on Church. He thrived on it. He became more eloquent, alive. He liked all the speaking, the engagement, he was good at it. He enjoyed the constant television appearances." Church loved to spar on television with Nixon's defenders; with his long-practiced debating skills, he usually won. Dine recalls one television appearance in which Church was paired against Republican senator Bob Dole, a staunch Nixon supporter. "Church turned to me and said, 'Dole is so unctuous.'"

Church was even invigorated by the process of preparing for television shows; Dine and Miller would grill Cooper and Church before their joint appearances on the Sunday talk shows.

With so much national attention, Church hired Wes Barthlemes, a former reporter and former aide to Robert Kennedy, to be his ghostwriter for a book that would be both an autobiography and an explanation of his views on foreign policy. "Fulbright had a book, and Church wanted one, too," noted Dine. But Church was so busy and so much in demand that he never committed enough time to it, and the book project died. (Surprisingly for a man who loved language and the written word, Church never wrote a book.)

Inevitably, Church's sudden fame led to "the discomfort of colleagues," as one former aide politely described the growing jealousy of his fellow senators. One reason the jealousy was so intense was that Church was becoming famous without ever having paid his dues as a true Senate insider. He had no love for the garrulous late-night poker games or drinking sessions that fueled the Senate; he usually went home at night for dinner.

As a result, Church had only a few real friendships with other senators. Those who didn't know him well saw only what he seemed to be on the surface — aloof, pretentious, enraptured by the sound of his own voice.

Becoming a Washington celebrity put new pressures on Church and his family. Forrest Church, who had finally reconciled with his father, planned to marry Amy Furth, his girlfriend from Stanford, in California on Memorial Day of 1970. The wedding date fell right in the middle of the Senate debate over the Cooper-Church Amendment, thus providing a test of Church's priorities — family or politics.

The Cooper-Church debate was transforming Frank Church into a star, so Frank and Bethine very nearly chose politics. They considered not going to the wedding. "For a while it looked like Congress might remain in session through the holiday and we would miss the wedding," Bethine wrote in her memoir. In the end, she wrote, "we were able to get away and arrived just in time," even though "things were really heating up in Washington."

When they arrived, Bethine was aghast to discover that Forrest and Amy had written pacifist wedding vows, which they had printed up as leaflets to distribute to the guests. Bethine didn't want anything to damage Frank Church's political fortunes. "The morning of the wedding I told Forrest that if they passed out those leaflets, I would not attend the ceremony," Bethine wrote. "We were getting hit from all sides about the Cooper-Church Amendment, which was being called defeatist, disloyal and worse. Forrest's leaflets threatened to cause a media frenzy." The wedding couple gave their vows but agreed not to distribute the leaflets; stories were written about their pacifist vows in *Stars and Stripes* and a newspaper in Idaho, but there was no significant coverage.

Church's modest suburban lifestyle also began to feel the heat of his fame. Even when he claimed he was trying to get away from official Washington to relax and recharge, he and Bethine still found ways to socialize with other political celebrities.

Church bought a small cabin near Gettysburg, Pennsylvania, as a weekend family getaway, which was supposed to serve as a rustic retreat in the East that gave the Churches a little taste of Idaho, with no phone to connect Frank to the office. He would go skeet shooting with Chase and his friends, and over dinner lead sing-alongs; he loved the songs from the musical *Man of La Mancha*.

But the cabin also became yet another place where Frank and Bethine could entertain famous guests. Henry Kimelman, an investor and hotel owner from the Virgin Islands who became Church's most important political fundraiser, later told of a barbecue at Church's cabin during the Nixon years that was attended by both Supreme Court Justice Potter Stewart and U.S. Attorney General Elliot Richardson.

Church was soon even engaging in after-dinner banter with his nemesis on Vietnam, Henry Kissinger. "He razzed Kissinger as the White House sex symbol," wrote Knight-Ridder about Church's star turn at the Washington Press Club dinner. "Until now, his boy scout image and political base in the Idaho boondocks haven't dramatized him on the national scene."

Unlike others in the Senate, Senate Majority Leader Mike Mansfield didn't mind Church's new celebrity status, and continued to allow him to take the lead in trying to end the war. He recognized that while Church was a publicity hound, he also had a deep moral conviction that the war was evil and must be stopped. Behind the scenes, Mansfield played a key role in shepherding the Cooper-Church Amendment through the Senate. "Mansfield said [to Church] you do this," Miller recalled. "You have the speaking ability. You have the energy."

Nixon hadn't resisted the first Cooper-Church Amendment in 1969, because it didn't really affect his war strategy. But he fought back hard against the 1970 Cooper-Church Amendment and its funding ban on military operations in Cambodia. He called the amendment a "slap in the face." According to notes later released by Nixon White House aide H. R. Haldeman, the president encouraged the American Legion to mount a campaign against Cooper-Church.

The American Legion of Idaho — of which Church was a member — called for the rest of Idaho's congressional delegation to defeat the "declaration of surrender" proposed by Cooper and Church. The legion commander characterized it as "a stab in the back of our boys in combat."

Nixon also pushed his allies in the Senate to accuse supporters of Cooper-Church of "knife-in-back disloyalty." Senator Robert Griffin, a Michigan Republican and a Nixon ally, warned that Cooper-Church would be "tying the hands of the commander in chief."

Facing stiff resistance from the White House and its allies, Church was willing to compromise. Quietly, Church, Cooper, and other key senators met with Kissinger at Blair House, across the street from the White House, to hammer out possible changes in the amendment that would satisfy Nixon.

But even as the White House fought back, the Cooper-Church Amendment was gaining strength in the Senate, in part because it represented a more moderate approach than a competing and more drastic measure known as the McGovern-Hatfield Amendment, which called for the end of all U.S. military operations in Vietnam by the end of the year and the withdrawal of all troops by the middle of 1971.

The debate over the Cooper-Church Amendment was putting much more pressure on Nixon than on Church, and in June 1970 the president blinked first; he announced that he would withdraw troops from Cambodia earlier than planned. Later in June, the Cooper-Church Amendment passed the Senate by a vote of 58 to 37. In September 1970, Church proclaimed on television that the doves had won.

Once U.S. combat operations in Cambodia were largely over, the political momentum behind the Cooper-Church Amendment began to slow, and it failed in the House of Representatives. A revised version finally passed Congress in December and was signed into law by Nixon in January 1971, when it no longer had any significant impact on U.S. operations.

But it did set an important precedent: for the first time, Congress had used its power of the purse to place limits on the president's war-making powers.

The legislation also finally repealed the Gulf of Tonkin Resolution, which Lyndon Johnson had used as a flimsy mandate for war in Vietnam and which Frank Church deeply regretted having supported.

Nixon was now on notice that Congress was rapidly losing patience with the war. *The St. Louis Post-Dispatch* wrote that "the passage of the Cooper-Church Amendment was a landmark reassertion of the Senate's constitutional responsibility in foreign affairs."

*　*　*

In October 1971 Church and Cooper introduced yet another Cooper-Church Amendment, and this time it directly targeted combat operations in Vietnam, rather than on the peripheral edges of the war. It called for a ban on further funding for the war in Vietnam except for the expense of withdrawing all remaining troops. Church was no longer interested in incremental measures. The amendment was rejected by only one vote in the Senate — a strong signal to Nixon that he was running out of time to end the war.

In January 1972, Nixon gave a nationally televised speech on the war, both to reveal that he had been engaged in secret peace talks with North Vietnam and to unveil a new peace proposal that held the promise of finally bringing American troops home.

But by then, Church had heard it all before. On the night of Nixon's speech, Church told reporters that Nixon was still refusing to take the steps necessary to end the war. Indeed, Nixon's speech and his supposed peace initiative were soon forgotten as the war escalated once again two months later. A massive North Vietnamese offensive, with thousands of troops slashing across the demilitarized zone between North and South Vietnam, caught the U.S. and South Vietnamese forces off guard. In response, U.S. warplanes once again began to bomb Hanoi, and the U.S. Navy mined North Vietnamese harbors.

With the war intensifying once again, Church pushed harder. He now formed a partnership with another moderate Republican, Senator Clifford Case from New Jersey. Case stepped in for Cooper, who had decided not to run for reelection in 1972 and begged off further involvement in Church's anti-war campaign. In April 1972, they cosponsored the Case-Church Amendment, cutting off all funding for the war in Vietnam. The funding cutoff would be contingent upon the release of American prisoners of war and an accounting of those missing in action. Case and Church later modified it to provide funding for four months to give the White House enough time for a total withdrawal.

But the Case-Church Amendment got snarled in the Senate with other amendments from its opponents that were designed to water it down. Kissinger then undercut the amendment when he issued his "October surprise"; just before the November presidential election, he announced that the U.S. and North Vietnamese were close to a peace agreement. A hellish American bombing campaign of North Vietnam in December 1972 subsequently forced the North Vietnamese to agree to the settlement's final terms, and the peace agreement was signed in January 1973.

Church's long fight to use the power of the purse to end the war had forced Nixon's hand. Historians now largely agree that the growing anti-war sentiment in Congress pressured Nixon to accelerate the peace talks and agree to the Paris peace deal with North Vietnam in January 1973, ending American involvement in the war and bringing U.S. troops and prisoners of war home.

"During the final negotiations with the Vietnamese over ending the war, culminating with the 1972 Christmas Bombings and the Paris Peace Accords in January 1973, the president knew that he only had a limited amount of time before Congress finally used the power of the purse to bring the war to an end—regardless of what the administration wanted," observed Princeton historian Julian Zelizer.

In fact, Frank Church has never received the credit he deserves for the critical role he played in forcing an end to American involvement in the Vietnam War. Mike Wetherell, a longtime aide, later wrote to Church that "there are literally thousands of young men alive who, but for your efforts, and those of others like you who spoke up early and strongly against the Vietnam war, would be lying wasted in some rice paddy in Vietnam."

As Nixon's first term neared its end, a few other Democratic liberals begrudgingly acknowledged that Church had been right about the war all along. In February 1972, at a press conference in which Church endorsed Senator Edmund Muskie for the Democratic nomination for president, the Maine Democrat praised Church's longtime opposition to the war, saying he wished he had followed Church's lead much earlier. "He [Church] influenced me finally to see it more closely," Muskie said.

The Vietnam War had served as Frank Church's crucible. He emerged from the war questioning whether the United States was still a force for good in the world. Church was now on a collision course with the national security state.

* * *

In the closing days of his long fight against the war in 1972, Frank Church took on another political task—helping a young Democrat named Joseph R. Biden Jr. in his long-shot bid to defeat Senator J. Caleb Boggs, a hawkish incumbent Republican senator from Delaware. Boggs was such a reliable vote for the Nixon Administration on Vietnam that Richard Nixon personally persuaded Boggs to run for reelection in 1972 after he had considered retirement. Frank

Church was eager to help defeat Boggs, so he lent three of his staffers — including Dine, his top foreign-policy aide — to the Biden campaign. Dine helped develop Biden's positions on Vietnam, which were similar to Church's views.

Biden defeated Boggs in the November 7, 1972, election, but on December 18, before Biden could be sworn in to office, Biden's wife, Neilia, and his baby daughter, Naomi, were killed in a car crash in Delaware. Biden's two sons were also in the car and were both badly injured. Traumatized by grief, Biden considered abandoning his newly won Senate seat.

Frank and Bethine Church played a critical role in persuading the future U.S. president not to quit the Senate. Frank Church directed some of his staffers, including the indefatigable Verda Barnes, to help Biden set up his new Senate office. "While my children were recovering, I did not want to go to the Senate, I really didn't," Biden told a small Boise audience while campaigning for president in 2019. "My brother was meeting with the Democratic governor-elect to appoint someone in my place. And it was Frank Church, and Bethine, and a guy from South Carolina and his wife, a guy named Fritz Hollings, and Mike Mansfield and his wife, who came to me, and said you got to stay. The fact was, they saved my sanity, they convinced me to stay."

Church also had a lasting influence on Biden's views on foreign policy and national security; echoes of Frank Church's speeches on Vietnam could be heard many years later, when Biden explained to the nation why he was withdrawing U.S. troops from a remote and unwinnable war in Afghanistan.

CHAPTER 8

"An enormous hue and cry"

FRANK CHURCH WAS finally famous. He had become a political star thanks to his long campaign to stop the Vietnam War. He had stood up to Richard Nixon at the height of his imperial presidency, and did more than any other member of Congress to rein in Nixon's war and bring about peace.

But celebrity status is fleeting in Washington. With U.S. troops and prisoners of war coming home following the January 1973 peace agreement between the United States and North Vietnam, the war in Southeast Asia began to recede from the headlines, while a new story began to dominate the American consciousness — the Watergate scandal.

As Watergate started to consume Washington, the capital's new stars were the congressional leaders, prosecutors, and journalists investigating the scandal. Frank Church was not among them. The celebrity status he had earned from waging war with Richard Nixon over Vietnam was not enough to get him included in the new congressional battle with Nixon over Watergate. In fact, it guaranteed that he would be shut out.

* * *

In early 1973, Senate Majority Leader Mike Mansfield decided to create a special committee to investigate the growing Watergate scandal, which had begun in June 1972 with the arrests of the

Watergate burglars the previous June. Mansfield knew that a Watergate select committee would come under enormous scrutiny, so he wanted a low-key Southern conservative to lead it — someone whom Republicans wouldn't immediately attack as being too partisan.

Instead of a liberal like Frank Church, whose fame was white-hot after Vietnam, Mansfield chose as committee chairman North Carolina Senator Sam Ervin, a conservative Democrat who had opposed civil rights and was close to retirement. The Senate Watergate committee was created in February 1973, and Ervin, its home-spun chairman, went on to lasting fame. It seemed that Frank Church, the hero of Cooper-Church, was now yesterday's news.

But even as he was shut out of Watergate, Church was conducting a major investigation of his own.

Radicalized by Vietnam, Church now wanted to go further than Cooper-Church had taken him; he wanted to investigate the sources of power that he believed were behind the rise of the permanent national security state that had led to endless war in Southeast Asia. He was convinced that the sources of that power were not just political or military, but economic and financial as well. So Church began a landmark investigation into the rising global power of America's corporate giants, and the trail he began to follow would ultimately lead him to the CIA. He would inadvertently begin to uncover the CIA's hidden power for the first time in his Senate career, and that would eventually lead to an even more ambitious congressional investigation of the CIA and the intelligence community — the Church Committee.

To counter Washington's imperial drift, Church realized, Congress had a powerful tool that it had failed to put to good use during the Vietnam War: the ability to investigate.

In early 1972 — months before Watergate — Frank Church began pushing the Senate leadership to let him launch a major investigation that he believed would expose the hidden forces that led America into Vietnam, forces he believed were beginning to transform the nation into a militaristic power. He wanted to start by investigating the postwar rise of the American multinational corporation, and how these new commercial behemoths were influencing — and perverting — U.S. foreign policy.

Church was eager to move beyond Vietnam and start investigating such wide-ranging sources of unaccountable power, but he lacked the standing in the Senate to launch any serious investigation on his own. Committee chairmen usually decided what to investigate, and Church had not yet become the chairman of any major Senate committee, powerful positions which were then still dominated by long-tenured Southerners. Even though Church was now in his third term, by early 1972 he was still just considered a back-bencher by the Senate's old barons. (In 1971 he became chairman of the Senate's special committee on aging, but it had little real power.) What's more, the Senate's leaders in the years immediately before Watergate were wary of high-profile, headline-grabbing investigations after the experience of the 1950s, when Senator Joseph McCarthy hijacked the Senate's investigative process to launch his paranoid, anti-Communist witch hunt.

Church had been involved with only one significant investigation: the McClellan Committee's probe of labor racketeering in the late 1950s. Church landed on the McClellan Committee in 1958, after Senator Pat McNamara — a Michigan Democrat who was a close ally of Walter Reuther, the legendary president of the United Auto Workers union — quit the committee in protest, complaining of its anti-labor bias. Church didn't like being on the committee either, and tried to keep his role to a minimum.

But Church had a bigger problem than a Senate seniority system that denied him a major chairmanship, or the Senate leadership's reluctance to launch another era of controversial investigations. Frank Church had an image problem inside the Senate. His prominent role in congressional efforts to end the war had not enhanced his power in the insular Senate or changed the way other Senators viewed him. He couldn't shake his reputation among other senators that he was a pretentious blowhard and publicity hound, in love with the sound of his own voice.

Democratic Senate leaders — particularly Senator J. William Fulbright, chairman of the Senate Foreign Relations Committee, who had emerged as one of the most influential lawmakers in the 1960s and early 1970s and a leading voice against the war in Vietnam — felt an intense personal dislike for him. Church thought he had a good relationship with Fulbright, but the truth was that after working closely with Church for years on the foreign relations committee, Fulbright didn't trust him.

"Senator Fulbright at one point said to me, 'You can't count on

Frank Church,'" recalled Carl Marcy, who served as Fulbright's chief of staff on the foreign relations committee from 1955 until 1973. "You can count on Senator Gore [future Vice President Al Gore's father], you can count on Senator Symington [Senator Stuart Symington, a Democrat from Missouri].

"What he meant was that if Symington or Gore...said they were going to do so-and-so, they'd do it," Marcy elaborated. "They would support him on the floor on an amendment or whatever it might be. Fulbright was never sure of Senator Church. Always the implication being, without his ever having said it, that Senator Church was a bit of an opportunist. If that meant that he had to change his position or create a doubt about something maybe Fulbright had been led to believe he was firm on, he'd shift."

Fulbright also may have been jealous of the press attention Church had received during the legislative fights over Vietnam. "I think some of it was that Church was a rising star," observes Dave Schmitz, a historian who has written extensively about Church's leading role in the congressional battles against the war. "Fulbright probably thought about all the things he had accomplished, and thought, what has Church really done legislatively?"

Top Church aide Tom Dine recalled that Fulbright's staff on the Senate Foreign Relations Committee would "almost on a daily basis, feed stories" to the *New York Times* to make Fulbright look good. Fulbright and his staffers resented Church for stealing the limelight from Fulbright. "They said Church is too camera ready," Dine recalled. "They were pissed that Church was getting too many headlines. Fulbright was jealous."

But another reason for the divide between Church and Fulbright was that Church now had a radical view of American foreign policy—and Fulbright didn't. Fulbright and the rest of the Democratic congressional leadership had grudgingly come to oppose the war in Vietnam, but they were not interested in challenging the status quo in Washington. Fulbright was still an establishment figure at heart, unwilling to push for the kind of fundamental change to America's role in the world that Church believed was necessary. So it's ironic that Fulbright's caution—his penchant for quiet backroom maneuvering—ultimately set the stage for Frank Church to take charge of his first major congressional investigation, one that would rock the foreign-policy establishment by exploring the dark side of corporate America's global power — and its secret connections to the CIA.

* * *

After chairing the Vietnam hearings of the Senate Foreign Relations Committee in 1966 (after being pushed to do so by Frank Church), Fulbright became the most recognizable face of the Senate's opposition to the Vietnam War. One unexpected consequence of Fulbright's public role as an anti-war leader was that whistleblowers started to approach him with secrets they believed needed to be exposed. In November 1969, Daniel Ellsberg, a RAND Corporation analyst who had turned against the Vietnam War, met with Fulbright and gave him a copy of the Pentagon Papers, the Defense Department's secret history of the war. Astonished by the trove of documents and the government's lies that they exposed, Fulbright initially promised Ellsberg that he would hold hearings and make the Pentagon Papers public.

But Fulbright lost his nerve; he was frozen with fear by the thought of publicly revealing stolen classified documents without government approval. He told Ellsberg that he had changed his mind, only to briefly revive the idea of disclosure after Nixon's invasion of Cambodia and the Kent State shootings in the summer of 1970. That fall, however, Fulbright once again backed off.

"Fulbright just let the idea of hearings fade away," Ellsberg recalled in an interview. "In December 1970, I went to see Fulbright again, and he said this [the Pentagon Papers] is just history."

In February 1971, Ellsberg turned to Senator George McGovern, who was also initially intrigued. But like Fulbright, McGovern ultimately refused to get involved with the Pentagon Papers. "He said he was going to run for president, so he couldn't do anything with them," Ellsberg said. Ellsberg then met with Senator Gaylord Nelson, a liberal Democrat from Wisconsin, and Senator Charles Mathias, a liberal Republican from Maryland, before finally deciding to take the Pentagon Papers to the New York Times.

After the New York Times began publishing the Pentagon Papers in June 1971, Fulbright realized, to his embarrassment, that they were the same documents Ellsberg had handed him nearly two years earlier. "The Pentagon Papers had come into the committee's possession a year or two before they appeared in the *New York Times*," Pat Holt, a top aide to Fulbright on the foreign relations committee, later admitted in an oral history interview with the Senate Historical Office. "The circumstances under which they came into the committee's possession were such that the committee felt some constraints about how it used them...Once they were published, a cry arose that the committee do something about them."

In September 1970, another whistleblower came to Fulbright with sensitive documents, this time a journalist unwilling to take the risk of publishing a story about them. Warren Unna, a reporter with PBS who had previously worked for the *Washington Post*, met with Fulbright and handed over a trove of explosive documents from inside ITT, a giant New York–based communications conglomerate that had conquered markets in one country after another at a time when American corporations had little foreign competition. ITT had used its international market power to buy politicians — and even whole governments — around the world. While AT&T held an iron grip on the domestic telephone business in the United States, ITT had grown into the dominant player in the overseas telephone business. It gained control of telephone networks in countries in Europe as well as the developing world — including Chile.

Owning the national phone system in Chile gave ITT enormous clout to ward off any political threats to its investments in the country. One such threat came in 1970, when Chile's telephone company became a candidate for government seizure and nationalization if socialist candidate Salvador Allende won that year's presidential election in Chile. ITT wasn't going to let that happen and appealed to its allies in the U.S. government for help.

In the months before Chile's election in September 1970, former CIA director John McCone, a member of ITT's board of directors, held a series of meetings with his successor at the CIA, Richard Helms, to discuss ITT's fears of a possible Allende victory, and to ask what the CIA and the Nixon Administration were going to do about it. The McCone-Helms meetings helped launch a collaboration between ITT and the CIA that began during the election campaign and continued after Allende became Chile's president. Among other things, the company offered to set up a secret fund to support a right-wing candidate against Allende, collaborated with the CIA to try to destabilize Chile's economy, and later provided funds to help finance a CIA-backed newspaper in Chile that spouted anti-Allende propaganda.

The documents that Warren Unna, the journalist-turned-whistleblower, handed to Fulbright revealed the broad scope of this plot: they showed that ITT was collaborating with the CIA in a secret campaign to stop socialist leader Salvador Allende from gaining power in Chile. Unna explained years later that he gave the documents to Fulbright rather than writing about them because "I could not publish them myself without compromising their source."

Fulbright responded to the ITT documents in the same way he had to the Pentagon Papers. He was initially astonished by what they revealed. Fulbright "had in his possession some Xeroxed memoranda from various people in the office of ITT in Washington," recalled Fulbright aide Pat Holt, "which indicated very clearly that ITT was going to great efforts to inspire some kind of activity on the part of the CIA."

But Fulbright once again moved cautiously. Instead of going public, Fulbright called Helms, the CIA director, who came to Fulbright's Capitol Hill office and denied that the CIA was involved in any effort to block Allende in Chile. That was good enough for Fulbright, who trusted Helms because the CIA director had been one of the only top officials during the Vietnam War who had told him that the war was not going well. Fulbright stored the ITT documents in the foreign relations committee's safe, just as he had the Pentagon Papers. But just like the Pentagon Papers, the ITT documents would soon come back to haunt Fulbright.

* * *

In February 1972, syndicated columnist Jack Anderson broke an explosive story about a corrupt quid pro quo between ITT and the Nixon Administration. Anderson, who was at the time the most famous investigative journalist in the nation, reported that he had obtained a secret memo from an ITT lobbyist in Washington revealing that the company had agreed to give $400,000 to help Nixon's reelection campaign pay for the Republican National Convention in 1972 in exchange for an agreement that the Justice Department would drop its antitrust opposition to ITT's acquisition of Hartford Fire Insurance.

Anderson's series of columns about the quid pro quo between ITT and Nixon's reelection campaign were published just as the Senate was considering the nomination of Richard Kleindienst to become Nixon's new attorney general. Anderson reported that Kleindienst had lied about his involvement in the case, and an outraged Kleindienst demanded that the Senate Judiciary Committee, which had already voted to approve his nomination, hold a new set of confirmation hearings so he could clear his name. The new hearings went on for weeks, and turned the ITT story white hot, with a horde of reporters trying to catch up with Anderson.

As Fulbright watched the ITT scandal burst open, he suddenly remembered the trove of explosive ITT documents locked in his safe. He had made the mistake of sitting on the Pentagon Papers, only to see them have an earth-shattering impact when they were finally published by the *New York Times;* he did not want to be embarrassed again.

Yet Fulbright also didn't want to go public with the ITT documents himself and face questions about how and when he had obtained them. So Fulbright ordered his aide, Pat Holt, to secretly leak all of the documents about ITT, the CIA, and Chile to Jack Anderson.

In March 1972, Jeff Brindle was a college intern working in Jack Anderson's Washington office when he took a call from Pat Holt. "He said he was from the Senate Foreign Relations Committee, and he said he wanted to drop some documents off, and wanted to do it in person," recalled Brindle in an interview. "He came up to the office, and I was the one who received them. It was about a half-inch-thick envelope with documents."

In his oral-history interview, conducted in 1980, Holt acted as if he had no idea how Anderson obtained the documents. "So the Judiciary Committee was inquiring into this [ITT's quid pro quo with Nixon and his presidential campaign] and lo and behold during those hearings Anderson followed up by publishing some of the ITT documents from September 1970 dealing with Chile."

Armed with the documents he had secretly been given by Holt at Fulbright's direction, Anderson wrote his first column about ITT, the CIA, and Chile in late March 1972. The column rocked Washington.

Frank Church read Anderson's column and realized that it

provided him with a perfect opportunity to push for the kind of investigation into modern corporate power that he had been thinking about for months. After Anderson reported on the ITT-Chile documents, "there was an enormous hue and cry and the Foreign Relations Committee felt called upon to involve itself in this," recalled Holt. "Frank Church, for about eighteen months at that point, had been fretting about the problem for American foreign policy posed by multinational corporations, and I had done some preliminary work on this. But neither Church nor I had brought the thing to a focus. Well, the Anderson revelations brought it to a focus."

Fulbright quickly agreed to create a new subcommittee devoted to investigating the ITT case — and, despite his disdain for him, to name Frank Church its chairman. It was an elegant way for Fulbright to hide his own role in having kept the ITT-CIA conspiracy a secret for so long.

Fulbright also agreed that the new Senate Subcommittee on Multinational Corporations could go beyond the ITT case to investigate other instances of corruption and excessive political influence wielded by U.S. companies around the world.

To jump-start the investigation of ITT and the CIA in Chile, Jack Anderson quietly agreed to share copies of his ITT-Chile documents with Frank Church and his new subcommittee staff. The documents thus came full circle: from Fulbright to Anderson and back to Church.

* * *

Pat Holt recommended six people for Church to interview as staff director of the new subcommittee. Among them was Jerry Levinson, a Latin America expert who had just coauthored a book about U.S. policy in the region.

Church hired Levinson, but he had to fight off the FBI and the CIA to do it. During its background check of Levinson, the FBI found that he had undergone psychoanalysis for eight years. Bethine Church later told Levinson that her husband had to overrule both the FBI and the CIA in order to hire him. Both agencies advised Church not to hire him because they saw psychoanalysis as a sign of instability, which made Levinson a security risk. Rejecting their antiquated prejudices, Church took the opposite view; he respected

Levinson for recognizing he needed help and sticking with his treatment. "It took a lot of guts for Church to hire me and then to stand by me," Levinson wrote in an unpublished memoir.

Church quickly integrated Levinson into his daily routine. Each morning, Levinson would drive his Honda over to Church's Bethesda house, Church would climb in, and the two men would carpool to work at the United States Senate. Each night, Levinson and Church would drive back to Bethesda together, and Church often stopped at Levinson's nearby home for drinks; Church almost always had a Black Russian. They would talk into the night. Sometimes their wives joined them for dinner.

What made their routine—and their relationship—so unusual was that Jerry Levinson was a Senate staffer who worked for Frank Church; it was rare for a United States senator to develop such a close friendship with an aide. But Levinson served a special role on Church's behalf: he ran the first major investigative panel that Church had ever chaired, and the two men bonded over their highly sensitive inquiry. Years before the creation of the Church Committee, Frank Church and Jerry Levinson were investigating the ties between corporate America and the national security state. Together they took on one sacred cow after another.

As he launched the investigation, Church still lacked Fulbright's support. After he was hired, Levinson was warned by Fulbright staffers that he shouldn't trust Church, and that he couldn't count on Church's support if his investigative work met political resistance. "When I first took the job, Carl Marcy and Pat Holt [Fulbright's top staffers] took me out to lunch and said, be careful of Church," recalled Levinson in an interview. "He won't protect you. He will leave you out on a limb."

Meanwhile, other important senators made it clear to Church's new staff director that he would face strict limits on how far he could pursue the probe into corporate power. When Levinson met with Senator Stuart Symington, a senior member of the foreign relations committee, the Missouri Democrat gave his blessing to the ITT investigation. But Symington quickly added that the new subcommittee should not "demonize" all American corporations.

When Levinson relayed to Church what Symington had said, Church understood the message. He explained to Levinson "that what Symington was saying was that it's ok to go after ITT, but don't go after my friends in St. Louis." Symington's warning was an early sign that Church's multinational investigation would be seen as a threat to the American establishment.

*   *   *

The multinational subcommittee was created in March 1972, but politics delayed Frank Church's ITT investigation. Under pressure from Nixon, Senator Hugh Scott — a Pennsylvania Republican who was the Senate Minority Leader — agreed to the creation of the sub-committee only on the condition that its ITT investigation be delayed until after the 1972 presidential election. The ITT story was then exploding in the press thanks to Jack Anderson's revelations, and Nixon did not want a congressional investigation that would keep the scandal on the front page throughout the presidential campaign. Fulbright agreed to the delay in order to avoid a partisan split on the foreign relations committee.

Just three months after Fulbright and Scott reached their accord, however, the Watergate scandal began. The Republican demands to delay the ITT inquiry until early 1973 meant that it would coincide with the Senate investigation of Watergate. As a result, Church's ITT investigation gained far more attention than it would have if it had begun a year earlier, since it became linked in the public's con-sciousness with the unfolding Watergate scandal. Church hadn't made it onto the Watergate committee, but he was still managing to benefit from it.

*   *   *

ITT was the perfect target for Frank Church's first investigation of the power of multinational corporations to skew U.S. foreign pol-icy. But as Church and his staff began to dig into ITT, they didn't realize they were missing a much larger story: ITT was really a minor player in the CIA's wide-ranging covert-action program in Chile to stop Allende from gaining power, and later to oust him from office.

Nixon had applied intense pressure on the CIA to mount an all-out secret effort against Allende. Under White House orders, the CIA launched a two-track strategy. The first called for an anti-Allende propaganda-and-disinformation campaign, bribes to Chil-ean politicians, and a damaging economic boycott by foreign corporations, like ITT. On the second, more secretive track, the CIA plotted with Chilean military leaders to attempt a coup and take over the government.

Even as Frank Church began his investigation into ITT, the CIA was working to sabotage Allende's government. Nixon feared the ITT investigation might lead Church to uncover what the CIA was really doing in Chile, and the president was determined to keep it secret. To maintain the cover-up, Nixon Administration officials who testified before Church's subcommittee would have to lie. Exposing their lies — and holding the officials who lied accountable — would ultimately become the central focus of Church's ITT investigation.

The subcommittee's high-profile showdown with ITT and the CIA appealed to both sides of Frank Church: the side that wanted to overturn the foreign-policy status quo and the side that was politically ambitious and eager for publicity. Church revealed his publicity-seeking side when, minutes before the subcommittee's first hearing was to start in March 1973, he congratulated Jerry Levinson on a successful hearing.

Levinson was confused; the hearing hadn't started yet. "How could it already be a great success?" Levinson wrote in his unpublished memoir. "And then I understood. All three television networks — ABC, NBC, and CBS — had set up on the left-hand side of the room, along with public broadcasting. Two press tables were full. The major print media were present with star reporters, the *New York Times*...the *Washington Post*...the *Wall Street Journal*." Frank Church was getting lots of attention, just the way he liked it.

CHAPTER 9

"As long as the KGB does it"

RICHARD HELMS WAS a CIA careerist, a smooth-talking WASP and Washington insider who socialized with all the right people, including compliant politicians and journalists who helped shield him from public view. He joined the OSS during World War II and then stayed at the CIA, rising to the top while becoming complicit in most of the Agency's worst, most abusive activities. Living in the world of secrets, he was Washington's ultimate *éminence grise*, once described as "socially correct, bureaucratically adept, and operationally nasty."

Richard Helms was also the first top CIA official to square off against Frank Church.

Helms was at the center of the Nixon Administration's cover-up of the CIA's covert role in Chile, and he repeatedly and blatantly lied to Congress about it. As a result, he became the central target of Frank Church's multinational subcommittee's investigation. It was the start of a long-running and extremely bitter feud between Church and Helms that would continue during the Church Committee and beyond to Helms's eventual prosecution by the Justice Department for lying to Congress. Helms represented everything about the CIA that Church came to hate: an amoral willingness to follow orders, to engage in operations with no regard for ethics or the law, and then a casual readiness to lie to Congress about it all. For his part, Helms came to see Church as a martinet, a publicity hound who failed to understand that his loyalty was to the president, not to members of Congress who couldn't keep secrets. Their diametrically opposed views of the role of the CIA in American society were about to collide.

* * *

The multinational subcommittee's investigation into ITT's alliance with the CIA in Chile in early 1973 came at the worst possible time for Richard Helms. He had two big problems: Richard Nixon and Watergate.

After the Watergate break-in on June 17, 1972, Richard Nixon was scrambling to contain the scandal and stage a cover-up, and he wanted the CIA to take the fall. Within days of the break-in and the arrest of the Watergate burglars, Nixon began pushing his aides to get Helms to shut down the FBI's investigation on national-security grounds; Helms could get the FBI off the trail by explaining away the break-in as part of a secret CIA operation. Helms recognized that he was being set up by Nixon, and engaged in passive-aggressive maneuvering, taking some tentative steps that aided Nixon while also stalling—before finally distancing the Agency from the White House and the scandal.

Angry that Helms had not been willing to use the CIA to help in the Watergate cover-up and eager to place a political loyalist in the CIA, Nixon ousted Helms as CIA director right after winning the presidential election in November 1972. But rather than push him out of the government entirely, Nixon named him ambassador to Iran. Nixon knew his man; Helms accepted the demotion and stayed on Nixon's team. But that meant that Helms would have to face Senate confirmation to be ambassador just as Church's subcommittee investigation into ITT, the CIA, and Chile was gearing up. Helms's confirmation hearings quickly merged with the multinational subcommittee inquiry, and Helms faced an intense grilling by Frank Church over Chile.

Helms may not have gone along with Nixon's Watergate cover-up, but he was willing to keep up the cover-up of the CIA's role in Chile. So he lied for Richard Nixon after all.

At his initial confirmation hearings to be ambassador to Iran, Helms was asked about Chile and the CIA, and lied, and Jerry Levinson was certain that Helms had lied. He wanted to have a shot at questioning Helms about Chile more carefully.

CIA director Richard Helms in the White House Cabinet Room, 1968.

What Levinson planned was revolutionary; no one on Capitol Hill had ever tried to take on Helms before. The CIA director had always received kid-glove treatment from Congress; he would whisper some selective bits of intelligence on Vietnam or the Soviet Union to a chosen few, and his congressional supporters would quietly make certain that his handling of the CIA was never subjected to any real scrutiny.

But Frank Church and Jerry Levinson wanted to bring those days to an abrupt end.

With Church's approval, Levinson prepared for a showdown with Helms. He came up with about 100 questions for the CIA director, all crafted to force him to reveal the truth about the CIA's involvement in Chile. In a March 6, 1973, closed-door hearing, Frank Church, armed with Levinson's questions, began to grill Helms and box him in.

"We have prepared," Church began, somewhat ominously, "a series of questions..."

Church's first question got straight to the point. "Mr. Helms, did the CIA attempt at any time to prevent Salvador Allende Gossens [Allende's full name] from being elected President of Chile in 1970?"

Helms replied, "No sir."

Church then began to dig further. "Now, following the election, and up to the time that the Congress of Chile cast its vote installing Allende as the new president, did the CIA attempt in any way to influence that vote?"

Helms asked, "Which vote?"

Church: "The vote of the [Chilean] Congress."

Helms: "No sir."

In answer to further questions from Church, Helms claimed that he didn't recall the policy positions on Chile of the 40 Committee, the Nixon Administration's group of top officials who dealt with covert-action programs. That was a lie; Helms knew that the 40 Committee had, in fact, been intimately involved in Nixon's anti-Allende plans.

Church drilled in. "In response to my first question when I asked you whether the—I will have to go back to that question— my first question was, did the CIA attempt to prevent Salvador Allende from being elected as president of Chile in 1970, and you answered that categorically and you said no. Now you say you can't remember what the policy was during the very period leading up to his selection by the Congress."

Helms tried to wriggle free of the perjury trap Church was setting for him:

"As I interpreted your first question, and as I understood the question, to which I answered no, did the CIA attempt to influence the election in Chile by putting money into opposition candidates, or whatever the question may have been, to keep Allende from being elected and the answer is no, and this I am relatively certain is the case."

Helms's effort to reframe Church's question and make it sound narrower than it really was immediately caught the suspicious attention of Senator Clifford Case, who called Helms out for his disingenuous efforts to confuse and deceive.

"I am not attempting to be devious, Senator Case," Helms answered. "I simply, there seems to be a general thrust in the questions that the CIA had a policy of putting money in, I assume, in favor of the candidates—"

Church then interrupted: "No, no—no question was asked in that way, Mr. Helms, not a question."

Church was just about to nail Helms inside a trap built of his own words when Stuart Symington came to Helms's rescue. Symington was aghast at how far Church was pushing to prove that Helms was lying and was engaged in a cover-up. By aggressively insisting on the truth about the CIA, Church was breaking with Senate decorum, and the old-school Symington wasn't having it.

"I would like to make a statement at this point," Symington said, interrupting Church just as he was about to ask Helms a follow-up question.

"We are now talking to the former head of the intelligence agency of the government of the United States."

Symington chided Church for his intense questioning of Helms about the CIA's involvement in Chile, insisting that Church seek such detailed answers from lower-level CIA officials instead—notably William Broe, who had been the chief of the CIA's Latin American operations. "Church and Case zeroed in on conflicts in Helms's testimony, and Symington stepped in to stop it," Levinson recalled in an interview. And then Symington tried "to divert us from Helms by saying we should talk to Broe."

Frank Church was getting too close to the truth. After the contentious hearing, Church fielded a call from Senator John McClellan of Arkansas, the longtime chairman of the powerful Senate Appropriations Committee who also chaired a CIA "oversight" panel that almost never met or held hearings. McClellan asked Church to come to his office. When Church arrived, he found James Schlesinger, the CIA's newly appointed director, was there with McClellan. With the new CIA director sitting with him, McClellan told Church he should back off on his investigation of the CIA and Chile—and specifically he should not seek Broe's testimony.

Church rejected McClellan's demands, and warned McClellan that one part of his investigation was to determine whether ITT should have received $92 million from the government's Overseas Private Investment Corporation, which provided U.S. companies with financing for their foreign operations. Church "told McClellan that if he wanted to be responsible for the ITT corporation receiving $92 million in taxpayer funds, that was his choice, but he, Church, was having no part of it," Levinson recounted in his unpublished memoir.

McClellan suddenly backed off. He "put his feet up on his

desk," Levinson recalled, "clasped his hands behind his neck, looked at Schlesinger, let out a long whistle, and then in his deepest rural Arkansas drawl, said, 'Nobody ever told me anything about ITT getting paid $92 million in U.S. taxpayer funds.'" McClellan then said Church would have no further problems with him or his CIA oversight panel. Broe was subsequently summoned to appear by Church, becoming the first CIA covert operative ever to testify before Congress. Although he talked about the CIA's collaboration with ITT in Chile, Broe likewise continued to conceal the broader Agency covert plan to overthrow Allende.

It would take time for the CIA cover-up on Chile to crack. It would finally break open thanks to a new Agency director.

* * *

In 1974, William Colby, the new CIA director, gave secret, closed-door testimony to a House committee that contradicted the earlier lies to the Senate about Chile by Helms and other top officials. Unlike Helms, Colby believed that Congress had the right to know the truth, and he was unwilling to perpetuate the cover-up.

Massachusetts Representative Michael Harrington was not on the House committee that heard Colby's testimony, but he insisted on being allowed to read it. Astonished by what Colby had revealed, Harrington told Church and Fulbright, then followed up by writing Fulbright a formal letter detailing Colby's testimony.

Harrington's letter quickly leaked to *New York Times* reporter Sy Hersh. After Hersh's story was published in September 1974, Levinson wrote a memo for Church that spelled out how Colby's testimony confirmed that Helms and others had lied to Congress.

"Colby is reported to have testified that the Nixon Administration authorized more than $8 million for covert activities by the Agency in Chile between 1970 and 1973 in an effort to make it impossible for President Salvador Allende Gossens to govern," Levinson wrote.

He added that "Ambassador Richard Helms, in the course of his confirmation hearing, committed perjury in stating that no money was passed to opponents of Allende and that no attempt was made in the September 1970 Chilean elections to prevent Allende from becoming president."

Levinson's memo immediately leaked to the press; Secretary of

State Henry Kissinger angrily tried to seek revenge on Levinson by pressuring friendly senators to call for Levinson's firing. Church "told me that was not going to happen," Levinson recalled. Church stood by his staff director in the midst of the media storm. Jerry Levinson had learned that Frank Church would not give in when he met powerful resistance to sensitive investigations. The warnings from Fulbright's aides that Church would not support his staff "was exactly the opposite of what Church was like," noted Levinson.

Levinson's memo was sent to the Justice Department along with testimony transcripts, and Justice Department officials came to interview Levinson about Helms's testimony. That began a long-running criminal investigation and prosecution of Helms for lying to Congress. Finally, in 1977, Richard Helms cut a plea deal with the Justice Department. He agreed to plead *no contest* to two counts of failing to answer questions fully, completely, and accurately, as required by law, during three Senate hearings in February and March 1973; in exchange, Helms received only a suspended sentence and a $2,000 fine.

Church was outraged that Helms received such a light sentence, but the Washington establishment, which had always protected Helms as one of its own, was elated. Church was widely criticized for going too far by pushing for Helms's prosecution, and for failing to recognize that Helms could not be expected to tell the truth to Congress.

* * *

Church's ITT investigation made him powerful enemies, who continued to try to target him even after Richard Nixon resigned from office. On November 11, 1974, John McCone, the former CIA director who was also an ITT board member, met with the new president, Gerald Ford, and Brent Scowcroft, then Ford's deputy National Security Advisor. During the meeting, they all began to complain about Frank Church.

"I wanted to talk about the CIA and the fact that its image is being tarnished, both here and in Europe," McCone told Ford, according to a memo about the meeting included in *Foreign Relations of the United States*, the State Department's official history of U.S. foreign policy. "People talk to me in a way far different from the way they did a few years ago...there must be an understanding on the Hill that we must keep [conducting covert action]...as long as the KGB does it." Ford responded by saying that "most of them on the Hill do [support covert action], but you get these zealots, together with some of the press, who just don't give a damn."

McCone then complained about Frank Church in particular. "I met with Senator Church before the [ITT-CIA-Chile] hearings and he understands, but then he shot barbed questions at me. I would hope you would meet with the Senate leadership..."

McCone had come to the White House to ask the president to rein in Frank Church. Long before he led the Church Committee, Frank Church was becoming radioactive to the intelligence community.

* * *

Just when Frank Church and Jerry Levinson were trying to decide what to investigate next after ITT, the CIA, and Helms, the answer came from one of the most arcane sections of the federal bureaucracy—the Securities and Exchange Commission.

After Watergate, the SEC conducted a series of investigations into corporate payoffs to President Nixon's reelection campaign that had been unearthed during the scandal. As SEC officials began to dig through the records of companies that had made payoffs to Nixon, they were surprised to find that many of the same companies had also been paying large bribes to foreign-government officials in order to do business overseas.

There was so much evidence of foreign bribes and payoffs by U.S. corporations that the SEC couldn't keep up. So Stanley Sporkin, a top enforcement official with the SEC, contacted Jerry Levinson and began to share the evidence with the multinational subcommittee.

Suddenly, Jerry Levinson and Frank Church had a major new investigative path to follow—evidence of American corporate bribery on a global scale.

Northrop Corporation, a big defense contractor in Southern California, came first; the company had created a slush fund to make illicit payments to the Nixon reelection campaign, and some of its money ended up being used as hush money for the Watergate burglars. When investigators subsequently discovered evidence that Northrop had made foreign bribes as well as domestic payoffs, Church and his staff pounced.

In June 1975, the subcommittee held its first public hearings on

Northrop. Church was able to coax Northrop chief executive Tom Jones into acknowledging that his company's foreign-bribery practices were patterned after the model established by Lockheed, the nation's largest defense company.

Church nudged Jones into publicly implicating Lockheed because Church already knew the answer. Levinson had met privately with a prominent defense-industry lawyer, who fingered Lockheed as the industry's role model for foreign bribery.

As the subcommittee peeled back the dark secrets of international corporate bribery, Lockheed soon became Church's leading target. Just before the Lockheed hearings began, the company's treasurer, Robert Waters, locked himself in his home in Valencia, California, and shot himself in the head.

The Lockheed scandal — one of the most far-reaching corporate scandals in modern history — had begun. Church later called the Lockheed story a "sordid tale of bribery, and of shadowy figures operating behind the scenes...a cast of characters out of a novel of international intrigue."

*　*　*

When he opened the Lockheed hearings, Church didn't pull any punches about how the criminal behavior by major corporations that his investigation was starting to uncover was perverting America's standing in the world.

"The bribes and payoffs associated with doing business abroad," Church said, "represent a pattern of crookedness that would make, in terms of scope and magnitude, crookedness in politics look like a Sunday school picnic." Lockheed chairman Dan Haughton tried to downplay the significance of his company's foreign payments, testifying that some were legitimate commissions and kickbacks rather than bribes. But Church immediately ridiculed him. "What's the difference between a bribe and a kickback?"

Haughton argued that a kickback is "something in the price that you return to the buyer. A bribe is where you ask for a service and you pay for it. That's how it comes through to me, though I'm no authority..."

"If you aren't an authority," Church replied acidly, "I don't know who is."

The scale of Lockheed's corruption was breathtaking. Church's investigation revealed that Lockheed had been engaged in a massive campaign of foreign bribery around the world at a time when the company was veering toward bankruptcy; indeed, Congress had approved a taxpayer-funded bailout in 1971. Lockheed executives had convinced themselves that foreign bribes were necessary to get foreign governments to buy Lockheed's poorly designed fighter planes and commercial airliners.

Lockheed bribed officials in Italy, the Netherlands, Japan, Saudi Arabia, West Germany, and Indonesia; the revelations about those payoffs by Church's multinational subcommittee triggered scandals and prolonged political crises in each of those nations. The Lockheed investigation had exposed so much corruption, joked a Church staffer, that it threatened to "bring down more governments in a few hours than Lenin had in a lifetime."

One of the highest-profile Europeans caught up in the scandal was also one of the most colorful: Prince Bernhard, the husband and prince consort of Queen Juliana of the Netherlands. Born in 1911 in Jena, Germany, Bernhard was from a minor, faded German royal family, the House of Lippe. He joined the SS in 1934 and would spend the rest of his life trying to play down his Nazi ties. He met Princess Juliana at the 1936 Winter Olympics in Bavaria, and they married in 1937, while her mother was still the Dutch queen. After Germany invaded the Netherlands in World War II, the Dutch royal family went into exile in England; Bernhard met Ian Fleming, the James Bond author who was then in British intelligence, and he flew three Allied combat missions using the pseudonym Wing Commander Gibbs. After the war he helped found the World Wildlife Fund, and served on the boards of KLM Royal Dutch Airlines and Fokker Aircraft, ties that made him an attractive target for bribes in the aerospace industry. He was a womanizer with two illegitimate children and a mistress in Paris, so Lockheed's money came in handy.

After the revelations from Frank Church's subcommittee that the prince had accepted bribes from Lockheed, Bernhard denied the accusations, but the Dutch still opened an investigation. They found no evidence that Bernhard had exerted influence on Lockheed's ability to obtain Dutch contracts, but concluded that he had "shown himself open to dishonorable favors and offers" and had "harmed the interests of the State." The Dutch government decided not to prosecute Bernhard, fearing such a move could ignite a constitutional crisis with the Dutch monarchy. But Bernhard was forced to resign from nearly all his military and business posts, save for his royal title of *Prince Consort*.

But it was in Japan that the revelations of Lockheed bribes had the biggest and longest-lasting political impact.

*   *   *

Mitsuyasu Maeno was a strange figure in 1970s Japan. He was a soft-core porn star, an amateur pilot, and an ultranationalist. His hero was Yoshio Kodama, a World War II–era war criminal, gangster, and right-wing power broker. Maeno loved "Song of the Race," a Kodama-authored underground nationalist anthem calling for a revival of Japan's militaristic past.

But Maeno's faith in his idol was shattered in early 1976, when Japan was rocked by revelations from Church's subcommittee that Lockheed had paid millions in bribes to Japanese officials between 1969 and 1975, including to former prime minister Kakuei Tanaka and to Kodama, who had served as Lockheed's bagman and go-between with Japan's political elite. Church voiced anger at Lockheed's decision to employ as its "secret agent" such a "prominent leader of Japan's ultra-right wing militarist political faction...In effect, we have had a foreign policy of the United States Government which has vigorously opposed this political line in Japan and a Lockheed foreign policy which has helped to keep it alive through large financial subsidies in support of the company's sales efforts. We had better make up our minds whether we are going to have a United States or a corporate foreign policy."

Maeno told friends that he was deeply disillusioned by Kodama: by taking bribes from the Americans, his former role model had betrayed both Japanese ultranationalism and the samurai code.

On March 23, 1976, Maeno traveled to Chofu Airport outside Tokyo, dressed like a World War II kamikaze pilot, and rented a small, Piper Cherokee plane. Maeno explained to airport personnel that he was working on a movie. He took off and headed for the Tokyo home of Yoshio Kodama. As he dived his plane earthward, Maeno yelled over his radio, "Long live the emperor! Banzai!" before slamming into the second floor of Kodama's house. The crash killed Maeno, injured two household servants, and started a fire. Kodama was unhurt.

Maeno's suicide attack on Kodama came in the midst of one of the biggest scandals in modern Japanese history, triggering protests in the streets of Tokyo and marches on Japan's parliament. The Lockheed bribery scandal laid bare the corruption at the heart of postwar Japanese politics and exposed the degree to which American corporations exploited it.

Church's subcommittee found that Tanaka, who served as prime minister from 1972 to 1974, had been bribed in exchange for using his influence to get All Nippon Airways to buy Lockheed L-1011 Tristar commercial airplanes instead of aircraft from its American rival, McDonnell Douglas. The impact of the Church investigation into multinational corporations reverberated in Japan long after the subcommittee finished its work. Tanaka was arrested in 1976 in connection with the Lockheed scandal, and his case wound its way through the Japanese courts for years. In 1983, a Tokyo court sentenced Tanaka to prison, but he appealed and never served any time before his death in 1993.

*　*　*

But even as his corporate investigations were having a global impact, Frank Church found that he was cutting too close to the bone, both in Washington and overseas. After holding hearings on Lockheed's payoffs in Japan, Church received a telegram warning him that a "special attack corps is alive in Japan," and that it was prepared to act if he didn't stop the hearings. The U.S. Embassy in Tokyo told Washington that the people behind the message were dangerous; among them were former Japanese kamikaze pilots who had survived World War II and who had now allied themselves with Japanese extremist groups. The message was considered a credible death threat. Secret Service agents checked Church's offices for bombs.

Meanwhile, key senators launched a counterattack against Church for going too far with his investigations of corporate America. They were fed up with what they believed was Church's gratuitous campaign against a key pillar of the American establishment, and faulted him for trying to curb the international influence of American multinational corporations, which they believed was a crucial element of America's global power.

Senator Jacob Javits, a New York Republican, and Senator Hubert

Humphrey, the Minnesota Democrat who had been Lyndon Johnson's vice president and the Democratic presidential nominee in 1968, both quit the multinational subcommittee to protest Church's aggressive investigations. Javits and Humphrey then tried to get the full Senate Foreign Relations Committee — the parent organization of Church's subcommittee — to block Church from providing information to foreign governments seeking to investigate the corrupt payoffs from American companies that he had uncovered.

Javits and Humphrey eventually won approval from the foreign relations committee to abolish the multinational subcommittee, so that no one else could ever again use it to launch the kind of aggressive investigations that Frank Church had conducted. It was replaced with a much more docile subcommittee on "foreign economic policy," which took a sympathetic attitude toward American corporations. Humphrey privately ridiculed Church as a "show horse," interested only in high-profile, sensationalist hearings.

But the criticism helped Church. It toughened him, and prepared him for the biggest challenge of his life — taking on the CIA, the FBI, and the White House in what would become known as the Church Committee.

CHAPTER 10

"We have stood watch"

ON MARCH 14, 1974, Frank Church briefly put aside his investigation of ITT, left the spreading Watergate scandal behind, and traveled to Burley, Idaho, a small town in southern Idaho 40 miles east of Twin Falls, for some old-fashioned retail politicking. He set up shop at the Cassia County Courthouse, where he held private, one-on-one meetings with any voter who showed up and who had problems with Medicare, the Veterans Administration, or any other part of the federal bureaucracy. He held a luncheon at the Pomerelle Room at Burley's Ponderosa Inn, and threw it open to anybody who wanted to come and ask him questions. In the afternoon he visited the Cassia County Senior Center, then held a public meeting in the evening at the Dworshak Elementary School.

While he was in town, the liberal icon of the Senate wasn't above throwing some crowd-pleasing red meat to the conservative voters of Burley. Frank Church wanted to show them he hadn't forgotten where he came from.

Church let everyone in Burley know that he had arrived in town late only because he stayed in Washington to vote against gun-control legislation in the Senate. That was a familiar refrain; Church loved to remind Idaho voters about his consistent and outspoken opposition to gun control, proof that he was not a doctrinaire liberal. Church could be very theatrical about his opposition to gun control: he once collected thousands of signatures from Idaho voters for a petition that opposed one particularly controversial gun-control measure, then personally—and with plenty of publicity—delivered the signatures to the Senate panel considering the legislation.

His position on guns repeatedly brought him criticism from liberals in Washington, but Church knew that guns were basic to the life and culture of Idaho, and opposing gun-control legislation was the price he was willing to pay to remain in the Senate. Tom Dine, a Church foreign-policy aide in the early 1970s, once asked Church: "You take on Vietnam, why not guns?" Church turned to Dine and asked: "Do you like your job? Because if I did that, I would be out of here."

Church was so strongly opposed to gun-control legislation, and spoke so ardently about it, that it was difficult to determine whether he was only motivated by political pragmatism or a genuine personal belief that gun rights should not be regulated. It is one of the few issues on which Church left room for doubt about his true motivations. "He was very pro-gun," remembered his son, Chase Church. But "he really didn't have time for hunting as an adult... he would often pose for campaign [photos] dressed for hunting and with a gun."

With his audience in Burley, Church doubled down on his anti-Washington talk, telling the lunch crowd at the Pomerelle Room that he would not allow the National Park Service to create a "Disneyland" at nearby City of Rocks, the majestic scenic area south of Burley that was about to become a national monument managed by the park service. Church vowed to kill the park service's proposal—controversial in southern Idaho—to minimize car traffic by ferrying tourists around City of Rocks in horse-drawn carriages. The park service, Church said, "gets carried away with itself." It should instead build a conventional visitors center "without a Disneyland for which there would be no money available anyway."

Frank Church's day in Burley was part of what his staffers liked to call his "courthouse tour sweep," a key element in Church's strategy to keep getting elected as a liberal Democrat in Idaho. Every six years, Church had to thread the needle of Idaho politics by convincing voters that, while he was a liberal on big issues like the Vietnam War, national security, and the environment, he still used his power to help individual constituents.

Church's county-courthouse tours had served him well for years, allowing him a chance to explain himself to voters and keep in touch with the political climate in Idaho. But in 1974, Mike Wetherell, one of Church's top campaign aides in Idaho, was worried.

Idaho was becoming even more conservative and more reliably Republican than it had been in the 1950s and 1960s, and Church's personal political visits back to the state were no longer having the same impact. They were too few and far between, and Church's national prominence was starting to make him seem too distant to Idaho voters. One day in Burley, no matter how successful, was not enough.

"There is an increasing feeling among people...that you don't spend enough time with them," Wetherell wrote in a private memo to Church in 1974. They "ask, where is Church? We never see him.

"There is only one way to overcome this problem and that is your presence in the state on a more frequent basis.

"You also have another handicap to overcome," Wetherell added. "You have mentioned this yourself. You have developed a star quality in the last few years. This star quality is an asset, but it is also a liability." People in Idaho now "call you Senator Church. You have to become good old Frank again, and the way to do that is to encourage it. When people come up and say hello Senator Church, you should encourage them to say Frank. The guy on the street has to feel comfortable with you again."

Local journalists were also starting to detect Church's political vulnerabilities. "Not all Idahoans are happy with the record of Frank Church," wrote the conservative *South Idaho Press* in March 1974, at about the same time Church visited Burley. "True, he is a leader in Washington and a respected political figure, but some of the home town constituents — the ones who elect him — are showing signs of discontent."

*   *   *

The gap between Church's growing national stature and his political strength at home in Idaho was starting to widen. And back in Washington, the gulf was also growing between Frank Church and other leading senators on the issues that mattered the most to Church — national security and foreign policy.

Church had been permanently scarred by Vietnam, while the rest of official Washington had happily gone back to business-as-usual once the war was over. Almost alone among American political leaders, Church saw Vietnam as a symptom of a deeper sickness in an increasingly militaristic foreign policy. The fear that America was turning into an empire rather than a republic was now a constant theme for Church.

"We stand in this year 1971 at the end of one decade of disillusion, with no good reason to believe we are not now embarked upon another," Church said in an October 29, 1971, speech on the Senate floor.

> Ten years ago, the leaders of the United States — and to a lesser degree the American people — were filled with zeal about their global goals. With supreme confidence both in our power and capacity to make effective use of it, we proclaimed the dawning of a new era in which America would preserve world peace, stem communism and lead the impoverished masses of mankind through the magic point of "takeoff" into a decade of development. To bring these glories to pass — so we allowed ourselves to believe — we had only to recognize the simple, central fact which Professor Walt Rostow [President Johnson's National Security Advisor] assured us would bring victory in Vietnam and success in all our other foreign enterprises, "the simple fact that we are the greatest power in the world — if we behave like it."
>
> Looking back on the sixties, no one can deny that we were indeed "the greatest power in the world" and that we surely did "behave like it" — if throwing our might and money around is the correct measure of "behaving like it." Nonetheless, we not only failed to accomplish what we set out to accomplish 10 years ago; we have been thrown for losses across the board. In the name of preserving peace, we have waged an endless war; in the guise of serving as sentinel for the "free world," we have stood watch while free governments gave way to military dictatorship in country after country, from one end of our vast hegemony to the other.

Church's radicalization left him increasingly isolated from Washington's foreign-policy elite, with which he had a long-running love-hate relationship.

He yearned to be fully accepted by the foreign-policy establishment — his dream was to be chairman of the Senate Foreign Relations Committee — even as he despised everything the elite stood for, and said so publicly and repeatedly. "Is it possible," Church wondered in a 1974 speech, "to insulate our constitutional and democratic processes at home from the kind of foreign policy we have conducted...a policy of almost uninterrupted cold war, hot war, and clandestine war?"

Richard Nixon and his global fixer, Henry Kissinger, embodied this abusive approach to the world, Church believed. Kissinger, serving as both Secretary of State and National Security Advisor, had seduced most congressional leaders — as well as the Washington press corps — and persuaded them to buy into his brand of foreign policy, called "realism." Worshipful reporters covering Kissinger compared him to Prince Klemens von Metternich — the clever and calculating foreign minister and chancellor of the Austro-Hungarian Empire, whom many had hailed as the architect of the balance of power in Europe in the early 19th century. When Kissinger was accused of lying about his involvement in the secret wiretapping of his aides, Kissinger threatened to resign rather than deal with a congressional inquiry; cowed congressional leaders backed off.

Church's attitude toward Kissinger was complicated. He was impressed by Kissinger's geopolitical skills, and his ability to pull off big power deals with China and the Soviets. Church aide Dine recalled that the *Christian Science Monitor* once asked every senator to fill out a survey describing their views on Kissinger and the Nixon Administration's foreign policy. Dine filled out the survey for Church, and included harsh criticism of Kissinger. But Church erased all of the criticism before sending it back to the newspaper.

Yet Church was also horrified by how Kissinger's brutal foreign policy sacrificed developing nations to deter the global Communism threat — and to expand an American empire. In fact, Church saw his subcommittee's investigation into ITT, the CIA, and Chile as a case study in the abuses of Kissinger-style foreign policy. He was convinced that Kissinger, like former CIA director Helms, had lied under oath about his involvement in Chile coup-plotting. Church took every opportunity he could to grill the elusive Kissinger, much to the chagrin of the foreign-policy establishment.

During one 1974 hearing of the full Senate Foreign Relations

Committee, Church sought to question Kissinger about the CIA and Chile, but committee chairman Fulbright ruled him out of order; the hearing was supposed to be limited to a discussion of U.S.-Soviet relations. Church "grasped his papers to his chest and angrily stalked out," the Associated Press reported.

Frustrated, Church wielded his small Senate Subcommittee on Multinational Corporations like a surgical knife, slicing open American national-security policy to expose its inner rot. He saw, as few others in Washington did at the time, that powerful business and financial forces were secretly influencing American foreign policy in ways that kept the United States on a path toward empire.

"Vietnam did radicalize him, and made him think about the role of multinational corporations in foreign policy," recalled Jerry Levinson, the staff director of the multinational subcommittee. "After Vietnam, he realized that there had been a lot of interest by multinational corporations in the continuation of the war."

At the time, Church considered the work of the multinational subcommittee to be among his most important achievements. In addition to his investigations of ITT and Chile and Lockheed's foreign payoffs, the Church subcommittee launched a wide-ranging investigation into the political and economic power wielded by the oil industry. With lucky timing, Church's investigators dug into Big Oil just as the Arab oil embargo hit the United States in the fall of 1973. Saudi Arabia and other Arab nations cut off oil shipments to the United States to protest U.S. support for Israel in the Arab-Israeli war in October, 1973. The embargo led to gasoline shortages, long lines at gas stations, and deep public anger toward Arab countries. Moving quickly, Church became the first congressional leader to examine the history of the U.S. oil industry's close ties to Saudi Arabia — and how that relationship had perverted American policy in the Middle East.

Church obtained an archive of documents from the National Security Council and the Justice Department that shed light on how, decades earlier, the Eisenhower Administration had secretly exempted the oil industry from antitrust laws, enabling major U.S. oil companies to form consortiums to control Middle Eastern oil. One giant consortium was set up in Iran, giving Big Oil control of Iranian crude following the CIA-backed coup in 1953 that ousted Mohammad Mossadeq, Iran's democratically elected prime minister.

The secret regulatory breaks for the oil industry had been justified on the grounds of national security, Church discovered. "The Cold War was used as a reason for excusing the big oil companies from the anti-trust laws," a Church staffer told the *New York Times* in 1974. "It was to keep Iran out of the hands of the Communists. This is a precursor to the problems we're having now."

Church was taking on powerful figures and giant companies that no one else in Congress wanted to confront, and his aggressive investigative approach was shaking up the Senate. Senator Henry Jackson, a Democrat from Washington state who was an avowed hawk and a defender of the national-security establishment, secretly worked with the CIA to try to blunt Church's investigation of Helms, ITT, and the CIA's role in Chile, according to an internal CIA history. Meanwhile, Senator Charles Percy, a moderate Republican from Illinois and a member of Church's Subcommittee on Multinational Corporations, recoiled at Church's aggressive investigation of the oil industry. (It was Church's radical approach to the role of the multinational subcommittee that later prompted Humphrey and Javits to get it abolished.)

Even Bethine Church worried that her husband was taking on too much by going after corporate America — just as she had worried about his early opposition to the Vietnam War. Levinson recalled overhearing a phone conversation between Church and his wife in which she told him he might be "asking for trouble from multinationals" by giving a speech tying corporate interests to militarism. Church responded by saying, "If I can't give a speech like this, then what the hell am I doing here?" recalled Levinson.

His wife eventually came around, even attending subcommittee hearings on the oil industry. During one hearing, reporters noticed her signaling to her husband from the audience that the hearing room was too hot, asking that he get someone to turn down the thermostat. Bethine was always ready to serve as Frank Church's fixer.

* * *

But even as Church was criticized by some senators for becoming too radical, his effective handling of his subcommittee's wide-ranging and sensitive inquiries quietly impressed the one man who really mattered: Senate Majority Leader Mike Mansfield.

Mansfield was the opposite of an elite establishment figure. As a 14-year-old during World War I, he ran away from his Montana home and lied about his age to join the Navy. He then served in the Army before switching to the Marines, serving in China in the 1920s.

The taciturn Mansfield blanched at Church's hunger for headlines. Unlike other senators, however, he admired Church's readiness to take on the power structure with his multinational investigation. Speaking at a dinner for Church in October 1973 in Boise, Mansfield said that "Frank Church stands out today as one unwilling...to remain within the comfortable confines of complacency." Mansfield also felt some kinship with Church as a fellow Democrat from the Northwest who had been an early and vocal critic of Vietnam. "Mansfield was the father figure, and Church was the next generation," observed Church aide Bill Miller.

Soon, Mansfield would turn to Church to run an even more explosive investigative committee.

Senator Mike Mansfield in the White House Cabinet Room, 1966.

Church's investigations into corporate power had been linked in the public consciousness to the much larger Watergate scandal, which finally led to President Richard Nixon's resignation in August 1974. That meant Church's investigative work had grabbed headlines, but it had kept him in Washington throughout much of 1974 — a year when he faced reelection.

The political outlook for Democrats in the mid-term elections of 1974 couldn't have been better. The year was dominated by a severe recession and the all-consuming Watergate scandal, climaxing with Nixon's resignation and followed by the deeply unpopular decision by the new Republican president, Gerald Ford, to pardon Nixon in September. All signs pointed to a Democratic landslide in November.

Church had fended off a recall attempt in 1967 and won a reelection campaign in the tumult of 1968, despite his controversial role as a leading dove on Vietnam. With the troops now home from Vietnam and the Republicans in retreat nationally, Church thought he could coast home in 1974.

At the time, Church and other Idaho Democrats could still count on large pockets of support scattered throughout the state. North Idaho, which was then heavily unionized with mine workers, was the strongest Democratic base. Democrats could also rely on the Lewiston area in central Idaho, where lumber workers and German Catholic wheat farmers had a tradition of voting Democratic. In the eastern part of the state, the factory town of Pocatello was another Democratic stronghold, along with Idaho Falls, which had experienced an influx of highly educated workers to a nearby federal atomic-energy facility. Boise was largely Republican, but the north end of town was Democratic. The Democratic formula for success in Idaho in the 1960s and 1970s, recalls John Greenfield, the party's state chairman from 1978 to 1979, was to generate strong voter turnout in those bastions while limiting the damage in the rest of the state.

Distracted by both his subcommittee investigation and Watergate, Frank Church made only short, hurried campaign visits back to Idaho, like his day in Burley. Forrest Church, now reconciled with his father, helped compensate for his father's absence by returning to Idaho to campaign heavily for him in 1974.

Church relied heavily on out-of-state campaign contributions, including from Hollywood. His strong support for Israel also attracted wealthy Jewish donors.

But Church was not taking his 1974 reelection campaign as seriously as he had his earlier races — nor as seriously as he should have. He was dangerously misreading the mood in Idaho. Job losses in the timber and mining industries were starting to lead to angry political fights and growing public support for right-wing causes, like greater commercial access to the federal government's huge landholdings in Idaho. The conservative backlash against the environmental movement was just beginning to build; it would coalesce in the late 1970s in the Sagebrush Rebellion.

Church's Republican challenger was Robert L. Smith, the chief of staff for Representative Steve Symms, an Idaho Republican who had first been elected to the House in 1972. Smith and Symms were old friends and ideological soulmates. Conservatives disgusted by what they saw as the leftward drift of the country in the early 1970s, Smith and Symms had both fantasized about emigrating to Australia. Instead, Symms ran for Congress, with Smith as his campaign manager. Symms's affable personality helped smooth the edges off his hard-right views, and his 1972 upset victory shook Idaho's more moderate Republican establishment. Symms, whose family owned a large orchard ranch in Canyon County, was ambitious and had his eyes on the Senate, but he wasn't ready to take on Church in 1974. He pushed Smith instead.

"I was back in Idaho to give a speech, and people were asking me if I was running for the Senate in 1974," recalled Symms in an interview. "I said no, but the guy who I think would be great would be Bob Smith, my chief of staff." Smith, for his part, remembered that Symms publicly endorsed him for the Senate seat before he even asked Smith if he was interested in running. "Symms gave a speech and said, 'Smith should run for Senate against Church,'" recalled Smith. "Without telling me." But Smith agreed, and returned to Idaho from Washington to launch his campaign.

While Smith was just as conservative as Symms, he lacked his innate political skills. He had never run for office before, and even he saw his race as a long shot. Church did not see Smith as a serious threat, and while Church publicly claimed that he was open to debating Smith, the two sides failed to reach an agreement on one.

"I wasn't that big a person that he felt he had to debate me," recalled Smith.

But Smith still went after Church, hammering away at his support for the creation of vast wilderness areas. "My major issue was that we should have multi-use forest management, rather than just having wilderness areas with no commercial uses," Smith recalled. "Church was for turning a lot of Idaho into a wilderness. I wanted to allow timber and mining, and Church said no, we need to go the John Muir way."

Smith also attacked Church for supporting the new Occupational Health and Safety Act, which Smith said was creating "petty nuisances" for small businesses.

Church's radicalization on national security and foreign policy easily could have damaged him in conservative Idaho, but Smith never focused on it. Some Church aides later expressed their astonishment that Church's belief that America was turning into a militaristic empire was ignored in the campaign.

"When I had to go back and look at his campaign in '74 in national-security and foreign-policy terms, I couldn't believe the lack of caution, the lack of political good sense, the kind of advanced careless George McGovern attitude that he took into that election," said William Bader, who later served as a Senate aide to Church despite having far more establishment views than Church. "If you catalogue some of the votes of Church on defense issues before the '74 campaign, you could retrospectively say, 'My God! Why did he do this?' I mean, this borders on the politically gratuitous."

But the fact that Idaho voters overlooked his foreign-policy work also had a downside for Church. Thanks to the Arab oil embargo, voters were angry at the big oil companies. But few in Idaho realized that Church had been conducting the first major congressional probe of oil-industry excesses.

Meanwhile, the conservative John Birch Society launched a disinformation campaign to smear Church's reputation. Its pamphlet *Frank Church: The Chameleon in the Senate* badly distorted Church's views; political columnist Jack Anderson said the pamphlet was like "quoting Abe Lincoln as saying he would carry on his work 'with malice,' without adding the words 'towards none.'"

At first, Church didn't want to respond, although he did defend longtime aide Verda Barnes against claims that she was a Communist sympathizer because of her support for Henry Wallace and the Progressive Party back in the 1940s.

But Church couldn't stay completely silent about the personal attacks on him, because questions about whether Church supported the United Farm Workers and Cesar Chavez's crop boycotts were causing even more trouble.

Rumors swirled that during the Idaho state Democratic convention in Sun Valley in 1972, Church had signed a petition supporting Chavez's lettuce boycott, stirring speculation that Church might support some future potato boycott, which would hit home in Idaho, by far the largest potato-producing state in the nation.

Church made the situation worse by claiming he didn't remember whether he had signed the petition or not. Verda Barnes tried to find the petition but could never locate a copy. Church eventually said he may have signed it "inadvertently," an answer that didn't satisfy anyone.

In the last few weeks of the campaign, Church's lead in the polls began to shrink. "Six to eight weeks out before the election, I was seeing signs that Smith was making inroads," campaign aid Mike Wetherell recalled in an interview. "I never thought that Church was going to lose to Smith. But I recognized that there were problems."

At the last minute, Church scrambled to fight back. He countered the attacks against him in detail in a large newspaper ad and an hour-long television address broadcast across Idaho. "Bob Smith has engaged in a campaign reminiscent of Watergate," read Church's newspaper ad. "He has twisted facts and spread falsehoods in an attack on Frank Church's good name and reputation." The ad accused Smith of refusing to denounce the John Birch Society's smear campaign, and said the idea that Church supported farm boycotts — particularly a potato boycott — was a "hoax."

In the end, Church won the election with nearly 56 percent of the vote, or 36,000 votes. While it was still a relatively comfortable win, it was Church's narrowest margin of victory since he was first elected in 1956. To Idaho political insiders, it suggested that Church was vulnerable.

"I was flabbergasted that the race was close," recalls Smith. "It was a surprising race."

Church knew he had narrowly escaped. "The 1974 campaign

was a very bad campaign," Church said later. "I made all of the mistakes you would think with experience you wouldn't make."

"Bob Smith came a little closer than we thought he would," recalled Cleve Corlett, who was Church's press secretary. "I would have to say that 1974 was a prelude to six years later, with Reagan and the rise of the right wing in 1980."

Still, with his win in 1974, Church became the second-longest tenured senator from Idaho in the state's history; only Borah had served longer. But Steve Symms was also reelected to his House seat, winning 58 percent of the vote, and it was obvious he was coming for Church. Privately, Church confided to Wetherell that "it is looking more and more like I will be the last Democrat elected to the Senate from Idaho."

* * *

By late 1974, Frank Church was at a crossroads, both in Idaho and in Washington.

His hold on his Senate seat seemed increasingly fragile, while his belief that America was becoming a militaristic empire placed him outside the Senate's mainstream.

What's more, he worried that his Senate career had so far been unfulfilled.

Church decided it was time to gamble. On a 1974 trip to Venezuela for the oil-industry investigation, he confided in Levinson that he was thinking about running for president in 1976.

But in December 1974, just after his narrow reelection, Church's plans suddenly became even more ambitious—and more complicated.

CHAPTER 11

"This will cost you the presidency"

WHEN JAMES SCHLESINGER became director of the Central Intelligence Agency in February 1973, he was a stranger to the spy agency. A Harvard-educated economist and former RAND Corporation analyst, Schlesinger had been chairman of the Atomic Energy Commission when President Richard Nixon surprisingly picked him to run the CIA, replacing Richard Helms.

Nixon wanted his own hatchet man at the CIA, and Schlesinger fit the bill. Schlesinger was arrogant and abrasive and made enemies everywhere, and he went to the CIA with a mandate from Nixon to chop heads.

But Schlesinger didn't expect to unearth the CIA's dark history.

By the time Schlesinger arrived at the CIA, the Watergate scandal was starting to overwhelm everything else in Washington. What was most troubling for Schlesinger was that there was mounting evidence that the CIA was caught up in the growing scandal to a greater extent than Agency officials had previously acknowledged. In the days after the Watergate break-in in June 1972, then–CIA director Richard Helms had engaged in a complicated dance to escape Richard Nixon's efforts to get the CIA to shut down the FBI's Watergate investigation by having Helms falsely claim that the break-in was part of a secret CIA operation. Helms later publicly denied any Agency involvement in Watergate.

But Schlesinger discovered that former CIA officers charged in connection with the Watergate burglary had received logistical support from the CIA when they got involved in the Nixon White House's wide-ranging illicit operations. At the request of a top Nixon aide, General Robert Cushman — deputy director of the CIA at the time — had authorized the Agency to provide support for E. Howard Hunt, a former CIA officer working for the Nixon White House's secret "Plumbers" unit, which was behind the Watergate break-in. Hunt had received logistical support in the Plumbers' 1971 illegal burglary of the Los Angeles office of Daniel Ellsberg's psychiatrist. Nixon and his lieutenants were looking for information they could use to discredit Ellsberg after he had leaked the Pentagon Papers. Helms also authorized the CIA to prepare a psychological profile of Ellsberg at the request of the White House.

Shocked, Schlesinger began to wonder what else the Agency was hiding. In May 1973 he ordered Agency officials to compile a report listing everything in the Agency's past — and present — that could be considered scandalous or illegal. He didn't want to be blindsided again, so he demanded that all of the CIA's questionable actions be unearthed, going back to the Agency's very founding. Schlesinger issued a directive ordering all "senior operating officials of this Agency to report to me immediately on any activities now going on, or that have gone on in the past, which might be construed to be outside the legislative charter of this agency." His order added that "I hereby direct every person presently employed by CIA to report to me on any such activities of which he has knowledge. I invite all ex-employees to do the same."

The wording of Schlesinger's order was vague, since the limits of what constituted acceptable activities under the CIA's "legislative charter" had been left purposefully hazy ever since the Agency's founding. Those limits had never really been tested before. The National Security Act of 1947 banned the CIA from having "police, subpoena, law-enforcement powers, or internal security functions," but the statutory language was otherwise so loose that it had not kept up with the dramatic expansion of the CIA's secret operations.

But experienced CIA officers understood what Schlesinger's directive meant. He wanted to know not only about any unreported illegal programs, but also about any unethical or embarrassing activities that CIA insiders knew could lead to what they called a "flap"—a damaging public disclosure. Schlesinger was asking for the Agency's dirty laundry.

The result was a report that came to be known as "the Family Jewels." It didn't cover all of the Agency's past abuses and criminal activity, but the list of the CIA's sins included in the report was still a long one. No one at the CIA had ever put together such a damning and dangerous file.

Schlesinger didn't stay at the CIA long enough to decide what to do with the Family Jewels report. He ran the Agency for a total of just 17 weeks, leaving in July 1973 to become Secretary of Defense as Nixon, besieged by Watergate, shuffled his lieutenants. So Schlesinger's successor at the CIA, William Colby, was left to deal with the Family Jewels.

The CIA never intended for the top-secret Family Jewels report to be made public. But in the aftermath of Watergate, with both Congress and the suddenly aggressive Washington press corps eager to discover the next scandal, the Family Jewels report was like a ticking time bomb hidden inside the CIA.

* * *

Seymour Hersh—described by *Rolling Stone* in the 1970s as "a hurricane of a man who seems to approach life as if it were a battlefield"—was a 32-year-old freelance journalist when he burst onto the national stage in 1969 with his Pulitzer Prize–winning exposé of the My Lai massacre in Vietnam. Hersh was a fast-talking force of nature ("he walks and talks like a speed freak but the energy is all natural; he doesn't even smoke," said *Rolling Stone*) who had learned his reporting skills at the legendary *City News Service* in his native Chicago. He cherished his independence as a freelancer and hated the sclerotic bureaucracy of large news organizations, like the Associated Press, where he had covered the Pentagon. But after My Lai, he feverishly kept breaking one big story after another, and was inevitably hired by the *New York Times*, charged with competing against Bob Woodward and Carl Bernstein of the *Washington Post* on Watergate.

Hersh, Woodward, and Bernstein battled furiously for Watergate scoops, but also came to respect one another, and sometimes quietly compared notes as the scandal grew. The three men were the vanguard of a new generation of investigative reporters, bringing fresh intensity and professionalism to a field once dominated by gossip-prone columnists like Drew Pearson—the columnist who two decades earlier had broken the story of Senator Herman Welker's involvement in the blackmail scheme that led to the suicide of Senator Lester Hunt.

But even as he was covering Watergate, Hersh was pursuing leads on another huge story: evidence of illegal activities at the CIA.

Hersh kept reporting on the CIA story through the closing days of Watergate and Nixon's resignation in August 1974, and then kept going through the fall and into the winter. In late December 1974, he conducted his final interviews—including with CIA director William Colby—and was ready to write his story. Hersh was such an independent rogue that he didn't start writing his massive project until the last minute, and was still writing well past midnight before its scheduled publication in the Sunday, December 22, edition of the *New York Times*. But he had committed the cardinal bureaucratic sin of failing to give his editors at the *Times* any warning of his story's immense length, leading to a night of legendary drama inside the *Times* that Hersh richly detailed in interviews and his 2018 memoir.

When a low-level night editor in New York saw the story's length, he called Hersh, who was still cranking out even more copy while sitting alone late at night in the Washington bureau. The editor told Hersh there wasn't enough space in the Sunday paper for his story.

Hersh went ballistic, and tried to track down Abe Rosenthal, the paper's mercurial executive editor. He called Rosenthal's home after 2 a.m. and got his wife on the phone. Hersh said he needed to talk to Rosenthal immediately, but his wife bitterly revealed that Rosenthal had left her, and that he was now living with his new girlfriend. Hersh then called the girlfriend—it was now almost 3 a.m.—and let the phone ring incessantly. Finally she answered, and brought Rosenthal to the phone. Rosenthal called the paper's night desk and got Hersh the space he needed.

On December 22, 1974, Hersh's story dominated the front page of the Sunday *New York Times* and was immediately seared into the national consciousness. In his memoir, Hersh described the CIA domestic-spying story as "the most explosive of my years at the *New York Times*."

The CIA, Hersh revealed, had for years secretly conducted a massive and illegal domestic-spying operation against anti-war activists and other dissidents. During the Vietnam War, Hersh reported that a special unit of the CIA, reporting directly to the Agency's director, had collected intelligence files on at least 10,000 American citizens. In addition, Hersh reported, a review of the CIA's files ordered the previous year by Schlesinger had "produced evidence of dozens of other illegal activities by members of the CIA inside the United States, beginning in the nineteen-fifties, including break-ins, wiretapping, and the surreptitious inspection of mail."

Hersh's CIA story was initially seen by many as the backstory to the Watergate scandal, which had reached its climax with Nixon's resignation just over four months earlier. The CIA's murky role in the Watergate scandal had never been fully explored by congressional investigators or the press, and Hersh was now laying out the proof that the Agency had engaged in illegal domestic operations.

In his story, Hersh hinted at a Watergate connection. "The disclosure of alleged illegal CIA activities is the first, possible connection to rumors that have been circulating in Washington for some time," Hersh wrote. "A number of mysterious burglaries and incidents have come to light since the break-in at Democratic party headquarters in the Watergate complex on June 17, 1972."

Hersh's story prompted Senator Howard Baker, a Tennessee Republican who had gained fame on the Senate Watergate Committee, to seek a renewed congressional inquiry into the CIA's connections to Watergate. Watergate "reeked of domestic operations" by the CIA, said Baker. "There's a whole range of unanswered questions." (Indeed, while serving on the Senate Watergate Committee, Baker had bombarded the CIA with questions about the Agency's involvement in Watergate, according to an internal CIA history.)

But Hersh's massive story went far beyond Watergate. It revealed a much more sprawling and ominous scandal, showing that the CIA had turned its intimidating foreign-intelligence powers inward on Americans. The story, which contained the most explosive allegations of illegal activities and widespread abuses committed by the CIA ever published in the American press up to that time, quickly set off a firestorm — and would soon lead to the formation of the Church Committee.

Calls for wide-ranging investigations of the CIA began within hours of the publication of Hersh's story; in his first follow-up story in the next day's *New York Times*, Hersh reported that Senator William Proxmire, a Wisconsin Democrat, was the first congressional leader to call for the Justice Department to investigate the CIA. Hersh's story was published just as President Ford was flying to Vail, Colorado, for his Christmas vacation, and Ford told reporters traveling with him on Air Force One that after reading Hersh's story, he had told CIA director William Colby that he would not tolerate such domestic spying by the CIA. He said that Colby had assured him that "nothing comparable" was currently going on at the Agency.

Meanwhile, the *Times* reported that James Angleton, the CIA's chief of counterintelligence who had been named in Hersh's story as having run the illegal domestic spying operation, had resigned.

In fact, Colby had fired Angleton just before Hersh's story appeared. Angleton was an aging, paranoid alcoholic who over the decades had built a strange, ad hoc empire deep inside the CIA. In addition to running the domestic-spying operation in the late 1960s, largely against anti-war activists, Angleton had for decades maintained personal control over all of the Agency's spy-hunting operations.

As counterintelligence chief, Angleton had paralyzed the CIA's efforts to spy on the Soviet Union by wrongly insisting that every new Russian defector who approached the CIA was an untrustworthy double agent. CIA officers involved in Russian operations who questioned Angleton's surreal counterintelligence methods were accused by Angleton of being Soviet moles. One CIA officer described him as a ghost: "I watched Angleton as he shuffled down the hall, six feet tall, his shoulders stooped as if supporting an enormous incubus of secrets, extremely thin, he was once described as a man who looks like his ectoplasm has run out."

Angleton had been protected by previous CIA directors, notably Helms. But Colby distrusted Angleton and had been planning to get rid of him because of his dysfunctional management of counterintelligence. With Hersh's story looming, Colby finally fired him. When the news of Angleton's ouster was made public, it appeared as if the CIA was cleaning house in response to the disclosures of its domestic abuses.

As the impact of Hersh's story kept growing, Ford and his aides realized they had to move quickly if they were to stay ahead of the demands for Congress to launch a major investigation. Henry

Kissinger, along with White House chief of staff Donald Rumsfeld and his deputy, Dick Cheney, held a series of meetings as they scrambled to craft the administration's response. Cheney took the lead as they sought to contain the emerging crisis. Ford announced that he had ordered Colby to write a report summarizing what was known about the CIA's past abuses.

But the early preemptive steps by the White House and the CIA couldn't stop the political firestorm created by Hersh's story. Within a week of the story's publication, the chairmen of four congressional committees announced plans for investigations into the CIA.

A few days later, a group of senators invited Hersh to talk to them privately at Senator Alan Cranston's apartment in the Watergate. The legislators wanted to know where the journalist thought a no-holds-barred congressional investigation might lead.

* * *

No one read Hersh's story about the CIA's history of domestic abuses with greater interest than Senate Majority Leader Mike Mansfield, who had long been frustrated by the fact that the CIA lacked any real congressional oversight. He had been pushing the Senate to create a CIA committee for more than 20 years.

Mansfield began his fight for a CIA committee in July 1953, just six months after he first came to the Senate. Joe McCarthy, then at the height of his red-baiting powers, was seeking to subpoena and investigate CIA official William P. Bundy, who was a Mansfield friend. Mansfield wanted to stop McCarthy's reckless attacks on the CIA while also establishing procedures for serious congressional oversight.

Mansfield failed, but he tried again the next year, warning that "once secrecy becomes sacrosanct, it invites abuse." Mansfield kept trying—and kept failing. He was finding it impossible to overcome the powerful forces protecting the CIA, including the Agency's many defenders within Congress itself. During the Eisenhower Administration, CIA director Allen Dulles and Senator Richard Russell of Georgia, the longtime leader of Southern Democrats in the Senate, helped set the pattern for the Agency's discreet and easygoing congressional relations that would continue into the 1970s. Russell privately handled many of the CIA's most sensitive matters through his fiefdom in the Senate Armed Services Committee; his steadfast opposition to any aggressive oversight stymied Mansfield.

Mansfield tried again in 1960, after the Russians shot down a CIA U-2 spy plane and it became clear that the Agency's secret photo-surveillance flights over the Soviet Union had little supervision from anyone outside the CIA. "Not a single member of the cabinet nor the President exercised any direct control whatsoever over the ill-fated U-2 flight at the critical moment at which it was launched," Mansfield said. The flight "owes its origin more to bureaucratic inertia, lack of coordination and control, and insensitivity to its potential diplomatic cost than it does to any conscious decision of politically responsible leadership."

But he failed again in 1960, and again in 1966 in the midst of the Vietnam War.

The first successful effort to legislate some modest CIA oversight passed Congress just days before Hersh's story was published. In the wake of Vietnam, Watergate, and revelations of the CIA's involvement in Chile — largely disclosed by Frank Church's multinational subcommittee investigation — Congress passed the Hughes-Ryan Act, requiring Congress to be notified of any new CIA covert-action programs. The bill had been winding its way through Congress for more than a year, and finally passed the Senate on December 17, 1974, and the House the next day — the week before Hersh's story was published. Ford signed the bill into law on December 30, as part of his effort to address the changing mood in both Congress and the nation amid the accusations of the CIA's domestic abuses detailed by Hersh in the *New York Times*.

But Hughes-Ryan had little impact. Though it formalized congressional covert-action notification, it did not change who in Congress was getting notified. At the time that Hersh's domestic-spying story was published, relations between the CIA and Congress were still handled through private, off-the-record meetings between a handful of House and Senate leaders and the CIA director — a clubby approach to "oversight" little changed since the days of Dulles and Russell in the 1950s. Vest-pocket subcommittees hidden inside larger committees pushed the CIA's secret needs through Congress. Few questions were ever asked.

By 1974, Mansfield had still not succeeded in creating a Senate intelligence committee that would conduct serious oversight. But with Hersh's story, Mansfield finally saw his chance.

* * *

Hersh's revelations about the CIA's domestic abuses came at the perfect time for Mansfield. The Democrats had just won a landslide victory in the 1974 post-Watergate midterm elections, giving them a 60-seat majority in the Senate and a 291-seat majority in the House. The Republicans still controlled the White House, but Gerald Ford was an unelected president who was in a weak position to take on such overwhelming Democratic power in Congress. More importantly, after Vietnam, Watergate, and Nixon's resignation, the country seemed to be in the mood for reform.

The Senate's old guard no longer had the power to stop Mansfield. So in January 1975, the Majority Leader pushed aside those senators who were eagerly talking about launching their own CIA investigations through existing committees, and rammed through a Senate resolution creating a new intelligence committee.

The committee that Mansfield created would be temporary, designed to "conduct an investigation...of the extent to which illegal, improper or unethical activities were undertaken by any agency of the federal government or by any persons, acting individually or in combination with others, with respect to any intelligence activity." The resolution passed the Senate by a vote of 82 to 4 on January 27, 1975. The new committee would be formally known as the Senate Select Committee to Study Governmental Operations with Respect to Intelligence Activities.

Mansfield knew who he wanted to chair the new CIA committee — Senator Philip Hart, a liberal Democrat from Michigan. Mansfield trusted Hart, and knew that he could navigate the political minefield the committee would inevitably face. Hart was also widely popular in the Senate — he was good friends with Senator James Eastland of Mississippi, one of the old Southern segregationists. Hart had earned the nickname "the Conscience of the Senate"; under Hart's leadership, Mansfield believed, the CIA committee could conduct a thorough investigation without causing too much partisan rancor. It was the same reasoning that Mansfield had used in 1973 when he chose Senator Sam Ervin to chair the Senate Watergate committee.

But Hart told Mansfield that he had cancer, and that he couldn't take on the chairmanship. So he recommended another candidate: "Hart said, 'I can't do it—why don't you give it to Frank Church? He wants this and he will do a good job,'" recalled Bill Miller, who served as the staff director of the Church Committee.

In fact, Church was already lobbying Mansfield for the chairmanship. He met with Mansfield and told the Majority Leader he wanted it. Church wanted it so badly that he was also lobbying other senators, something that Church usually found distasteful and rarely did. *New York Times* photographer George Thames later recalled taking photographs during a meeting of Democratic senators when Church walked up to Senator John Stennis of Mississippi and sought his support for Church's bid to lead the new committee.

* * *

Just as Church began his full-court press to win the chairmanship of the CIA committee, he was also taking his first, quiet steps to run for president in 1976. In fact, he had already begun to set up his campaign organization before meeting with Mansfield about the CIA committee.

In late 1974 and early 1975, Church later recalled, it became clear that the most prominent national Democrats were out of contention for the presidential race in 1976. Senator Ted Kennedy had decided it was too soon after his 1969 Chappaquiddick scandal, which centered around Kennedy's efforts to cover up his negligent (and probably drunken) driving in a car crash on an island just off Martha's Vineyard that led to the death of a young woman trapped when the car sank. Meanwhile, Senator Hubert Humphrey, the former vice president and 1968 candidate, and 1972 nominee Senator George McGovern, were both considered painful reminders of the Democratic Party's recent defeats. It looked like the 1976 presidential race would be wide-open on the Democratic side. "It was beginning to become apparent the race would provide an opportunity for Democrats who had not been national candidates before, like Mo Udall, Birch Bayh, Sarge Shriver, Jimmy Carter—who at that time was the least thought-about of all," Church recalled years later. "I thought, if these people can run...why not give it a try?"

So Church and his key supporters set up an exploratory committee in January 1975.

Carl Burke, Church's longtime friend from Boise who had managed his Senate campaigns, recalled that while Democrats in Washington and New York had been urging Church to run for president for several years, Church did not seriously consider the prospect until 1975. But just after he started gearing up for the presidential race, Church decided to seek the CIA committee chairmanship as well.

"Then the investigation came up," Church said later. "I went to Mansfield. I wanted to manage that investigation because I felt so keenly that there is no threat to freedom like the internal threat... the kind that leads to fascism." When he met with Mansfield to sell himself, "he [Mansfield] listened, he neither said yes or no," Church recalled.

At some point during their discussions, Mansfield asked Church about his presidential ambitions — and made it clear that Church could not run for president at the same time he was running the CIA committee. Church readily agreed.

"Church went to Mansfield" to ask for the chairmanship, recalled Bill Miller. "Mansfield told him, 'This will cost you the presidency.'"

"Mansfield was very suspicious of Church's ambitions," observed Tom Dine, Church's foreign-policy aide in the early 1970s. "Mansfield was suspicious because Church liked the limelight."

But in the end, Mansfield of Montana gave Church of Idaho the job. "A Westerner looking out for a Westerner," noted Dine.

Church recalled that Mansfield was maddeningly noncommittal until the very end. During their private meeting, during which Church asked for the chairmanship, Mansfield said, "I'll consider it," Church recalled. "And he never said one word to me about it. Then when the committee was established, Mansfield sent a list of his nominees [for Democratic committee members] to the [Senate] desk. And I was the most senior member that he chose, which meant that I would be chairman."

Ever since, there have been conflicting accounts of the precise wording of Church's promise to Mansfield that he would not run for president while running the committee. Church's critics believe that he made a blanket promise to Mansfield that, if named committee chairman, he would not run for president in 1976. But Church later said that he only promised that he wouldn't run for president until after the committee had completed its work. He insisted that he hadn't agreed to completely rule out a presidential bid in 1976. "It was understood, whether it was implicit or explicit, that I would not be running for president while I was conducting the investigation," Church said in a later interview.

By parsing his words and placing a careful caveat on his promise, Church left himself open to harsh criticism and deep suspicions about his motives for seeking the chairmanship of the CIA committee. It would lead to skeptical press coverage of the committee's investigations, fed by White House and CIA officials who sought to discredit the committee's work by painting it as nothing more than a vehicle for Church's upcoming presidential campaign.

There had always been two sides to Frank Church — the reformer and the politician. At the most important moment in his career, Church couldn't choose between the two, between his genuine moral outrage over the CIA's abuses and the growth of an American empire, and his own political ambitions. And so, in the most fateful decision of his career, he would try to do both: run what would become known to history as the Church Committee, and run for president.

PART TWO

"We doubt that any other country would have the courage"

1975

CHAPTER 12

"A delicate balance"

FRANK CHURCH WAS a loner in the Senate.

He had never played any role in the Senate's leadership, and he had refused to immerse himself in the male-dominated culture of drinking, poker-playing, and womanizing that was still the trademark of the Senate in the mid-20th century.

Bryce Nelson, who worked for Church in the late 1950s and early 1960s, went with Church to see a Federico Fellini film, and as they were leaving the movie theater in Washington he asked Church whether the hedonistic lifestyle depicted by Fellini would appeal to him. "He said yes, it would," Nelson recalled.

But that was just an idle, passing thought. Nelson also recalled walking to the Senate with Church from his office when Church turned to him and expressed disgust with many of his Senate colleagues. "He said that there were a lot of Senators who had the view that your skill with women reflected your skill with legislation. They all admired other senators who fooled around."

Church had only a handful of genuine friends among other senators — Wisconsin liberal Gaylord Nelson was one — and didn't go out of his way to cultivate close ties with many others. He usually found it difficult to ask other senators for their votes, or even to tell other members of his own committee what to do.

"I found Church to be shy," observed F. A. O. "Fritz" Schwarz, who served as chief counsel of the Church Committee. "It was funny, he would be out front, he would love to make speeches, but in person he was shy. He wouldn't lobby other senators; when we dealt with the other senators on the committee, I had to do a lot of it. He would say, they are senators, they can make up their minds. It was odd."

So Church was not the kind of senator to object to the back-handed, almost insulting manner in which Mike Mansfield had given him the chairmanship of the new intelligence committee. Nor did Church resist as Mansfield chose the committee's members without any input from him.

Just as he had done earlier with the Senate Watergate Commit-tee, Mansfield was determined to shape the new intelligence com-mittee himself. He quietly cut a deal with Senator Hugh Scott, the Pennsylvania Republican who was Senate Minority Leader, to nar-rowly divide the committee, with six Democrats and five Republi-cans, even though the Democrats had a lopsided majority of 60 seats in the Senate at the time.

The Republicans on the committee were a mix of conservatives, moderates, and liberals, and were more divided than the Demo-crats. Senator John Tower, a staunch conservative and the first Republican elected to the Senate from Texas since Reconstruction, was the ranking Republican on the committee. He was joined by Senator Barry Goldwater of Arizona, the onetime presidential can-didate and iconic conservative standard-bearer, who had been a critic of Frank Church since the Cooper-Church amendments and the Vietnam War. But Tower and Goldwater were outnumbered on the committee by moderate and liberal Republicans — Senator How-ard Baker of Tennessee, Senator Charles Mathias of Maryland, and Senator Richard Schweiker of Pennsylvania. (Baker, for his part, was a wild card; he joined the committee because he wanted to get to the bottom of the CIA's role in Watergate, yet at the same time he was maneuvering for a Senate GOP leadership post and didn't want to upset his fellow Republican senators.)

Hugh Scott, the Senate Minority Leader, was close to the Ford White House and had chosen Tower to serve as the ranking Repub-lican to act as a tough and prickly foil to Frank Church. Tower was widely disliked in the Senate, and his assignment to the committee was meant as a reminder to Frank Church that the White House was keeping an eye on him. "Tower was there to watch Frank Church," recalled Bill Miller, the Church Committee's staff director. "That was his job, to keep Frank Church honest."

In his 1991 memoir, *Consequences*, Tower wrote that Scott had chosen him to act as the "damage control officer" on the committee, and that Scott expected him to do his best to protect Republican interests. But Tower also knew that he didn't have much power to slow down Church and the Democrats; he and Goldwater couldn't even count on the support of the committee's three other Republicans, who often sided with Church and the Democrats on the need for an aggressive investigation.

The Democrats on the committee were more unified than the Republicans, but they too had to contend with personal rivalries and unique personalities. In addition to Church, Mansfield chose as the Democratic committee members liberals Walter Mondale of Minnesota and Philip Hart of Michigan, balanced by two Southern Democrats, Walter "Dee" Huddleston of Kentucky and Robert Morgan of North Carolina. Finally, for youth, Mansfield added Gary Hart, who was then just 38 and had just been elected to the Senate from Colorado in the 1974 Democratic landslide.

Church, Mondale, and Gary Hart would be the Democrats who became most heavily involved in the committee and its investigations. Hart, who had first gained national prominence as the brash young manager of Senator George McGovern's 1972 presidential campaign, had been in the Senate for only three weeks when Mansfield stunned him by selecting him for the committee. Mansfield "walked up to me on the floor and said he was putting me on the committee," recalled Hart. "He said, 'Frank is running it. You're going to look into the CIA. Do a good job.'"

One thing that many of the Democrats and Republicans on the committee had in common was that they had served in the military in World War II. Phil Hart had been wounded on Utah Beach on D-Day. Walter Huddleston was a tank gunner at the Remagen Bridge the day it was captured, giving the Americans a way across the Rhine. John Tower had served on an amphibious gunboat in the Pacific. And Charles Mathias was a Navy officer in the Pacific who had toured Hiroshima and Nagasaki right after the Japanese surrender, witnessing the atomic devastation of those two cities.

Church Committee meeting. Senator Frank Church is in the center. On his right is Senator Philip Hart, then Senator Walter Mondale and Senator Walter (Dee) Huddleston. On Church's left are Senator John Tower, Senator Howard Baker, a partially hidden Senator Barry Goldwater, and Senator Richard Schweiker. Behind Church are Church Committee chief counsel F. A. O. "Fritz" Schwarz and Republican counsel Curt Smothers.

While Church was the only member of the committee who had been an intelligence officer, their military experience still gave many of the committee members a basic, pragmatic understanding of the uses and misuses of intelligence. "Without a doubt, World War II had a major impact on my views of national security issues," Tower later wrote.

They were also all white men. At the time, the Senate was still essentially a white man's club; there were no women in the Senate, and only one Black man, one Hispanic, and two Asian-Americans. This lack of Black or other minority senators would make a significant difference as the committee's investigation into the FBI deepened during the year to come.

* * *

Mansfield very deliberately did not include any senators who had been involved in the Senate's old, cozy relationship with the CIA.

"When Mansfield put together the committee, he did it with great care," recalled Mondale in an interview. "He knew the personalities of everyone involved."

Mondale was a Minnesota Democrat and Humphrey's protégé; he had briefly considered running for president in 1976, but had abandoned those plans in 1974. Searching for something meaningful to do in the Senate instead, he jumped at the chance to join what became known as the Church Committee. Mondale recalled (in one in a series of interviews conducted over several years before he died in 2021) that "I needed something to do and this came along, and the issue was perfect for me. The whole issue of how do we keep this government strong enough to deal with our adversaries but still protect the liberties of Americans is what we are still struggling with."

Mondale wanted to focus on the FBI, so Church created a domestic task force for Mondale to run. It was one of several early moves to broaden the committee's scope beyond merely the CIA in order to investigate the entire intelligence community — including the FBI, the National Security Agency, military intelligence, and other agencies.

Church readily agreed that the committee should expand its investigation. But he had never been particularly interested in the FBI, so putting Mondale in charge of the FBI investigation allowed him to keep his own focus on the CIA. "That's the way Church wanted to do it," Mondale recalled, when asked how he took the lead on the committee's probe of the FBI. It fit with Mondale's interest in "how the issues we uncovered affected domestic policy," he recalled. "There were a lot of things that showed that the rights of American citizens had been abused."

Giving Mondale such a prominent leadership role on the committee was an intriguing decision by Church. It was already clear by early 1975, when the committee was created, that Church and Mondale were political rivals, with both vying for national leadership of the liberal wing of the Democratic Party. By the summer of 1976, Church and Mondale would square off in a competition to be Jimmy Carter's running mate, after the former Georgia governor came out of nowhere to win the Democratic presidential nomination.

Gary Hart, meanwhile, was particularly excited by getting assigned to the committee by Mansfield. Hart quickly dived into the investigation of the CIA. "The mystery of it was intriguing," recalled Hart in one of several extensive interviews. For Hart, the Church Committee was both a serious investigation and an adventure into the world of espionage.

*   *   *

Fascinated by the CIA's dark arts, Gary Hart acted independently and aggressively to dig into the committee's investigation. As a Senate newcomer, Hart was so eager that he began to meet privately and on his own with William Colby, the CIA director, who at the time was more willing to cooperate with the new Church Committee than any other senior official in the Ford Administration.

Like former CIA director Helms, Colby had served in the OSS during World War II; he parachuted behind enemy lines in both France and Norway. A Princeton graduate, he was part of the generation of Ivy Leaguers who dominated the CIA in its early years, but his later career was largely shaped by the Vietnam War. He served as CIA station chief in Saigon and later supervised the CIA's Phoenix Program in Vietnam, widely criticized as little more than an assassination program. Colby later defended Phoenix as "much-misunderstood," but as a Catholic, he may secretly have felt compelled to cooperate with Church's investigation as a form of penance for his involvement in the blood-soaked program. Colby's cooperation with Church would eventually put him directly at odds with the Ford White House, as well as with Helms and the old-boy network within the CIA.

When Gary Hart began to meet privately with Colby, Frank Church didn't try to stop Hart's freelancing. The result was one of the most interesting early avenues in the committee's investigation.

Hart asked Colby for help. The Church Committee had learned that in the early 1960s, the CIA had hired a mysterious European hit man, code-named QJWIN, first to try to assassinate former Congo prime minister Patrice Lumumba — and, later, Cuban leader Fidel Castro. Hart told Colby that he wanted to meet QJWIN, and Colby told him that he would see what he could do.

In the summer of 1975, Hart traveled to Moscow as part of a congressional delegation. On his last day in Moscow, a man from the U.S. embassy walked up to Hart at a reception and handed him an envelope. Inside was a note, obviously from the CIA, that said a man will meet you in Amsterdam about the request you made to Colby.

On his way back to Washington from Moscow, Hart stopped off in Amsterdam and waited for further instructions. In the middle of a dinner out in Amsterdam, he was given a message to go to the bar in his hotel at 11 p.m. that night. When Hart arrived at the bar, a man tapped him on the shoulder, then guided him to a corner table.

The man was John Stein, then the CIA's chief of European operations. Stein told Hart that the CIA had contacted QJ-WIN, who was then living under a false identity in Europe. Stein said the Agency had told QJ-WIN that a "friend of ours wants to talk to you about the past," Hart recalled. The hit man asked if the request for a meeting had anything to do with the congressional inquiries into the CIA then underway in Washington. Told that it did, QJ-WIN got up and left—refusing to meet Hart.

But Hart wasn't done with his independent investigative work. He persuaded Church to let him create and run his own subcommittee of the Church Committee. Its mandate would be to investigate the intelligence community's performance in connection with President Kennedy's assassination. (Richard Schweiker joined Hart as the subcommittee's Republican.)

Hart didn't believe the CIA was involved in the assassination, but he was troubled that the Agency hadn't shared everything it knew with the Warren Commission when the latter conducted its investigation of Kennedy's killing. Hart had dinner with James Angleton, the ousted CIA counterintelligence chief, who talked cryptically about the slaying by quoting from Bible verse John 14:2.

"I asked Angleton, 'Do we know everything about the Kennedy assassination?'" recalled Hart in an interview. "And Angleton looked at me and said, 'In my father's house, there are many mansions.'" (In other words, the CIA was a big and secretive organization with a long history and many layers, so anything was possible.) "I had to laugh," Hart recalled, "because I had been a divinity student, and I knew the reference."

The capstone to Hart's independent work on the Church Committee would come a year later, when he sought to investigate the gruesome gangland-style murder of one of the committee's witnesses.

*   *   *

Despite his orders from Senate Republican leader Hugh Scott to spy on Frank Church, John Tower soon found that he and Church got along better than he expected. As the committee was gearing up in February 1975, Church and Tower met jointly for the first time with CIA director Colby, and together the two men pushed Colby to provide access to Agency documents, and also to allow the committee to conduct interviews with current and former CIA officers. The relationship between Church and Tower was a sign that in its early days, before polarizing rancor set in over some key issues, the Church Committee would benefit from a level of bipartisanship that would be unheard of in Congress in later decades.

In March, Church and Tower went to the White House together to meet with Ford and his aides, and they jointly pushed the president to give the committee access to a list of key documents, including many from the National Security Council. The White House had anticipated that Church would use the meeting to demand documents; a White House memo prepared for Ford for the meeting, which has since been publicly released, reminded the president to "not commit yourself either to cooperate fully or to provide any specific categories of information. You should avoid negotiating with the senators or dealing in specifics."

But Church was able to push hard thanks to the bipartisan support he had on the committee. "I consider that any investigation that Tower and I agree on should be a source of satisfaction all around," Church told Ford, adding, "Tower and I are in agreement" on the committee's document demands."

"It is an unusual team," Ford responded.

Indeed, Tower and Church were working so well together during the committee's early weeks that Tower was later attacked viciously by conservative *New York Times* columnist William Safire, who wrote that "Tower has made a doormat out of himself." But Tower knew that Frank Church had the nation behind him when the committee started its work in early 1975. The Vietnam War and Watergate had generated enormous public mistrust of government—and a pent-up demand to uncover the government's dark side. Tower didn't like it, but he knew that he and the Ford White

Senator Frank Church and Senator John Tower meet with President Gerald Ford in the Oval Office in March 1975.

House were on the wrong side of the political wave. The United States had created a national-security state with virtually no debate after World War II, and now the public was finally demanding that debate.

* * *

Church Committee members from both parties were also keenly aware that they were at a watershed moment in the history of American national security. "I had been shaken by the loss of public trust after Vietnam, and I was still offended by Nixon's abuse of public office," Mondale wrote in his 2010 memoir, explaining his interest in joining the committee. "I still believed in government as a force for good, but I wasn't sure how long we were going to be able to hang on to the public's confidence. This was a question of whether large, powerful agencies of the executive branch and even the White House were going to obey the law and make themselves accountable."

Church saw the committee's task as to act as a kind of constitutional convention, debating the proper balance between national security and civil liberties. "A free society depends upon maintaining a delicate balance between preserving individual freedom, on the one hand, and maintaining a good order on the other, and if that equilibrium ever tips too far in one direction, it results in tyranny," Church said on the CBS News program *Face the Nation* on February 2, 1975, soon after being named chairman of the committee. "If it tips too far in the other, it results in anarchy.

"So ours is a very delicate mission, to determine how we must maintain that balance, because there is no more important goal than the preservation of freedom in this country."

CHAPTER 13

"The dirty facts"

WITH SO MUCH riding on the intelligence investigation, Frank Church decided in early 1975 to put his presidential ambitions on the back burner — at least temporarily.

Loch Johnson, a 33-year-old assistant professor of political science at Ohio University, was on a research trip to Washington in early 1975 when he stopped by Frank Church's Senate office to talk. He had worked for Church years earlier on a fellowship during the Vietnam War, and now he asked Church if he could join the staff of the new CIA committee. Johnson admitted to Church that he didn't know much about the CIA, and Church replied that "we'd learn together." Church's comment was evidence that he hadn't known much about the CIA himself before leading the Church Committee, because Congress had never before conducted any significant oversight of the Agency.

Loch Johnson quickly became one of Church's most trusted staffers, serving as his "designee" — personal representative — on the Church Committee. That gave Johnson much-broader access to both the committee's work and Frank Church's personal political plans than almost any other staffer. Johnson was one of the few people who bridged the gap between Frank Church the committee chairman and Frank Church the potential presidential candidate.

Johnson recalled going to dinner at Church's house just after the committee's formation and meeting Church's campaign brain

Church aide Loch Johnson with his wife, Leena Johnson, in 1976.

trust. Among the guests were Carl Burke, Church's old friend from Boise who was planning to manage Church's presidential campaign, and Henry Kimelman, a wealthy hotel owner and investor from the Virgin Islands. (Kimelman, the finance chairman for George McGovern's 1972 presidential campaign, was planning to be the chief fundraiser of Church's campaign.) Over dinner, Johnson was struck by the fact that Church was still considering running for president even though he had just been named chairman of the new committee.

But Church was being indecisive. He recognized the new committee's significance and gravity, and the historic role he was being asked to play as its chairman. At the same time, he hoped that running the committee's investigation would increase his national stature and propel him to the presidency. Yet, as he bounced back and forth, he also knew that the intelligence investigation could complicate his future and might prove to be a political albatross.

Church's inability to make up his mind about the presidency irritated his key supporters, who were ready to commit to him. Kimelman wondered whether Church was using his role on the new intelligence committee as an excuse, because he wasn't really prepared to commit to the arduous task of running for president. "I admired and respected Frank Church," Kimelman later wrote, "yet there was a lingering doubt in my mind as to whether he possessed the necessary ego and passion to be the leader of the free world... And as the campaign drew nearer, it sometimes seemed to me that inside himself, Frank was hanging back from the cruel demands of a presidential race."

Soon after the dinner meeting, Church finally told his family, aides, and supporters that he was suspending his plans for a campaign in order to focus on the intelligence investigation.

But Church didn't close the door entirely. When the committee was created in January 1975, the Senate had given it a nine-month life span, meaning it had to complete its work by September. So even as he suspended his campaign, Church privately harbored the faint hope that he could revive his presidential bid once the committee's work was finished, launching his bid before the end of 1975.

In the meantime, Church took full advantage of the national attention he was getting as chairman of the new committee — publicity that still might help propel his presidential campaign. Posing for photographs that would accompany a *New York Times* feature about him after he was named chairman, Church agreed to the photographer's request that he stand beside the portrait of William Borah, his childhood political role model, which hung on Church's office wall. As the photographer lined up both Church and Borah, Bethine Church, hovering nearby, urged the photographer to "get both of their chins jutting out."

*　*　*

Among Church's initial tasks as chairman was to hire a staff to conduct the new committee's investigation, but his lack of experience in running such a large organization led to problems almost immediately. He hired his two most important staffers with little thought about how the pair would mesh and collaborate.

As staff director, Church hired Bill Miller, a genteel, straitlaced former U.S. Foreign Service officer who had previously worked for Church in the Senate. As the committee's counsel, he hired F. A. O. "Fritz" Schwarz, a long-haired, aggressive New York lawyer and scion of the famous F. A. O. Schwarz toy store company. (Schwarz's

F. A. O. "Fritz" Schwarz around the time of his work
on the Church Committee.

father had sold the company after realizing that Fritz and his
brother had no interest in running the business, but that didn't stop
Church Committee staffers from giving Fritz a nickname they used
behind his back: *Toys*.)

Frank Church had hired Miller first, deciding only later that the
committee also needed a powerful chief counsel — a structure mod-
eled after the Senate Watergate committee. He then hired Schwarz
after meeting him just once, and then only after a number of other
candidates had turned down the job.

Church was initially looking for a high-profile Washington
legal figure to be chief counsel, but Burke Marshall, who had been
Assistant Attorney General for Civil Rights during the Kennedy
Administration, urged him to hire Schwarz. Marshall got to know
Schwarz in the late 1960s, when Marshall was general counsel of
IBM and Cravath and Swaine was IBM's outside counsel fighting

the government's huge antitrust case against the computer giant. Fritz Schwarz's work at Cravath and Swaine on the IBM antitrust case had impressed Marshall. The pair had also worked together on criminal-justice reform issues in New York as volunteers with the Vera Institute of Justice, so Marshall knew that Schwarz had an interest in public service.

Church asked Marshall to see if Schwarz was interested. When Marshall called, Schwarz immediately said yes.

"It came completely out of the blue," Schwarz said in an interview. "I had never met a single one of the senators before being asked to take the job. I got a telephone call one afternoon. I was at my law firm here in New York. It was a call from Burke Marshall who said that he had been asked to ask me if I would be interested in talking about the job. It took me about five seconds to conclude yes. About two or three days after that, I went down to Washington and had a meeting with Senator Church alone for maybe three quarters of an hour and then with all the other Democratic senators, except Mondale. Probably the next morning, Senator Church called me up back in New York and said they would like me to do it."

The contrast in personalities between Miller and Schwarz was immediately obvious to everyone working for the committee. "My impression of Miller was that he was a nice guy, but probably a little too soft-spoken and gentle," recalled Richard Betts, a Church Committee staffer and later a professor of political science at Columbia University. "He didn't strike me as dynamic or on the cutting edge. Schwarz was more hard-charging, always pressing on things."

Miller and Schwarz represented the two sides of Church's personality. Miller reflected the Frank Church who was a politician yearning for status and acceptance from the establishment. Schwarz represented the post-Vietnam Frank Church who was a radical eager to overturn the militaristic, imperialistic status quo. Their differences very nearly derailed the Church Committee's investigation before it even began.

* * *

Frank Church already knew Bill Miller well by the time he chose him to be the committee's staff director. Church had first met him when Miller was working for Senator John Cooper; Miller played an important role in crafting the Vietnam War–era Cooper-Church Amendments. Church later hired Miller as staff director of a special Senate committee that Church chaired to scrutinize the history of how presidents had used emergency powers.

Church became fascinated by that arcane subject after learning how certain presidential emergency orders, some dating back more than a century, had been used to perpetuate the war in Vietnam despite growing congressional opposition. The Nixon Administration, for example, had at one point claimed the right to keep troops in Cambodia even without congressional funding thanks to an 1861 emergency power allowing the Army to buy feed for its horses during the Civil War even if Congress hadn't approved the funds.

As staff director of the emergency-powers special committee, Miller showed a penchant for obscure research; he later said his work on that committee "really was one of those creative things without any pressure."

But Miller's personality and experience did not give him the skills needed to run an aggressive congressional investigation of the CIA and FBI. In fact, Miller didn't believe the Church Committee should launch an aggressive investigation at all. He believed that the committee should be policy-oriented and should focus on researching the history of the intelligence community to find lessons that the Senate could then use as the basis for future legislation to reform America's spy agencies. In other words, the Church Committee should be like the emergency-powers committee.

Miller's plan for the committee was to seek testimony from current and former top officials from the White House, State Department, Pentagon, CIA, FBI, and other agencies — and ask them what reforms were needed to improve the intelligence community. This "wise men" strategy, Miller believed, would receive bipartisan support while avoiding a protracted fight with the Ford White House and the CIA over access to the classified documents required for a more intensive investigation.

"Church understood, in fact the whole group understood, that if this thing was going to work at all, it had to be bipartisan," Miller said in 1984. "You had to work with people who were very protective of the intelligence agencies and very suspicious of anyone looking into that area of things."

Miller's strategy of limiting the committee's work to a series of

nonconfrontational hearings in which former officials offered recommendations for reform had another, unstated advantage: it
meant the committee could be finished quickly, giving Frank Church
time to run for president.

*　*　*

Fritz Schwarz wanted the Church Committee to do the exact
opposite of everything Miller proposed. Schwarz had agreed to join
the committee because he was eager to conduct an aggressive,
Watergate-style investigation to uncover the worst abuses that the
CIA, FBI, and other agencies had been hiding for decades. He was convinced that the only way the Church Committee could gain public
support to rein in the intelligence community was to show the
nation the unvarnished truth about its past abuses—and to show
Americans that they had been fed lies for decades about the CIA
and the FBI. Schwarz had spent his career as a litigator at Cravath
and Swaine, one of New York's premier law firms, and he knew that
the way to persuade a jury was to build a case with unassailable
evidence.

Schwarz was angry and frustrated that Frank Church seemed to
be letting Miller pursue a much softer approach. Schwarz later said
he felt he had been misled by Church when he took the job, because
he had no idea he was going to have to fight Miller for control over
the committee's strategy and direction. "I had the clear impression
from Senator Church that I was going to be completely running
things," Schwarz later said. "Miller was to take care of administrative matters. I was amazed during these early weeks."

"Bill Miller and I were extremely different people," recalled
Schwarz in an interview. "Bill was less interested in getting what I
called 'the dirty facts,' which I thought we had to get in order to
gain public support. My view was without facts that showed misconduct, we would never get support from the public or even the
Congress for reforms."

Miller "thought we could do it without letting the dirty laundry
come out," Schwarz added. "He was more interested in getting
input from the wise men."

The fight between Miller and Schwarz became so critical to the
direction of the committee that some of the senators on the committee weighed in—on Schwarz's side.

"Bill Miller...thought we could conduct our investigation mainly through interviews with agents and agency officials, then put the story together without digging around in the sewer for facts," recalled Mondale. "That view was not shared by the committee's chief counsel, F. A. O. Schwarz, who came down from New York to join the committee's staff. Schwarz was a litigator at heart, an investigator, and he felt we had to see the files, get the documents, start digging, then draft the questions and call witnesses. Fritz argued that without exposing specifics we couldn't document a case for genuine reform. Most of us endorsed Schwarz's strategy."

*   *   *

With conflict looming and no coordination between the two men, Miller and Schwarz both began to hire staffers, quickly leading to the creation of rival camps on the committee staff.

To suit his interest in historical research and policy recommendations, Miller hired academics and foreign-policy experts, many with government experience. Schwarz scoured New York law firms for young litigators like himself. "Fritz put out a call to his Harvard Law School classmates, and to partners at New York law firms, and they were picking good young associates in their firms," recalled Church Committee staffer Barbara Banoff. "I was an associate litigator, and I got on the committee because a partner at my firm in New York had been a law school classmate of Fritz, and he recommended me."

The result was that the staff was divided into two distinct personality types—the quiet, professorial foreign-policy experts versus the brash New York lawyers.

"It became obvious to me within days of arriving on the staff that there was tension between Miller and Schwarz," recalled Frederick Baron, a young Church Committee staffer who worked closely with Schwarz. "Bill had that foreign service and academic orientation, and he knew how things worked in the Senate, and how hearings were done, and he brought in a lot of people with foreign policy academic credentials. And there was Fritz, who had arrived thinking this was primarily an investigation, like a big piece of litigation. Fritz was so outrageously talented that he did not doubt that he was there to be the master investigator."

At first, Miller had an advantage over Schwarz because he had already filled many of the senior staff positions with people who agreed with his soft strategy.

The feud broke into the open during a staff meeting, when Miller's allies in senior posts angrily complained about a Schwarz demand that he be allowed to place lawyers in key positions in every section of the committee staff. The Miller allies protested that Schwarz's plan was nothing more than a blatant power grab. Schwarz responded by slamming his hand down on a table, shouting: "I'm not going to sit here and take these accusations."

Miller and Schwarz took their differences to Church; finally forced to choose, Church sided with Schwarz. He told both men he wanted the committee to pursue an aggressive investigative strategy.

"We took that argument to Church, and Church said yes, we have to get the facts," recalled Schwarz in an interview. "To Bill's credit, even though that's not how he would have done things, he went along with it."

"Church felt that boring hearings would not attract the attention of the American people and create pressure for reform; that took some drama," Loch Johnson recalled in an interview. What Bill Miller failed to understand, Johnson says, is that "democracy is a battle between those who have no real sense of the Constitution and its checks-and-balances, on the one hand, and those who truly value the rule of law and the dangers of unbridled power, on the other hand."

Siding with Schwarz was one of the most consequential decisions Church made as committee chairman. If he had sided with Miller and approved a soft, nonconfrontational strategy, the Church Committee would have long since been forgotten by history.

* * *

After winning the showdown with Miller, Schwarz emerged as the committee's most dominant staffer. Miller retained his title as staff director, but Schwarz became the de facto leader of the staff.

Miller gamely acquiesced to Schwarz's leadership role, working behind the scenes to smooth relations with committee Republicans and the White House. But even as Miller began to cooperate with Schwarz, his allies on the committee remained bitter, especially as they saw their own roles being overshadowed by Schwarz and his legion of lawyers. They remained convinced that Schwarz's focus on headline-hunting investigations was a distraction from a more sober study of the intelligence community.

"I was seriously opposed to the way that F. A. O. Schwarz was taking the committee and taking Church with it," Miller ally William Bader said in a 1987 interview. "Turning that committee, or trying to turn that committee into some kind of investigatory circus. I think in a lot of corners of the United States, people said, Church? What's Church doing with that committee? He's grandstanding."

Bringing in Schwarz "created a more antagonistic relationship with the intelligence community," David Aaron, a Church Committee staffer and Miller supporter, recalled in an interview. "Miller didn't want to do that. Miller wanted to reform the community, point out some mistakes, and get to the bottom of the problems, but do it in a way that the intelligence community cooperated with. And Schwarz wanted to do it in a more adversarial way...Schwarz managed to put on a good show, and that's exactly what Church wanted."

The lingering divisions within the staff led Schwarz to rely heavily on the lawyers he had hired to conduct the committee's investigations. The foreign-policy experts brought in by Miller retained their senior-staff titles, but many of them faded into the background, almost as if they had gone on strike. "A lot of those people [Miller's allies] kind of sat back after the fight," recalled Baron. "It felt like all the energy was on the investigative side. It's where the drama was, and where the facts came out."

On the Republican side, Senator Tower depended on his long-time aide Charles Kirbow, while Senator Baker relied heavily on aides Howard Liebengood and Mike Madigan. Curt Smothers was the Republican counsel, and the highest-ranking Black member of the committee staff. (Liebengood's son became an officer with the U.S. Capitol Police, and was one of two Capitol Police officers to commit suicide after the insurrection at the U.S. Capitol on January 6, 2021.)

Under Schwarz's leadership, the Church Committee staff ballooned to about 120, with 75 professional researchers, investigators, and lawyers and 45 clerical and administrative staffers. There were also 14 outside consultants, bringing the staff total to 134. They were crowded into cubicles built in the same auditorium in the Dirksen Senate Office Building that had served as the office of the Senate Watergate Committee.

It was a modern-style cubicle farm, and many of the lawyers on the committee staff were not used to it. "You could hear everybody; it was one huge room," recalled former Church Committee staffer Paul Michel, a lawyer who later became a federal judge. "Twenty people on the phone talking to 20 different potential witnesses...I came from a very structured environment as a local prosecutor. When I came to the Church Committee and walked into that crazy place with people yelling and talking on the phone at the same time, it was very chaotic, very noisy, very confusing to me."

If the Church Committee's staff was riven by internal strife, however, a parallel probe in the House was in even worse shape.

* * *

By early 1975, the House of Representatives, like the Senate, was eager to launch its own investigation into the CIA. The Democrats had picked up 49 House seats in their 1974 midterm landslide, and many of the newly elected House Democrats were liberals eager for reform.

While Mike Mansfield chose Frank Church to lead the Senate investigation, the House stuck with Representative Lucien Nedzi, a Michigan Democrat and the chairman of the House Armed Services subcommittee on intelligence.

Nedzi played both sides in Washington's bitter new political wars over intelligence. On one level, Nedzi was an old-school congressional overseer who had never asked the CIA too many questions and had never pressed the Agency to make significant changes. Nedzi's long-standing subcommittee on intelligence had been a rubber stamp for the spy agency for decades; Nedzi was much more acceptable to the CIA than Frank Church. In a CIA memo written in March 1975, a CIA officer dealing with a House investigator complained that the staffer was reluctant to develop a "cordial working relationship" with the CIA and was pursuing an "adversarial" relationship instead. "He does not reflect Mr. Nedzi's will in this respect," the CIA officer wrote.

But Nedzi was also quietly talking to Sy Hersh as he investigated the CIA for the *New York Times*. To complicate matters further, Nedzi had developed a back-channel relationship with William Colby and kept the CIA director informed about Hersh and his reporting on the Agency's domestic abuses.

Before Hersh's December 1974 story was published, Nedzi told Colby that he had talked to Hersh, and that the reporter had used the word "jewels" to describe what he had learned about the CIA's abuses—a clear reference to the Family Jewels report ordered by ex-CIA director James Schlesinger. "He is going back to that meeting we had in which you briefed me on all the—he used the same term, incidentally, jewels," Nedzi told Colby, according to an internal CIA history about Colby's tenure as CIA director. "I wonder where he got that word," Colby wondered. "It was used by [only] a few people around here." Clearly, Nedzi had been briefed on the Family Jewels well before Hersh's story—but had not used his House subcommittee to launch an investigation of the CIA's past abuses.

After Hersh's story was published, Nedzi publicly downplayed its significance, even though he had clearly been one of Hersh's sources for the story. Nedzi told reporters that as far as he knew, the domestic activities of the CIA had not been as extensive as reported in the *New York Times*, and that it was unclear any laws had been violated. "The statute is vague and although the Agency has overstepped itself, whether or not some activities are illegal is a matter of definition and judgment," Nedzi told a reporter with the Knight-Ridder newspaper chain in late December 1974.

Congressman Nedzi's leading role in the House investigation of the CIA became untenable in June 1975, when the *New York Times* revealed that despite having been briefed on the CIA's abuses more than a year earlier, Nedzi had not informed the House—or called for any congressional investigation—before Hersh's story was published. Nedzi had also failed to tell the other members of the newly formed House investigative committee that he had long since been briefed by the CIA on the abuses they were beginning to investigate.

The revelation upended the House investigation of the CIA, which was supposedly running in parallel to the Senate's Church Committee. Nedzi offered to resign his chairmanship, but in a show of support the House voted to reject his resignation; flummoxed House Democrats briefly considered abandoning the investigation completely.

In July, the House leadership finally decided to continue the investigation with a new committee chairman, Representative Otis Pike of New York. Pike was a moderate Democrat from Long Island who had conducted a House investigation of North Korea's 1968 capture of a Navy spy ship, the *USS Pueblo*. The House investigation would soon be known as the "Pike Committee," the counterpart to the Church Committee. But the tumult over Nedzi and the near-collapse of the House investigation meant that Otis Pike was running months behind Frank Church.

* * *

While the Senate and House committees suffered through early struggles, the Ford White House was initially determined to block them from mounting any serious investigations of the intelligence community at all. Dick Cheney, then the deputy White House chief of staff, spearheaded the Ford Administration's hostile approach to Congress. His resistance would pose an important, early test for Frank Church and the Church Committee.

After Sy Hersh's domestic-spying story was published in December 1974, President Ford had offered only a muddled response to the rising calls for congressional investigations of the CIA. Frustrated, Cheney tried to take the lead in a crisis that was rapidly spinning out of control. He argued that Ford must get ahead of Congress by creating his own commission to investigate the CIA.

Cheney and his boss, chief of staff Donald Rumsfeld, quickly settled on the members of the commission (including Ronald Reagan, who was then just ending his two terms as governor of California) and wrote an executive order for the president to sign in January 1975, to create the commission and define its scope. The commission would be chaired by Vice President Nelson Rockefeller.

But even Ford's creation of the Rockefeller Commission could not slow down the momentum on Capitol Hill for aggressive congressional investigations. Kissinger, trying to motivate Ford to fight back, darkly warned the president that the demand for congressional investigations was "worse than in the days of McCarthy."

Once it became clear that the Rockefeller Commission was not deterring Congress, Cheney fell back to yet another line of defense. He took charge of a White House effort to control how much information the new Church Committee's investigators could obtain from the CIA and other agencies.

But Cheney had trouble getting the White House to focus on stopping Frank Church. In personal notes—written on March 24,

1975, and preserved in Ford's presidential library—Cheney lamented that "at the present time, we have no clear guidelines, no coherent strategy developed for responding to congressional requests generated by their investigation of the intelligence community."

Cheney's campaign to stonewall Church was running into President Ford's personal reluctance to get drawn into another major showdown with Congress so soon after Watergate. Ford did not want a legal battle over congressional access to White House documents that would end up at the Supreme Court. It was just one year earlier that the Court had ruled unanimously against President Nixon, forcing him to turn over the Oval Office recordings that revealed his involvement in the Watergate cover-up, ending his presidency.

Still, Cheney kept working on ideas he could use to counter Church. In the same set of notes he wrote in March, under the heading "processing of requests," Cheney wrote that the White House needed to develop "categories of activities and/or documents where executive privilege is involved."

In other words, Dick Cheney wanted President Ford to claim that executive privilege barred Frank Church from gaining access to

President Gerald Ford, with Dick Cheney in the background. As deputy White House chief of staff, Cheney fought a losing battle to block the Church Committee's access to White House and CIA documents.

huge caches of government documents needed for his investigation. But it would be up to Ford to decide whether he wanted to wage that battle with Congress.

As Frank Church sought access to White House and CIA documents, Gary Hart proposed a way to test the Ford Administration's willingness to provide material: each of the senators on the Church Committee should personally ask for the files the government had on them. But Barry Goldwater quickly killed the idea. "Goldwater said, 'Dammit, I don't want to know what they have on me,'" Hart recalled.

CHAPTER 14

"Like what?" "Like assassinations."

FRANK CHURCH HAD made the critical decision to side with Fritz Schwarz and use the Church Committee to conduct an aggressive investigation. The problem now was simple — where to start?

The CIA had avoided any real congressional oversight for three decades; there were countless past abuses that could be examined. There was so much to investigate that the real danger for Frank Church was that his committee could become overwhelmed and pursue unfocused, superficial inquiries of too many issues. "It's such a large mandate we're going to have to narrow down on certain focal points," Church told reporters soon after launching the committee.

Fortunately, President Gerald Ford provided Frank Church with the answer.

* * *

On January 16, 1975, President Ford met with *New York Times* executive editor Abe Rosenthal and other top editors from the paper to talk about the fallout from Sy Hersh's domestic-spying story, published the previous month. Hersh was not invited to the meeting.

Ford talked about his plans for a presidential commission, chaired by Vice President Rockefeller and stacked with conservatives like former California governor Ronald Reagan. Rosenthal asked Ford why he had chosen "such an obviously loaded commission." Ford replied that said he had chosen people whom he could trust to keep secrets that deserved to remain secret.

"Like what?" Rosenthal asked.

"Like assassinations," Ford blurted out.

The president had only just learned about the CIA's past assassination plots in the days after Hersh's story, when Henry Kissinger warned him over the Christmas holidays that more-troubling abuses might come tumbling out of the CIA.

But after Ford's comment about assassinations, he quickly followed up by saying: "That's off the record."

Rosenthal and the other *Times* editors were stunned that Ford had disclosed something so explosive that had not been revealed in Hersh's December story.

But Rosenthal also felt obliged to go along with Ford's assertion that his comments were off the record, which he interpreted to mean that the *New York Times* could not report on the CIA's involvement in assassinations.

But not every *Times* leader agreed. Tom Wicker, the reporter who years earlier had embarrassed Frank Church in front of Senator Richard Russell, had risen to become a *Times* columnist and associate editor, and he told Rosenthal that they should tell Hersh what Ford had said. Wicker then decided to tell Hersh himself.

Wicker not only told Hersh about Ford's comments about the CIA and assassinations, but also that Rosenthal had agreed not to publish the disclosure. After talking to Wicker, Hersh did some quick reporting and discovered that Fidel Castro was one of the foreign leaders the CIA had tried to kill. But he knew Rosenthal would never let him publish the story, so he decided to leak it to another news organization. Hersh went to his friend and neighbor in Washington, Daniel Schorr of CBS News, and told him what he knew about Ford's comments — and what he had subsequently discovered about the CIA and Castro. Schorr was soon able to confirm and break the news. The CIA's involvement in assassination plots suddenly became the biggest and most explosive element of the widening intelligence scandal.

Ford, now backtracking rapidly from his disclosure to the *New York Times*, tried to keep his newly created Rockefeller Commission from investigating the CIA's assassination plots. The commission's members were happy to give Ford the whitewash he desired. In addition to staunch conservatives like Reagan, other commission members had close ties to the intelligence community, and were not interested in rocking the boat. General Lyman Lemnitzer had been chairman of the Joint Chiefs of Staff during the Bay of Pigs, while Douglas Dillon had helped set up the Office of Strategic Services during World War II. Rockefeller had been on the President's Foreign Intelligence Advisory Board during the Nixon Administration. There were no members of Congress on the commission.

In his memoir, Colby recounted a conversation he had with Rockefeller that showed just how reluctant the commission was to conduct an aggressive investigation. After Colby testified before the commission, Rockefeller came up to him and plaintively asked, "Bill, do you really have to present all this material to us? We realize that there are secrets that you fellows need to keep and so nobody here is going to take it amiss if you feel that there are some questions you can't answer quite as fully as you seem to feel you have to."

But the commission's executive director, David Belin, refused to play along. He was determined to pursue a serious investigation. Belin had been a lawyer on the Warren Commission that investigated the assassination of President Kennedy—an experience that made him determined to investigate the new allegations of the CIA's involvement in the assassinations of foreign leaders. Undaunted by the incurious attitude of his fellow commission members, Belin began to push to get access to government documents that could help him tell the story of the CIA's assassination schemes.

But Dick Cheney and Henry Kissinger kept throwing obstacles in Belin's path. Even after securing tentative approval to include the CIA's assassination plots in the commission's investigation, Belin was not given full access to White House and CIA documents, and was warned that it would still be up to the White House to decide whether any of his work on the issue ever saw the light of day. White House Counsel Philip Buchen wrote that "once you complete your investigation in that regard, you should advise the president of the outcome, through me, and then it can be decided whether the subject should eventually be included as an integral part of the Commission's final report."

The Rockefeller Commission completed its work on an accelerated schedule in the spring of 1975. Ford had made it clear to

Rockefeller that he wanted a quick report concluding that mistakes were made but they had been corrected, and Rockefeller delivered.

But there was one problem for the White House — Belin. He had written a chapter in the commission's final report on the CIA's assassination schemes. In May, just before the commission was to publicly release its final report, the White House demanded that the assassination chapter be withdrawn.

The commission gave in. The report was released on June 6, 1975, without the chapter on assassinations. Belin reportedly considered holding a press conference of his own to denounce the decision, but Cheney blocked him from going public. The final report included a misleading paragraph suggesting that the commission had wanted to investigate the CIA's assassination plots, but didn't have time.

"Allegations that the CIA had been involved in plans to assassinate certain leaders of foreign countries came to the Commission's attention shortly after its inquiry was under way," the report stated. "Although it was unclear whether or not those allegations fell within the scope of the Commission's authority, the Commission directed an inquiry be undertaken. The President concurred in this

Vice President Nelson Rockefeller meets with President Gerald Ford in the Oval Office before the official release of the Rockefeller Commission's report.

approach. The Commission's staff began the required inquiry, but time did not permit a full investigation before this report was due. The President therefore requested that the materials in the possession of the Commission which bear on these allegations be turned over to him. This has been done." Other sections of the report had also been rewritten or severely edited to soften the criticism of the CIA.

By the time Cheney and Kissinger had successfully blocked the publication of Belin's chapter, Frank Church and Fritz Schwarz had decided to make the CIA's assassination plots the first thing the Church Committee would investigate. It was just the sort of ugly and violent CIA abuse that Church wanted to expose, showing how the Agency conducted potentially illegal operations that could undermine U.S. foreign policy with virtually no independent supervision. It would bring home, in graphic detail, the need for congressional oversight of America's spies.

What's more, Church saw that the assassination story was now dominating the headlines, and new revelations were emerging almost daily as investigative reporters began to dig. Church's investigation of the CIA's efforts to kill foreign leaders would get plenty of press attention.

* * *

On May 9, 1975, the Church Committee met and agreed to launch an investigation into the CIA's assassination plots. Loch Johnson, in his first-person account of the Church Committee, *A Season of Inquiry*, said the decision was perhaps the committee's most important of the entire investigation. After months of false starts, the Church Committee now had a central focus for the opening phase of its investigation. "At last the staff knew the senators' top priority," Johnson wrote.

But Church and the committee staff had to continually fight for access to documents, while also pushing to interview officials who knew about or had been involved in the assassination schemes. The Ford Administration tried to delay delivering documents in the hope that "stalling, coupled with the Senate's deadline for completing the job, would result in pallid, half-baked findings," observed Fritz Schwarz in his book *Democracy in the Dark*.

But surprisingly, Church received strong, bipartisan support from the committee to fight back against White House efforts to limit the committee's access to documents. During one committee meeting, Walter Mondale said that Church should tell White House officials that if they continued to drag their feet, Church would respond by getting the Senate to extend the committee's life for as long as it took to obtain the documents. John Tower, the ranking Republican senator on the committee, immediately said he agreed with Mondale. (Church later did get approval to extend the life of the committee. Its deadline to complete its work was extended from September 1975 to the end of February 1976.)

With bipartisan support, Church was able to negotiate from a position of strength, and so he rejected a CIA demand that the Agency be allowed to "monitor" the Church Committee's interviews with current and former officials. And, after Church personally applied pressure and threatened to issue subpoenas, the White House finally relented and agreed to turn over the materials that the Rockefeller Commission had on the CIA and its assassination plots.

President Ford had thus decided to ignore Dick Cheney's calls to stonewall Frank Church. Cheney's constant refrain for the need to pursue a scorched-earth strategy in dealing with the Church Committee was badly out of touch with Ford's views, who was willing to resist some congressional demands but wasn't eager to engage in a bitter showdown with the Church Committee. After Watergate, Ford was seeking a truce with the Democratic-controlled Congress, so he ultimately gave Frank Church what he wanted.

"Under your instructions," White House aide Jack Marsh later wrote in a memo to Ford, "the various intelligence agencies provided... complete access to all documents" related to the Church Committee's investigation of the CIA's plots to assassinate foreign leaders.

* * *

Frederick Baron, the Church Committee staffer who worked closely with Fritz Schwarz, was assigned to go to the White House Situation Room and sift through the first tranche of documents on Cuba and the CIA's plots to kill Castro. The White House had agreed to give Baron only an hour to go through five boxes of documents and pick a handful for the committee to review.

"I started reading, and it was astounding," recalls Baron. "It was all there, the whole history, all these documents with code words that nobody had ever heard of before. The more I read, the more I realized I couldn't agree to just list a few documents. So instead, I went back to see Fritz Schwarz and I told him this is a gold mine, we need everything. Fritz immediately understood and that's what we pushed for, and we got it."

Meanwhile, the CIA under Colby was actually becoming even more cooperative than the White House. After meeting with Church and Tower, and trying to accommodate the freelancing Gary Hart, Colby began to give the committee staff broad access to Agency documents.

"Colby was a key player, because he himself I think had decided the Agency had gone far afield," Church later recalled. "He believed from the beginning that it was possible to cooperate with my committee." In the same unpublished interview, Church even suggested that he had developed a secret back channel with Colby, one that has never before been documented: "We met with each other many times before the committee began its work."

Under Colby, the CIA created a special coordinating unit to deal with the Church Committee's requests, and Colby named a long-time Agency official, Seymour Bolten, to act as the Agency's liaison with the Church Committee. (Bolten's son, Joshua, later became White House chief of staff under President George W. Bush.) With a green light from Colby, Church Committee staffers began to hunt through the recesses of the CIA throughout the spring and summer of 1975, cranking through ancient microfiche machines to view copies of old CIA cables related to the Agency's plots to assassinate foreign leaders.

For its investigation into the CIA's assassination plots, the Church Committee ultimately took sworn testimony from more than 75 witnesses and gained access to thousands of pages of raw, classified files from the White House, CIA, FBI, and Pentagon, as well as the presidential libraries of Eisenhower, Kennedy, and Johnson. A key document was the CIA Inspector General's 1967 report on the Agency's assassination plots, an internal probe that had been kept secret from Congress.

To be sure, the CIA resisted many of the committee's document demands. Repelled by Colby's relative openness, a number of Agency officers dragged their feet rather than cooperate fully with the Church Committee. David Phillips, a longtime CIA officer, was so disgusted that he retired in 1975 in order to launch a public campaign attacking Frank Church and the CIA's other critics. Phillips created a network of retired CIA officers to conduct coordinated public attacks on Church, taking advantage of the media's sudden hunger to interview CIA veterans about the congressional investigations.

But through fits and starts, the Church Committee investigators gained access to far more classified documents than they had ever expected. "We would find some documents, and then we would go back and ask for more," recalls Baron. "They would resist, and then we would go back and forth." For Fritz Schwarz and his team of lawyers, parrying with the White House and CIA over documents felt familiar—like the discovery process in civil litigation. They were good at it, and they usually beat the White House and the CIA.

* * *

Church's decision to focus on the CIA's assassination plots was fiercely opposed by many of the staffers on the Church Committee—led by the same staffers who had backed Bill Miller in his showdown against Fritz Schwarz. They thought a focus on the assassination plots distracted from a broader study of the CIA's history and operations; it was a continuation of the earlier argument between Schwarz and Miller over whether the Church Committee should view itself as an investigative committee at all. Miller later called the assassination issue a "red herring," and claimed that the CIA wanted the committee to focus on assassinations so the committee would "stay away from the other stuff, the real work" of the Agency.

"I think where he [Church] was so importantly mis-served by F. A. O. Schwarz was in directing the committee's attention, and thus Church's attention, to this assassinations gambit," added Miller ally William Bader.

Church ignored the critics on his staff and created a small unit, with three committee members—John Tower, Gary Hart, and himself—combined with a very small but intense group of about 15 staffers, led by Fritz Schwarz, to delve into the CIA's assassination plots. Schwarz's work with Church on the investigation of the CIA's assassination plots ultimately solidified his control over the committee's staff, while Miller faded further into the background.

*　*　*

Church and this small team left the rest of the committee behind and went back into the CIA's dark history, back to a time when there were virtually no rules governing the spy agency.

The CIA, as Church and his investigators would soon discover, had plotted to assassinate foreign leaders all around the world, but Fidel Castro had been the Agency's number-one target. The CIA was so determined to assassinate Castro that the Agency considered eight different plots to kill him, including some bone-headed schemes involving exploding cigars, a scuba diving suit laced with toxin, and an exploding conch shell placed off the Cuban shore where Castro liked to scuba dive.

The CIA even forged an alliance with the Mafia to assassinate Castro; indeed, untangling the story behind the CIA-Mafia alliance would become one of the landmark investigations of the Church Committee.

Thanks to the Church Committee's detailed and comprehensive investigation, the CIA's alliance with the Mafia to kill Castro has since become the most infamous episode in the Agency's history. The CIA's decision in the early 1960s to work with the mob to murder the leader of a foreign country revealed the degree to which CIA officials believed there were no rules they had to follow, and no limits on what they could do or who they could do it with. They believed they could get away with anything.

They had good reason to believe it, because at the time, there was no one in Washington willing to rein in the Agency, and no one in Congress who had any interest in finding out what the CIA was doing. Operating in total secrecy and with no independent supervision, the CIA had drifted so far from its 1947 charter that joining forces with the mob no longer seemed unreasonable.

CHAPTER 15

"I had been asked by my government to solicit his cooperation"

THE CIA-MAFIA ALLIANCE began with a very bureaucratic meeting.

In August 1960, Richard Bissell, the chief of the CIA's espionage operations, met with Sheffield Edwards, the CIA's chief of security, to discuss a plan to kill Cuba's leader, Fidel Castro. Edwards later said there was a "studied avoidance" of the use of the term assassination in the meeting, but both men knew what they were talking about. They decided to get the Mafia — they called it "the Gambling Syndicate" — to help them do it.

Bissell asked Edwards to find a way to contact the Mafia. Edwards immediately thought of Robert Maheu.

Bob Maheu wasn't a mobster, but he was just disreputable enough that Edwards figured he would know how to get in touch with the Mafia. In fact, Maheu had just the right combination of connections and temperament to act as a bridge between the Mafia and the CIA. He was a former FBI agent who had quickly found J. Edgar Hoover's bureau to be too confining, and instead set up shop as a private investigator in Washington, using his FBI connections to land rich clients; he later became a confidential aide to his wealthiest client: the reclusive Howard Hughes.

At the same time, Maheu secured a secret contract from the CIA to quietly handle a series of highly questionable operations the Agency wanted done, but didn't want to do itself. Jim O'Connell, an official in the CIA's office of security, assigned Maheu to handle "cutout" operations, "jobs with which the company could not be officially connected," Maheu later wrote in his memoir.

In the 1950s, for example, the CIA assigned Maheu to blackmail Sukarno, the Indonesian president, because the Eisenhower Administration thought he was too independent, and not sufficiently pro-American. When the CIA was instructed to discredit Sukarno, they turned to Maheu to handle the job.

The Agency believed that Sukarno was having an affair with a Russian woman he had met on a visit to Moscow and who had later visited him in Indonesia. The CIA believed she was a KGB plant, and wanted to find a way to use the relationship for propaganda purposes, to discredit and politically weaken Sukarno.

The CIA didn't have conclusive evidence of Sukarno's relationship with the woman, so the Agency decided to fabricate a smoking gun. Sheffield Edwards asked Maheu to produce a movie with lookalikes of Sukarno and the Russian woman, and have them stage a bedroom scene. It was the 1950s version of a Deep Fake.

Since Maheu was also working for Howard Hughes and commuting between Washington and Los Angeles, he had developed an impressive network of Hollywood connections. He recruited Bing Crosby, the singer then at the peak of his career, and his brother Larry Crosby to help him produce the film. Their work for the CIA came decades before *Argo* — the CIA's fake movie that served as a cover to get Americans out of Iran in 1980.

Maheu and the Crosby brothers arranged to use a small studio and a production crew, and shot a five-minute film with the lookalikes. Maheu got the undersheriff of Los Angeles County to pressure a female informant to play the Russian, while a man who worked for his investigative firm played Sukarno. The CIA never released the five-minute movie, probably because it would have been too easy to tell it wasn't really Sukarno. Instead, the Agency distributed a few still photographs in which the actors were carefully positioned to leave the impression that it was Sukarno, then arranged for the images to be published in Indonesia and elsewhere around the world.

The CIA's sordid campaign didn't have much impact on Sukarno, who stayed in power for another decade. Yet it was considered a success by the CIA, and it cemented Maheu's relationship with the Agency. He now had a well-earned reputation at the CIA that he was willing to take on the Agency's dirtiest work, no questions asked.

* * *

The CIA had hired Maheu to destroy the reputation of a foreign leader, so Edwards figured he might be willing to help kill one, too. It turned out he was right. After meeting with Jim O'Connell and Edwards, Maheu agreed in 1960 to lead the Castro plot, and to get the Mafia to work with him.

As Maheu began to build a team of mobsters who could help him kill Castro, he immediately thought of one mobster in particular — someone he had met the year before, under unusual circumstances.

In 1959, Maheu had been offered some quick cash and a free weekend in Las Vegas if he would serve a subpoena on Beldon Katleman, the owner of the El Rancho Casino, who was caught up in a bitter legal battle and had eluded previous process servers. Maheu didn't yet have any connections in Las Vegas, so he called his old college friend Edward Bennett Williams, a high-powered lawyer with a list of powerful clients in organized crime. With a couple of phone calls, Williams arranged a room for Maheu at the sold-out El Rancho and a meeting with a man named Johnny Rosselli.

Maheu met Rosselli in the lobby of the El Rancho, and Rosselli invited him to have drinks with the El Rancho's owner, Katleman; Maheu didn't tell Rosselli he had a subpoena in his pocket ready to serve on Katleman.

But when Rosselli introduced him to Katleman, who was sitting with Hollywood star Zsa Zsa Gabor, Maheu decided not to serve the subpoena. He still didn't know who Rosselli was, but he knew that he was a friend of Edward Bennett Williams, and he didn't want to anger Rosselli by taking advantage of his introduction to Katleman.

Maheu's decision paid off. Rosselli, who turned out to be one of Hollywood's most famous gangsters, later heard about Maheu's decision to keep the subpoena in his pocket and not serve Katleman, and he thought that showed Maheu had some style. The two began having lunch regularly in Los Angeles.

As soon as Edwards and O'Connell asked Maheu to build a hit team with the Mafia, Maheu knew he wanted Rosselli. So in August 1960 — not long after Bissell and Edwards held their first meeting at CIA headquarters about forging a CIA-Mafia alliance — Maheu called Rosselli and asked him to meet him for lunch at the Brown Derby, one of Rosselli's favorite Hollywood hangouts.

Maheu probably didn't realize it, but by approaching Rosselli he had chosen one of the few gangsters in the country who could help him act as an intermediary between the Mafia and the CIA.

While Rosselli had a long-standing affiliation with the Chicago outfit going back to the days of Al Capone, he was also tied to the local Los Angeles mob of Jack Dragna. Rosselli also did criminal deals on the side on his own. He was a kind of freelance mobster, who had come to know almost everybody in organized crime while managing to avoid making powerful enemies. Rosselli was a bridge between mob families, so he could also serve as a bridge between the criminal world and the world of intelligence. In fact, by the time he started working for the CIA, Johnny Rosselli had lived one of the most unique lives in Mafia history.

*   *   *

Like most everyone in golden-age Hollywood, Johnny Rosselli reinvented himself after arriving in Los Angeles. But his reinvention was much more complete than that of any movie star. He lied about his background his entire life, concealing his immigrant origins from both the Mafia and the government. Even the CIA didn't know the truth about him.

The first federal criminal record of the career criminal known as Johnny Rosselli stated he was born in Chicago, to parents Vincenzo and Maria Rosselli, and that his first name had been anglicized from the original *Giovanni*. "I was born in Chicago in 1905," Rosselli told the Kefauver Committee investigating organized crime in 1950. That was a lie, backed up by a falsified birth certificate planted by Rosselli in Chicago city records to mask his true name and origin.

Johnny Rosselli was in fact Filippo Sacco, born in 1905 in Esperia, Italy, a village between Rome and Naples in the Province of Frosinone. He came up with the name Johnny Rosselli when he was young in order to hide his immigrant status and his early crimes,

Johnny Rosselli, a roguish gangster involved in the Mafia's secret alliance with the CIA to try to kill Cuban leader Fidel Castro, walks past reporters as he leaves Capitol Hill after testifying to the Church Committee.

and he stuck with it throughout his life in the mob. By the late 1920s he was a gangster and rumrunner with considerable status in Los Angeles, both in the mob and in Hollywood.

Rosselli was five foot eight and had good looks and charisma, but he had also earned a reputation as a tough fighter and gunman. Prohibition's illegal liquor trade was in full swing in Los Angeles as gangs smuggled shipments from the coast inland or robbed rival gangs of their loot. Rosselli did plenty of both. But he learned to bury the evidence of his violence just deep enough to move easily in Hollywood circles, where he was considered both charming and slightly dangerous.

During his 1950 testimony to the Kefauver Committee—one of

the very few times he talked about himself in public — Rosselli was asked whether he had been in the liquor business during Prohibition:

"In some manner, yes," Rosselli said.

"Would you state what manner?" he was asked.

"Very, very, very small...other than just buying and selling a little liquor here and there."

"You were first known as a tough guy, is that right?"

"I wouldn't say it that way," Rosselli answered. "I got into a few minor scrapes, fistfights as a young fellow, and naturally those things go on, and if you stand on your own toes and fight back you soon get that kind of reputation. The man who is thrown out in the street, that is what happens, naturally."

By the mid-1950s, Rosselli's focus turned from Los Angeles to Las Vegas. Rosselli transformed himself into the Chicago mob's man in Vegas; his loyalty was now to Chicago mob boss Sam Giancana. He kept an eye on the opening of the Tropicana, which was secretly backed by the Chicago mob, and then got rewarded with some of the concessions gushing money out of the hotel and casino, according to *Handsome Johnny*, a 2018 biography of Rosselli. When Maheu and Rosselli first met, Rosselli was at the peak of his power, known as an important fixer in Las Vegas.

Maheu later told the Church Committee that when he met Rosselli, he didn't know the full extent of his mob ties, but added that "it was certainly evident to me that he was able to accomplish things in Las Vegas when nobody else seemed to get the same kind of attention."

* * *

Before Maheu approached Rosselli, Jim O'Connell, Maheu's CIA handler for the Castro operation, told him not to tell Rosselli that the CIA was behind the plot. Instead, O'Connell told him to say that the plan was backed by rich businessmen angered by the loss of their operations in Cuba, and that they were prepared to pay $150,000 for the hit.

But Maheu ignored O'Connell. If he was going to talk to the mob about killing Castro, he didn't want to start by lying to them. He immediately told Rosselli that the government was backing the plan. "I informed him that I had been asked by my government to solicit his cooperation in this particular venture," Maheu told the

Church Committee. Similarly, Rosselli testified before the Church Committee that during their initial meeting at the Brown Derby, Maheu told him that "high government officials" needed his cooperation in getting rid of Castro. Rosselli quickly agreed to get involved in the plot, and shortly after, he and Maheu met with O'Connell in New York in September 1960. Maheu told Rosselli that O'Connell was with the CIA.

Once he had agreed to work with the CIA, Rosselli turned to Sam Giancana, the Chicago boss he was working for so lucratively at the Tropicana in Las Vegas, and asked him to join him.

Giancana agreed, but he knew that in order to conduct a hit on Fidel Castro, they also had to get Santo Trafficante Jr. on board.

Chicago mobster Sam Giancana, who was recruited by Johnny Rosselli to join the Mafia's secret alliance with the CIA to kill Cuban leader Fidel Castro.

Trafficante was a Tampa-based Florida mob boss who had been the power behind the hotels and casinos in Cuba before Castro took over, and he was now tightening his grip on mob businesses in Miami as well. Trafficante was the only one of the four with serious contacts in Cuba.

Rosselli introduced Giancana to Maheu as *Sam Gold* and Trafficante as simply *Joe*. Maheu later said he discovered their true identities only a few weeks later, when he read a story in *Parade* magazine that listed the top ten mobsters in America. Both Giancana and Trafficante were on the list.

Maheu and Rosselli set up shop in Miami, first at the Kenilworth Hotel, where Arthur Godfrey's television show was filmed, and later at the glitzy Fontainebleau Hotel on Miami Beach, where they took a five-room suite with a kitchen and dining room and were joined by Giancana and occasionally by Trafficante. They drank champagne while Giancana had beluga caviar flown in from New York. Maheu cooked spare ribs in their suite. Their gathering resembled a scene from that year's *Ocean's Eleven* — except they were there to kill the leader of a foreign country on behalf of the Central Intelligence Agency.

*   *   *

The CIA originally thought the Mafia could arrange for someone to shoot Castro, but Giancana quickly vetoed that idea. Whoever shot Castro would almost certainly be captured or killed immediately afterward. No one could be recruited for such a suicide mission, Giancana argued. He wanted to use poison pills that could be slipped into Castro's food or drink.

The initial plan worked out by the CIA-Mafia gang was for "Joe" — Trafficante — to travel to Cuba and get in touch with his contacts who could help put the assassination plot in motion. At the time the CIA-Mafia alliance was started, Castro had not yet closed all of the casinos in Havana, and Trafficante still had reasons to travel to Cuba. Giancana claimed that Juan Orta, Castro's disaffected private secretary, had previously received kickbacks from the Mob to protect its casino interests, and had since lost that income and needed money, so he could be persuaded to help kill Castro.

The CIA's Technical Services Division was asked to produce poison pills, and came up with what Maheu later described as "colorless, round, gelatinlike" capsules filled with botulin.

The CIA's Jim O'Connell later recalled that he handed the pills over to Rosselli. (although Maheu recalled in his memoir that he was given the pills by the CIA, then turned them over to Rosselli and Giancana.) The pills were then passed to Trafficante, who in turn got them to Orta in Cuba. But after several weeks of dithering, Orta admitted that he had lost his nerve. He refused to go through with the poisoning.

Trafficante then said they should try Dr. Anthony Varona, a leader in the Cuban exile community in Miami, who Trafficante said could recruit someone close to Castro to poison him. Varona was frustrated with the ineffectiveness of the exile community in Miami and agreed to take on the assassination mission, but demanded $10,000 and communications equipment for his organization first. Varona, however, didn't have any more success than Orta.

Meanwhile, a comedic subplot was threatening to upend the CIA-Mafia alliance. Sam Giancana was in the midst of a long-running affair with singer Phyllis McGuire, a member of the singing group the McGuire Sisters. McGuire was appearing in Las Vegas while Giancana was in Miami, and Giancana suspected she was also sleeping with comedian Dan Rowan—later famous as the co-star of *Rowan & Martin's Laugh-In,* a hit television show in the late 1960s. The jealous Giancana told Maheu he was leaving to go to Las Vegas and check up on McGuire.

To placate Giancana and get him to stay in Miami and continue to work on the Castro plot, Maheu hired Ed DuBois, a Miami private investigator, to spy on McGuire and Rowan in Las Vegas. Maheu also called Sheffield Edwards at the CIA to ask if the Agency could provide a sensitive microphone that could be attached to the wall of a room adjoining Rowan's hotel suite. The Agency refused the request, but volunteered to pay $1,000 for Maheu to hire someone to do the eavesdropping.

Arthur Balletti, the operative sent by DuBois to Las Vegas, didn't follow Maheu's directions, and placed a tap directly on Rowan's hotel room phone.

A hotel maid soon discovered Balletti's surveillance equipment in his room, and he was arrested by the local sheriff. Balletti called Maheu in Miami and Rosselli paid Balletti's bail, creating a paper trail that linked the illegal wiretapping of Dan Rowan to Maheu, Rosselli, and their Miami operation.

The FBI sent agents to Miami to question Maheu, who quickly turned to Sheffield Edwards at the CIA for help. Edwards then told the FBI that the CIA would object to Maheu's prosecution in the Rowan wiretapping case because it could expose sensitive information about the CIA.

Maheu was not charged. But the FBI, alerted by the wiretapping of Dan Rowan, began to unravel what the CIA and the Mafia were doing together in Miami.

Once the FBI uncovered the CIA's secret alliance with the Mafia, the Bureau began to dig further — and made an even more explosive discovery. Judith Campbell, a beautiful young woman from Los Angeles, had been sleeping with both Giancana and President John F. Kennedy. Campbell had been introduced to Kennedy by Frank Sinatra.

FBI Director J. Edgar Hoover took full advantage of the explosive information his agents had gathered on the CIA, the mob — and now the president. In February 1962, Hoover sent a memo to the president's younger brother, Attorney General Robert F. Kennedy, and to Kenneth O'Donnell, special assistant to President Kennedy, revealing that the FBI knew all about the connections between Johnny Rosselli, Judith Campbell, Sam Giancana, and John F. Kennedy. Hoover's memo noted that the FBI had discovered records of phone calls between Campbell and the White House.

Hoover followed up by meeting privately with President Kennedy at the White House on March 22, 1962. During that meeting, Hoover almost certainly told Kennedy what he knew about the CIA-Mafia scheme as well as Kennedy's connection to Judith Campbell, according to several historical accounts, including *From the Secret Files of J. Edgar Hoover* by Athan Theoharis and *Enemies*, a history of the FBI by Tim Weiner. Hoover had a follow-up meeting with Attorney General Kennedy as well.

Hoover's raw political blackmail worked. Once Hoover told President Kennedy how much he knew about his secrets, it became nearly impossible for the Kennedy Administration to rein in Hoover and the FBI.

* * *

The CIA temporarily suspended its campaign to kill Castro after the Bay of Pigs — the April 1961 Agency-backed invasion of Cuba by a small unit of Cuban exiles that quickly turned into a disaster. Humiliated by the debacle and furious at the Agency for pressuring him to go through with the plan, President Kennedy pushed out CIA Director Allen Dulles; his deputy, General Charles Cabell; and espionage chief Richard Bissell.

But Kennedy could not abide the notion that Castro had bested him at the Bay of Pigs. Before long the White House was once again putting pressure on the CIA about Castro. Soon, the Agency got back in the business of trying to kill the Cuban leader.

William Harvey—an overweight, alcoholic CIA officer who openly rebelled whenever he thought the Agency bureaucracy was getting in the way of his spy operations—was now put in charge. Despite his many flaws, Harvey was already a legend within the CIA's clandestine espionage service. He had run the CIA's base in Berlin and was in charge of the Agency's Berlin tunnel, a daring operation to dig from West Berlin to East Berlin to tap into underground cables that carried Russian communications back to Moscow.

Before Bissell left the Agency, he talked to Harvey about reviving the suspended CIA-Mafia alliance. In April 1962, Harvey asked Sheffield Edwards to put him in touch with Rosselli.

Rosselli, who was probably still working with Trafficante, reconnected with Varona, the Cuban exile leader. Harvey gave Rosselli a new batch of poison pills to pass to Varona, who vowed to kill not only Fidel Castro but his brother Raul—and Che Guevara as well. But once again Varona demanded payment up front, and this time around he wanted weapons for his exile group.

Harvey arranged for the transfer of $5,000 worth of explosives, weapons, and other gear, the matériel to be stashed for Varona in a U-Haul truck in a Miami parking lot. Rosselli and the CIA's Jim O'Connell watched from across the street as the weapons-laden truck was picked up.

In May 1962, Rosselli informed Harvey that Varona had dispatched a three-man team to Cuba, carrying both the CIA's poison pills and its guns. But once again, nothing happened.

In September, Rosselli told Harvey that Varona was planning to send a second team to Cuba to penetrate Castro's security. But this second team never even left for Cuba, and Harvey finally realized that Varona would never come through. He shut down the operation and in early 1963 directed Rosselli to cut off communications with Varona and the Cubans.

After abandoning its plans to use the Mafia, the CIA still pursued other means of trying to kill Castro. Perhaps the CIA's most ominous assassination effort came when it worked with Rolando Cubela Secades, a Cuban revolutionary leader who had grown disenchanted with Castro. In a secret meeting in Paris on November 22, 1963, the CIA gave Secades a hypodermic syringe, disguised as a ballpoint pen, that could be used to inject Castro with poison. The meeting was underway just as President John F. Kennedy was assassinated in Dallas.

As they investigated the CIA's Castro plots, questions about the possible connection between the Agency's efforts to kill Castro and the assassination of President Kennedy worried several members of the Church Committee, and helped fuel Gary Hart's interest in creating a subcommittee to investigate the CIA and the Kennedy assassination. The CIA's plots to kill Castro have been caught up in conspiracy theories about the assassination of President Kennedy ever since.

* * *

Questions about exactly who authorized the assassination plots against Fidel Castro and how the orders were issued would plague the Church Committee. The CIA's efforts to work with the Mafia to kill Castro started under President Dwight Eisenhower and were renewed under President John F. Kennedy, and both presidents were masters of plausible deniability. Thus the Church Committee, faced with conflicting evidence and testimony, struggled to determine whether either president actually gave the orders to kill Castro.

Looking back today, there is little doubt that both Eisenhower and Kennedy secretly made it clear to the CIA that they wanted the Agency to kill Castro. Throughout his presidency, Eisenhower had turned to the CIA to achieve foreign-policy objectives by covert means so he didn't have to go to war. By authorizing the CIA to sponsor coups in Iran and Guatemala in the early 1950s, Eisenhower had transformed the CIA from an Agency designed to collect foreign intelligence and avoid another Pearl Harbor into one focused on covert action around the world. Killing Castro was an extension of how Eisenhower had used the Agency throughout his presidency.

215

Kennedy came to share Eisenhower's belief that the CIA existed to serve as a presidential weapon — particularly when it came to Cuba. "We cannot overemphasize the extent to which responsible Agency officers felt themselves subject to the Kennedy Administration's severe pressures to do something about Castro and his regime," stated a 1967 CIA Inspector General's report about the CIA's anti-Castro plotting.

But when the Church Committee tried to unravel these issues for the first time in the 1970s, presidential accountability for CIA plots to kill Castro and other foreign leaders became the most contentious subject dividing committee members, and threatened to rip the committee apart along partisan lines. Conservative Republican senators, led by Barry Goldwater, accused Frank Church and the committee's Democratic majority of trying to protect John Kennedy's legacy at a time when Ted Kennedy, his younger brother, was a powerful member of the Senate — and a possible presidential contender.

The Kennedy family legacy loomed over the Church Committee and was a burden for Frank Church. When the committee was created in January 1975, Frank Church initially thought his investigation would pick up where Watergate had left off the year before, focusing on the crimes of Richard Nixon. Instead, Church soon discovered that the sins of the CIA and other intelligence agencies went back decades, to their founding, and encompassed both Republican and Democratic administrations. "I don't think we understood at first that it would not be just Nixon" that the committee would investigate, recalled Walter Mondale.

That damning realization finally led to a difficult question: was the disgraced Richard Nixon really that different from his predecessors in the White House? The question would become central to the Church Committee's investigation of the postwar era. But first the Church Committee would have to unravel the stories behind the CIA's assassination plots against Castro and other foreign leaders — and that meant tracking down and interviewing everyone involved.

One of the key figures the committee wanted to question was Sam Giancana, to talk to the Chicago mobster about his role in the CIA-Mafia alliance to try to kill Castro. In June 1975, Church Committee staffer Patrick Shea arranged to travel to Chicago to interview Giancana. Shea had originally planned to meet with Giancana a couple of weeks earlier, but the meeting had been delayed because Giancana had to go to Houston for gall-bladder surgery. Once Giancana returned to Chicago, Giancana's lawyer agreed with Shea on a new schedule for the interview. "Then I got a call at about 4 in the morning, and it was the U.S. Marshal who was going to travel with me," recalled Shea in an interview. "The marshal said, 'It looks like we aren't going to Chicago.

" 'Sam Giancana was just killed.' "

CHAPTER 16

"Who will rid me of this man?"

AT 11:53 P.M. on June 19, 1975, police officers in the Chicago suburb of Oak Park, Illinois, arrived at 1147 South Wenonah Avenue, a
1930s-era five-bedroom house with an art deco tiled roof that was
the home of Chicago mobster Sam Giancana.

The firemen in an ambulance unit who had first responded
showed the police officers to the basement, where they had discovered a shooting victim lying dead on the floor. The body of the
67-year-old Giancana, who was listed on the police report as five
foot nine and 170 pounds, was lying on his back in a pool of blood,
with his left leg crossed over his right, his arms outstretched. The
basement's kitchen area was brightly lit, and the police noted that a
frying pan, on the stove's right rear burner, was filled with food that
was still warm. (Reporters later determined that Giancana had been
cooking sausages and escarole.) A sixteen-ounce bottle of the diet
soft drink Tab sat on the kitchen table, along with an ashtray and a
cigar. The police found six .22 caliber shells in the kitchen. Giancana
had been shot in the head and neck seven times. Two officers from
the Chicago police department's organized crime intelligence unit
had been parked in front of the house conducting surveillance of
Giancana that night, but said they hadn't seen or heard anything.

The next morning, Frank Church was in Lewiston, Idaho, to
speak at a ceremony marking the opening of the Lower Granite

Dam, part of the billion-dollar Lower Snake River Seaway, which was to provide a new water connection for shipping between Idaho and the Pacific Ocean. Church attended the opening despite his long-standing opposition to the Lower Granite Dam. Six years earlier he had proposed a moratorium on dam building on the Snake River above Lewiston, and had included in his proposal a halt to further construction on the Lower Granite Dam. But he had lost that fight, and Church, ever sensitive to the politics of Idaho, thought that attending the dam's opening ceremony was important enough that he had left Washington during one of the most intense periods of the Church Committee's investigation. Church may have been taking on the national-security state, but he was still a U.S. Senator from Idaho, and Lewiston and surrounding Nez Perce County were then strongly Democratic — and an important part of Church's political base.

"This was a big deal in Lewiston," recalled former Church aide Mike Wetherell. "Church was very popular in Lewiston, and the local paper, the *Lewiston Tribune*, was very supportive of him. He had a lot of friends in Lewiston. It would not even have occurred to us that he shouldn't attend."

But the reporters who crowded around Church in Lewiston that day didn't want to talk to him about the Lower Granite Dam. They wanted to ask him about Sam Giancana's murder the night before, and its impact on the Church Committee's investigation of the CIA's alliance with the Mafia to assassinate Cuban dictator Fidel Castro.

Church immediately sought to downplay the impact of Giancana's killing on the investigation. He told the reporters that he gave "no credence" to the idea that the CIA was in any way involved with Giancana's murder. The CIA would not have had a reason to order a hit on Giancana to silence him, Church said, because his committee's investigation was rapidly progressing, and the committee "already is in possession of the facts, and we have other sources."

But in the wake of Giancana's killing, Church said the committee should consider whether to provide protection for its other witnesses. "I don't want to speculate on who might be in jeopardy, but witnesses associated with the underworld would be the ones we might consider would fall in that category."

* * *

Giancana's murder rattled the Church Committee. It was unprecedented for a witness in a major congressional investigation to be murdered. Yet the committee did not conduct its own investigation into whether Giancana had been murdered to silence him just before he was about to testify before the committee.

This failure to act raised some concerns among committee staffers, but they were already investigating so many leads on so many fronts that they quickly moved on.

"I remember thinking, don't we have to do something about Giancana's killing?" recalls Church Committee staffer Frederick Baron. "But I don't remember any discussion at the committee about how this is our business. The committee was already so overloaded."

Added committee staffer Patrick Shea: "That was a quagmire the committee didn't want to get into."

Frank Church told the press he considered the killing a local-police matter: "As to the assassination of Mr. Giancana, we don't know who did it, or why it was done," Church told reporters in Washington a few days after he was first asked about the case in Idaho. "And it is the responsibility of the local police to investigate that particular murder."

Frank Church gave such a low-key public response immediately after Giancana's killing because he didn't want anything, not even the murder of one of its witnesses, to get in the way of the Church Committee.

* * *

Frank Church was now at the peak of his career; he knew this was his moment, and Sam Giancana's murder couldn't deter from that. Frank Church was famous again. This time the fame was far more intense than what he had previously experienced during Vietnam and the battle over Cooper-Church. Now, Frank Church was everywhere; in the summer of 1975 he seemed even bigger than the Senate.

He was running the nation's biggest investigation since Watergate, and that inevitably placed him squarely in the conversation about the 1976 presidential race. Church did nothing to discourage such speculation, despite his pledge to Senate Majority Leader Mike Mansfield not to run until after the committee finished its work.

His dual role—investigator and potential candidate—attracted more national attention than ever before.

"Senator Church looks different off camera," wrote Louise Sweeney in an in-depth profile of Church in the *Christian Science Monitor* in July 1975. "On camera, answering volatile questions, he is formal, guarded, his eyes hooded, almost scholarly, with a certain heaviness of manner and appearance which are deceptive. In person, he is trim, ebullient, tall (6 ft) with a tan face that grins easily, brown eyes...and a warmth that the camera somehow doesn't catch. The one constant, off camera or on, is the voice, a soft baritone that falls in measured cadences like lines from Tennyson, with no slang...That sound you may hear off in the wings is Frank Church clearing his throat for a TV summer."

Even as the Idaho senator tried to downplay its significance, Sam Giancana's murder added a slightly dangerous edge to the emerging national image of Frank Church. Giancana's killing also gave a nervous energy to Church's investigation of the CIA's plots to assassinate foreign leaders, particularly the CIA-Mafia alliance to kill Castro, which by the summer of 1975 had become the centerpiece of the Church Committee's work.

While it wasn't known exactly who killed Giancana or why, his murder had all the markings of a Mafia hit. Tony Accardo, who was then the boss of the Chicago mob, was widely believed to have either ordered or sanctioned the killing, after years of barely tolerating Giancana's garish and excessively public life. Constant FBI surveillance in the early 1960s—in spite of his work with the CIA—had nearly driven Giancana insane, and after a year in prison on contempt charges he was forced out of power from the Chicago mob and into exile in Mexico.

In 1974, Mexican authorities kicked him out of the country and turned him over to the FBI at the border, and he was brought back to Chicago for questioning about the murder of his former associate Richard Cain, and also to appear before a federal grand jury to answer questions about mob-related matters dating back to the years before he left for Mexico.

Still, the FBI didn't believe Giancana was murdered because of his grand-jury testimony, because he wasn't revealing anything about the Chicago mob. On the day after Giancana's murder, two FBI agents met with the Oak Park police and said that, "in the opinion of [the] U.S. Attorney and the FBI, most of what [Giancana said to the grand jury] were untruths, and the FBI had requested the U.S. Attorney to indict him for perjury." The FBI agents told the Oak Park police that, before he was killed, they had been hoping to get a perjury indictment against Giancana "in a week or two." The FBI agents "felt the grand jury was not a significant factor" in his murder, the Oak Park police files state.

The day after Giancana's murder, Church had told reporters in Idaho that he thought Giancana might have been murdered to stop him from talking to the federal grand jury in Chicago. But privately, Church still wasn't sure. Months later—despite his initial public statements downplaying the significance of the killing—Church quietly asked Justice Department officials to tell him what they knew about Giancana's murder, and whether they thought his killing was related to the Church Committee's investigation.

The Oak Park police handling the murder investigation also weren't sure why Giancana was killed. Confronted with a murder case involving a high-profile mobster and plenty of unanswered questions swirling in the press about Giancana's role in the CIA-Mafia alliance to assassinate Fidel Castro, the Oak Park police called the CIA.

On June 21, 1975, Oak Park's deputy police chief called Angus Thuermer, an assistant to CIA director Colby, to talk about the Giancana murder. The deputy chief told Thuermer that he "would appreciate any statement his organization could make [in] reference to certain allegations made by the newspapers regarding a possible connection of the CIA in the death of Sam Giancana."

Thuermer "stated that he would like to make a quote of the statement made by William E. Colby, director, Central Intelligence Agency of the United States, 'we have nothing to do with it,'" according to Oak Park police records. Thuermer then quoted an Agency spokesman who had told reporters that the notion of any CIA involvement in Giancana's murder was "total Tommy rot." But Thuermer's dismissive comments only addressed the question of whether the CIA had murdered Giancana, while ignoring the issue of why Giancana was killed.

The following year, the Justice Department finally responded to Frank Church's request for information about the Giancana murder. In February 1976, Richard Thornburgh, then the Assistant Attorney

General for the Justice Department's Criminal Division, wrote a letter to Church stating that "all the information which we have received through the present date indicates that this was a gangland slaying intended to settle problems within the syndicate [the Mafia]."

Giancana's murder has never been solved. In 2006, the Illinois State Police Laboratory conducted DNA tests on evidence collected in the Giancana murder investigation. The tests identified DNA from a male who was not Giancana, but those samples returned no DNA matches, according to Oak Park police files.

Theories about the motive have abounded ever since the murder. Giancana may have angered the Chicago mob because of his grand-jury testimony, or he may have angered the mob because of his upcoming testimony before the Church Committee. He had also reportedly alienated some Chicago mobsters during his time in Mexico by setting up gambling operations in Central America and Iran without cutting them in on the profits.

It seems possible that all of those issues were factors; a Mafia hit on a longtime, high-profile mobster like Giancana probably isn't done for just one reason. Giancana had been too reckless, too unpredictable, too public, and too selfish for more than a decade, and now he was back in town, talking to prosecutors and to Congress. Tony Accardo was probably fed up with all of it.

The unsolved murder of Sam Giancana has haunted the legacy of the Church Committee ever since. Yet the real problem for Frank Church was that while Sam Giancana was the first of his witnesses to wind up dead, he wasn't the last.

*   *   *

In the immediate aftermath of Sam Giancana's murder, Pat Shea and Republican staffer Mike Madigan interviewed Johnny Rosselli in preparation for his formal testimony before the full Church Committee. To keep their interview secret, they met Rosselli in a suite at the Watergate Hotel rather than on Capitol Hill. Rosselli, shaken by Giancana's murder a few days earlier, demanded that the hotel-suite curtains be kept closed while they talked. Over two days, Rosselli explained to Shea and Madigan that he was proud of his work with the CIA, and that he had considered it his patriotic duty to help the spy agency try to get rid of Castro.

On June 24, 1975, Shea guided Rosselli through the basement

of the U.S. Capitol, eluding the press on his way to a secure hearing room; there Rosselli gave his formal testimony, once again insisting that he had done his patriotic duty. "He was absolutely captivating," recalls committee staffer Frederick Baron, who attended the closed hearing. "He looked like a movie star, totally dapper and well-tailored. And he had that husky Mafia voice. He seemed utterly sophisticated, and he had charm and intelligence. He was basically trying to say, you may not sympathize with my career path, but I was being asked to perform my patriotic duty."

"He was relaxed, almost congenial, cooperative to a fault, saying we were just trying to help the government and the country," recalled Gary Hart, who also attended the hearing. "It was all patriotism. He wrapped himself in the flag."

After the hearing, Shea and the Capitol Police escorted Rosselli out of the Capitol, but this time they faced a media horde. Rosselli briefly soaked in the attention; he was beaming. "It was his moment of glory," recalled Shea.

Shea was able to navigate Rosselli and his lawyer through the crowd of reporters to his car, then drove them from Capitol Hill to downtown Washington. After Shea parked and dropped them off on K Street downtown, Rosselli shook Shea's hand, thanked him for his help, and then added ominously as he walked away, "I'm not going to be around much longer."

* * *

Frank Church decided that all of the hearings concerning the CIA's assassination plots would be closed to the press and the public. Sensitive to criticism that he was bent on grabbing headlines, Church wanted to prove that he could conduct the highly charged assassination inquiry without any television cameras present. As a result, the press missed the pattern that developed in the closed hearings, in which CIA officials involved with the assassination plots repeatedly stated that they had been following presidential orders, while a parade of White House aides from each administration categorically denied that the presidents had intended the CIA to engage in assassination.

Richard Bissell, the CIA official who was one of the architects of the CIA's alliance with the Mafia to assassinate Castro, testified that he believed President Kennedy knew the Agency was plotting to kill Castro. Though Bissell had never talked to President Kennedy about the plots himself, he said he strongly believed that CIA Director Allen Dulles had briefed both President Eisenhower and later President Kennedy; he said Dulles may have briefed Kennedy right after the 1960 election, even before Kennedy took office. (The CIA-Mafia alliance began in 1960, while Eisenhower was still president.) "I believe at some stage the President and the President-elect both were advised that such an operation had been planned and was being attempted...I would guess through some channel by Allen Dulles," Bissell told the committee. (Dulles was dead by the time of the Church Committee.)

North Carolina Democratic Senator Robert Morgan responded to Bissell by saying that "it's a serious matter to attribute knowledge of this sort to the President of the United States, especially one who cannot speak for himself...I gather that you think it came out [that Kennedy was told], but because of the seriousness of the accusation you are just being extremely cautious. Is that a fair assumption to make?"

"That is very close to a fair assumption, sir," replied Bissell. "It's just that I have no direct knowledge, firsthand knowledge, of his [Kennedy's] being advised, but my belief is that he knew of it."

George Smathers — a former Democratic senator from Florida who had been one of John Kennedy's closest party-loving friends while they were both in the Senate, and later when Kennedy was president — provided testimony to the committee that seemed to come close to proving Kennedy's knowledge of the CIA's assassination plots against Castro.

Smathers, who had been fiercely anti-Castro and became an expert on Latin American issues while in the Senate, told the committee about a private conversation with Kennedy on the White House lawn in 1961. President Kennedy "asked me what reaction I thought there would be throughout South America were Fidel Castro to be assassinated," Smathers testified. "I told the President that even as much as I disliked Fidel Castro, that I did not think it would be a good idea for there to be even considered an assassination of Fidel Castro, and the President of the United States completely agreed with me that it would be a very unwise thing to do, the reason obviously being that no matter who did it and no matter how it was done and no matter what, that the United States would receive full credit for it and it would work to his great disadvantage with all of the other countries in Central and South America. I disapproved of it, and he completely disapproved of the idea."

The fact that Kennedy asked Smathers what he thought about assassinating Castro suggests the president was eager to talk to his friend about the CIA's secret plots but couldn't quite bring himself to do so, especially after Smathers made it clear that he thought killing Castro would be a terrible idea. That episode also may help explain a later conversation that Smathers told the Church Committee that he had with Kennedy, when he shut down any further talk of Cuba: "Smathers said that on a later occasion he had tried to discuss Cuba with President Kennedy, [but] the president had made it clear to Smathers that he should not raise the subject with him again."

During his testimony before the Church Committee, former CIA director Helms explained how presidents indirectly got the CIA to conduct assassination plots without issuing explicit orders. In questioning Helms, Senator Charles Mathias drew upon the story of Thomas Becket, the Archbishop of Canterbury, who was murdered in 1170 by supporters of King Henry II, after the English king had supposedly asked aloud whether anyone would get rid of Becket for him.

"Let me draw an example from history," offered Mathias, while questioning Helms. "When Thomas Becket was proving to be an annoyance, the King said, who will rid me of this man. He didn't say to somebody, go out and murder him. He said who will rid me of this man and let it go at that."

"That is a warming reference to the problem," replied Helms.

"You feel that spans the generations and the centuries?" asked Mathias.

"I think it does, sir," responded Helms.

"And that is typical of the kind of thing which might be said, which might be taken by the [CIA] director or by anybody else as Presidential authorization to go forward?"

"That is right," Helms replied. "But in answer to that, I realize that one sort of grows up in [the] tradition of the time, and I think that any of us would have found it very difficult to discuss assassinations with a President...I just think we all had the feeling that we're hired to keep those things out of the Oval Office."

"Yet at the same time you felt that some spark had been transmitted that that was within the permissible limits?" asked Mathias.

"Yes," said Helms, "and if he [Castro] had disappeared from the scene, they would not have been unhappy."

By contrast, all of the top Eisenhower and Kennedy Administration officials who testified claimed that they had no knowledge of any assassination plans against Castro or any other foreign leader, and they did not believe that either President Eisenhower or President Kennedy knew about or approved any such schemes.

Gordon Gray, Eisenhower's special assistant for national security affairs, said the "Special Group"—the group of senior administration officials who oversaw covert operations for Eisenhower—never approved any plan to assassinate Castro. Gray added that "I do not believe that Mr. Dulles would have gone independently to [Eisenhower] with such a proposal...without my knowing about it from Mr. Dulles." Gray also said that he never talked with Eisenhower about any plans to assassinate Castro.

Andrew Goodpaster, another top national-security aide to Eisenhower, added that Eisenhower never told him about any assassination plots. and believed that he was so close to Eisenhower on a daily basis that if such plots had been raised with Eisenhower, he would have learned of it. Goodpaster added that after the crisis over the Soviet downing of a U-2 spy plane operated by the CIA in the spring of 1960, the White House had reviewed and tightened its procedures for approving CIA operations. He also said that while Secretary of State John Foster Dulles was a confidant of Eisenhower's, his younger brother Allen Dulles was not.

Former Kennedy Administration officials offered similar denials. Secretary of State Dean Rusk and Secretary of Defense Robert McNamara both said they had never heard of any such plots, while Roswell Gilpatric, who had been Deputy Secretary of Defense, said that Kennedy's Special Group, the Kennedy Administration's team of senior officials that dealt with covert action operations against Cuba, never considered the assassination of Castro to be within its mandate. General Maxwell Taylor, who chaired Special Group meetings on Operation *Mongoose*—the Kennedy Administration's covert-action plan to undermine the Castro regime—said he "never heard of an assassination effort against Castro and that he never raised the question of assassination with anyone." McGeorge Bundy, who had been Kennedy's national security adviser, said it was his conviction that "no one in the Kennedy Administration in the White House or in the cabinet ever gave any authorization or approval or instruction of any kind for any effort to assassinate anyone by the CIA."

There was thus a standoff between the assertions of presidential authorization by CIA officials and the categorical denials of such presidential approval from presidential aides. The issues surrounding presidential knowledge and direction of the assassination plots would later lead to the biggest political controversy Frank Church faced over his leadership of the committee. In fact, questions about President Kennedy's involvement would soon get very awkward.

CHAPTER 17

"The White House, can I help you?"

THE CHURCH COMMITTEE'S investigation into the CIA's alliance with the Mafia to kill Castro took a dramatic turn late in the summer of 1975, when a brash new Republican staffer began digging where no one else on the staff had looked.

Andy Postal was a 26-year-old long-haired lawyer and self-described "radical young man," a libertarian who had joined the Republican staff of the Church Committee in July, just after Rosselli's testimony. He began to probe the connections between the Kennedy White House and the CIA-Mafia anti-Castro alliance more aggressively than any other Church Committee staffers had done, looking beyond the documents turned over to the committee by the CIA and the White House.

His break came after the Justice Department let Postal review old organized-crime case files involving Giancana and Rosselli.

"Over Labor Day weekend, I went to DOJ to review those files," Postal recalled in an interview. "They locked me in a room with a desk that took up most of the room with two feet of paper of raw FBI files." He noticed that the FBI files included telephone-call records, so "I started to make a record of who was calling whom."

Hours later, Postal noticed that an associate of both Giancana and Rosselli by the name of Judy Campbell had been making phone calls to a number in Washington, D.C. That night, he decided to call the Washington number. He was shocked when the person answering the phone announced, "The White House, can I help you?"

Postal had found evidence of the connections between Judith Campbell, Sam Giancana, and President John Kennedy—the same connections that J. Edgar Hoover had secretly discovered and used against John and Robert Kennedy back in 1962.

For Postal, the phone records raised an explosive question: had Judith Campbell, mistress to both President Kennedy and Sam Giancana, served as an intermediary between Giancana and Kennedy while the CIA was working with Giancana to kill Castro?

"I went home, got drunk, and tried to figure out what to do with this," recalls Postal.

The next day, Postal went to see Curt Smothers, the Church Committee's Republican counsel. "I said, let's go for a walk, we have to talk outside." (In the auditorium that served as the Church Committee office, with staffers and their desks crowded together, it was difficult to hold a truly confidential conversation.) Once clear of potential eavesdroppers, Postal told Smothers that Judy Campbell had called the White House seven times from the same phone numbers being used by the gangsters working for the CIA from 1960 to 1962.

Postal wrote a memo and presented findings that upended the Church Committee's investigation into the CIA's assassination plots. Suddenly the committee found itself unearthing the truth about the private life of President John F. Kennedy.

Democrats on the committee were quietly stunned; Republicans were quietly gleeful. Some Democratic senators and staff grumbled that the committee they had expected to be a sequel to Watergate, investigating Nixon–era intelligence abuses, was being hijacked by the Republicans in an effort to discredit the Kennedys, the mythic heroes of liberal America. "There were Kennedy people sprinkled throughout the committee," trying to protect the Kennedy legacy, recalled Postal.

But Frank Church told Postal to keep going, to keep digging, even if that meant embarrassing the Kennedys. "I thought Frank Church was a really stand-up guy," Postal said.

Church was keenly aware of the perception that he was close to the Kennedys, so he refused to block the investigation of Judith Campbell or any other element of the CIA's plots to kill Castro during the Kennedy Administration.

Gary Hart's opinion was that Church really had no choice but to support Postal's investigation. "I think Frank would have been very cognizant of one fact — that the committee's report would have been useless if the Republicans didn't join," Hart said. "He couldn't bend over backward to protect the Kennedys and do that. That would have brought the committee into disrepute and reduced its success. I think Frank felt that we had to reform the intelligence community, and to get that done, he had to get unanimity on the committee."

Fritz Schwarz added that he believes Frank Church's reputation as a Kennedy true believer was exaggerated. "I was in Church's office once, and he had a bust of Kennedy sitting there," Schwarz recalled. "So I asked him who was the most impressive person you ever dealt with, and he said in a flash Lyndon Johnson." Schwarz believed that Church wasn't overawed by Kennedy, and so wasn't willing to block an investigation that might tarnish his legacy.

With the green light from Church, Andy Postal teamed up with David Bushong, another Republican staffer, and continued to pursue the Judith Campbell connection. "We subpoenaed the White House telephone records that were up in Boston" at the John F. Kennedy Presidential Library, Postal recalled. "I had initially found seven calls, but the White House records showed 70 calls" made by Campbell to Kennedy. "Ultimately, the committee couldn't ignore what we found," Postal adds.

It took time for the committee staff to find Judith Campbell — she had remarried and was now living in Southern California as Judith Exner. Bushong recalled in an interview that he went to California to serve her with a subpoena to testify before the Church Committee, but mistakenly served her sister instead. He then got a call from Robert Maheu, who told him that he could accept service on the subpoena for Judith Campbell and would arrange for her to fly to Washington to testify. Bushong was never sure why Maheu got involved in arranging Campbell's testimony.

After Judith Campbell agreed to travel to Washington, Democratic and Republican staffers secretly conducted a joint interview of her on September 20 in a room in the Russell Senate Office Building.

So far, the press did not yet know about Judith Campbell, but Church was concerned that her story might leak after her testimony.

Judith Campbell Exner, former girlfriend of both Sam Giancana and President John F. Kennedy.

So Bill Miller assigned Pat Shea to sit in on the Campbell interview. Miller told Shea that once the interview was over, he was to grab the only copy of the interview transcript from the stenographer and then immediately place it in a committee safe to which only a small handful of staffers had access.

During the interview, it quickly became clear that in the early 1960s, Judith Campbell had been a beautiful young woman with intoxicating connections in both Hollywood and Washington, but had never played any role as an intermediary between John Kennedy and Sam Giancana.

"At any point during your friendship with Mr. Giancana and Mr. Rosselli, did either Mr. Giancana or Mr. Rosselli ever ask you to

232

communicate messages to the President or anyone else in government?" asked Curt Smothers.

"No."

"Did they ever ask you to make contact or arrange any meetings or discussions between themselves and anyone in government?"

"No."

"Did you ever hear Mr. Rosselli or Mr. Giancana speak about, either to you or [did you overhear] them speak about, any connection with…the CIA?"

"No."

"It is also your testimony that you did not talk to the President on behalf of Mr. Giancana or Mr. Rosselli?"

"No, I did not."

Near the end of the interview, Fritz Schwarz told the other staffers that he and Smothers, his Republican counterpart, had agreed with Campbell and her lawyer that the actual "subject matter of the conversations between this witness and President Kennedy is irrelevant to the matter under investigation by the committee." In other words, Schwarz and Smothers had agreed to bar any questions about her sexual relationship with Kennedy.

Despite Campbell's denials that she was a Kennedy-Giancana go-between, the committee called Johnny Rosselli back for another interview to question him about her — specifically, whether Campbell had played any role in the CIA-Mafia alliance.

Two days after Judith Campbell was interviewed, Postal and Bushong questioned Rosselli in a suite at the Watergate Hotel. This time, Rosselli was angry that the staffers were trying to drag Judith Campbell into the investigation.

When Postal and Bushong asked him about dates and times that he may have seen Judith Campbell, Rosselli complained that "I'm not going to start guessing at times about a young lady that does not even belong in this whole conversation, or who did what to whom, or where. It is a little disgusting to me, because I do not really like to talk about these things, women…You are talking about the White House and Judith Campbell and all this. This is none of my affair."

Postal and Bushong pressed. "Did there come a time when you became aware that Judith Campbell had made the acquaintance of John Kennedy?"

"I will not answer that question."

They kept asking, and finally Rosselli said, "Among the jet set in Hollywood and the United States, yes, it was common knowledge that she was friendly with the president."

They asked whether he had ever used Judith Campbell as an intermediary with Giancana: "Did you ever give Judy a message for Sam?"

"I would not give my mother a message to give to Sam," Rosselli replied.

During a break in the questioning, Bushong noticed that Rosselli was wearing an expensive watch, and told him he thought it was the most beautiful watch he had ever seen.

"Lucky gave me that," Rosselli replied. He flipped the watch over. On the inside was an inscription from legendary mobster Lucky Luciano.

Postal and Bushong also interviewed Kenneth O'Donnell, one of President Kennedy's closest aides, about Judith Campbell. She had told them that she had met O'Donnell at the Democratic National Convention in Los Angeles in 1960, when Kennedy won the presidential nomination. But O'Donnell was even more resentful of the questioning about Campbell than Rosselli.

"You are on a dead-end street!" O'Donnell snapped.

*　*　*

With so much anger and resentment building over their investigation of the Kennedys, the CIA, and the Mafia, Andy Postal and David Bushong became suspicious that they were starting to face serious personal threats. Postal was walking down the street in Washington one evening when he was accosted by two men, one of whom pulled a .45 caliber pistol from his belt. "The next 40 seconds felt like three years," Postal said. He shoved one of the men and ran out into the street. "I dove over one car, rolled under another car, and these guys looked at me like I'm crazy. They ran away. I told the committee security guy the next day."

The incident was almost certainly a common mugging attempt, and had nothing to do with Postal's work on the Church Committee. But he became jumpy. So did Bushong, who became convinced that he saw Johnny Rosselli in a car following him on his way to work one day. Bushong said he asked Rosselli about it during a break in their questioning, and that Rosselli seemed to confirm that he had followed him.

*   *   *

After the investigation was complete, there was a quiet, intense debate involving Frank Church and a few other senators and staff about what to write about Judith Campbell and her relationships with Kennedy and Giancana in the committee's report on the CIA's assassination plots. They also debated whether to actually name her.

They decided to seek the advice of Senator Phil Hart, who was widely respected by both Democratic and Republican senators. Hart was then at Bethesda Naval Hospital, receiving treatment for the cancer that would kill him just over a year later, in December 1976.

Burt Wides, Hart's personal staffer on the Church Committee, went to the hospital to ask him what the committee should do.

"I went out to see Hart at the hospital, and I said, 'A lot of senators want to know what you think they should do,'" recalled Wides. "He thought about it for a minute, then said, 'Find out first if she has any young children who would be impacted by going public with it.' He was a first-class guy. Nobody else had thought of that." After Wides relayed Hart's comments to the other senators, Church decided not to name Campbell. No one on the Church Committee ever checked to see if Campbell had any children, but Church and the other committee members understood that Phil Hart was simply reminding them to think of Campbell in human terms. (Campbell did not in fact have any children from her two marriages, but she did have a child. She had become pregnant in the 1960s during an affair with a Hollywood producer. Campbell placed the baby up for adoption, and she and her son would not reconnect until the late 1980s.)

In the report on its investigation into the CIA assassination plots, the Church Committee only identified Campbell as a "close friend" of President Kennedy. She was not named, and the report did not even say whether the "close friend" was a man or a woman.

"Evidence before the Committee indicates that a close friend of President Kennedy had frequent contact with the President from the end of 1960 through mid-1962," the assassination report stated. "FBI reports and testimony indicate that the President's friend was also a close friend of John Rosselli and Sam Giancana and saw them often during this same period."

Church justified the kid-gloves approach by arguing there was no evidence that Campbell had played any role in the CIA-Mafia alliance, and that she had not acted as an intermediary between Giancana and Kennedy. (In her 1977 memoir, Campbell wrote that she did not act as an intermediary, confirming her earlier testimony to the Church Committee. But in sensational interviews years later, she changed her story, claiming that she had lied to the Church Committee when she said she wasn't a Kennedy-Giancana go-between. Her later claims were discredited.)

Despite the turmoil inside the Church Committee over Judith Campbell and the Kennedy connection, the committee's assassination report provided a comprehensive investigation of the CIA-Mafia alliance during the Eisenhower and Kennedy Administrations. Decades later, virtually all of the facts publicly known about it are still those originally unearthed by the Church Committee.

But before the committee's report on the CIA's assassination plots was published, Frank Church faced an unpleasant task—so unpleasant that he didn't want to do it himself.

* * *

While Frank Church was running the Church Committee in 1975, the assassinations of John and Bobby Kennedy were still fresh in the national consciousness, and the Kennedy name—and the Kennedy machine—still dominated the Democratic Party. And, despite the Chappaquiddick scandal in 1969, Senator Ted Kennedy was widely expected to run for president at some point in the near future. So Frank Church decided that Ted Kennedy should be given advanced warning about the committee's findings about Judith Campbell, Sam Giancana, and President Kennedy.

"We had a meeting of the Democratic caucus of the committee," recalled Gary Hart, "and Frank said we've got to talk to Senator Kennedy about it. I said I'd be happy to talk to him. Church encouraged me to go reveal what we had to Ted. Either Frank didn't want to do it himself, or had decided not to."

Hart found a moment when Ted Kennedy was by himself on the floor of the Senate, walked up beside him and quietly told him what the Church Committee had discovered about Judith Campbell and President Kennedy. When Hart was finished, Kennedy looked at him, said thank you, and walked away. To Hart it seemed obvious that Ted Kennedy already knew the story—and had been waiting years for it to be revealed.

Separately, Walter Mondale—who did not know that Hart had talked to Kennedy—decided he should tell Kennedy what the committee had discovered as well. "That was not a very productive conversation," Mondale recalled in an interview. "I talked to Ted in the Senate cloakroom. He didn't want to get into it. I didn't know what to do with it...he knew what I was talking about. As soon as I brought it up, he responded immediately." (Hart and Mondale did not know that Ted Kennedy had been with his brother in Las Vegas when John first met Judith Campbell—and that Ted had also tried to sleep with her, until she chose his brother over him. In her 1977 memoir, Campbell said she met John Kennedy in Las Vegas in February 1960, when both he and Ted Kennedy were at Frank Sinatra's table in the lounge of the Sands Hotel and Casino. Campbell wrote that later on the same night they met, Ted Kennedy came to her hotel room and awkwardly tried to put the moves on her. She resisted—then fell for his older brother instead.)

There were also other, smaller ways in which the Kennedy circle was handled with special care by Frank Church and the Church Committee. "We took testimony from [former Kennedy national security adviser] McGeorge Bundy, asking about any National Security Council meetings during the Kennedy Administration in which there were discussions of assassinations," recalled Frederick Baron, who worked closely with Fritz Schwarz on the committee staff. "Fritz, who knew him, arranged a dinner with him and me at the Hay Adams [a luxury hotel opposite the White House] the night before he was going to testify before the committee. It was more like Bundy was his [Fritz's] client rather than a witness, and Fritz was a comforting presence."

"I may have gone to dinner with Bundy before he testified," countered Schwarz, "but I tried to meet with most witnesses before they testified, to talk to them. Meeting with Bundy was not out of the ordinary."

While these modest accommodations to the Kennedy circle did not blunt the Church Committee's aggressive investigation, they were still misguided, since they came just as Frank Church was about to face increasing partisan attacks accusing him of protecting the Kennedy legacy.

*　*　*

During the early months of the Church Committee, relatively little partisan in-fighting had broken out among the committee members. John Tower, the ranking Republican, had proven to be a disappointment to the Ford White House and the Republican leaders in the Senate, who had expected him to try to act as an obstacle to Frank Church's investigative efforts. Instead, Tower and most of the other Republicans on the committee had cooperated with the Democrats on most issues.

But by August 1975, Barry Goldwater—the most conservative Republican on the committee—was becoming increasingly irritated by Frank Church, and he was ready to lash out. Goldwater was angered by what Church had told the press in July in a sound bite that would become Church's most controversial statement of the entire investigation.

In a closed committee hearing on July 18, John Eisenhower, President Eisenhower's son who had also been a White House aide to his father, testified that President Eisenhower never told him of any CIA activity involving any assassination plans, and certainly not an attempt to assassinate Fidel Castro. John Eisenhower said he believed his father would have confided in him if he knew about any such plots, since he had previously told him even bigger secrets. He said his father told him about the atomic bomb in July 1945, the month before it was dropped on Japan, and had also told him about the CIA's U-2 flights years before the Soviets shot down one of the high-altitude spy planes, publicly exposing the surveillance program.

After listening to John Eisenhower's testimony, Frank Church stopped to talk to the press gathered outside the hearing room, and said that the committee had so far found "no hard evidence linking any former presidents to the CIA's plots to assassinate foreign leaders." He added that it was "a very real possibility" that the CIA had tried to kill foreign leaders without presidential authorization. The CIA "may have been behaving like a rogue elephant on a rampage," Church said.

Despite the fact that Frank Church used the rogue elephant line after a closed hearing about Eisenhower, Goldwater was convinced that Church's blanket statement that there was no conclusive evidence that any president had ordered an assassination plot was a clever tactic designed to protect the legacy of John F. Kennedy.

Church had, in fact, picked up the phrase from a former Kennedy aide. Church privately told Loch Johnson that he got the rogue elephant line from McGeorge Bundy when the two had breakfast together — probably around the same time that Fritz Schwarz had dinner with Bundy.

"I'm very much afraid that this may lead to a contest in the committee between those who want to make sure nobody blames President Kennedy and those who want to tell the truth," Goldwater said in August. "Specifically, it appears that efforts are being made to divorce President Kennedy and his brother, former Attorney General Robert Kennedy, from the assassination attempts made on Fidel Castro in the 1960s."

Goldwater added that the committee's investigation had determined that "since World War II, presidents have directly or indirectly approved all actions taken by the CIA which have been the subject of [the Church Committee's] investigation. The CIA was at all times acting within the law or had every reason to believe it was acting legally in taking action on behalf of Presidents Eisenhower, Kennedy, Johnson, and Nixon. Any other conclusion is based on wishful thinking or political ax-grinding. In the early 60s, President Kennedy and his brother had every right to perceive that the nation's best interest lay in the removal of Fidel Castro. Castro's removal seemed necessary, if not vital, in those days, and was supported by all responsible officials in Washington."

Goldwater's criticism marked the first major, headline-grabbing break between the committee's Democrats and Republicans since the Church Committee had been created.

At first, Church responded only tersely to Goldwater's charges that he was soft-pedaling the committee's findings on the Kennedys. "I'm just at a loss to know what the senator means," Church told reporters. "All the committee is interested in is telling the truth, and we're doing our best to do it."

When he appeared on *Meet the Press* a few days later, Church offered a more expansive response to Goldwater.

"I have said before, and repeat today...the committee has no hard evidence linking these assassination plots with any former President or with the former Attorney General or other high administration officials," Church said. "We have had witnesses who, admitting that they do not possess personal knowledge, have nonetheless expressed the opinion that these plots were known to and authorized by the highest authority. By the same token, we have had many witnesses who have expressed the contrary opinion, and we have circumstantial evidence that suggests the contrary. Now, these men are dead. They can't speak up for themselves, and I certainly would not be a party to any finding that would make them parties to these plots, that would attribute guilt to them in the absence of clear and convincing evidence. I think this is a question that the committee will not be able to provide a definitive answer for, though we have done our best—looked at all of the evidence available."

Church added that "I do think that when you see the evidence, it will bear out the fact that there has been a good deal of looseness in the control of the CIA over all of these past administrations, and that is one of the reforms I think the committee will advocate."

Church was then asked whether he regretted using the phrase "rogue elephant," which had triggered so much controversy.

Church said he regretted only that his phrase had been misconstrued. "Because I used the term 'elephant,' Barry Goldwater—who is my good friend and a man I admire very much, a member of the committee—said to me, 'Frank, the next time you feel constrained to characterize the CIA, why don't you call it a wild jackass?'"

Gary Hart remembered that once Goldwater began to focus more of his attention on the committee's finding that the Castro-assassination plots began under Eisenhower, not Kennedy, he moderated his criticism. "That kind of calmed Barry down a bit," Hart recalled.

Ultimately, Goldwater signed the committee's assassination report along with the Democratic majority, saying he did so primarily because "I am greatly appreciative of the dedicated work done by the Senate members of the committee and the complete staff."

Still, Frank Church failed to recognize how Goldwater's criticism that his committee tried to protect the Kennedys would spread within conservative circles, and would affect the perception of the committee's work and his own reputation.

Conservative columnist William Safire was particularly brutal in his attacks on Church and the committee, which he dubbed the "Church Coverup Committee."

"The dead body of Sam Giancana lies across Frank Church's path to the presidency," Safire wrote.

* * *

The Judith Campbell story was too good and too salacious to be kept a secret for long, and it inevitably leaked to the press, despite the fact that the Church Committee had decided not to identify her. Andy Postal and David Bushong, the Republican staffers who had investigated the Campbell case, "had to insist that we didn't leak this," Postal recalls. "I threatened to publicly insist that everyone on the committee take a lie-detector test."

Deeply angered by the leak, Frank Church ordered staffer Pat Shea to launch a leak investigation inside the committee. "Church was furious, and he wanted to polygraph everybody," recalls Shea. "Bill Miller said no, we're not going to do that." Instead, Shea commandeered an old film-projection room in the upper reaches of the auditorium that served as the committee's office. One by one, committee staffers trudged up to the small room, where Shea asked each to sign an affidavit saying they had not leaked the Campbell information. Five staffers refused to sign.

"I went and briefed Church, and told him that we had five who hadn't signed," recalled Shea. "I told him that if you give me a week, I can figure out who leaked."

Church then went to a senators-only meeting of the committee. When he emerged from the meeting, he found Shea and asked him to walk with him. Privately, Church told Shea to drop the leak investigation.

"He said the senators had come to an agreement that we're not going to do anything" about the leak, Shea recalled. Church didn't provide Shea with any further details, but Shea assumes that the senators had decided they didn't want the truth about the leak to be revealed.

* * *

The Church Committee's members and staff liked to boast that they were very disciplined when it came to protecting classified information, and that their committee, unlike the Pike Committee in the House, had few leaks. They believed that it was important for them to prove that Congress could conduct oversight of the intelligence community without publicly revealing secrets.

But of course, there were plenty of leaks and apparent security breaches. Daniel O'Flaherty, a Church Committee staffer, resigned after being confronted by the FBI; he had been overheard discussing the Church Committee's business in a Washington restaurant. "I inadvertently disclosed material that had been classified and immediately resigned," O'Flaherty said in response to a request for comment for this book. "No one asked me to resign, let alone forced me to. I was there only four months, so I have little to say about the committee's work."

The committee also developed a symbiotic relationship with key journalists, bartering information between the two sides. After Frank Church and John Tower found out that *60 Minutes* was preparing a story about the CIA and assassinations, Pat Shea met with CBS correspondent Dan Rather. "Church and Tower didn't want to be scooped by CBS, so we talked about what each of us had found," recalled Shea. "I told [Rather] about which assassinations we were looking into."

Frank Church also became a constant media presence, and footage from his press briefings and television interviews in 1975 show that he relished the media's glare.

Yet his frequent public appearances began to grate on other members of the committee, and so when both Church and Mondale gave high-profile speeches that included details about the committee's work, Gary Hart got fed up. Hart went to Mansfield and told him that he was going to quit the committee unless all of the publicity-seeking stopped.

"I got upset with Church and Mondale for breaking the code of silence on public comments," recalled Hart. "I thought that was the end of the committee. I thought there would be a rebellion. And I went to Mansfield and said if this is going to go on, I don't want to be on the committee. I thought it would destroy the credibility of congressional oversight."

Mansfield told Hart to stick with the committee, and said that he would take care of it. The publicity-seeking was soon toned down. "I would guess he [Mansfield] had a talk with Church and Mondale."

But even a toned-down Frank Church continued to embrace the headlines and fame that he was garnering as committee chairman.

*   *   *

One advantage of all the press coverage was that the Church Committee was flooded with tips, leads, and gossip — including from celebrities.

Marlon Brando, who had befriended Frank Church when he became a leading opponent of the Vietnam War, called the Church Committee and talked with Pat Shea. Brando told Shea that the committee should investigate the FBI's infiltration of the American Indian Movement, a group of Native American activists engaged in a long-running battle with federal agents at the Pine Ridge reservation in the 1970s. (Two years earlier, Brando had declined an Oscar for his performance in *The Godfather* as a protest against the way Hollywood portrayed Native Americans, and had a Native American activist speak in his place. It was the most controversial moment in Academy history until 2022, when actor Will Smith stormed onstage to slap comedian Chris Rock for making a joke about Smith's wife.)

The committee also interviewed E. Howard Hunt, who had become a celebrity thanks to his prominent role in the Watergate scandal. Frederick Baron traveled to interview Hunt at the federal prison camp at Eglin Air Force Base in Florida, where he was then serving his Watergate-related sentence. Hunt, a former CIA officer, told Baron that he knew that the CIA had created an assassination squad in the early 1950s.

David Aaron, a Church Committee staffer, recalled that after Judith Campbell's story became public, he got a call from Marlene Dietrich's agent. The agent told Aaron that after she read about Judith Campbell, Dietrich wanted to tell the Church Committee about her own experience with President Kennedy. The agent said that Dietrich had been performing on stage in Washington when she got a call from the White House, inviting her to lunch with President Kennedy. They had lunch in Kennedy's private quarters, and Kennedy then asked her to sleep with him, which she did. After sex, Kennedy asked Dietrich if she had also slept with his father, Joseph Kennedy Sr., and she said no. Kennedy then said of his father: "I knew he was lying!"

"I think Dietrich wanted us to know this story because she was jealous of Judith Campbell" and all the attention she was getting, recalled Aaron.

*   *   *

At the height of the Church Committee's investigation of the CIA's assassination plots in the summer of 1975, eight of Frank Church's most loyal aides secretly gathered at the Washington apartment of Verda Barnes, Church's longtime political aide, for a strategy session about the 1976 presidential campaign. The July 30 meeting had to be kept secret because of Frank Church's promise to Mike Mansfield that he would not run for president until the committee's work was complete. But Church knew about and approved of the strategy session, and received a confidential memo afterward detailing the political recommendations and advice of his aides.

In addition to Verda Barnes, the Church aides and advisers at the meeting included Jerry Levinson, the staff director of Church's multinational subcommittee; Mike Wetherell, a Church aide who was an expert on Idaho politics; and Loch Johnson, Church's personal representative on the Church Committee staff. They brainstormed for four hours about the looming presidential race, and concluded that Ted Kennedy was the biggest obstacle to Church's chances of winning the 1976 Democratic presidential nomination.

"It was the consensus of the group that, barring a Kennedy entry into the race or a serious problem with the CIA investigation, that the nomination is wide open and that you have as good a chance as any of the current candidates to claim it," wrote Wetherell in a memo to Church.

The belief among his closest advisers that Ted Kennedy stood in the way of Frank Church's presidential ambitions was a sign that Church was not as beholden to the Kennedy family as Barry Goldwater and the conservative critics of the Church Committee believed.

But the group also stressed that Church still faced a major problem of his own making that he might not be able to resolve: his promise to Mansfield not to campaign during the investigation. "All agreed that we face a serious dilemma," Wetherell wrote. "You cannot announce or even allow the formation of a [presidential campaign] committee because of the CIA investigation. As the campaign law currently reads, no fundraising or expenditures in excess of $1,000 can be made on your behalf unless such a [campaign] committee is authorized.

"The CIA committee is in many ways both your major current asset and liability in any race," Wetherell continued. "All [attendees of the strategy session] agreed that one of your major assets is that your image is one of an honorable and honest man. Any action to promote your candidacy which appeared less than honest and honorable would immediately undercut one of your main assets."

Given Church's promise to Mansfield, the group agreed that Church was very limited in what he could do, and that "no funds could be expended or raised" for a campaign. He could, however, accept speaking invitations in states that would be important in 1976, and make "courtesy" phone calls to Democratic leaders whenever he traveled to give speeches in their states. He should also hold lunches with experts on the economy — an issue on which Church's knowledge was woefully inadequate.

Those recommendations didn't call for Church to do much more than what a prominent senator would routinely do, even one not running for president.

The secret meeting and the follow-up memo did not spur Frank Church to launch a presidential campaign in the summer of 1975. He delayed again. The Church Committee was unearthing so many abuses committed by the CIA and other agencies that Church already knew the committee could never finish its work on the original schedule, and that he had to get Senate approval for an extension of the committee's life.

Mike Wetherell had hoped the strategy session and follow-up memo would prod Church to start the complicated process of launching a presidential campaign, but Church refused, repeatedly reminding Wetherell of his promise to Mansfield. "I was encouraging him to get in the race early enough so that he could run in the Massachusetts primary [scheduled for March 2 in 1976]," recalled Wetherell. "I thought he needed to win an eastern state. But he said he couldn't do it."

Betty Beale, a syndicated Washington society columnist, caught up with Church at a Washington garden party not long before the secret campaign strategy session held by the Church staffers at Verda Barnes's apartment, and casually got Church to make revealing remarks about his thinking about both running for president and the Church Committee.

Church grimly told her that he couldn't think about running for president until "I'm through with this thing," meaning the Church Committee's investigations.

"It may explode."

CHAPTER 18

"We met your man in the Congo"

IN THE SUMMER of 1975, while the press covering the Church Committee focused on what had so far become public about the committee's investigation into the CIA's efforts to assassinate Fidel Castro, the committee was more quietly conducting comprehensive investigations of four other CIA assassination plots that revealed a long pattern of criminality in American national security policy that had never been fully disclosed or curbed. The CIA plots targeted Patrice Lumumba in Congo; Ngo Dinh Diem in South Vietnam; Rafael Trujillo in the Dominican Republic; and General Rene Schneider in Chile, and combined, took place over four consecutive presidential administrations — Eisenhower, Kennedy, Johnson, and Nixon. The horrific stories disclosed by the committee's investigations of the four cases confirmed Frank Church's belief that the United States was not always a force for good in the world, and that the rise of an unaccountable and permanent national-security state was perverting American foreign policy.

For Frank Church, the two cases that personally resonated the most involved Congo and Chile.

* * *

When Frank Church gained access to the CIA's files on the Agency's plots to assassinate foreign leaders, he came across a familiar name: Congo's former prime minister, Patrice Lumumba. That brought back memories for Church of his trip to Congo in December 1960, in the midst of the political crisis that led to Lumumba's assassination a month later.

Just after he was elected president in November 1960, John F. Kennedy wanted to send a message that he planned to make Africa a higher priority in U.S. foreign policy. He therefore asked Frank Church and two other Democratic senators to tour Africa on his behalf. Bethine Church made the trip with her husband; the couple didn't mind leaving their children behind for five weeks. Frank and Bethine Church frequently talked about how they put family above politics, but the truth was that sometimes politics won.

They would be joined by Ted Kennedy, the president-elect's younger brother. Ted Kennedy had not yet been elected to the Senate, but his presence on the trip would signal the delegation's significance to African leaders. "My brother, after the 1960 campaign, urged that I go to Africa to find out what was happening there, and I spent five and a half weeks there with...Frank Church" and other senators, Ted Kennedy later recalled.

The most important stop on their eight-nation trip was Congo, where a sudden declaration of independence from Belgium in June 1960—after eight decades of brutal colonial rule—had led to a bloody struggle for control of the mineral-rich country, a battle that frequently dominated the headlines in the United States in the midst of the 1960 presidential campaign between Kennedy and Nixon. The ongoing crisis in Congo was the reason Kennedy believed it was time to pay more attention to Africa.

In his final months in office, Eisenhower saw the Congo crisis as the latest front in America's Cold War battle with the Soviet Union, and he was determined to use the CIA to covertly intervene just as he was also then trying to do in Cuba, and just as he had done earlier in his presidency in Iran and Guatemala.

Eisenhower's views were shared by Secretary of State John Foster Dulles and his brother, CIA director Allen Dulles. They all feared that Africa's newly independent nations were betraying America's interests by declaring neutrality in the Cold War. Excerpts from National Security Council meetings reveal the true resentment Eisenhower felt about de-colonization in Africa: the president told his staff that the global movement for independence from European powers was "a destructive hurricane."

Patrice Lumumba was the charismatic leader of the independence movement in Congo, and became prime minister when the country declared independence. But Belgium and the corporate interests that controlled Congo's vast mineral wealth, along with Congo's white colonial power structure, were not ready to cede their control over the country. When the Belgian-backed commanders of the white-controlled repressive colonial gendarmerie refused to make any changes to reflect the nation's independence, the Black rank-and-file of the security force mutinied. Attacks on whites and white-owned property by the mutineers gave Congo's white power structure, Belgium, and the United States and other major Western nations the justification they wanted to counter Congo's independence—and Lumumba's new government.

Patrice Lumumba, Congo's independence leader who was forced from power in a CIA-backed coup and then assassinated.

With Belgium's support, the mining regions of Katanga and South Kasai seceded from the newly independent Congo, and the United Nations sent troops to Congo, essentially to protect Western interests and the secessionist regions.

Lumumba traveled to the United States to seek military support from Eisenhower; when Washington refused, a desperate Lumumba turned to Moscow. Lumumba was no communist, but his decision to seek Soviet help, followed by the arrival in Congo of Soviet military advisers, turned the West solidly against him. Eisenhower became determined to get rid of him.

By September 1960, Lumumba had been ousted from power in a CIA-backed coup. But he continued to struggle to regain power, and was left in a kind of political limbo, guarded by United Nations troops who blocked his capture by the new Congolese government.

But Eisenhower feared Lumumba was so charismatic and had so much popular support that he could still reemerge as Congo's leader. And so by the time Frank Church arrived in Congo in December, the CIA was trying to kill Lumumba.

Frank and Bethine Church didn't know anything about the machinations underway behind the scenes when they arrived in Congo's capital, Léopoldville (now Kinshasa). "In Léopoldville we met the American ambassador to the Congo, Claire Timberlake, who was an absolute case," recalled Bethine Church in her memoir. "He and his wife wanted us to think that everything was going along just as normally as could be...he insisted we take a shopping trip, as if we were in the middle of Paris, although we had to have an escort. Unlike other places in Africa, very few people were in the marketplace, and you could tell things were amiss."

At a dinner at the embassy, "I met a man named Mr. Thomas, from southern Idaho, who said he was a lawyer there on business," Bethine wrote. "Well, I knew there was no law business to conduct in Léopoldville. I whispered to Frank that he had just met a CIA agent...When Frank got back to the States, he had a debriefing with the CIA director, Allen Dulles. At one point, Frank said to him, 'oh by the way, we met your man in the Congo.' Dulles was stunned and Frank just let it go."

The Congo crisis dominated Frank Church's discussions at the next leg of his Africa trip when he landed in Lagos, Nigeria. Church had lunch at the home of Robert Fleming, an official with the

Rockefeller Brothers Fund, a Rockefeller family philanthropic organization, and met prominent Nigerian businessman Bank Anthony, who had been trying to gather international support for the Lumumba government in Congo. Anthony had tried to get Fleming to persuade the Rockefellers to use their financial and political influence to assist Lumumba's government in preventing the Congolese mining provinces from seceding; Anthony argued that supporting Lumumba would bolster American prestige in Africa. No assistance came.

After meeting Church, Anthony stayed in touch. He later implored Church to push Washington to support Lumumba's release from house arrest.

But at the time of his 1960 trip to Congo, Church still shared Kennedy's hawkish, Cold War view of the world, which really wasn't much different from the views held by Eisenhower and the Dulles brothers. Church, like Kennedy, saw Lumumba as an obstacle to Western efforts to stabilize Congo and fend off Soviet influence in Africa. After returning home, Church described the ousted prime minister as a polarizing figure. Church told reporters it would be easier "to establish a legitimate government in the Congo without including Lumumba."

Political activist and economist Donna Allen wrote to Church on February 12, 1961, to chastise the Idaho senator for those comments. Refusing to restore the democratically elected Lumumba, she argued, would only sow instability. "The Lumumba government is still the only democratically-elected government there is unless or until another election is held," Allen wrote. "We cannot change their government to secure policies we prefer."

Church wrote back to Allen just two days later, but refused to concede that Lumumba was necessary to the creation of a credible government in Congo. "I intended to make no implication inconsistent with your own definition of a 'legitimate' government," he wrote. That same month, the coup-installed Congolese government revealed that Lumumba had been killed, but refused to provide details.

By 1975, when the Church Committee uncovered the CIA's efforts to assassinate Lumumba, Frank Church — radicalized in his foreign-policy views of American militarism and imperialism — no longer saw the Congo crisis and Patrice Lumumba through a Kennedy-style Cold War lens. Instead, he now viewed the CIA's Congo plot as a prime example of how the United States had for decades allowed anti-Communist paranoia to warp its actions around the world. He also seemed to understand that an investigation of the Lumumba case would help him explore his own journey from Cold Warrior to fierce opponent of American imperialism.

* * *

The Church Committee managed to gain access to the entire archive of secret cables between CIA headquarters and the CIA station in Congo during the period when the Agency, under pressure from Eisenhower, was plotting to kill Lumumba. The cables laid out the chilling story of how assassinating Lumumba became a bureaucratic imperative in the American government.

Larry Devlin, the CIA's station chief in Leopoldville during the Congo crisis, stoked the Eisenhower administration's paranoia about the Soviet presence in Congo with his cables back to headquarters. On August 18, 1960, he wrote a cable stating that "Embassy and Station believe Congo experiencing classic Communist effort takeover government... anti-west forces rapidly increasing power Congo and there may be little time left in which take action to avoid another Cuba."

That cable triggered panic in Washington. At a top-secret meeting of the National Security Council that same day, Eisenhower made it clear that he wanted Lumumba assassinated. He used language that represented the most explicit presidential directive to kill a foreign leader found in any of the five cases investigated by the Church Committee.

"The evidence indicates that it is likely that President Eisenhower's expression of strong concern about Lumumba at a meeting of the National Security Council on August 18, 1960 was taken by [CIA director] Allen Dulles as authority to assassinate Lumumba," stated the Church Committee's interim report on the CIA assassination plots. "Indeed, one NSC staff member present at the August 18 meeting believed that he witnessed a presidential order to assassinate Lumumba."

Robert Johnson, the NSC staff member, told the committee that during that meeting, "President Eisenhower said something — I can no longer remember his words — that came across to me as an order for the assassination of Lumumba who was then at the center of political conflict and controversy in the Congo. There was no discussion. The meeting simply moved on. [But] I remember my sense of that moment quite clearly, because the President's statement came as a great shock to me...I was convinced at the time, and remained convinced when I thought about it later, that the President's statement was intended as an order for the assassination of Lumumba. [But] I must confess that in thinking about the incident more recently I have had some doubts."

During an August 25 meeting of Eisenhower's Special Group, the top officials involved in covert action decision-making, Gordon Gray, the president's special assistant for national security affairs, said that Eisenhower "had expressed extremely strong feelings on the necessity for very straightforward action in this situation." The Special Group then agreed not to rule out "consideration of any particular kind of activity which might contribute to getting rid of Lumumba."

The following day, Allen Dulles sent a cable to Devlin in Léopoldville saying that "In high quarters here it is the clear-cut conclusion that if [Lumumba] continues to hold high office the inevitable result will at best be chaos and at worst pave the way to communist takeover...his removal must be an urgent and prime objective and that under existing conditions this should be a high priority of our covert action."

Richard Bissell, the CIA's chief of clandestine operations who was deeply involved in the Agency's assassination plots at the time, later wrote in his memoir that "while the meaning of the [Dulles cable to Devlin] may seem open to interpretation, in that period of history its meaning would have been clear." Eisenhower had ordered Lumumba's assassination.

Devlin reported back to CIA headquarters that he was already meeting with Congolese political leaders who were interested in assassinating Lumumba, but they wanted small arms from the CIA.

Meanwhile, Bissell turned to the CIA's chief poisoner to kill Lumumba. Bissell asked CIA scientist Sidney Gottlieb to come up with a method to poison Lumumba without its being traced back to the CIA. Bissell told Gottlieb that the assignment came from the highest authority—which Gottlieb later testified to the Church Committee that he had assumed meant the president.

Gottlieb reviewed what was available at the U.S. Army

Chemical Corps installation at Fort Detrick, Maryland, and selected a toxin that "was supposed to produce a disease that was indigenous to that part of Africa and that could be fatal," he later told the Church Committee. In late September 1960, Gottlieb traveled to Léopoldville, where he met with Devlin, using the agreed-upon code that he was "Joe from Paris."

He then gave Devlin the toxin—along with rubber gloves, a mask, and a syringe—for use against Lumumba. Gottlieb explained to Devlin that the toxin had to be injected into Lumumba's food or something else that he would swallow.

When Gottlieb handed him the poison with which to kill Lumumba, Devlin felt ambushed. So he contacted CIA headquarters, which confirmed the order to poison Lumumba. Devlin later told the Church Committee that Gottlieb told him the order came straight from Eisenhower.

Devlin didn't want to carry out the assassination, he testified. "I looked upon the Agency as an executive arm of the Presidency," he told the Church Committee. "Therefore, I suppose I thought that it was an order issued in due form from an authorized authority. On the other hand, I looked at it as a kind of operation that I could do without—that I thought that probably the Agency and the U.S. government could get along without. I didn't regard Lumumba as the kind of person who was going to bring on World War III...I saw him as a danger to the political position of the United States in Africa, but nothing more than that."

Devlin claimed that he used bureaucratic tactics to slow-roll the CIA's assassination plot. After meeting with Gottlieb, "my mind was racing," Devlin wrote in his 2007 memoir. "I realized that I could never assassinate Lumumba. It would have been murder. While I could have justified the assassination of Hitler to myself, Lumumba's case was not the same. It would have been morally wrong. Further, even if I tried to assassinate Lumumba, which I had no intention of doing, and bungled the operation, it would be a disaster for the embassy, the Agency, and the U.S. government. It would seriously complicate our relations with the Third World, where it would be exploited by the Soviet Union."

Still, the CIA cable traffic reveals that Devlin never told his superiors he wouldn't carry out the assassination. Instead, he sent a series of cables explaining his "exploratory steps in furtherance of the assassination plot," the Church Committee report states. He sent cables that were "progress reports on his attempts to find access to Lumumba," Devlin told the Church Committee, including a plan to place a Congolese agent close to Lumumba while the former prime minister was under house arrest.

Devlin's claims that he wasn't really trying to assassinate Lumumba were belied by cables that "indicate that he planned to continue his efforts to implement the operation and sought the resources to do so successfully," the Church Committee determined. "The central point remains that [Devlin] planned to continue the assassination effort by whatever means."

Church Committee staffers who questioned Devlin were never quite sure what to believe about him. "When Devlin was in the room, he was being perfectly gentlemanly, but I had no assurance that I was hearing the whole truth," recalled committee staffer Frederick Baron.

Devlin continued to insist that he had only acted as if he was going along with the assassination plot, while in fact he was trying to use bureaucratic means to stop it. "I have been severely criticized for my role in Lumumba's removal from office and his eventual death," Devlin wrote in his memoir. "I can understand the repugnance that some people will feel when they learn of the [CIA] operation. I believed then and I believe now that it was an ill-conceived and unnecessary operation, an operation that demonstrated President Eisenhower's lack of a clear understanding of the situation...I am aware that some people believe I should have rejected the order to implement the operation, but I do not regret the way I handled it. At the time, I realized that a refusal to obey what I believed to be an order from the president would have resulted in my immediate recall...on balance, I thought that it was better to play the time-honored bureaucratic game of stall and delay."

Devlin testified that he placed the poison in an office safe in the CIA station, then later dumped it in the Congo River.

* * *

Devlin's delays with the poison plot prompted CIA headquarters to try other methods. Justin O'Donnell, a senior CIA officer, testified to the Church Committee that in October 1960 he was called in to a meeting with Bissell, who told him to "eliminate Lumumba."

255

O'Donnell refused the order, but he did agree to travel to Congo to find a way to draw Lumumba out of his house arrest, where he was surrounded by UN peacekeeping troops, so he could then be captured by forces loyal to his enemies.

The Agency also sent QJ-WIN, the European hit man whom Gary Hart had tried to meet in Amsterdam. Another agent, codenamed WI-ROGUE and described as a "stateless soldier of fortune," was also sent to Léopoldville by the CIA, but only after the Agency had provided him "with plastic surgery and a toupee so that Europeans traveling in the Congo would not recognize him," according to the Church Committee report. WI-ROGUE then asked QJ-WIN to join an "execution squad" in Congo.

QJ-WIN arrived in Léopoldville in November and sought to "pierce both Congolese and U.N. guards" in order to gain access to Lumumba, either to assassinate him or to free him so that he could later be captured by other forces.

But before QJ-WIN could act, Lumumba slipped out of UN custody and tried to make his way to Stanleyville [modern-day Kisangani], his base of support in eastern Congo. QJ-WIN became "anxious" to pursue Lumumba to Stanleyville, and "expressed desire execute plan by himself" against Lumumba, according to a CIA cable quoted in the Church Committee report. But Lumumba was captured on his way to Stanleyville by forces loyal to the regime that had ousted him, and was transferred to the Belgian-backed secessionist state of Katanga. On January 17, 1961, Patrice Lumumba was secretly executed by a Katangan firing squad under Belgian supervision. Belgian police later chopped up his body and dumped the parts into a vat of acid. The details of Lumumba's death would not be fully known for another 40 years.

The Church Committee concluded that while the CIA tried to assassinate Lumumba, the Agency did not kill him. Still, the CIA knew that if Lumumba was captured by the forces of the new, coup-installed Congolese government, he would probably be turned over to the secessionist government of Katanga, which would certainly kill him. So the CIA's efforts to lure him out of his house arrest, or track him down as he made his way to his Stanleyville sanctuary, could be seen as indirect attempts to aid and abet his murder.

The CIA's "Congo station had advance knowledge of the [post-coup] government's plan to transport Lumumba into the hands of his bitterest enemies where he was likely to be killed," the Church Committee report stated. There was also evidence that the CIA had at least attempted to help Congolese troops capture Lumumba as he fled to Stanleyville. A CIA cable from Léopoldville stated that Agency officers were working with the new Congolese government to block roads and alert troops along Lumumba's possible escape routes. Devlin told the Church Committee that he had talked with Congolese officers about the routes Lumumba might take to Stanleyville, but that he had not been a "major assistance in tracking down Lumumba prior to his capture." Justin O'Donnell, the CIA officer assigned to lure Lumumba out of house arrest, told the Church Committee that the Agency had played no role in Lumumba's eventual decision to slip away to Stanleyville.

Still, there was no doubt that the CIA had tried to kill Lumumba — and that it had done all it could to encourage and support those who eventually succeeded in doing so. The Eisenhower Administration, the CIA, the United Nations, and the Belgian government all wanted to be rid of Lumumba. "In fact, Lumumba's assassination was the culmination of six months of intervention by the West in the Congo," observed Belgian writer Ludo De Witte in his landmark 1999 book, *The Assassination of Lumumba.*

In 2001 a Belgian parliamentary inquiry issued a report finding that Belgium bore a "moral responsibility" for Lumumba's killing. In 2018 a square in Brussels was renamed for Patrice Lumumba.

* * *

Apart from Vietnam, few foreign-policy issues loomed as large in Frank Church's career as did Chile. Church's first major congressional investigation was of ITT's secret collaboration with the CIA in Chile, and that investigation ultimately helped unravel the bigger and far darker scandal of the Nixon Administration's secret plot to foment a coup against Chile's socialist president, Salvador Allende. Richard Helms had lied to Church's multinational subcommittee in an unsuccessful effort to stop Frank Church from discovering the Agency's broader coup-plotting, and Church had then pushed for Helms to be prosecuted for perjury. Church's success with the ITT inquiry also helped convince Mike Mansfield that Church could handle the broader investigation of the CIA and the intelligence community. The Church Committee's investigation of CIA efforts to eliminate Chilean general René Schneider, along with a broader inquiry by the committee into the Agency's covert action to overthrow Allende, served as sequels to Church's ITT investigation.

On September 4, 1970, Allende had come in first in the Chilean presidential election, but since he had not gained an outright majority, Chile's Congress had to choose the winner. That congressional action, scheduled for late October 1970, was supposed to be a pro forma certification of Allende, the first-place candidate. But Richard Nixon wanted to use the intervening weeks to stop Allende from coming to power.

The Nixon Administration pursued a two-track strategy. The first track included a campaign of propaganda and disinformation against Allende, as well as bribes to key players on Chile's political scene and boycotts and economic pressure from multinational American corporations with operations in Chile, such as ITT.

The second and far more secretive track called for a CIA-backed military coup.

In a White House meeting on September 15, 1970, with National Security Advisor Henry Kissinger, Attorney General John Mitchell, and CIA Director Richard Helms, Nixon ordered Helms to secretly foment a military coup to stop Allende from becoming Chile's president.

Helms later testified to the Church Committee that he recalled coming away from the September 15 meeting with [the] "impression that the President came down very hard, that he wanted something done and he didn't much care how, and that he was prepared to make money available. This was a pretty all-inclusive order. If I ever carried a marshal's baton in my knapsack out of the Oval Office, it was that day."

Helms and the other CIA officials involved didn't think they had much of a chance of mounting a successful coup — but none of them expressed any moral qualms about following Nixon's orders.

The CIA had some contacts in the Chilean Army willing to stage a coup. But the Chilean military officers told the Americans that a coup couldn't succeed because General Rene Schneider, the Army's commander in chief, would never agree to a military takeover. Schneider, loyal to Chile's constitution, would never allow the military to be used to subvert the nation's democracy. Thus, "as a result of his strong constitutional stand, the removal of General

Schneider became a necessary ingredient in the coup plans of all the Chilean conspirators," stated the Church Committee's assassination report. The CIA saw its task as overcoming "the apolitical constitutional-oriented inertia of the Chilean military."

On October 19, a group of Chilean military officers supported by the CIA tried to kidnap Schneider, but failed; their second attempt the next day failed as well. On October 22, the CIA gave the group a cache of machine guns and ammunition to use in another attempt.

Later that day, Schneider was mortally wounded in an attempted kidnapping. Ambushed while in his car, Schneider pulled out his gun and fought back but was shot by the would-be kidnappers.

The Church Committee concluded that the kidnappers who killed Schneider were from a different group of military officers than the ones the CIA had supplied with weapons the night before. But the CIA was still very familiar with the group of Chilean officers who did kill Schneider. In fact, it was led by retired Chilean general Roberto Viaux, whom the CIA had initially supported as its best hope to lead a coup. After first supporting Viaux, however, the CIA later discouraged his coup plotting, because the Agency realized that Viaux lacked the power or standing in Chile to successfully stage a military takeover. Another Chilean general told the CIA that Viaux was a "general without an army," according to a CIA cable.

Still, the CIA wanted to keep Viaux and his group on standby to join a larger, more effective coup if it could be organized by other military officers. While the CIA believed that a Viaux-backed "mini-coup at this juncture would be counterproductive" and wanted him to "postpone his plans," the Agency still wanted to encourage "him in a suitable manner to maintain his posture so that he may join larger movement later if it materializes." The Agency wanted "to encourage Viaux to expand and refine his coup planning. Gain some influence over his actions." As a result, the CIA remained in contact with Viaux, and knew about his plans to kidnap Schneider. In mid-October, the CIA station in Chile sent a cable to CIA headquarters stating that "Viaux intends to kidnap Generals Schneider and Prats (Schneider's deputy) within the next 48 hours in order to precipitate a coup."

The CIA later claimed it wasn't involved in Schneider's killing because the murder was not committed by the group that had just received weapons from the Agency. That was a laughable alibi; the CIA had worked with Viaux, kept in touch with him, knew his kidnap plans, and wanted someone to get rid of Schneider. And it was obvious that any kidnapping plot could have a murderous end.

Frank Church was personally outraged by the CIA's attempts to eliminate Schneider. His murder raised deep moral issues for Church; the CIA wanted to get rid of Schneider because he obeyed Chile's constitution, adhered to the rule of law, and refused to lead a military coup against the democratically elected Allende. The CIA plot against Schneider was thus a perversion of everything America claimed that it stood for.

* * *

When he testified in closed session before the Church Committee, former CIA director Helms claimed he had nothing to do with Schneider's murder, and tried to walk back his earlier statement that he had left the September 15 meeting with Nixon carrying a "marshal's baton." Gary Hart asked Helms whether he thought "the kind of carte blanche mandate you carried, the marshal's baton that you carried out in a knapsack to stop Allende from assuming office" included a presidential mandate to assassinate Schneider — or Allende.

"Well, not in my mind," Helms said. "Because when I became director, I had already made up my mind that we weren't going to have any of that business when I was director. I had made that clear to my fellows and I think they will tell you this."

Henry Kissinger also claimed that he had nothing to do with the Schneider murder, but went further to insist that he didn't even know about the CIA's efforts to foment a military coup. Kissinger and his deputy, General Alexander Haig, both told the Church Committee that on October 15, 1970, the White House ordered the CIA to stand down and suspend any further efforts to stage a military coup. But Thomas Karamessines, the chief of the CIA's clandestine service at the time, disputed Kissinger's claims that he didn't know what the Agency was doing in Chile, and the Church Committee found records of frequent meetings and conversations between Kissinger and Karamessines during the period when Karamessines said he was briefing Kissinger on Chile.

"The testimony given to the committee by Henry Kissinger and General Haig conflicts with that given by CIA officials," the Church Committee report on assassinations stated. "Both [Kissinger and Haig] testified that after [October 15] they were neither informed of nor authorized CIA Track II activities, including the kidnap plans of General Schneider and the passage of weapons to the military plotters. By contrast, CIA officials testified that they operated before and after October 15 with the knowledge and approval of the White House. The conflict pertains directly to the period after October 15, but it bears on the degree of communication between the White House and the CIA in the earlier period as well."

After the Church Committee's interim report on assassinations was published, Richard Nixon agreed to answer a series of written questions from the committee, many of them concerning Chile. At the time, Nixon was the only former president still alive who had been in office during any of the CIA assassination plots investigated by the Church Committee. The committee published an addendum to the assassination report that included Nixon's answers.

Nixon denied that he had ever ordered a military coup in Chile. He insisted that the September 1970 White House meeting, in which Helms said he carried a "marshal's baton" out of the Oval Office, was merely to discuss "the prospect of Salvador Allende's election to the presidency of Chile," and that he wanted the "CIA to determine whether it was possible for a political opponent of Mr. Allende to be elected President by the Chilean Congress."

Nixon also said he was unaware that his September 15 meeting with Helms had prompted the CIA to attempt to foment a military coup in Chile; that he did not know the CIA had tried to arrange the kidnapping of Schneider; and that he did not know the CIA had provided machine guns for a kidnapping attempt.

"Mr. Nixon's statements...contrast with evidence received previously by the committee," the Church Committee report stated. "All CIA officials stated that they interpreted President Nixon's September 15 instruction as a directive to promote a military coup in Chile."

*   *   *

Even before the CIA's role was investigated and disclosed by the Church Committee, the assassination of Schneider backfired on

Nixon, the CIA, and the Chilean coup-plotters. Rather than smooth the way for a coup to block Allende from gaining power, Schneider's killing immediately triggered the declaration of martial law in Chile and the appointment of Schneider's pro-constitution deputy as the new Army commander. His violent death rallied the Chilean Army "firmly behind the flag of constitutionalism," according to a CIA cable at the time. On October 24, Chile's Congress confirmed Allende as president.

It would be another three years before a CIA-backed coup against Allende would succeed.

Clandestine-service chief Karamessines told the Church Committee that the Nixon Administration's Track II—its efforts to foment a coup in Chile—never stopped after Allende took office. The CIA continued to try to undermine Allende until the Chilean military finally succeeded in 1973. "What we were told to do in effect was, well Allende is now President...we were told to continue our efforts. Stay alert and do what we could to contribute to the eventual achievement of the objectives and purposes of Track II."

On September 11, 1973, Allende died during a military coup in which Chilean general Augusto Pinochet come to power. The military claimed Allende had committed suicide. Pinochet became a ruthless dictator who tortured and executed thousands of political dissidents and other Chileans who got in his way.

The Schneider assassination had been just the beginning of a dark, repressive era that the CIA and Richard Nixon helped impose on Chile, and so the Church Committee also investigated the broader CIA covert action that ultimately led to the 1973 coup.

Chile was one of several covert-action operations investigated by the committee, but it was the only one on which it held hearings and discussed in its reports. Colby, the CIA director who had been relatively cooperative with the Church Committee, sought to block any investigation into the Agency's covert-action operations. Frank Church struggled to get Colby to change his mind, but ultimately Church had to compromise. He agreed with the CIA to limit the committee's public discussion of covert action to a single case, and Church chose Chile.

As part of the Chile covert-action investigation, committee staffer Rick Inderfurth interviewed Orlando Letelier, Chile's foreign minister under Allende, who in 1975 was living in exile in Washington. Letelier had arrived in the United States in 1974 after a year's imprisonment and torture in Pinochet's concentration camps; only international diplomatic pressure had secured his release. Since his arrival in Washington, he had become a leading dissident voice against Pinochet's dictatorship.

In the summer of 1975, Inderfurth and another committee staffer visited Letelier at his home in Bethesda, Maryland — the same Washington suburb where Frank Church lived. They asked Letelier about the de-stabilizing effect on the Allende government of the Nixon Administration's overt and covert policies in the years leading up to the 1973 coup. Letelier helped provide valuable insights and context for the Church Committee's investigation of the CIA and Chile. But even while he lived in Washington and spoke with congressional investigators, Letelier still wasn't safe from Pinochet.

On September 21, 1976, Letelier was killed by a car bomb as he drove to work through Sheridan Circle in downtown Washington. Ronni Moffitt, an American woman who was his co-worker at the Institute for Policy Studies, a Washington think tank, was riding to work with him and was also killed. Moffitt's husband, Michael, who was sitting in the car's back seat, was thrown from the vehicle by the blast and survived.

Sam Giancana, and now Orlando Letelier; the assassination of Chile's former foreign minister on the streets of Washington marked yet another murder of a Church Committee witness.

Since Letelier did not testify in public in the Church Committee's hearings on Chile, it has not previously been disclosed that the committee interviewed Letelier. It is not known whether the Pinochet regime knew that Letelier had been talking to the Church Committee, but Pinochet was clearly furious over Letelier's more public efforts to lobby Congress to take action against the Pinochet regime. In June 1976, just months before Letelier's killing, Pinochet met with Secretary of State Henry Kissinger and complained that dissidents in Washington were spreading lies about his human-rights record. And he singled out Letelier, saying "Letelier has access to Congress," according to a declassified transcript of their conversation excerpted in The Pinochet File, a 2003 book by Peter Kornbluh.

Eventually, the FBI identified as one of the key figures in the

Letelier assassination Michael Townley, an American agent for the Pinochet regime's Operation Condor, a vicious program to assassinate Chilean dissidents around the world. Operation Condor was run by DINA, the Chilean secret police. Pinochet remained in power until 1990, long after the Church Committee's investigation of the CIA's role in ousting Allende.

CHAPTER 19

"What the president wanted to happen"

IN A PERIOD of just a few short months, the Church Committee had performed a herculean task; it had won a battle with Dick Cheney and the Ford White House for access to thousands of highly classified documents, had conducted interviews with most of the key figures from four administrations, and had written a comprehensive report that contained astonishing details about the CIA's efforts to assassinate foreign leaders. With its awkwardly named "Interim Report" on the "Alleged Assassination Plots Involving Foreign Leaders," Frank Church and his committee had pulled back the curtain on some of the most atrocious and criminal activities ever conducted by the U.S. intelligence community.

The layers of detail unearthed by the committee's investigation — and, critically, the interviews with key participants in meetings directly with each president — provided strong circumstantial evidence that each of the five plots studied by the committee had received at least indirect presidential authorization.

And yet the Interim Report's conclusion stuck to Frank Church's earlier public assertions that there was no ironclad proof that the CIA had been ordered to conduct assassinations by any of the presidents. The report's conclusion read as if Church was trying to prove that, despite the evidence gathered by his own investigators, his "rogue elephant" statement had been correct after all.

"The committee has endeavored to explore as fully as possible...how and why the plots happened, whether they were authorized and if so at what level," the report stated.

> The picture that emerges from the evidence is not a clear one. This may be due to the system of deniability and the consequent state of the evidence, which even after our long investigation remains conflicting and inconclusive. Or it may be that there were in fact serious shortcomings in the system of authorization so that an activity such as assassination could have been undertaken by an agency of the United States government without express authority. The committee finds that the system of executive command and control was so ambiguous that it is difficult to be certain at what levels assassination activity was known and authorized. This situation creates the disturbing prospect that government officials might have undertaken the assassination plots without it having been uncontrovertibly clear that there was explicit authorization from the presidents.

Did Frank Church intervene to soften the conclusion, perhaps in a bipartisan deal covering both Democratic and Republican presidents?

Fritz Schwarz, who was the primary author of the committee's assassination report, said the conclusions reflected his own thinking at the time about the level of the evidence of presidential authorization obtained by the committee. "Frank Church did not intervene on the way the conclusions of the assassination report were written," Schwarz said in an interview. "None of the other senators intervened either. I wrote the conclusions myself, with no intervention."

Schwarz says that, at the time, he believed that "the evidence of presidential orders was murky." But in the years after the Church Committee completed its work, "My thinking on that evolved," Schwarz added. "I progressively became more convinced that the presidents probably did know. As time went by, I became more convinced of that."

In the end, the Interim Report has stood the test of time. Even decades later, most of what is known about the CIA's plots to assassinate foreign leaders was first disclosed by the Church Committee.* Despite the way the conclusion was written and the intense media coverage at the time of Frank Church's "rogue elephant" comments, the wealth of facts unearthed and revealed in the 364-page Interim Report clearly points to presidential authorization, or at least presidential knowledge, of the assassination plots.

"When you put it all together, all of the evidence is laid out in the report," notes committee staffer Frederick Baron. "There wasn't an effort to keep any of the evidence out of the report. We included all of the evidence and the conclusions were obvious. I think any reasonable reader...had to conclude that the CIA was not out on their own, that it was made crystal clear this is what the president wanted to happen."

* * *

While all of the Church Committee's hearings on the CIA's assassination plots were held in closed session, Frank Church believed that the report on the committee's investigation should be made public, and he planned to publish it months before the committee's final reports on the rest of its work were completed. But when the Ford White House and the CIA saw the details packed into the assassination report, they panicked—and launched a last-minute effort to stop its publication.

Ford sent a letter to each member of the Church Committee urging them not to make the report public, arguing that it would damage

---

* Daniel Ellsberg, the Rand Corporation analyst who leaked the Pentagon Papers in 1971, played an intriguing and previously undisclosed role in the Church Committee's investigation of the assassinations of foreign leaders. Ellsberg said in an interview that he met privately with Frank Church in 1975 while the Church Committee was conducting its investigation of the assassination plots. Ellsberg said that during their meeting, he handed Church a manila envelope containing copies of a series of top secret cables that he had obtained. The cables were between the American embassy in Saigon and the Kennedy White House, and related to the U.S. role in the planning of the 1963 coup against South Vietnamese president Diem that resulted in his assassination. The section of the Church Committee's interim report on assassinations dealing with the Diem case repeatedly cites as key sources of information both the Pentagon Papers and cables from 1963 between the embassy in Saigon and the Kennedy White House. It is not clear if the report relied on the cables Ellsberg handed to Church, or whether the Church Committee separately obtained the cable traffic from the government.

national security. And, after quietly cooperating with Frank Church for most of the year, CIA director Colby held a press conference at the CIA to complain that the report included the names of CIA officers who would be endangered if their identities were made public. Meanwhile, Sidney Gottlieb—the CIA scientist who brought the poison to Larry Devlin so he could kill Patrice Lumumba—anonymously filed a lawsuit in federal court to block the Church Committee from naming him.

In order to avoid a last-minute delay in the report's publication, Frank Church agreed to take the names of Gottlieb and a few other CIA officers out of the report. Instead, they were given pseudonyms, thought up quickly by Church Committee staffers. Sidney Gottlieb was called "Joseph Scheider," Larry Devlin was "Victor Hedgman," and Justin O'Donnell was "Michael Mulroney."

"I flipped through the phone book looking for names to use as pseudonyms that looked similar to their real names," recalls Baron.

But Church resisted other Colby demands as excessive, and he refused to remove the names of senior CIA officials as well as the identities of the outsiders in the CIA-Mafia alliance, among them Bob Maheu, Johnny Rosselli, and Santo Trafficante.

With the White House and CIA campaigning to block the report, Church went to the full Senate to seek a vote authorizing the report's release.

On November 20, 1975, the full Senate held a rare closed session to debate whether the assassination report should be made public. A transcript of the closed session reveals that Frank Church used all of his oratorical powers to make the case for the report's release.

"We have spent months drafting and redrafting this report to make sure the evidence was stated fairly and completely," Church told the Senate.

> Meeting first in a subcommittee composed of Senator Tower, Senator Hart of Colorado and myself, and then in the full committee, our descriptions of the assassination plots are all carefully documented...we believe the public is entitled to know what the instrumentalities of their government have done. We believe that our recommendations can be judged only in the light of the factual record. We believe the

truth about the assassination charges should be told because democracy depends upon an informed electorate. Truth is the very anchor of our democracy.

We wrestled long and hard with the contention that the facts disclosed in this report should be kept secret since they are embarrassing to the United States. We concluded that despite any temporary injury to our national reputation, foreign peoples will, upon sober reflection, respect the United States more for keeping faith with its democratic ideals than they will condemn us for the misconduct revealed. We doubt that any other country would have the courage to make such a disclosure, and I personally believe this to be the unique strength of the American Republic...Any effort to keep the truth from the American public could only have the effect of increasing the corrosive cynicism about government, which is such a threat to our society today.

Despite Church's plea, as well as supportive statements from other members of the committee, the Senate session broke down into squabbling over Senate rules and whether Congress had the right to release classified information over the president's objections. A big problem for many senators was that they hadn't been given a chance to read the report before the day of the vote. Senate Majority Leader Mike Mansfield, concerned that the vote might be so close that it would be embarrassing for the Church Committee, decided to abandon plans for a vote, abruptly ending the closed session.

Church, asserting that he never really needed the full Senate's approval, published the report that same day, angering Senate Republicans as well as the White House. But the episode was embarrassing for Church, and was an early sign that support for Church's efforts to take on the national-security state was very fragile.

CHAPTER 20

"The abyss from which there is no return"

WHILE THE CHURCH Committee focused its first few months on investigating the CIA's assassination plots against foreign leaders, below the radar, plenty of other lines of inquiry were also underway. So much bad behavior in the intelligence community had gone unsupervised by Congress for so long that committee staffers scrambled to keep up as they sought to uncover the full scope of the abuses and illegal activities that had been ignored for so long. It was like trying to air out a house that had been shuttered for 30 years.

Yet those quiet but intense investigations would begin to bear fruit just as the Church Committee geared up for its first public hearings in September 1975. The work would include inquiries into domestic-spying and mind-control programs—and an intensive examination of one of the strangest characters in the history of the CIA.

* * *

A mysterious figure loomed large in the national imagination as the Church Committee began its work in early 1975. James Jesus Angleton, the CIA's longtime head of counterintelligence, had been named in Sy Hersh's landmark December 1974 domestic-spying story as a key player in the Agency's illicit activities. Angleton had previously been unknown outside the dark world of spies and counterspies, but now he was flushed from his life in the shadows, and he was suddenly an object of media fascination — and a prime early target of the Church Committee's CIA investigation. With Angleton's name everywhere, Gary Hart sought him out for dinner for their cryptic talk about the CIA and the Kennedy assassination.

Loch Johnson was assigned by Fritz Schwarz, the committee's chief counsel, to meet Angleton and find out more about him and his subterranean counterintelligence empire. To get ready for the committee's public hearings, when Frank Church hoped to turn Angleton into a star witness, Johnson was told to see whether he could get Angleton to talk about the illegal CIA operations he had secretly run.

Loch Johnson was about to launch on an unexpected journey with one of the strangest men in Washington.

James Angleton had been born in Boise in 1917, seven years before Frank Church. But unlike Church, Angleton left Idaho behind when he was still a young boy. His father, James Hugh Angleton, known as Hugh, was a sales agent for the National Cash Register Company, and he moved his family to Dayton, Ohio, in 1927, when he became a vice president at the company's headquarters. Hugh Angleton's breakthrough financial success came when he personally bought out NCR's Italian operations, moving his family to Milan in 1933.

With his father now wealthy, James Angleton was sent to private school in England, then to Yale University and Harvard Law School, and during World War II he joined the OSS, America's wartime spy service. After the war, Angleton joined its successor, the CIA, when it was created in 1947, and stayed for the rest of his career. Over the decades, he amassed a bureaucratic empire of hybrid parts that placed him in charge of both counterintelligence and the CIA's relationship with Israel.

Angleton was a baroque character, attracted to — and easily swayed by — fabulists and con artists. While in college in the late 1930s, Angleton sought out American poet Ezra Pound, who was then living in Italy and had become an ardent anti-Semite and propagandist for Mussolini and Hitler. Pound befriended the college boy, then tried to get money out of Angleton's rich father. (At the end of World War II, Pound was arrested in Italy by American forces for treason.)

In the OSS and the CIA, Angleton's mentor was Kim Philby, a smooth-talking officer from MI-6, the British intelligence service, who was secretly a Russian double agent. When Philby's betrayal of the West was revealed, Angleton was crushed, and he descended into paranoia. Angleton came to believe that Russian moles were everywhere in the CIA, and anyone who disagreed with him was subject to suspicion — and investigation by Angleton's counterintelligence office.

Angleton's paranoia was fed by yet another con man, Anatoliy Golitsyn, a KGB officer who defected in 1961. Golitsyn enjoyed the gravy train that came with being the CIA's most coveted Russian defector, and didn't want any other defector to cross over and outshine him. Angleton fell for Golitsyn's story that any KGB officer who defected after him would be a double agent sent to discredit him.

When KGB officer Yuri Nosenko defected to the CIA in 1964 and said that the KGB had nothing to do with President Kennedy's assassination the year before, Angleton was immediately suspicious, and the CIA secretly imprisoned Nosenko in a specially-built bunker for three years without ever charging him with a crime. The Nosenko case underscored the degree to which the CIA's Soviet operations were paralyzed for decades by Angleton-driven witch hunts.

William Colby was the first CIA director to recognize the damage Angleton had wreaked. Angleton was stunned when Colby fired him just days before Hersh's domestic-spying story appeared in December 1974. By the time the Church Committee was created, Angleton was out of the CIA, bitter and adrift.

*   *   *

In the early summer of 1975, Loch Johnson called the CIA's legislative liaison to set up a meeting with Angleton. Surprisingly, Angleton agreed, and invited Johnson to lunch at one of his favorite haunts, the Army-Navy Club, a staid old Washington fixture a few blocks from the White House.

Angleton was still just 57 when he met Johnson, but the ravages of chain-smoking and alcoholism made him look 20 years older.

Dressed in a fusty, out-of-date three-piece suit, Angleton settled into the club, lit up a cigarette, and ordered a kir — a French cocktail he told Johnson he had discovered in long drinking sessions with the mayor of Marseille.

Over lunch, Johnson tried to focus their discussion on what Angleton could tell him about the CIA's domestic-spying program, code-named Operation Chaos, the Agency's illegal mail-opening program, code-named HT-LINGUAL, and the Huston Plan, a Nixon-era proposal to get every agency in the intelligence community to target their spying efforts on anti-war protesters. But all Angleton really wanted to do was recount old stories about Golitsyn and Nosenko. He was still obsessed with his witch hunts.

Johnson didn't give up. He and Angleton regularly got together for lunch during the summer and early fall of 1975; Johnson recalls that they met about seven times. As he drank more heavily, Angleton became more expansive about the CIA and counterintelligence. He seemed to enjoy tutoring "his innocent young charge on counterintelligence tradecraft and lore," Johnson recalled. Meanwhile, Angleton made misleading claims minimizing his role in Operation Chaos and in the CIA's mail-opening program. Johnson wrote a memo about their discussions after each lunch, and they were usually filled with Angleton's tales of counterintelligence heroics.

After one lunch, Angleton took Johnson for a long drive in his Mercedes, pumping up the volume of the opera he loved to play on his stereo — which, he maintained, had been custom-designed for his car by NASA. "He was very nice to me, very cordial, probably because he was trying to find out what the Church Committee was up to."

But by their last few meetings, Angleton was drinking more — he was up to five glasses of kir — and by the end of each lunch he was slurring his words and lashing out at Frank Church and the committee's investigation. "At one of our later lunches, he started venting that the Church Committee was destroying U.S. intelligence," Johnson remembered. "He jumped out of his chair, put on his black hat, and stormed out of the club, loudly complaining that 'Washington is a jungle!' It was totally strange."

By the end, Angleton suggested to Johnson that Church was acting at the direction of the Soviets; it was the same kind of accusation he had made against all of his enemies inside the CIA. "It got to be extremely boring after a while," recalled Johnson.

Above all, what Angleton revealed to Johnson was the CIA's utter dysfunction. James Jesus Angleton, the CIA's supposed mastermind of counterintelligence and the evil genius behind its illegal operations, was just an old drunk. And Frank Church was about to expose him in humiliating fashion.

*   *   *

For all his bluster during his lunches with Johnson, Angleton wilted under grilling by Frank Church during his public testimony before the full Church Committee on September 24, 1975. In a sworn deposition taken by Johnson a few days earlier in the Carroll Arms Hotel, an old hotel on Capitol Hill where the Church Committee conducted some of its private interviews and confidential depositions, Angleton had said that "it is inconceivable that a secret intelligence arm of the government has to comply with all the overt orders of the government."

During the full committee hearing—one of the committee's first public sessions—Church jumped on that line from the transcript of Angleton's deposition; it cut to the heart of whether the CIA could be held accountable by either presidents or Congress. For Church, it seemed to vindicate his "rogue elephant" description of the CIA that had caused him so much grief.

During his questioning of Angleton, Church showed rare flashes of anger.

"You said, 'It is inconceivable that a secret intelligence arm of the government has to comply with all of the overt orders of the government,'" Church said to Angleton, repeating for the entire nation the line from Angleton's deposition.

Realizing how bad it sounded out loud and in public, Angleton backtracked. "I withdraw the statement," he hurriedly told Church.

"Do you retract that statement now, or do you merely regard it as imprudent?" Church fired back. "Did you not mean it when you said it the first time? When you said it to us, did you mean it or did you not mean it? You are unwilling to say whether or not you meant it when you said it."

"I would say that the entire speculation should not have been indulged." Angleton appeared scattered, and had now climbed down completely.

During a break in the hearing, a shaken Angleton walked past

Former CIA counterintelligence chief James Jesus Angleton testifies before the Church Committee.

Bethine Church, sitting in the audience. "Angleton walked down the aisle and, noticing me, shot me a look the likes of which I had never seen," Bethine wrote in her memoir. "I then understood the phrase 'if looks could kill.'"

* * *

Bill Miller, the Church Committee's staff director, had originally divided the staff into task forces, with each one assigned to a different agency in the intelligence community. That structure had largely been overshadowed when Fritz Schwarz took control of the committee, placing the investigative focus and energy on the CIA assassination plots. Some of the task forces never really recovered from that shift.

The team assigned to investigate military intelligence, for instance, accomplished little. It was headed by Alton Quanbeck, a former Air Force pilot best known for triggering a major diplomatic incident in 1950 during the Korean War, when he mistakenly bombed an air base inside the Soviet Union rather than his assigned targets in North Korea. Quanbeck recalled in an interview that he "got sidetracked" from his military-intelligence assignment on the Church

Committee when he was pulled off to help with the inquiry into the CIA's plot against General René Schneider in Chile.

But some teams quietly kept working and made stunning discoveries while working on their own. The group assigned to the National Security Agency was a prime example; while technically part of the moribund military task force, the NSA group worked separately and launched an aggressive investigation of the most secretive agency in the U.S. government, with little guidance or interference from the Church Committee's leadership. The result was a series of astonishing revelations of illegal activities at the NSA — disclosures that would help define the Church Committee's historic legacy.

*   *   *

By the time he joined the Church Committee staff and began to investigate the NSA, Britt Snider already had experience investigating intelligence abuses. After serving in the Army in Vietnam, Snider came to Washington looking for a job on Capitol Hill, was hired by Senator Sam Ervin, and soon went to work on an investigation led by Ervin into evidence that the Army had conducted a domestic-spying program. After switching to the Church Committee, Snider was first assigned to the CIA assassination probe, but shifted to the small group inside the military task force that was trying to investigate the NSA. Soon Snider and the rest of the team assigned to the NSA, which is part of the Department of Defense, was the tail wagging the dog of the Church Committee's military task force.

It was hard to figure out where to begin. The NSA was like a black box; its existence was barely acknowledged by the government, and it had managed to stay out of the headlines while disclosures about the CIA's abuses led to the creation of the Church Committee. Congress had never before made any effort to find out what the NSA was doing, and there were even some senators on the Church Committee who were nervous about having the committee launch any investigation of the NSA at all.

"I felt like I was shooting in the dark for a while," Snider recalled in an interview. He started delving into the NSA by meeting with staffers from the Senate armed services and appropriations committees, both of which had nominal authority to oversee the agency. But Snider soon discovered that the two Senate committees each had only one staffer assigned to dealing with the NSA—and they just handled the agency's budget. They did no oversight. "They didn't even see oversight as their job," said Snider. "They basically just put the money through Congress for the NSA every year."

Snider was joined on the Church Committee's NSA team by Peter Fenn, the childhood Bethesda friend of Forrest Church who had grown up and joined the Church Committee staff, and Eric Richard, who joined the committee staff in the summer of 1975 right after graduating from Harvard Law School. Richard was intrigued by the prospect of investigating the NSA in part because he had studied in the Soviet Union while in college, and had seen what it was like to live under an oppressive police state with intimidating surveillance powers. "That gave me a strong incentive to not have a KGB in America," recalled Richard in an interview. Investigating the NSA "raised a lot of issues the law had not clearly addressed, and there was a lot of room for creative thought."

The team's first break came from the Rockefeller Commission. As the presidential commission issued its final report and was shutting down in the spring of 1975, it turned over its copy of the CIA's secret "Family Jewels" report to the Church Committee, cataloging the agency's past abuses. Snider noticed references to the NSA buried in the report—one said the CIA had provided the NSA with an office in New York for a program to copy telegrams, and another revealed that the CIA had asked the NSA to spy on the communications of anti-war protesters who had been placed on a watchlist. Snider started looking into the former, while Peter Fenn and Eric Richard investigated the latter.

As part of his inquiry, Snider kept trying to get a briefing from the NSA, or at least get his written questions answered. When the NSA finally responded, the agency insisted that it would only brief Frank Church and John Tower—the chairman and ranking minority member of the committee. It eventually relented and agreed to a briefing for Snider by one lowly NSA staffer.

The briefer admitted to Snider that, through a highly secretive program code-named SHAMROCK, the NSA had been collecting international telegrams going in and out of New York between Americans and overseas recipients. Couriers regularly delivered magnetic tapes containing the telegrams from New York to NSA headquarters at Ford Meade, in Maryland. That explained the NSA's office in New York. But the NSA staffer briefing Snider knew little about the program beyond the fact that it had been abandoned earlier in 1975 — because, he insisted, it had produced little of intelligence value. When Snider kept grilling the briefer with more detailed questions, the exasperated NSA staffer finally told Snider to go find "Dr. Tordella."

Dr. Louis Tordella, the longest-serving civilian deputy director in the NSA's history, was a secret legend within the agency. A math professor before World War II, Tordella was a Navy code-breaker during World War II and never left after the war; he joined the NSA when it was created in 1952. As deputy director from 1958 until 1974, Tordella knew all of the NSA's secrets. General officers rotated in and out of the job of NSA director on their way to other military postings, but Tordella stayed — and became the agency's de facto czar.

After decades of operating without oversight, the NSA — like the other major agencies in the intelligence community — had developed its own incestuous cult of personality. The CIA had James Angleton, the FBI had J. Edgar Hoover, and the NSA had Louis Tordella. "It was Dr. Tordella who had really been running the place," said Snider.

* * *

Tordella had finally retired a few months before Snider went to see him on a Sunday afternoon at his relatively modest yet comfortable white house on a tree-lined street in Bethesda, Maryland.

Tordella was in his mid-60s, about six feet tall and largely bald, with a sallow complexion. He greeted Snider dressed informally in an open-collar shirt, and ushered Snider out to a sunporch on the back of the house where they could sit and talk.

At first Tordella was suspicious. He looked at Snider with a sort of steely-eyed squint, either because he was trying to figure Snider out, or to show his displeasure with the interview.

"It was a bit disconcerting to me at the beginning, but, as we talked, he began to relax, and his squints became less frequent and less pronounced," recalled Snider. Tordella spent the first hour asking Snider about his background, and probing to find out what the Church Committee was doing. He then asked Snider what he already knew about SHAMROCK.

"He asked me, what do you got already?" Snider recalled. Tordella was trying to gauge how much to say.

"I told him what I knew, and he was just grimacing that I already knew about some things." Tordella cautiously began to talk, but was careful to leave out certain key details; he did not tell Snider that he was the person who had asked the CIA to give the NSA an office in New York, the incident that Snider had discovered in the Family Jewels report.

Over the next four or five hours, as the two sat alone on the porch, with Snider furiously taking notes, Tordella walked Snider through the history of SHAMROCK. The secret program began in the immediate aftermath of World War II, when the government decided to continue its wartime operation to intercept international telegram traffic. Starting in August 1945 and continuing until May 1975, the NSA obtained copies of millions of international telegrams sent to or from the United States, as well as telegrams that transited the United States from one foreign country to another. SHAMROCK had been the government's largest communications intercept program affecting Americans at the time.

Tordella told Snider that his main concern about the Church Committee investigation was the possibility that the telecommunications companies that had cooperated with the NSA would be publicly identified and could face legal action for participating in an illegal domestic spying operation. "Tordella was worried that no American company would ever cooperate with the NSA again," Snider said. The issue of whether to identify the companies involved in SHAMROCK would later become a central issue within the Church Committee, as the senators and staff debated how to handle the NSA investigation.

Yet by talking to Snider, Tordella sent a signal to the NSA to cooperate with the Church Committee — at least on a limited, grudging basis. "They didn't resist my requests as much anymore," recalled Snider. And there was another, hidden reason why the NSA finally agreed to cooperate with the Church Committee. Months before Snider and his team began to investigate the NSA, the Rockefeller Commission had also secretly discovered the NSA's domestic-spying operations. The Rockefeller Commission did not publicly disclose the existence of the NSA programs in its final public report in June 1975 — and did not even tell the Church

Committee what it had found. Yet the Rockefeller Commission did inform the Justice Department that it had uncovered NSA domestic-spying programs that appeared to violate the law. That prompted the Justice Department to secretly launch a review to determine whether NSA officials who had been involved in the operations should be prosecuted. Thus by the time Britt Snider and his team were beginning to ask questions, NSA officials had already been investigated by the Rockefeller Commission. It would take the Justice Department another two years to abandon the idea of prosecuting NSA officials — and even then, Justice Department officials kept the matter secret.

The three telecommunications companies involved with the NSA's SHAMROCK program — RCA Global, ITT World Communications, and Western Union International — were leery of Snider, but they eventually agreed to cooperate, permitting the Church Committee to take depositions of key company officials.

Snider also wanted to find out who had approved SHAMROCK, but the program was so old and had survived so many presidential administrations that it was difficult to determine. It wasn't until the NSA investigation was nearly finished that Snider received a batch of documents from the office of the Secretary of Defense, revealing meetings of senior officials over several administrations in which SHAMROCK was discussed — and its continuation approved.

* * *

While Snider investigated SHAMROCK, Peter Fenn and Eric Richard had been trying to figure out the other tantalizing lead from the Family Jewels report: how the CIA got the NSA to spy on Americans who had been placed on a CIA watchlist. That led them to MINARET — and to a whistleblower.

In 1967 the NSA had begun to monitor the international communications of Americans on the CIA watch list, primarily anti-war and civil-rights activists. In 1969 the agency gave the program the code name MINARET. The NSA was so determined to keep its involvement in the illegal program secret that the NSA's name was not even mentioned on the classified intelligence reports based on the MINARET intercepts. The NSA told Fenn and Richard that the program had been discontinued in 1973, when NSA director Lew Allen became concerned about its legality.

While Fenn and Richard were uncovering MINARET, James Bamford was a young law student and a Navy reservist. Before law school, Bamford had been on active duty, serving in an NSA unit at the Navy's Pacific headquarters in Hawaii. During his reserve duty in October 1974, he was assigned for two weeks of active duty at an NSA listening post at Sabana Seca, Puerto Rico. The station was supposed to be monitoring telephone traffic in Cuba, but during Bamford's brief stint there, an intercept operator let him listen into a telephone conversation between Americans that he was monitoring. Bamford asked the operator whether they overheard Americans regularly, and he said they did on some assignments.

Back at law school, Bamford had a part-time job with a local prosecutor's office, where he dealt with a case involving a warrant for a wiretap. He began to wonder what legal authority governed the NSA in Puerto Rico, where intercept operators were listening to American conversations. He couldn't find anything in the law library, so in the summer of 1975 he called the Church Committee.

Bamford met with Fenn and told him about his experience in Puerto Rico — proof that the NSA had been lying when it claimed that its programs targeting Americans had long since been shut down. Bamford feared being publicly identified because he was still in the Navy reserve, so Frank Church received his confidential testimony in his personal hideaway office in the Capitol Building. "They were keeping me very secret," recalls Bamford. "They didn't want to bring me before the full committee."

Fenn and another committee staffer flew to Puerto Rico and toured the NSA facility to confirm Bamford's account. Bamford's experience as a whistleblower for the Church Committee changed his life: he became a renowned author and journalist, and continued to investigate the NSA for his breakthrough 1982 book, *The Puzzle Palace*, as well as in later books.

* * *

Frank Church pushed for the Church Committee to hold public hearings on the National Security Agency, and also to publicly identify the telecommunication companies that worked with the NSA in the committee's final report. Church won on both issues, but it wasn't easy. He had to face down complaints from Attorney General Edward Levi and Secretary of Defense James Schlesinger, both of whom urged the committee not to hold public hearings. John Tower initially sided with Levi and Schlesinger, but Tower gave in and Church prevailed without having to hold a formal committee vote.

Surprisingly, Britt Snider was strongly opposed to publicly identifying the telecommunication companies. After leading the NSA investigation and taking depositions by company executives, Snider had come to accept the arguments for shielding their identities that Louis Tordella had laid out during their first meeting. "I had become persuaded not to name the companies, because I had really looked into it, and they didn't get anything for doing it — they did it because they were asked [to] by the government," recalled Snider in an interview. "There was a real concern that they would be sued, and I just thought that if they were identified then you won't have companies working with the intelligence community."

Snider met with Fritz Schwarz and presented his arguments against naming the companies. Schwarz disagreed with Snider, because he believed that the companies should be held accountable, and Frank Church sided with Schwarz in favor of naming the companies. The Church Committee held public hearings about the NSA, and published a report detailing SHAMROCK and MINARET and identifying the private companies that had secretly helped the government illegally spy on Americans.

Ultimately, the NSA investigation became one of the landmark achievements of the Church Committee. For the first time, the NSA was brought, kicking and screaming, into the daylight. In the process, Frank Church issued one of the most memorable — and most prescient — public statements of his entire career.

"In the need to develop a capacity to know what potential enemies are doing," Church said on *Meet the Press* on August 17, 1975, "the United States government has perfected a technological capability that enables us to monitor the messages that go through the air.

> These messages are between ships at sea, they could be between units, military units in the field; we have a very extensive capability of intercepting messages wherever they may be in the airwaves. That is necessary and important to the United States as we look abroad at enemies or potential enemies. We must know. At the same time that capability at

any time could be turned around on the American people and no American would have any privacy left, such is the capability to monitor everything: telephone conversations, telegrams, it doesn't matter. There would be no place to hide. If this government ever became a tyranny, if a dictator ever took charge in this country, the technological capacity that the intelligence community has given the government could enable it to impose total tyranny, and there would be no way to fight back because the most careful effort to combine together in resistance to the government, no matter how privately it was done, is within the reach of the government to know. Such is the capability of this technology.

Now, why is this investigation important? I will tell you why. Because I don't want to see this country ever go across the bridge. I know the capacity that is there to make tyranny total in America, and we must see to it that this agency and all agencies that possess this technology operate within the law and under proper supervision, so that we never cross over that abyss. That is the abyss from which there is no return.

CHAPTER 21

"Under a double shadow"

TERRY LENZNER SWAGGERED into the Church Committee's office like he owned the place. In a way, he did.

Lenzner—edgy, staccato-talking, and charismatic—had been the assistant chief counsel of the Senate Watergate Committee when its staff had occupied the same auditorium in the Dirksen Senate Office Building that now housed the Church Committee.

As he swept in, he yelled over at a staffer seated at one of the desks lining the auditorium's dais: "DeOreo, when are you going to come with me and do a real investigation?" Mary DeOreo, a Church Committee researcher, had worked for Lenzner in a similar job on the Watergate Committee. It was Lenzner's way of announcing to everyone within earshot that he didn't think much of the Church Committee—or its investigation.

"Lenzner," Fritz Schwarz recalled in disgust, "was a pain in the ass."

A year after Richard Nixon's resignation, Terry Lenzner was now back in the Dirksen auditorium—but this time he was on the other side. Lenzner was now in private practice as a lawyer, and was representing CIA scientist Sidney Gottlieb, the man responsible for some of the worst abuses ever committed by the CIA—and who was the subject of an investigation by the Church Committee.

Gottlieb had already come to the committee's attention as the

CIA scientist who traveled to Congo to deliver the toxin intended to be used to assassinate Patrice Lumumba.

But the Church Committee now realized that Gottlieb was much more than a supporting character in the CIA's assassination plots. Beginning in the early 1950s, Gottlieb had been the secret architect of the Agency's Cold War mind-control experiments with drugs, and had left behind a trail of death and destruction that the CIA had tried to keep hidden for decades.

Gottlieb's biggest mind-control program was code-named MK-ULTRA, and through that program and others, he became obsessed with the supposed mind-control potential of one new drug in particular—LSD. In violation of medical ethics, Gottlieb began to test LSD on unwitting subjects, pursuing his fantasy that LSD would allow him to unlock and control minds. Gottlieb, who was not a medical doctor, brought no scientific rigor to his harrowing experiments.

The story of the CIA, Sidney Gottlieb, and LSD has long since passed into American cultural lore, while MK-ULTRA has become a catchphrase widely used as a synonym for governmental abuse. Sidney Gottlieb, meanwhile, has gone down in history as America's Cold War Doctor Evil.

The CIA's mind-control experiments were just beginning to come to light when Frank Church began his work. But no one took on Sidney Gottlieb until the Church Committee.

* * *

The son of Eastern European Jewish immigrants, Gottlieb was born in 1918 in New York. Bullied as a boy for his club foot and stutter (according to *Poisoner in Chief*, Stephen Kinzer's 2019 biography of Gottlieb), he later resented being physically disqualified for military service during World War II.

Gottlieb received a PhD in biochemistry and held posts with both the Agriculture Department and the Food and Drug Administration before joining the CIA in 1951, where he took charge of the Agency's new efforts to develop mind-control drugs.

Shortly after the CIA's founding, Allen Dulles, then a senior CIA official, had become convinced that the Soviet Union had been experimenting with drugs and other techniques to control people's minds or extract secrets. Dulles helped create secret projects, code-named Bluebird and Artichoke, to conduct brutal interrogation experiments on prisoners of war and other "expendables" at black sites in Germany, Japan, and elsewhere.

Dulles tasked top CIA officials Frank Wisner, Richard Helms, and later James Angleton to oversee Bluebird, and these senior managers were among the two dozen or so CIA officers who knew of the existence of Bluebird's successor, MK-ULTRA.

After joining the CIA, Gottlieb began searching for a "truth serum." He and other CIA chemists tested marijuana on themselves, even mixing it in their food, but found it was too weak for use in interrogations. A series of other drugs — cocaine, heroin, and mescaline — were also rejected. Gottlieb finally hit upon LSD, and decided, based on no real evidence, that it was the wonder drug that could allow him to control minds.

In 1953, Gottlieb — supported by Helms, one of the Agency's rising stars — proposed MK-ULTRA, which would focus mainly on LSD as the mind-control drug of choice. Dulles, who by then had become CIA director, approved the program and cut through nearly every established CIA procedure to ensure MK-ULTRA was approved, fully funded, and kept secret even within the Agency.

Throughout the 1950s, Gottlieb and his team drugged an unknown number of people with LSD, often unwittingly, hoping that it would unlock methods to brainwash them. Mental abuse, sensory deprivation, and other forms of torture were used on unwilling victims during MK-ULTRA projects to determine how they would respond under the influence of LSD.

The CIA provided drugs and funding to colleges, military bases, hospitals, and prisons to operate as fronts to test both willing and unwilling subjects. The MK-ULTRA program had 149 "subprojects"; in one subproject 100 people at a mental hospital in Canada were unwittingly drugged. During an experiment at a prison in Lexington, Kentucky, a group of seven addicts coerced into MK-ULTRA were kept high on LSD for 77 consecutive days.

Gottlieb hired former narcotics agent George Hunter White in 1952 to run safe houses in New York City where people drugged with LSD could be secretly observed. White stalked Greenwich Village looking for people to drug with LSD, luring them back to safe houses where they could be monitored. Gottlieb and White later duplicated this model in San Francisco, calling it Operation Midnight Climax.

The true number of those who were killed or suffered severe physical or mental damage from MK-ULTRA is not known. But one infamous case stands out—and gave Frank Church the opening he needed.

* * *

In 1973, President Richard Nixon ousted CIA director Helms. With his longtime protector leaving, Gottlieb decided to retire as well. But before he left, Gottlieb was determined to cover up his many abuses and potential crimes. With the approval of Helms, Gottlieb destroyed most of the files of MK-ULTRA. Gottlieb "came to me and said that he was retiring and that I was retiring, and he thought it would be a good idea if these files were destroyed," Helms later told the Church Committee.

The destruction of the files meant that the names of most of the victims of MK-ULTRA were lost to history. And that made the case of Frank Olson—an Army biowarfare expert, and the one victim of MK-ULTRA whose name was known—even more significant for investigators. With Frank Olson, the Church Committee could put a face to the abuses of the CIA drug program.

Frank Olson knew many of the secrets of the overlapping Army and CIA drug programs; he had attended sessions at CIA black sites where people were fed drugs or tortured to death. But there are indications he was turning against the abusive nature of the drug programs; in 1953, citing stress, he stepped down as acting chief of the Special Operations Division, a joint Army-CIA drug unit at Camp Detrick in Frederick, Maryland.

On November 18, 1953, Olson was among a group of scientists involved in the secret drug program whom Gottlieb invited to a retreat at a cabin near Deep Creek Lake, in western Maryland. During the retreat, Robert Lashbrook, Gottlieb's deputy, offered Cointreau to the scientists—all of them unaware that the French liqueur had been laced with LSD. Olson was unwittingly dosed with approximately 70 micrograms of LSD.

Twenty minutes after Olson and the other scientists drank the Cointreau, Gottlieb informed them they had been drugged with LSD.

Olson made it home to Frederick the next day, but something was clearly wrong. He told his wife that he had "made a terrible mistake," but did not elaborate. Olson returned to work at Camp Detrick the following Monday, but he was agitated and seemed to be in a poor mental condition.

The next day he was still in terrible shape. Vincent Ruwet, who had taken command of the Special Operations Division when Olson stepped down, took Olson to see Gottlieb.

Gottlieb undoubtedly now considered Olson to be a security threat, based on his mental condition and how much he knew. Whether he now began to plot to murder Olson in order to silence him is an open question.

Gottlieb ordered Ruwet and Lashbrook to take Olson to New York to see Dr. Harold Abramson, who worked with the CIA on its mind-control drug programs and knew about MK-ULTRA. Abramson was not a psychiatrist; he could offer no real treatment for Olson. Instead, he was Sidney Gottlieb's medical fixer.

After seeing Abramson and staying overnight in New York, Olson, Ruwet, and Lashbrook flew back to Washington, but Olson's condition worsened. Gottlieb met with them, then told Lashbrook to take Olson back to New York. They went to see Abramson at his home on Long Island, spent the night at a guest house nearby, then drove back to Manhattan the next day. That night, Lashbrook and Olson checked into the same 10th-floor room in the Statler Hotel. Olson plunged to his death from the hotel-room window at 2:25 a.m. on Saturday, November 28. It was Thanksgiving weekend.

Whether Olson committed suicide or was pushed by someone from the CIA, eager to silence a potential whistleblower, has never been determined. The CIA hushed the whole thing up and lied to Olson's family about what had happened. In an interview, Eric Olson, Frank's son, said he is still convinced his father was murdered to silence him and cover up the CIA's crimes. "He was extracted from this family," said Eric Olson. "He was extracted to New York. He was essentially kidnapped, and then he was thrown out the window. A suicide makes no sense."

Despite Olson's death, Gottlieb and the CIA continued experimenting with LSD, and MK-ULTRA wasn't scaled back until 1963, following a damning but secret report by the CIA's Inspector General. The agency didn't end all of its LSD experiments until 1967.

Gottlieb's destruction of the MK-ULTRA files made future investigations of the program far more difficult. After he retired, Gottlieb and his wife left the United States for extended post-retirement travel, and were in India when the Church Committee was created in 1975. Gottlieb was clearly trying to hide from his past, and he might have eluded the Church Committee if not for the earlier work of the Rockefeller Commission.

*   *   *

The Rockefeller Commission was deeply flawed and suppressed many of its most explosive findings; under pressure from the White House, it eliminated the chapter on the CIA's assassination plots from its final report, and then kept its findings on the NSA secret.

But the commission's final report still had some surprisingly strong elements, including an examination of Operation Chaos, the CIA's domestic spying program that had been disclosed in Sy Hersh's December 1974 story in the *New York Times*, and the CIA's illegal mail opening program. But perhaps the Rockefeller Commission's biggest revelation was the existence of the CIA mind-control drug program.

Despite the best efforts of Vice President Nelson Rockefeller, who tried to steer the committee away from sensitive topics, the commission found out about the drug program; without being asked, CIA director William Colby told the commission about the CIA's deadly experiments with LSD.

The Rockefeller Commission's final report included a description of the drug program that was vague and brief, and only took up about two pages, but it was long enough to include a bare bones description of the events surrounding the death of Frank Olson in New York:

"On one occasion during the early phases of this program [in 1953] LSD was administered to an employee of the Department of the Army without his knowledge while he was attending a meeting with CIA personnel working on the drug project," the Rockefeller Commission's final report stated. "Prior to receiving the LSD, the subject had participated in discussions where the testing of such substances on unsuspecting subjects was agreed to in principle. However, this individual was not made aware that he had been given LSD until about 20 minutes after it had been administered.

He developed serious side effects and was sent to New York with a CIA escort for psychiatric treatment. Several days later, he jumped from a tenth-floor window of his room and died as a result."

The Rockefeller Commission report did not name Olson or Sidney Gottlieb or anyone else associated with the program. It did not even reveal the name of the program, MK-ULTRA. It also included errors: Olson did not, for example, receive psychiatric treatment in New York. The report explained its failure to provide more details in part by stating that "all persons directly involved in the early phases of the program were either out of the country and not available for interview, or were deceased." (The Rockefeller Commission had not gotten Sidney Gottlieb to return to the United States to talk.)

In July 1975, a month after the Rockefeller Commission report was released, the Olson family went public. Olson's wife and children realized that the unidentified Department of the Army employee who fell to his death in New York mentioned in the report had to be Frank Olson.

In a July 9 interview with Sy Hersh, followed the next day by a press conference, the Olson family expressed bitterness that the CIA had left them in the dark for so long. A family statement, quoted in Hersh's story, said that "since 1953, we have struggled to understand Frank Olson's death as an inexplicable 'suicide.' At the time he died, Frank Olson's wife was 38 years old, his eldest son was nine years old, his daughter seven and his youngest son five. Now, 22 years later, we learn that this death was the result of CIA negligence and illegality on a scale difficult to contemplate.

"Suddenly, we learn that Alice Olson's being left in early adulthood to raise a family alone, her children left to grow up without a father—we learn that these deprivations were not necessary. And we suddenly learn that for 22 years we were lied to, led to believe that Frank Olson had a fatal nervous breakdown. Thus, Frank Olson's children grew up under a double shadow, the shadow of their father's suicide and the shadowy inexplicability of that act."

Within days, public outrage over the Frank Olson case grew so intense that President Ford invited the Olson family to the Oval Office. White House press secretary Ron Nessen told reporters later that day that Ford had asked to meet the family to express his sympathy and to apologize to them on behalf of the government.

President Gerald Ford with Alice Olson, the widow of Frank Olson, upon her family's visit to the Oval Office.

The White House also said Ford had promised to provide the Olsons with access to information on the case, and had asked Attorney General Edward Levi to meet with the family's lawyers to discuss "the claims they wish to assert against the CIA." A few days later, the Olsons went to CIA headquarters to meet with CIA director Colby, who gave them a limited number of documents related to the case.

* * *

The Church Committee was eager to conduct a more aggressive investigation of Sidney Gottlieb and MK-ULTRA than the Rockefeller Commission had done, and refused to accept the excuse that Gottlieb was traveling overseas. The committee demanded that he show up for questioning.

Frank Church had agreed to take Gottlieb's name out of the report on the CIA's plots to assassinate foreign leaders, in order to avoid a lengthy lawsuit that would delay the report's publication. But Church refused to withhold Gottlieb's name from the section of its final report on MK-ULTRA, so Gottlieb was in the odd position of being named in one part of the committee's investigation but not in another. The press ignored his pseudonym and named Gottlieb in connection with Church Committee's investigations of both the assassination plots and MK-ULTRA.

At Lenzner's urging, Gottlieb agreed to testify before the Church Committee—but only in exchange for legal immunity from prosecution. The fact that the CIA had destroyed most of the records of MK-ULTRA made it critical for the Church Committee to question him, so Church agreed to give Gottlieb immunity in return for his testimony.

That would lead to a face-off between Gottlieb and Elliot Maxwell, a young Church Committee staffer assigned to deal with the CIA scientist only when no one else was available.

Maxwell had been a third-year student at Yale Law School when he was recruited to join the committee in February 1975. He had written a law-review article questioning the constitutionality of the way in which the CIA was funded; quoted in the *New York Times*, the piece attracted attention in Washington just as the Church Committee was hiring. Maxwell was first assigned to study the legal authorities of the CIA and other intelligence agencies, picking up where his law-review article left off. He scrutinized the CIA's budget, and heard indirectly that experts at the Office of Management and Budget were impressed with his budget analysis.

Maxwell later became a kind of utility player for the committee, handling jobs not taken by anyone else. But by far his most daunting task was to interview Sidney Gottlieb and investigate MK-ULTRA. What made the job even more complicated was that, to question Gottlieb, Maxwell had to go up against Terry Lenzner.

"Terry was a pit bull, his style was very aggressive, and his suspicions of people were legion," recalled Maxwell. "He was going to protect his guy." Lenzner fought every step of the way to limit Maxwell's questioning of Gottlieb.

When Maxwell finally sat down and faced Gottlieb to take his deposition, he found it difficult to believe the unassuming man before him could have committed such heinous acts.

"You had a sense of a guy who was thoughtful and smart, and who didn't come across as arrogant or contemptuous, which made it all the more confusing to think about what happened," recalled Maxwell. "I didn't have the sense that I was in the presence of unbridled evil. I think he believed that he had made difficult

Sidney Gottlieb (left), who ran the CIA's MK-ULTRA LSD program and supplied poisons for assassinations, with his flamboyant lawyer, Terry Lenzner
(right).

choices. I found him to be a complicated character." Gottlieb per-
sonified the concept of "the banality of evil," a phrase Hannah
Arendt had coined in writing about the trial of Nazi war criminal
Adolf Eichmann, who came across as a bland bureaucrat in his
1961 trial in Israel.

When Gottlieb testified before the full Church Committee in
closed session, he was shaken when Senator Richard Schweiker
showed him a CIA memo and asked him to comment on it. Elliot
Maxwell had unearthed the memo from the CIA's files; it was from
a CIA organization euphemistically named the "Health Alteration
Committee."

Gottlieb panicked, and told Lenzner that he needed a break.
The committee took a recess, and Lenzner and Gottlieb went to a
small room nearby to talk.

Gottlieb began to stretch, and do tai chi, to try to relax. He told
Lenzner that the memo Schweiker had shown him bothered him so
much because it related to an assassination plot that had been

successful, but which had not been discovered by the Church Committee during its investigation of the CIA's assassination plots. Gottlieb had sent a scarf infected with tuberculosis to an Iraqi colonel, he revealed to Lenzner. The colonel wore it — and died two weeks later.

Lenzner helped Gottlieb figure out how to avoid revealing the truth in his testimony. When the hearing resumed, Schweiker did not know enough to cut through Gottlieb's evasions. Lenzner thus had helped his client cover up a murder. The truth wasn't revealed until Lenzner published his memoir in 2015.

Maxwell also deposed former CIA director Helms, Gottlieb's mentor during MK-ULTRA. "Helms was one of these witnesses where, if you asked about a specific action or operation, his response would be, do you have any paper that connects me to that?" recalled Maxwell. "Then if you kept pressing, he would say I don't remember that. After I questioned him, someone told me that Helms said that if he thought some kid would have the right to question him under oath, he wouldn't have believed it."

Maxwell wrote the section of the Church Committee's final report dealing with Olson, Gottlieb, and MK-ULTRA. In many ways, the work was an extension of his earlier study of the CIA's legal grounding. How did Agency officials decide that drugging American citizens without their knowledge was both legal and within the mandate of the CIA? Gottlieb's long-running drug programs revealed "a failure of the CIA's leadership to pay adequate attention to the rights of individuals," wrote Maxwell in the committee's final report.

> Though it was known that the testing was dangerous, the lives of subjects were placed in jeopardy and their rights were ignored during the ten years of testing which followed Dr. Olson's death. Although it was clear that the laws of the United States were being violated, the testing continued. While the individuals involved in the Olson experiment were admonished by the director, at the same time they were also told that they were not being reprimanded, and that their bad judgment would not be made part of their personnel records. When the covert testing project was terminated in 1963, none of the individuals involved were subject to any disciplinary action.

With its disclosures, the Church Committee helped open the floodgates on MK-ULTRA, leading to new investigations and a steady flow of new information about the secret government LSD and interrogation experiments. Maxwell cooperated with staffers working for Senator Ted Kennedy, who used a health subcommittee that he chaired to hold hearings in which the Olson family testified in September 1975; two years later, Kennedy conducted a much larger investigation into the CIA's human drug-testing programs.

Meanwhile, other researchers and reporters continued to dig. John Marks was a former foreign-service officer and Senate staffer who was best known as the co-author of former CIA staffer Victor Marchetti's 1974 book, *The CIA and the Cult of Intelligence*, a best-seller that the CIA went to court to censor. In 1977, Marks filed a Freedom of Information Act request with the CIA for any remaining documents related to MK-ULTRA, and a responsive CIA archivist uncovered thousands of pages of expense reports in a CIA warehouse that identified many of MK-ULTRA's programs. Those documents formed the basis for Marks's 1979 book, *The Search for the Manchurian Candidate*.

In 1976, the Olson family received $750,000 in compensation through a private bill in Congress; President Ford had recommended $1.25 million, but Congress reduced the total payment.

Eric Olson still doesn't believe the truth about what happened to his father has ever come out. "This story of my father's murder is not tellable by an American, because Cold War triumphalism always stands in the way."

Elliot Maxwell also doesn't feel like he ever figured out all of the mysteries of Sidney Gottlieb and MK-ULTRA. As the only Church Committee staffer assigned to investigate MK-ULTRA, and the only one assigned to write the committee's report on the program, Maxwell was stretched too thin to dig as much as he would have liked. The Church Committee's focus on the CIA's assassination plots to kill foreign leaders left fewer staff and resources for investigating other CIA programs.

"I never felt that I understood sufficiently what happened in MK-ULTRA," Maxwell said. "I'm sure I could have learned more with more time and help.

"But I thought the big lessons could be learned pretty easily," he added. "The destruction of documents, the unwitting testing of people—you don't have to know too much more than that to understand that they engaged in a process in which they didn't give a shit about these people."

The Church Committee's domestic task force was about to discover another set of horrors at the FBI as well.

CHAPTER 22

"The man who made a police state out of America"

AN FBI AGENT ushered Mark Gitenstein into a vacant office in the Justice Department's headquarters building, then left him alone. As the agent walked out, Gitenstein scanned the room. There was a small table and a chair, but no desk. The office seemed like it had been shuttered for years.

But along the room's outer wall sat a line of aging file cabinets. Gitenstein walked over and pulled open one cabinet, then another. He realized with a jolt that the file cabinets held the long-rumored secret files of J. Edgar Hoover. He had finally found the Federal Bureau of Investigation's holy grail.

It was 1975, and Mark Gitenstein was a young lawyer, still in his 20s, and a newly hired staffer on the Church Committee. A reporter had given him a tip that led him on a journey to find Hoover's secret files. Now, with a push from Senator Walter Mondale—a leading member of the Church Committee—the FBI had finally agreed to reveal their secret hiding place to Gitenstein.

Gitenstein soon discovered that there were actually two separate sets of Hoover files. The first was entitled "Official and Confidential," and the second was "Personal and Confidential." The "Official and Confidential" files appeared to be complete, but most of the "Personal and Confidential" files were missing. Arranged alphabetically, the "Personal and Confidential" files only included volumes

"A" through "C." It seemed to Gitenstein that someone had tried to get rid of the Personal and Confidential files in a hurry — possibly just after J. Edgar Hoover's death in 1972 — but hadn't finished the job.

As Gitenstein read, he could understand why they were never supposed to see the light of day. The "Personal and Confidential" files that remained were explosive. Under "B," Gitenstein discovered a memo about "black bag jobs" — the FBI's nickname for illegal wiretaps and break-ins.

In order to find out what happened to the rest of Hoover's files, Gitenstein and Mary DeOreo, another Church Committee staffer, paid a visit to Hoover's longtime secretary, Helen Gandy, at her Washington home. Gandy had worked for Hoover beginning in 1918, and was widely known to have been the guardian of all of Hoover's secrets. But she refused to give Gitenstein and DeOreo any straight answers about the fate of Hoover's missing files. "We got nothing from her," DeOreo recalled. "She is there serving us tea, acting like she is your dear great-aunt. And we got nothing."

The truth was that Gandy had destroyed Hoover's personal files. Gandy later testified before a House committee that she had taken Hoover's personal files home and "tore them up, put them in boxes, and they were taken away to be shredded."

DeOreo faced other obstacles when she reviewed the Hoover files, perhaps because she was a woman. While reading through the "Official and Confidential" files at FBI headquarters, DeOreo came across an envelope that had been placed amid the files. When she opened it, she saw with a shudder that it was filled with extremely graphic photographs from the autopsy of Robert F. Kennedy. She looked over at the FBI agent assigned to monitor her. DeOreo could tell that he had been "waiting for me to find that."

Despite the obstacles, DeOreo and Gitenstein continued to dig. Gradually, Gitenstein grew more and more excited as he read through the surviving files. They offered the Church Committee a road map for its investigation of the domestic abuses of the FBI — just as the Family Jewels had given the committee a path to follow in its investigation of the CIA.

*   *   *

The Church Committee was originally created to investigate the CIA, but almost immediately it became obvious that its investigation had to go far beyond the Agency. It couldn't just be "the CIA committee," as some wanted to call it. Any serious investigation of the government's corruption, criminality, and violations of the rights of American citizens would have to include the FBI.

The FBI had avoided any real oversight for much longer than the CIA. Even disclosures in the press in the early 1970s about the FBI's widespread domestic abuses targeting the anti-war movement during the Vietnam War hadn't been enough to get Congress to investigate the Bureau. Hoover, the FBI's first and only director, had run the Bureau since 1924 — before it was even called the FBI — and he was simply too popular, too well-connected, too powerful, too intimidating, and too frightening. Rarely did members of Congress or presidents confront him.

To be sure, the FBI was part of the Justice Department, and the attorney general was nominally Hoover's boss. But the FBI was Hoover's private fiefdom. Eight presidents and 16 attorneys general came and went while Hoover was FBI director; for nearly 50 years, J. Edgar Hoover was a specter hanging over Washington, and politicians criticized him only in hushed tones.

It would be up to the Church Committee to finally conduct the first real investigation of the FBI in its history. And that could happen only because J. Edgar Hoover was finally dead.

Frank Church had long been skeptical of J. Edgar Hoover, even at the peak of his power in the 1950s, when Hoover's zealous anti-Communism helped cement his alliances throughout Washington's political establishment. In 1958, Bryce Nelson, then a college intern and later an aide in Frank Church's Senate office, was driving through downtown Washington with Church when they passed the FBI's headquarters. Church pointed at the FBI's offices and said sardonically, "There's J. Edgar Hoover's lair — the man who made a police state out of America."

"Church would criticize Hoover in private," said Nelson in an interview. "Church was really quite a radical person for the age, especially given his geographic background. He was more radical and antiestablishment than he let on. He would say that a lot of senators just wanted approval from Hoover, to help them deal with right-wing voters. But I don't think he ever was public about his feelings about Hoover" in the late 1950s or early 1960s, added Nelson.

Church kept his criticism of Hoover quiet for years and didn't try to publicly challenge Hoover's personal control over the FBI. Hoover had carefully cultivated close relationships with many of the most influential leaders in Congress, making it difficult for a lone senator like Church to raise questions about Hoover or his FBI. Church wasn't willing to spend his hard-won political capital on a fight with Hoover that he knew he couldn't win.

During Church's first few years in the Senate, he had protected his political flank not only by avoiding direct conflicts with the FBI, but also by dealing carefully — almost subserviently — with Hoover himself.

In 1961, just three years after he offered his biting criticism of Hoover privately to Bryce Nelson, Church sent a letter to Hoover and attached an article from the Twin Falls (Idaho) *Times-News* that described a local meeting in which a tape recording had been played of Ronald Reagan charging that Communists were infiltrating all phases of the government. (Reagan was then a Hollywood celebrity, just starting to rise in conservative Republican politics.)

In his letter, Church asked Hoover softball questions about Reagan's red-baiting comments. "Do you have any evidence that would support Mr. Reagan's charges as made in this article that Communists are infiltrating all phases of the government? If so, are you in a position to tell me what steps are being taken to remove these persons from any government positions that they may be holding?"

Hoover responded with a letter stating that he welcomed the opportunity to "respond to your questions about the Communist menace. In view of your concern, may I point out that the Communists have tried to infiltrate every part of our society, but they have not achieved substantial success because of our internal security programs; the investigation, arrest and prosecution of a number of Party functionaries; and the rising tide of public opposition to the communist movement."

Church's exchange with Hoover was clearly designed to help Church politically; it provided him with a written record documenting his anti-Communist bona fides for the benefit of conservative Idaho voters. Avoiding any fights with Hoover paid off for Church. Throughout the late 1960s and early 1970s, Church's leading role as an opponent of the Vietnam War did not significantly damage his relationship with the FBI. In June 1972, an FBI internal memo stated rather benignly that "we have enjoyed limited cordial relations with Senator Church in the past."

* * *

Frank Church was hardly alone in Washington in offering Hoover deference in public while denigrating him in private. Presidents dating back to Franklin Roosevelt had been wary of Hoover as well, and most had given him a wide berth, rarely intervening in the way he ran the FBI. Hoover became so intoxicated by his power and status that he began to style his memos to FBI field offices as coming from the "Seat of Government."

Hoover was such a master of Washington bureaucratic in-fighting that he rarely lost turf battles; one of his few major defeats came in the aftermath of World War II, at the hands of President Harry Truman. It was a bitter loss with long-lasting and damaging effects.

Truman distrusted Hoover's power, and unlike other presidents was willing to take on Hoover and rein him in. Despite Hoover's strong opposition, Truman pushed for and won congressional passage of the National Security Act of 1947, which created the CIA and blocked Hoover and the FBI from playing a major role in foreign intelligence. As a result, the FBI had to abandon its extensive operations in Latin America, built up both before and during World War II.

Hoover then bitterly sought revenge against Truman by secretly aiding his Republican opponent, New York governor Thomas Dewey, in the 1948 president campaign. Hoover provided Dewey with FBI files that he thought would boost the Republican; he was shaken when Dewey lost. After Truman finally left office in 1953, Hoover joined with Herbert Brownell, President Eisenhower's new Republican attorney general, in a partisan attack on the former president. Testifying before the Senate, both Hoover and Brownell accused Truman of having ignored FBI reports in 1946 that one of his appointees was suspected of being a Soviet agent.

No subsequent president dared to take on Hoover as forcefully as Truman did. But Hoover also never really got over his defeat in the turf war over the creation of the CIA, and he remained an intractable bureaucratic foe of the Agency for the rest of his career. Hoover's personal hatred of the CIA led to a poisonous relationship between the FBI and CIA, accounting for many of the deep-seated problems in the U.S. intelligence community that the Church Committee later uncovered.

Hoover solidified his relationship with Congress during the early Cold War, when he secretly aided right-wing demagogues on Capitol Hill eager to use anti-Communist red-baiting for political gain. In the late 1940s, Hoover confidentially helped the infamous House Un-American Activities Committee (HUAC) in its anti-Communist witch hunt in Hollywood, which led to actors, screenwriters, and other artists being blacklisted from the movie industry. On the condition that the FBI's cooperation remain secret, Hoover shared raw FBI files with the committee, fueling the witch hunt with unverified reports filled with gossip and inaccurate conclusions.

The FBI also secretly aided Richard Nixon, then a young California Republican congressman, when he helped lead HUAC's investigation of former State Department official Alger Hiss, who had been accused of being a Soviet spy by Whittaker Chambers, a journalist and former Communist spy who had broken with the Communist underground in the United States. Initially, Hoover also helped Senator Joseph McCarthy, who launched his red-baiting witch hunt in 1950, but Hoover later distanced himself from McCarthy as he grew wary of his recklessness.

The FBI's secret channel to Congress insulated Hoover from congressional scrutiny. But Hoover also relied on fear to hold sway over both the White House and Congress — fear among presidents and congressional leaders that Hoover would use the dirt routinely collected by the FBI against any politician who got in his way.

He used that hidden power most effectively against President John F. Kennedy.

* * *

The FBI first spied on Kennedy during World War II, when, as a young Navy officer, Kennedy had an affair with Inga Arvad, a married Danish journalist then working for a newspaper in Washington. Kennedy, the son of the former U.S. ambassador to Great Britain, met Arvad while he was stationed in Washington, at about the same time that the FBI separately heard a rumor that Arvad might be a Nazi agent. It was a specious claim that apparently traced back to a photograph of her with Hitler at the 1936 Olympic Games in Berlin, when she was working for a Danish newspaper.

But gossip about her was enough to get the FBI to start spying on Arvad, and the bureau then intensified the surveillance by wiretapping her trysts with Kennedy, even as it became obvious that she was not a German spy.

When Kennedy won the Democratic presidential nomination in July 1960, FBI officials prepared a memo for Hoover summarizing everything the Bureau had on Kennedy, including the Arvad affair. Hoover's file on President Kennedy and his brother, Attorney General Robert F. Kennedy, grew after the FBI uncovered the CIA scheme to work with the Mafia to kill Castro — which in turn led the FBI to discover the connection between President Kennedy and Judith Campbell.

Hoover's complex network of political alliances, along with the fear he engendered, helped to keep him in power throughout his life. He was able to survive periodic disclosures in the press about the FBI's abuses, as well as rumors about his own personal life, particularly whether the never-married Hoover — who persecuted gays in government for decades — might be homosexual himself. (Clyde Tolson, his longtime deputy, was his constant companion.) Hoover's connections continued to insulate him into the early 1970s, even after the rise of the anti-war and civil rights movements and the 1960s cultural revolution had made him look like a relic from the past.

Hoover's power was tested in March 1971, when anti-war dissidents broke into an FBI office in Media, Pennsylvania, and seized secret documents revealing the existence of covert FBI programs to harass, disrupt, and spy on anti-war groups. Calling themselves the Citizen's Commission to Investigate the FBI, the group mailed selected documents to two liberal members of Congress and several reporters. But Hoover's influence over Congress was still so strong that, immediately after receiving the documents in the mail, both congressmen — Senator George McGovern, a South Dakota Democrat, and Representative Parren Mitchell, a Democrat from Maryland — returned the documents to the FBI. (A month earlier, McGovern, who was then positioning himself for a presidential run in 1972, had also declined to do anything with the Pentagon Papers when he was approached by whistleblower Daniel Ellsberg.)

Meanwhile, Hoover's influence with the press remained powerful as well. *Washington Post* reporter Betty Medsger had received some of the stolen FBI documents by mail, but publisher Katherine

Graham initially opposed the publication of a story based on them, leading to a hurried internal debate by the paper's top management. The debate at the *Post* took place more than a year before the Watergate scandal, and the *Post* was not yet the aggressive institution committed to high-risk investigative reporting that it later became.

After a day of deliberation, Graham was persuaded by *Post* executive editor Ben Bradlee to publish a story based on the documents. "If it hadn't been for Bradlee, I don't think Graham would have published the story," Medsger said in an interview. "I am absolutely certain of that." But even after the *Post* and others finally reported on the FBI documents, Congress did not hold any hearings or investigate the new evidence of the FBI's domestic abuses. Without any investigation by Congress and only limited coverage in the press, the story uncovered by the Media, Pennsylvania, burglars largely faded away. It briefly resurfaced in December 1973, when NBC News reporter Carl Stern obtained additional FBI documents about the Bureau's domestic abuses. But his story was overwhelmed by the ongoing Watergate scandal.

Hoover remained FBI director until the day he died on May 2, 1972. His power was on display even in death: Congress voted to have his body lie in state in the Capitol Rotunda, an honor granted to only 21 others before him, including presidents. Chief Justice Warren Burger gave a eulogy that perhaps inadvertently laid bare the FBI's cult of personality. Burger said that Hoover's FBI had become an "institution that is, in a very real sense, the lengthened shadow of a man."

After Hoover's death, President Nixon passed over FBI insiders and chose L. Patrick Gray, a Nixon loyalist who had served on Nixon's staff when he was vice president, to become the FBI's acting director. That meant the FBI was being run by a Nixon lackey when the Watergate burglars were arrested in June 1972. Mark Felt, one of the FBI insiders passed over by Nixon when Hoover died, became Deep Throat, the legendary anonymous source for the *Washington Post* during Watergate.

Under constant pressure from the Nixon White House to support the Watergate cover-up, Gray collaborated by undermining the FBI's Watergate investigation. He kept the White House informed of virtually every move that FBI agents were making in the case, and agreed to White House orders to personally destroy documents from the safe of Watergate figure E. Howard Hunt. Gray was forced to resign in 1973 after his betrayal of the FBI came to light. Nixon was brought down by Watergate a year later.

By 1975, Hoover's death, the Watergate scandal, and Nixon's resignation all combined to provide an opening for the newly created Church Committee to investigate the FBI.

*   *   *

Mark Gitenstein and the domestic task force operated separately from the bulk of the Church Committee; they were not drawn into the committee's early investigation of the CIA assassination plots against foreign leaders, and instead kept their focus on the FBI. They considered Senator Walter Mondale, the head of the domestic task force, to be their boss, and rarely saw Church. "I dealt with Mondale," recalled Gitenstein (who went on to become a longtime aide and adviser to Joe Biden). "I hardly ever dealt with Church. Church wasn't really interested in the FBI and the domestic side."

"I had almost no contact with Church," added Barbara Banoff, who led the Church Committee's investigation of COINTELPRO, the FBI program to harass and disrupt civil-rights and anti-war groups in the 1960s.

Church's decision to turn over the investigation of the FBI to Mondale led to a split within the Church Committee staff, between those who were most loyal to Church and those who were aligned with Mondale. The Mondale loyalists — primarily those involved with the FBI investigation and the domestic task force — became quietly but harshly critical of Church, and felt that Mondale had not received enough credit for his leadership, particularly during the committee's final stages. That was when the Church Committee finally held hearings on the FBI, after its hearings on the CIA.

"I had a low opinion of Frank Church," recalls Banoff. She complained that Church tried to take credit for the FBI investigation even though Mondale was in charge of it. "I think he [Church] was basically a pompous, pious hypocrite."

A sense that they were a team apart from the rest of the Church Committee would help fuel the domestic task force's drive to uncover some of the worst abuses in the history of the FBI. The task force's most historic achievement was its investigation of the FBI's long-running harassment, surveillance, and abuse of the Reverend Martin Luther King Jr.

CHAPTER 23

"No holds were barred"

WHILE THE CHURCH Committee's inquiry into the CIA was highlighted by disclosures about the Agency's efforts to assassinate Castro, the committee's investigation of the FBI was headlined by revelations about the FBI's long campaign to spy on and discredit the Reverend Martin Luther King Jr. The FBI's persecution of King was arguably the most infamous episode in the Bureau's history — an abuse of such historic proportions that the FBI is still struggling with its legacy more than 50 years later.

The Church Committee's investigation brought to light for the first time the full scope of the FBI's abusive campaign of spying and unrelenting harassment of King. "Martin Luther King, Jr. was the target of an intensive campaign by the Federal Bureau of Investigation to 'neutralize' him as an effective civil rights leader," the Church Committee stated in the opening lines of its case study of the FBI and King. "In the words of the man in charge of the FBI's 'war' against Dr. King" [William Sullivan, who ran the FBI's intelligence division and testified before the committee], "No holds were barred. We have used (similar) techniques against Soviet agents. (The same methods were) brought home against any organization against which we were targeted. We did not differentiate. This is a rough, tough business."

These revelations forced a long-overdue reckoning at the FBI, and they constituted one of the Church Committee's greatest achievements. But the committee's FBI-King investigation might never have happened without Mike Epstein.

Epstein was one of the first Church Committee staffers assigned to the domestic task force and its investigation of the FBI, and he came to the assignment with invaluable knowledge and experience.

Born in New Bedford, Massachusetts, Epstein was the son of a local newspaper reporter, and credited his exposure to his father's work covering courts in New Bedford for his interest in the law. After law school at Boston University, Epstein was part of the flood of young lawyers and other staffers from Massachusetts who joined the Kennedy Administration. He went to work for the Justice Department in 1962 as a prosecuting attorney and special assistant to Attorney General Robert Kennedy.

During his years working for Kennedy at the Justice Department, Epstein heard bits and pieces about how the FBI had wiretapped King. He was convinced that there was a major scandal behind the office gossip, and he began to investigate the case as soon as he joined the Church Committee.

Mark Gitenstein's discovery of the secret Hoover files gave the Church Committee an outline of what it should investigate at the FBI. But Epstein's intense personal interest in unraveling the story behind the FBI's campaign against King helped the Church Committee focus on a specific case that could illustrate the broader pattern of abuses the committee uncovered at the FBI.

John Elliff, the chief of the Church Committee's domestic task force, said that Epstein started working on the King case even before the rest of the committee staff was hired. "He had the personal experience from his work in the '60s in the Justice Department... He had come up with the document request...I didn't assign him that. He was already doing that."

Epstein's inside knowledge of how the Justice Department of the early 1960s worked quickly paid off; he began to develop a network of insider sources from both the FBI and the Justice Department who guided his investigation. Declassified FBI documents show that the FBI officials assigned in 1975 to monitor the Church Committee and its investigation of the FBI were shaken by how much Epstein quickly began finding out about the King case. They struggled to keep up with Epstein, at one point discovering that he had been conducting a series of informal and damning interviews with former FBI agents without the Bureau's knowledge. Impressively, Epstein managed to stay ahead of his FBI minders as he was ripping open the truth about the ugliest chapter in the FBI's history.

*　*　*

Like everything else at the FBI, J. Edgar Hoover was personally responsible for the Bureau's harassment and abuse of Martin Luther King. Hoover's lifelong paranoia about Communism, combined with his deep racial prejudice, created his poisonous obsession with trying to destroy King, just as King was emerging as the most important leader of the Civil Rights Movement.

Hoover justified his campaign against King by claiming that he had Communist ties. One of King's closest associates, Stanley Levison, had been a leading member of the Communist Party in New York before joining the Civil Rights Movement, while Jack O'Dell, a King aide, had also been in the Party. Proving that Levison and O'Dell had not relinquished those ties became Hoover's obsession. The FBI director's racist views, meanwhile, prevented him from seeing any reason for the rise of the Civil Rights Movement other than as a Russian plot to sabotage America.

Hoover's hatred of King only grew after King publicly criticized the FBI in a November 1962 interview with the *New York Times*, complaining that FBI agents had sided with segregationists and local police during a civil rights campaign in Albany, Georgia, and had failed to adequately investigate beatings and other acts of intimidation against civil rights activists.

"One of the great problems we face with the FBI in the South is that the agents are white Southerners who have been influenced by the mores of the community," King said in the *Times* interview. "To maintain their status, they have to be friendly with the local police and people who are promoting segregation."

King's comments infuriated Hoover, and hardened Hoover's belief that he was a Communist puppet. Hoover became more determined than ever to destroy the civil-rights leader. Hoover believed that "King was an instrument of the Communist party, and he wanted it proved that King had a relationship with the Soviet bloc," William Sullivan later wrote in his memoir. Hoover was irate when Sullivan's intelligence division reported that there was no evidence that King or his organization were under Communist influence.

Hoover first began monitoring King in the late 1950s, after King rose to prominence as the leader of the Montgomery, Alabama, bus-boycott campaign. But Hoover launched his most intense and poisonous campaign targeting King during the Kennedy Administration, when Hoover began wiretapping King—with the knowledge of President Kennedy and the approval of Attorney General Robert Kennedy.

* * *

The story of how Hoover pressured the Kennedys into going along with his secret campaign against the civil-rights leader ultimately leads back to the CIA's efforts to use the Mafia to kill Castro. After the FBI had uncovered the CIA-Mafia scheme and the connections among President Kennedy, Judith Campbell, Sam Giancana, and Johnny Rosselli, Hoover almost certainly used that information against both the president and his brother, the attorney general—converting his knowledge into power over them, and ensuring that they would go along with his schemes against King.

In a private meeting with President Kennedy at the White House on March 22, 1962, Hoover almost certainly told Kennedy what he had learned about the CIA-Mafia scheme, as well as Kennedy's connection to Judith Campbell. The evidence comes in part from an FBI memo written two days earlier: in the March 20 memo, FBI assistant director Courtney Evans, the Bureau's White House liaison, wrote to FBI assistant director Alan Belmont and included "a restatement of information relating to telephone calls made to President's Secretary [Evelyn Lincoln] from Judith Campbell's Los Angeles residence. This is being submitted as the director may desire to bear this information in mind in connection with his forthcoming appointment with the President. Enclosure: Information has been developed that Judith E. Campbell, a free-lance artist has associated with prominent underworld figures Sam Giancana of Chicago and John Roselli [sic] of Los Angeles...A review of telephone toll calls from Campbell's Los Angeles residence disclosures that on November 7 and 15, 1962, calls were made to Evelyn Lincoln, the president's secretary at the White House. Telephone calls were charged to residence Campbell rented in Palm Springs."

After Hoover told Kennedy how much he knew about his

secrets, it became nearly impossible for the Kennedy Administration to rein in Hoover and the FBI. The following year, Attorney General Robert Kennedy—with whom Hoover had a follow-up meeting after his White House showdown with JFK—agreed to approve a series of FBI wiretaps on King.

There is no conclusive evidence that President Kennedy and his brother went along with Hoover's investigation of King because Hoover was blackmailing the Kennedys. But it does seem clear that the Kennedys feared Hoover's power and didn't want to cross him. "The suspicion was that Hoover had something on everybody, and the Kennedys were just—they were ripe for being blackmailed," observed Church Committee staffer Mary DeOreo. Ultimately, the Kennedys gave in to Hoover's demands to investigate King without really contesting Hoover's claims that Stanley Levison and Jack O'Dell posed a Communist threat in King's inner circle.

Throughout 1962 and 1963, Hoover regularly sent Robert Kennedy FBI reports and memos about Martin Luther King, the Communist Party, and Levison and O'Dell. By mid-1963, Kennedy was growing increasingly concerned about the FBI reports alleging Communist influence over King, not necessarily because he believed the reports, but because he feared that Hoover might leak them to the press and his congressional allies, while also claiming that the Kennedy Administration had ignored them. The Kennedys feared Hoover's ability to wield disinformation and propaganda.

At the time, the Kennedys were trying to craft civil-rights legislation, and believed that if they rejected Hoover's demands for a more aggressive investigation of King, the FBI director would use the FBI's secret reports on Levison and O'Dell to torpedo their civil rights bill. In fact, white Southern leaders were already echoing Hoover, publicly stoking Communist fears about King and threatening to derail congressional action on civil rights. Mississippi governor Ross Barnett testified before the Senate that civil-rights legislation would be part of the "world Communist conspiracy to divide and conquer our country from within."

But neither Hoover nor the Kennedys were prepared for how fast events were to move on civil rights during 1963, transforming King into a historic figure even as the FBI was secretly trying to destroy him.

* * *

In early 1963, King and the Southern Christian Leadership Conference (he was the group's president) launched a nonviolent protest campaign in Birmingham, Alabama. Arrested and imprisoned in April, King wrote his famous "Letter from Birmingham Jail," in which he defended his strategy of nonviolent civil disobedience. "Nonviolent direct action seeks to create such a crisis and foster such a tension that a community which has constantly refused to negotiate is forced to confront the issue," he wrote. "It seeks so to dramatize the issue that it can no longer be ignored."

The protests prompted a vicious response from the Birmingham police, led by the city's infamous police commissioner, Eugene "Bull" Connor. The Birmingham police turned dogs and fire hoses on the demonstrators, and television footage and newspaper photographs of the repression in May 1963 led many white Americans to become more sympathetic to King and his movement.

A month later, in June 1963, Alabama's segregationist governor, George Wallace, personally stood in the doorway to a University of Alabama campus building to block two African-American students from registering for classes, as a federal court had ordered. Television cameras captured Wallace's standoff with Deputy Attorney General Nicholas Katzenbach, who had been sent to enforce the court order, and the obstinacy of Southern white racism was on display nationwide.

Moved to action that night, President Kennedy gave his greatest speech on racial justice when he told the nation in a televised address that he would ask Congress to pass comprehensive civil-rights legislation. "We are confronted primarily with a moral issue," said Kennedy. "It is as old as the scriptures and is as clear as the American Constitution."

On August 28, 1963, King reached his most iconic moment when he led the March on Washington for Jobs and Freedom and gave his "I Have a Dream" speech at the Lincoln Memorial, with one of the most memorable lines in modern American history: "I have a dream that my four little children will one day live in a nation where they will not be judged by the color of their skin but by the content of their character."

King's heroic 1963 campaign vaulted civil rights into an urgent national issue. "In the summer of 1963 a need and a time and a circumstance and the mood of a people came together," King later wrote. But Hoover's FBI only saw that King's rise made him more dangerous.

Just days before King's "I Have a Dream" speech in August, William Sullivan's FBI intelligence division sent Hoover a report concluding that the Communist Party had failed to achieve any significant influence within the civil-rights movement.

Hoover lacerated Sullivan. He responded that "this memo reminds me vividly of those I received when Castro took over Cuba. You contended then that Castro and his cohorts were not Communists and not influenced by Communists. Time alone proved you wrong."

Chastened, Sullivan wrote a follow-up memo to his staff right after King's speech, making it clear that the intelligence division had to satisfy Hoover's increasing demands to aggressively investigate King.

"The Director is correct," Sullivan wrote. "We were completely wrong about believing the evidence was not sufficient to determine some years ago that Fidel Castro was not a communist or under communist influence. In investigating and writing about communism and the American Negro, we had better remember this and profit by the lesson it should teach us. Personally, I believe, in the light of King's powerful demagogic speech yesterday, he stands head and shoulders above all other Negro leaders put together when it comes to influencing great masses of Negroes. We must mark him now, if we have not done so before, as the most dangerous Negro of the future in this nation from the standpoint of communism, the Negro, and national security."

Sullivan later explained that he wrote memos expressing enthusiasm for the campaign against King because he was under constant pressure from Hoover, and that nothing he said would have changed Hoover's mind. "No one, not the Kennedys and certainly not anyone at the bureau, could stop the surveillance and harassment to which King was subjected until his death in 1968," Sullivan wrote in his memoir. "Hundreds of memos were written to Hoover during those years, from all the top men at the bureau, including me, all of us telling Hoover that King was a dangerous menace and that

Hoover was doing the right thing, all of them telling Hoover what he wanted to hear."

* * *

Despite the fact that President Kennedy was now publicly aligned with King on civil rights, Attorney General Robert Kennedy would, before 1963 was over, secretly give his approval for Hoover's surveillance of King.

In July 1963, just a month after President Kennedy's soaring televised speech on civil rights, Bobby Kennedy suggested to his FBI liaison that he was ready to authorize the FBI to wiretap King. Kennedy then waffled, and days later decided against the surveillance.

With Kennedy on the fence, Hoover pushed. Finally, Kennedy gave his approval in October, and the FBI began wiretapping King's home telephone as well as the offices of the Southern Christian Leadership Conference.

Edwin Guthman, Robert Kennedy's press secretary at the Justice Department, told the Church Committee that Kennedy had told him that he approved the wiretaps in October 1963 because "he felt that if he did not do it, Mr. Hoover would move to impede or block the civil rights bill." Guthman also said that Kennedy told him that "he felt that he might as well settle the matter of whether [Levison] did have the influence on King that the FBI contended."

Part of the hidden allure for the Kennedy White House of the FBI's investigation of King was also that Hoover made sure to pass on gossip about King's strategy for the civil rights movement, in addition to the supposed evidence of Communist influence. The FBI would report on meetings between King and his advisers in which they were planning the strategy for the Southern Christian Leadership Conference. "There was a funny kind of quid pro quo going on, which is, okay, you go ahead and you gather the information and at the same time you share it. Whatever you are getting, you share it. That was one of the reasons that I think that Hoover stayed untouched for so long," observed former Church Committee staffer DeOreo.

But not everyone in government was taken in by Hoover. Burke Marshall, who led the Civil Rights Division of the Justice Department in the Kennedy Administration (and who had recommended Fritz Schwarz to be the Church Committee's chief counsel) told the

Church Committee that the FBI reports were "of no use — it was stupid information. I was in touch with [King] all the time." King would tell Marshall "all kinds of information that went way beyond what was reported by the bureau."

But that didn't stop Hoover and the FBI.

* * *

On December 23, 1963 — a month after President Kennedy's assassination — William Sullivan led a nine-hour meeting at FBI headquarters to plot a new, more aggressive anti-King strategy. The FBI was now moving far beyond simply wiretapping King. It was launching a full-fledged campaign to harass, discredit, and destroy King. That effort continued until King was assassinated in 1968.

For a start, the FBI supplemented the telephone wiretaps that had been authorized by Robert Kennedy with hidden microphones in King's hotel rooms whenever he traveled, beginning in January 1964 with King's room at the Willard Hotel in Washington. The constant electronic surveillance provided the FBI with evidence of King's extramarital affairs, which changed the focus of the FBI investigation. The FBI lost interest in trying to prove King's nonexistent communist ties, and now bore down on his personal life. A Justice Department review later concluded that "the purposes behind [the FBI's long investigation of King] became twisted."

Sullivan told the Church Committee that the FBI shifted to a more aggressive strategy against King, one that focused on destroying his personal reputation, because that was "Mr. Hoover's policy." Asked whether he or any other FBI officials objected to these tactics, Sullivan said, "Not to my recollection. I was not ready at that time to collide with him. Everybody in the division went right along with Hoover's policy. I do not recall anybody ever raising a question...Never once did I hear anybody, including myself, raise the question, is this course of action which we have agreed upon lawful, is it legal, is it ethical or moral? We never gave any thought to this realm of reasoning."

A week after Sullivan's conference meeting to plot King's destruction, King was named *Time* magazine's Man of the Year for 1963, angering Hoover.

In January 1964, just days after the FBI had installed microphones in one of King's hotel rooms for the first time, Sullivan wrote a memo suggesting that the FBI would soon be able to destroy King. Sullivan recommended that the FBI engineer King's replacement with a more malleable "national Negro leader."

"It should be clear to all of us that Martin Luther King must, at some propitious point in the future, be revealed to the people of this country and to his Negro followers as being what he actually is — a fraud, demagogue and scoundrel," Sullivan wrote. "When the true facts concerning his activities are presented, such should be enough, if handled properly, to take him off his pedestal and to reduce him completely in influence."

Once King was out of the way, Sullivan recommended that the FBI arrange for his successor to be Samuel Pierce, an African-American lawyer who later became Secretary of Housing and Urban Development in the Reagan Administration. Sullivan included Pierce's biography with his memo. Pierce told the Church Committee that he was never contacted by the FBI about its replacement plans. Pierce was not identified by name by the Church Committee, after Church and the committee members concluded that it would be unfair to identify him since he had not been part of the FBI's plotting. Pierce's name surfaced only later; Sullivan named him in his memoir.

After he entered office following John Kennedy's assassination, President Lyndon Johnson became convinced that the FBI's allegations that King was under communist influence, still the official justification for the FBI's investigation of King, had no real basis. But Johnson allowed the FBI to continue to target King, even after the Bureau revealed to one of the president's top aides in January 1964 that the probe had begun to focus on King's personal life. FBI officials showed LBJ aide Walter Jenkins a memo summarizing the contents of the first few tape recordings from King's hotel rooms. The FBI also shared the same material with Robert Kennedy in March 1964, in order "to remove all doubt from the Attorney General's mind as to the type of person King is." (Robert Kennedy remained attorney general under Johnson after his brother's assassination, until September 1964, when he resigned to run for the Senate from New York.)

Johnson didn't stop Hoover from continuing to spy on King. He viewed information as power, and so Johnson wanted to know everything the FBI had on both his friends and his enemies.

Throughout his presidency, Johnson repeatedly and illegally used the FBI to spy on a wide range of domestic targets of his choosing; he wasn't about to rein in J. Edgar Hoover when the director was proving so useful. And, like the Kennedys, Johnson wanted to make sure he knew everything about King, in particular, while he was pushing civil-rights legislation.

Johnson signed the landmark Civil Rights Act of 1964 into law on July 2, 1964, during a White House ceremony with King standing right behind him—even though the president knew the FBI was spying on King and trying to discredit him at the time.

Johnson went along with the FBI campaign against King because he was "very concerned that his embracing the civil rights movement and of Martin Luther King personally would not backfire politically," Bill Moyers, who served as Johnson's White House press secretary, later told the Church Committee. "He didn't want to have a Southern racist senator produce something that would be politically embarrassing to the President and to the civil rights movement. We had lots of conversations about that. Johnson, as everybody knows, bordered on paranoia about his enemies or about being trapped by other people's activities over which he had no responsibility."

In October 1964, King was awarded the Nobel Peace Prize—once again infuriating Hoover, who responded by escalating his public attacks on King. He told a group of women reporters in Washington that King was "the most notorious liar in the country."

Sullivan sought to placate Hoover by ordering up what amounted to a highlight reel of recordings from King's hotel rooms, providing graphic audio evidence of his extramarital affairs. On November 21, Sullivan personally prepared a package containing the recordings, along with an anonymous letter. Sullivan then arranged for an FBI agent to fly to Miami with the package and mail it to King in Atlanta with no return address.

The letter and tape recordings were designed to persuade King to commit suicide. "King, there is only one thing left for you to do," the letter stated. "You know what it is. You have just 34 days in which to do it. There is but one way out for you."

The package was set aside, unopened, when it arrived at King's office, and King had still not seen it when he met with Hoover in Washington on December 1 in a bid to make peace with the FBI director. King then traveled to Oslo to deliver his Nobel-acceptance speech on December 10. It wasn't until January 1965 that the black-mail package reached King's wife, and King made the painful realization that the FBI's campaign against him had hit a dangerous new low.

Andrew Young, a King aide at the time, told the Church Committee that "the disturbing thing to Martin was that he felt somebody was trying to get him to commit suicide, and because it was a tape of a meeting in Washington and the postmark was from Florida, we assumed nobody had the capacity to do that other than the Federal Bureau of Investigation."

*   *   *

With his home and office phones tapped, microphones installed in his hotel rooms, and FBI agents conducting physical surveillance, King's life was under constant FBI scrutiny. But spying on King was just part of the FBI's multiyear campaign to discredit King and cut him off from financial support.

FBI officials regularly sought out hand-picked journalists to smear King, while they also tried to stop colleges from granting honorary degrees to King by meeting privately with campus officials to pass on dirt. Any major organization that made contributions to King and the Southern Christian Leadership Conference would also get visits from FBI officials, who would use their smear tactics to cut off King's funding. After he briefed one top official at a major religious group, Sullivan proudly reported that the official had assured him King would never again receive "one single dollar" from his organization.

Andrew Young, King's aide, told the Church Committee that FBI agents would spread lies with donors, telling them that King had a secret Swiss bank account, and that he had taken funds earmarked for the March on Washington for his personal use.

The Church Committee concluded that "the FBI's discrediting programs" had an "unquestionable" impact on the civil rights movement. "The material stayed in the political bloodstream all the way through to the time of Dr. King's death, and even after," Harry Wachtel, one of King's legal counsels, told the committee.

The FBI's heavy-handed tactics were not always successful. When the FBI found out that King was planning to travel to Rome, where he would be granted an audience with Pope Paul VI, an FBI official hurriedly met with New York archbishop Francis Spellman and asked him to intervene with the Vatican to block the meeting. The ploy didn't work: the pope met with King in September 1964. FBI officials also failed in their efforts to pressure a magazine to kill an article by King.

But the FBI's power was only tested. The Internal Revenue Service gave in to FBI demands to hand over five years' worth of King's tax returns, as well as those of the Southern Christian Leadership Conference. The FBI failed to find any financial irregularities — but they didn't give up.

The FBI's campaign against King waned between 1965 and early 1967, but intensified again when King began to speak out against the Vietnam War. On April 4, 1967, King spoke at Riverside Church in New York and said that the U.S. government was the "greatest purveyor of violence in the world today." At a press conference, he called for Black Americans and "all white people of goodwill" to boycott the war and become conscientious objectors. In response, the FBI concluded that King's new anti-war stance proved that he was under Communist influence, and the Bureau again sent a report to the White House and the Justice Department summarizing the dirt the FBI had collected, "to remind top level officials in government of the wholly disreputable character of King."

In late March 1968, when King traveled to Memphis to support a sanitation workers' strike, the FBI reported that he was staying at a Holiday Inn. Sullivan's intelligence division recommended in a memo that an article be planted in a "cooperative news source" that while he was in Memphis to support the sanitation workers' strike, King had stayed at the "plush," "white-owned" Holiday Inn, rather than the Black-owned Lorraine Hotel. The next time he returned to Memphis, he stayed at the Lorraine.

On April 4, King was assassinated on the balcony of his room at the Lorraine. The Church Committee concluded there was no evidence that the FBI was responsible for his move from the Holiday Inn to the Lorraine.

* * *

The full extent of the FBI's campaign against Martin Luther King remained largely hidden from view until after the civil-rights leader's death. Ironically, the first limited disclosure came from the FBI itself — as part of a campaign to damage the 1968 presidential campaign of Robert Kennedy.

By May 1968, a month after King's assassination, Robert Kennedy was a leading candidate for the Democratic presidential nomination. Both President Lyndon Johnson, who had announced he would not run for reelection, and J. Edgar Hoover shared a hatred for Kennedy, and both were eager to see his campaign fail. So Deke DeLoach, the FBI's White House liaison and thus the key intermediary between Hoover and Johnson, met for lunch with syndicated columnist Drew Pearson and Jack Anderson, then a reporter on Pearson's staff. DeLoach told them that when Kennedy was attorney general, he had authorized the FBI to wiretap King. DeLoach provided Pearson with FBI documents to prove the story. It was an orchestrated leak designed to stop Kennedy's political momentum. "I suspect Deke was prompted by the president to talk to me," Pearson wrote in his private diaries, which were published after his death.

Pearson's column disclosing that Kennedy had ordered King's wiretapping ran just days before the critical Democratic primary in California, which would help determine whether Kennedy won his party's presidential nomination. A Kennedy campaign aide remarked that they had expected "a last-minute smear story which couldn't be answered," Pearson wrote in his diaries after the column was published.

Kennedy won the California primary — but was assassinated just after his victory. Pearson's scoop revealing that Kennedy had authorized the FBI to wiretap Martin Luther King Jr was largely forgotten amid the grief and tumult of 1968. What's more, Pearson's column had been wildly out of context, revealing nothing about the FBI's vicious campaign against King. The full story was lost to history — until the Church Committee.

Epstein's digging allowed the Church Committee to publish the first comprehensive investigation of the FBI's harassment of King. Included in its final report, the committee's King investigation has stood the test of time. Most of what is known about the case can still be traced back to the committee's investigation led by Mike Epstein.

The FBI was forever befuddled by Epstein and his investigation. Lish Whitson — the FBI agent William Sullivan had sent to Miami to mail the blackmail package and suicide note to King — reported in a panic once in 1975 to FBI headquarters that Epstein knew the full story. "Whitson asked Epstein how he got the story," an FBI memo later recounted. "Epstein merely laughed and did not reply to the question."

The Church Committee's investigation finally forced the Justice Department to investigate the FBI's campaign against King. A special Justice Department task force issued a report in 1977 that echoed the Church Committee's findings.

Today, all FBI agent trainees are sent on a mandatory visit to the King memorial in Washington, D.C., and are given a lecture on the FBI's abusive campaign against him.

*   *   *

While Epstein focused on the King case, Arthur Jefferson, a young Black lawyer on the Church Committee's domestic task force, was eager to launch an even more sensitive and potentially more explosive investigation: an inquiry into the 1969 murder of Black Panther Party leader Fred Hampton by the Chicago police.

At 4:45 a.m. on December 4, 1969, Hampton was killed — along with Mark Clark, another member of the Black Panther Party — during a raid on a Chicago apartment by police officers assigned to the Cook County State's Attorney's Office. Hampton was only 21 years old.

While the raid was carried out by local law enforcement, it had actually been the culmination of a campaign of harassment, disruption, and surveillance of the Black Panther Party by the FBI. J. Edgar Hoover feared that the charismatic young Hampton could be an effective leader of the Black Panthers. The FBI's Chicago field office had an informant close to Hampton: William O'Neal, the chief of security for the Illinois Black Panther Party. O'Neal gave the FBI Hampton's schedule, location, a list of other Black Panther Party members who used his apartment, and an inventory of the weapons stored there, as well as a detailed floor plan of the apartment — including a note locating "Fred's bed."

During the raid, between 83 and 99 shots were fired, but only one came from a Black Panther weapon, which may have discharged when Mark Clark was shot. Hampton never made it out of bed. He had probably been drugged before the raid, and may have

Fred Hampton, the charismatic young leader of the Black Panthers, in Chicago, before he was murdered in a raid by the Chicago police backed by the FBI.

died in his sleep. The FBI said that the raid had been based on information furnished by an informant, and awarded O'Neal a special payment of $300.

The Chicago police had carried out the execution of Fred Hampton under the direction of the FBI. Arthur Jefferson, one of the few Black staffers on the Church Committee, wanted the committee's domestic task force to investigate the case just as aggressively as the committee's FBI team was investigating the King case. But Jefferson was blocked from conducting any investigation of the Hampton case.

In an interview, Walter Mondale, who oversaw the committee's FBI investigation, said he did not recall the issue of whether to investigate the Hampton case ever being raised. But other committee staffers remember quite clearly that Jefferson was thwarted. "He was very interested in getting into the Fred Hampton murder and the FBI, and I honestly don't know why it never happened," recalled Jim Dick, a Church Committee staffer on the domestic task force who sat next to Jefferson in the committee office. "I remember him talking about wanting to do it, but it didn't happen. I assume somebody discouraged him from doing it." Staffer Barbara Banoff also

Fred Hampton's bloody bed after the Chicago police
raid in which he was murdered.

recalled that Jefferson wanted to investigate Fred Hampton's murder but was discouraged from doing so. Jefferson died in 2011.

By seeking to conduct an investigation of Fred Hampton's murder, Jefferson was pushing the boundaries of what was politically
acceptable in Congress at the time. In 1975, an intense investigation
of the Fred Hampton case would have been politically radioactive —
and far more controversial for the Church Committee than its investigation of the FBI's harassment of King. Hampton was at that time a
politically unsympathetic character for white America, and Jefferson's failed efforts to probe the Hampton murder suggests that the

fact that all of the senators on the Church Committee were white influenced what the panel chose to investigate.

But Jefferson was still able to conduct a broader investigation into how the FBI used its COINTELPRO program to disrupt and discredit the Black Panther Party. Jefferson's detailed investigation, entitled "The FBI's Covert Action Program to Destroy the Black Panther Party," was one of the supplementary staff reports released in tandem with the Church Committee's final report. Many of the facts it uncovered are still central to what is known about the FBI's harassment and disruption of the Black Panther Party.

"Although the claimed purpose of the Bureau's COINTELPRO tactics was to prevent violence, some of the FBI's tactics against the BPP were clearly intended to foster violence, and many others could reasonably have been expected to cause violence," the report stated. "For example, the FBI's efforts to intensify the degree of animosity between the BPP and the Blackstone Rangers, a Chicago street gang, included sending an anonymous letter to the gang's leader falsely informing him that the Chicago Panthers had 'a hit out' on him. The stated intent of the letter was to induce the Ranger leader to 'take reprisals against' the Panther leadership."

On April 30, 1976, Arthur Jefferson and John Elliff represented the Church Committee in a meeting with the FBI to discuss the draft of the committee's report on its investigation into the FBI and the Black Panthers. In his draft, Jefferson had written that the FBI sent an anonymous letter to the Ranger leader claiming the Panthers planned to kill him. "This is an incorrect statement because the word *kill* was not used in the letter sent to the gang leader," Bureau officials told Jefferson, according to an FBI memo describing their meeting. "The letter sent to the gang leader stated, 'The brothers that run the Panthers blame you for blocking their thing and there's supposed to be a hit out on you'...The word 'kill' should be replaced with the word actually used, 'hit.' "

Jefferson and Elliff agreed to the change. But Arthur Jefferson refused to be silenced—either by the FBI or by the Church Committee. On May 25, 1976, after the Church Committee had completed its work, the FBI's Los Angeles field office reported to FBI headquarters that Arthur Jefferson, "allegedly a former staffer of the Senate Select Committee," would be testifying for the defense in a trial of Black Panthers on the West Coast. "Jefferson is testifying concerning FBI actions taken nationwide to disrupt BPP activities."

* * *

When Frank Church spoke publicly about the Church Committee's investigation of the FBI in the fall of 1975, he seemed to be taking himself to task for having joined in Washington's collective failure to hold J. Edgar Hoover accountable for so many years.

"If fault is to be found" with the FBI, Church said, "it does not rest in the Bureau alone. It is to be found also in the long line of Attorneys General, Presidents, and Congresses who have given power and responsibility to the FBI, but have failed to give it adequate guidance, direction, and control."

PART THREE

"A volcano cannot be capped"

1975–1984

CHAPTER 24

"Vindicated and pleased"

THE CHURCH COMMITTEE had so many moving parts, and was working on so many different inquiries, mostly behind closed doors, that it was difficult throughout much of 1975 for the press and the public to get a complete picture of the committee's work. By September, for example, the committee had completed its closed-door hearings on CIA plots to assassinate foreign leaders, but it had not yet released its interim report on the assassination plots. So as the Church Committee's public hearings in its other investigations began in September, it still wasn't completely clear to outsiders what the committee had been doing all year.

Frank Church regretted that the committee had not held any public hearings on the assassination investigation, since it represented the committee's most comprehensive and most cinematic inquiry, filled with CIA agents plotting with Mafia bosses — along with a cameo appearance by a presidential mistress. But though he knew the publicity would have been spectacular, he also knew he would have been accused of grandstanding.

Yet the irony was that by keeping the assassination hearings closed, he faced accusations of a cover-up. Enough had leaked out about the committee's investigation into the CIA's efforts to kill Castro during the Kennedy Administration that the press charged that Church was trying to keep it out of the public eye in order to protect the Kennedy legacy.

"For Church, the critical question is the handling of the prickly Kennedy issue," wrote political columnist Jack Germond in September 1975, just before the public hearings began. "Church began the inquiry in a flush of post-Watergate promises to seek out the evidence in public hearings before the eyes of the nation. But when it became clear that the central issue would be who ordered the assassination of which foreign leader and when, Church's commitment to public hearings went up in smoke."

Church grumbled that he was in a no-win situation. When he held open hearings, the press said he was showboating to hype his possible run for the presidency. When he held closed hearings, pundits said he was engaged in a cover-up. "The assassination matter would have been unprecedented box office," Church insisted in an interview with the *New York Times*. "It would have been the most sensational hearings held in this century."

Church addressed the criticism of the secrecy during his opening statement at the committee's first public hearing in September — the hearing on shellfish toxins where Church famously held up the CIA dart gun for all the world to see. "The committee has not held public hearings prior to this time because of its concentration on charges that the CIA has been involved in assassination plots directed against certain foreign leaders," Church said. "In that investigation the committee has...compiled a record on the assassination issue alone that compares in size to the entire investigation of the Senate Watergate Committee. Because of the serious damage that protracted public hearings on such a subject could do to the United States in its relations with foreign governments, the committee chose to conduct these hearings behind closed doors."

*   *   *

Unable to go public with the lurid tales uncovered in the assassination investigation, Frank Church and his staff scrambled to find another story that would capture the public's imagination and grab headlines in the committee's first public hearing. The problem was that so much of the committee's staff and resources had been devoted to the assassination probe that, with less than a month to go before the public hearings were scheduled to start in September, none of the other big investigations were ready to go public.

Church thought about starting with hearings on the FBI, but the staffers investigating the Bureau reported they weren't ready. Church then considered kicking off with hearings about the Huston Plan—the Nixon White House proposal to have government intelligence agencies spy more aggressively on American citizens. But the existence of the Huston Plan had been disclosed during the Watergate scandal, and Church suspected that the press would not think it newsworthy.

Finally in late August, CIA director William Colby revealed to Church that the Agency had illegally kept a supply of shellfish toxins for five years after President Nixon had ordered its destruction. The toxins had been kept for use in suicide pills and assassinations, which would be carried out with a dart gun. Colby told Church that the CIA had just launched its own internal investigation.

Church quickly saw that the shellfish toxins could make for a good opening round of hearings. The story was new, the toxins were frightening, the dart gun would make good theater, and the fact that the CIA had ignored a presidential order to destroy the poisons fit in with Church's belief that the CIA acted like a rogue elephant. "Church felt sort of vindicated and pleased," by the toxins case, observed Fritz Schwarz. "It fit in with Church's view during the assassinations investigation that the CIA was willing to go its own way." Now that Church had his show-opener, he told the staff to prepare for public hearings on shellfish toxins as fast as possible.

*　*　*

On the morning of the first hearing, Frank Church called Fritz Schwarz into his office and told him that he wanted him to take a leading role in the questioning of Colby. After Senators Church and Tower had made their opening remarks and Church had theatrically asked Colby to turn over the dart gun, he told Schwarz, he wanted him to take over much of the detailed questioning.

Schwarz was stunned; senators never deferred to their staff at such high-profile hearings. Staffers were supposed to remain anonymous while the senators grabbed all the attention and glory. Church's decision to give Schwarz such a prominent role contradicted the media narrative that Church cared only about publicity for himself. "About an hour or two before the hearing, Church told me that I was going to [take a leading role in questioning Colby]," recalled Schwarz. "He said, my colleagues don't know how to question, so I want you to do it."

Schwarz wound up performing so well that Church had him take a leading role in questioning during almost every one of the committee's public hearings. With Schwarz taking on such a conspicuous role, Curt Smothers, the Republican counsel, told him he needed to improve his shaggy appearance. Smothers took him shopping to buy a better suit.

* * *

The first day of the Church Committee hearings had the drama and trappings of the Senate's Watergate hearings two years earlier, but with a twist: Paul Duke, who covered the hearings for public television, noted that each senator on the Church Committee arrived with "a fat orange-colored notebook, crammed with classified material about the CIA, all marked top secret."

But while the press packed the Senate Caucus Room just as they had during Watergate, the public's attendance was more lackluster.

Fritz Schwarz, the Church Committee's chief counsel, greets CIA director William Colby before the start of the Church Committee's first public hearing. Mitchell Rogovin, a left-leaning lawyer hired by Colby to be the CIA's special counsel to help the Agency deal with the Church Committee, is in the background.

The members of the Church Committee take their seats as the first public hearing begins. Seated from left to right are Frank Church, Curt Smothers, and Howard Baker.

Despite the committee's dramatic focus on spies and long-secret abuses, scandals, and crimes, the seats in the audience reserved for the general public were only about two-thirds full, Duke noted. During the early days of Watergate, seats at the Senate Watergate Committee hearings had been the hardest tickets to get in Washington, with long lines snaking out of the hearing room. The audience was often sprinkled with celebrities, like John Lennon and Yoko Ono. Inevitably, the press judged public interest in the Church Committee by the impossible standards set during the Watergate scandal, when the entire nation was riveted by the Shakespearean tragedy of Richard Nixon's fall.

"There were in fact no long lines," Paul Duke noted after the first Church Committee hearing. "As someone said, after what has happened in this country during the past two years, there are no more future shocks." The shadow of Watergate always fell across the Church Committee.

*   *   *

Colby was furious with what he saw as Church's grandstanding with the dart gun at the start of the first hearing. Employing his old-style WASP language, he wrote in his memoir that the dart gun episode during the hearing was "the wildest hugger-mugger." But Colby quickly calmed down, and by the time he gave his own testimony during the hearing, he had composed himself enough to present a nuanced view of the Church Committee's work, suggesting an understanding of the need both for greater congressional oversight and for a reassessment of the intelligence community's role in American society.

"We are engaged in these investigations, Mr. Chairman," Colby said, "in resolving the dilemma between the necessary secrets of intelligence and the equally necessary exposure of our government's workings to our people and their representatives, to insure that they respond to the people's will."

Later, Colby complimented Church for the way his committee had handled its work. "In fairness...I have to add that this ghastly day [featuring the dart-gun episode] was an exception to the otherwise generally responsible and serious approach taken by the Church Committee," Colby wrote in his memoir.

But Colby's career could not survive the Church Committee's investigation — particularly the public spectacle of the dart gun at the first hearing. While Colby had resisted the Church Committee on some things, like its efforts to investigate the CIA's covert-action operations, the Ford White House saw Colby as far too accommodating of Frank Church.

William Colby had embraced the need for intelligence reform and greater congressional oversight. For those sins, he was fired by President Ford in November 1975.

"From the outset I had been, of course, aware that many in the administration did not approve of my cooperative approach to the investigations, and I had felt myself increasingly isolated from the White House 'team' as the year progressed," Colby wrote in his memoir. "But I could not and would not change my basic approach, I believed in the Constitution; I believed in the Congress' constitutional right to investigate the intelligence community; and I believed that, as head of that community, I was required by the Constitution to cooperate with the Congress."

On November 12, 1975, just days after he had been fired by Ford, Colby wrote a surprising personal note to Church Committee staffer Patrick Shea, quoting Robert Frost's poem "The Tuft of

Flowers": "I particularly like the final words of Frost that 'men work together...whether they work together or apart,'" Colby wrote to Shea. "I think this clearly expresses our American way of doing business in the separation of powers provided by the Constitution. When each does his work as well as he can, the whole nation benefits, even though they must stay apart."

Ford announced that Colby would be replaced by George Herbert Walker Bush. (Colby agreed to stay on the job until January). At the time, Bush was chief of the U.S. Liaison Office in China, making him the de-facto ambassador, but he was best known in Washington for having chaired the Republican National Committee during Watergate, when he served as a full-throated apologist for scandal-plagued Richard Nixon.

Frank Church was outraged that Ford's response to the Church Committee's investigative findings was to fire the man who had cooperated with Congress and install a Republican partisan eager to do Ford's bidding. "I find the President's appointment astonishing," Church said in a speech on the Senate floor in November 1975.

> The Senate and the House Committees, not to mention the President's own commission on intelligence, have labored for months reviewing the problems of intelligence agencies. These problems have been plentiful, and the areas for new legislation are many. Still, the prospects for starting afresh are good, and I have viewed the chances to restore public trust and confidence in the CIA with considerable optimism.
>
> But this is no way to begin the restoration...Let us not undermine the good work of the Rockefeller Commission and the Committees of the House and Senate by placing a former party chairman at the head of a highly sensitive intelligence agency. Let us not make a travesty out of our efforts to reform the CIA.

It wasn't just the Ford White House that turned on Colby for telling the truth. Many CIA officers vilified Colby for having cooperated with Frank Church and Congress, and at the same time they lionized Richard Helms for having lied to Church and Congress.

In fact, Helms had a very different view of the Church Committee than his successor. The former CIA director testified repeatedly during the Church Committee's closed hearings and later in its public hearings, and he also came under criminal investigation for lying about the CIA's involvement in Chile during his earlier testimony to Frank Church's multinational subcommittee. Helms hated Frank Church.

"It remains my opinion that Senator Church operated his committee at a level of self-serving hypocrisy unusual even for other run-of-the-mill presidential hopefuls," Helms wrote bitterly in his memoir.

The Colby-Helms divide would define the culture of the CIA for a generation, shaping how the Agency dealt with Congress for decades.

CHAPTER 25

"As dangerous as any stimulant"

THE CHURCH COMMITTEE'S second round of hearings, in late September, was highlighted by the grilling of Tom Huston, the author of the infamous Huston Plan. Despite Church's fears that the Huston Plan hearings might lack punch, they actually provided critical insight into the Nixon-era plot to illegally spy on Americans.

Of equal importance to Frank Church was that with its investigation and hearings into the Huston Plan, the Church Committee was finally playing the role that Church had for so long hoped — as a sequel to Watergate. Church could finally breathe a sigh of relief; the Huston Plan involved Richard Nixon, not John Kennedy.

The Watergate investigation had only glancingly dealt with the Huston Plan, but the Church Committee discovered the plan's true purpose. It was to provide White House cover and legitimacy for the FBI, CIA, and other agencies that wanted to revive or continue preexisting domestic-spying programs.

In June 1970, with anti-war protests growing around the country following the invasion of Cambodia and the Kent State shootings, President Nixon began pushing the intelligence community to spy more aggressively on the anti-war movement. Nixon was convinced that anti-war dissidents were Communist puppets controlled by Moscow, and he wanted proof. Tom Huston, a young White House lawyer, was assigned to coordinate the intelligence community's response, but it soon became clear that he was in way over his head.

William Sullivan, the FBI's wily intelligence chief, cleverly manipulated Huston to help him circumvent FBI director J. Edgar Hoover's opposition to more aggressive domestic spying by the Bureau. By 1970, the aging Hoover had grown cautious; he was no longer willing to conduct the kind of aggressive and lawless domestic-spying operations that had been his hallmark earlier in his career. That frustrated Sullivan, and so he saw Nixon's demands for action as a way to revive the FBI's domestic-intelligence programs. Huston became Sullivan's protégé, while the CIA and the NSA also filled Huston with novel ideas for domestic intelligence — which in fact were the very programs they were already secretly running without explicit presidential authorization. The FBI, CIA, and NSA all considered eager young Tom Huston as a pawn they could slyly use to obtain presidential authority and legitimacy for their illicit programs.

J. Edgar Hoover killed the Huston Plan as soon as he saw it. He recognized it for what it was — a power grab by Sullivan — and he made it clear to Attorney General John Mitchell and President Nixon that he couldn't support it. Nixon, who had approved the plan days earlier, was unwilling to take on Hoover, so he quickly reversed course and abandoned the proposal. But even after the Huston Plan was rejected by Nixon, the intelligence community secretly went back to running their domestic-spying operations without White House approval.

By the time he testified before the Church Committee, Huston recognized that he had been played by the intelligence community, and that he had been wrongly characterized during Watergate as the mastermind of an illegal White House spying operation. During Watergate, Huston was the villain; during the Church Committee hearings, he was the patsy.

"The impression," the bespectacled Huston said in testimony to the Church Committee, "is that I kind of sat down here and created out of whole cloth an entire array of new techniques to exploit and infringe upon the civil liberties of the American people, and that I forced it down Dick Helms' throat and I blackjacked Admiral [Noel] Gayler [director of the NSA at the time of the Huston Plan] and I really used my heavy weight on all of these poor little professional intelligence people and forced them into coming up with all of this."

"The President and Mr. Huston, it appears, were deceived by the intelligence officials," Frank Church agreed. "The intelligence agencies paid no heed to the revocation [of the Huston Plan]. As in the case of the shellfish toxin, the decision of the President seemed to matter little."

* * *

The ease with which the CIA and other agencies continued to operate programs without presidential knowledge or approval revealed their appalling lack of internal oversight. During a hearing on the CIA's illicit mail-opening program, Senator Richard Schweiker had a remarkable exchange with Gordon Stewart, the CIA's Inspector General in the 1960s, which revealed in stunning fashion that oversight within the CIA was nonexistent. The clueless Stewart admitted to Schweiker that, besides the mail-opening program, he never uncovered any other illegal programs at the CIA. He also admitted that while he wrote a report to the CIA director recommending that the mail-opening program be stopped, he did no follow-up — and did not even tell the CIA's general counsel about it.

Except for the mail-opening program, "You never came across any other illegal activities?" an astonished Schweiker asked Stewart.

"That is quite correct," Stewart replied.

"How do you account for what we are finding now in our House and Senate Intelligence Committees?" the Pennsylvania Republican asked. "Was this a lack of communication, or compartmentalization? Where did the breakdown occur?"

"Could you be specific, Senator?" Stewart asked.

"Well, we have been holding a number of hearings. We had a hearing here a while ago where a presidential order was violated on shellfish toxin. We have been holding a number of other hearings where the CIA was not complying with the law of the land. And my question is, how do you account for the discrepancies that are now coming to light when you are saying that during your tenure you really did not find any other illegal activities? I am a little bit confused. You are saying obviously that you did not know about them, but are you now maintaining there were no other illegal activities going on during your tenure as Inspector General?"

"No sir, I'm not maintaining that. I simply say that in the course of our surveys, which I explained we took [at] about the rate of one every five years, we had in fact not come upon other illegal activities that I recall and about which we reported."

Stewart's testimony underscored the desperate need for congressional oversight of the CIA. But the Church Committee's hearings on the NSA would show that even with greater congressional oversight, it was still going to be difficult to get intelligence officials to tell the truth.

The Church Committee's hearings on the National Security Agency marked a historic first: the director of the NSA testified in public before Congress. Lieutenant General Lew Allen Jr., the NSA director, publicly acknowledged the existence of the MINARET program, through which the NSA had illegally tapped the international communications of Americans who had been placed on a CIA watch list.

Allen was widely credited for his public appearance — but he was hiding a dangerous secret. What Allen kept hidden during the hearing was that two senators sitting on the committee — Frank Church and Howard Baker — were among the prominent Americans who had been spied on during MINARET. Also spied on by the NSA were Martin Luther King and fellow civil-rights leader Whitney Young; Muhammad Ali; *New York Times* journalist Tom Wicker; and Art Buchwald, a *Washington Post* humor columnist who had regularly irritated President Richard Nixon.

Yet the Church Committee never discovered that Church and Baker had been spied upon under MINARET. That was not publicly revealed until 2013, when an internal NSA history was partially declassified. The disclosure that the NSA had spied on Church and Baker would have had explosive ramifications for the Church Committee had it been divulged at the time of the committee's investigation of the NSA.

*　*　*

Although the Ford White House didn't block the NSA director from testifying in public, it drew the line on the Church Committee's public hearings on covert action. Even though Church had reached a deal with the White House and the CIA to make public the committee's investigation into the Nixon-era covert action in Chile — and only that covert action — Secretary of State Henry Kissinger refused to testify about Chile in public, perhaps fearful of falling into the perjury trap that had already ensnared Richard Helms. Ford prohibited anyone else from the administration to testify either; even William Colby refused to cooperate with Church. Some committee staffers pushed Church to subpoena Kissinger, but the senator didn't believe he would have the backing of the full Senate if he launched a long legal battle with Kissinger, who had many allies on Capitol Hill.

But Church also didn't believe there was enough time left for the committee to take on additional procedural battles. The Church Committee was running out of time — it was scheduled to go out of existence at the end of February 1976 — and Church was also quietly weighing how soon he could launch his presidential bid.

Mitchell Rogovin, Colby's counsel, later told the *New York Times* that what the CIA most wanted to protect from the Church Committee was its covert-action arm. The Agency was adamant about guarding the secrets of covert action, both to prevent political damage from disclosures of past operations and to retain the ability to conduct such operations in the future. (Even as the Church Committee pursued its investigation, the CIA was engaged in a new covert action in Angola.)

The Church Committee's CIA task force did not push back against the Agency resistance. The task force conducted six covert-action case studies, including Chile, but the task force agreed with the CIA that five of them — in Congo, Greece, Indonesia, Laos, and Vietnam — would not be made public. Only the Chile case study would be the subject of public hearings.

The agreement was a bad deal for the Church Committee. Although Frank Church approved it, the agreement reflected the soft approach toward the intelligence community preferred by Bill Miller and his close aide, William Bader, who ran the CIA task force. This task force was completely separate from the Fritz Schwarz team that had investigated the CIA's assassination plots against foreign leaders. It was no accident that the most explosive disclosures about the Agency came from Schwarz's separate assassination investigation, rather than from Bader and the CIA task force.

With Frank Church's approval, Bader and the CIA task force gave in on other issues as well. They agreed not to name any of the American journalists who had secret relationships with the CIA, and not to publicly identify the U.S. corporations, academic institutions, and labor unions that cooperated with the Agency. That marked a reversal for the committee, since it identified the companies that cooperated with the NSA's domestic-spying operations.

339

Joe DiGenova—the Republican Church Committee staffer who would later become Donald Trump's lawyer—recalled in an interview that the committee discovered CIA files revealing a relationship between the CIA and AFL-CIO president George Meany. But the Church Committee did not make it public. "George Meany would go overseas and get debriefed by the CIA, and he cooperated with the Agency," recalled DiGenova. "The Democrats on the committee didn't want that disclosed."

While the Church Committee may not have delved into Meany's case, his Agency ties were hardly a secret by the time of the committee's investigation in 1975. In 1967, for example, Drew Pearson and Jack Anderson reported that, under Meany, the AFL-CIO's International Affairs Department had received funding from the CIA, while in 1974, *CounterSpy*—a leftist, anti-CIA magazine—revealed that Meany had cooperated with the CIA to infiltrate labor organizations overseas. Other former committee staffers do not recall the issue, but DiGenova is certainly right that committee Democrats were not eager to focus on the CIA's ties to the most powerful labor leader in the nation.

*　　*　　*

Without officials from the Ford administration or the CIA willing to testify during the public hearings on covert action, the committee found a surprising replacement. David Phillips, the former CIA officer who had retired in order to wage a public campaign against the Church Committee, agreed to testify before the committee. Phillips, who had created a new alumni association for retired CIA officials, was a constant thorn in the side of Frank Church, attacking the congressional investigations into the CIA intelligence community on every television show that would have him. It was thus stunning that he agreed to testify before the committee—and to do so in a hearing boycotted by the White House and the CIA.

During his testimony, Phillips actually offered some provocative suggestions on how to reform and reorganize covert-action operations. His thoughtful testimony seemed utterly at odds with the public persona he had created as Frank Church's nemesis. Phillips recommended that covert-action operations be split off from the CIA and placed in a new, separate organization with a staff of only 100 people. Keeping it that small, Phillips argued, would guarantee that the U.S. launched only small, manageable covert operations. And housing it in a separate organization, he added, would make it easier for Congress to conduct effective oversight.

"All U.S covert action eggs then would be in one small basket, a basket which could be watched very carefully," Phillips said... "A joint congressional committee should find such a unit easy to monitor...The office I propose would call on expertise derived from experience. It would not employ airlines or mercenaries or exotic paraphernalia, but would need the capability to provide friends with imaginative advice and what British intelligence officers have sometimes called 'King George's cavalry' — money. Covert action is a stimulating business, a heady experience for those who sponsor it and for its practitioners. If not used in moderation, it is as dangerous as any stimulant."

But Walter Mondale was so disgusted by what the Church Committee had uncovered that he questioned whether the United States should engage in covert action at all. "The record shows that there is an almost uncontrollable tendency to play God with other societies," Mondale said during the hearings. It is naive to believe, he added, "that we can manipulate, control, and direct another society secretly with a few dollars or a few guns or a few bucks or a few lives in a way that we know we would never be controlled by another society that attempted the same tactics on us."

*   *   *

As the Church Committee's investigations and hearings into the CIA, the NSA, and other agencies began to wrap up in the fall of 1975, the domestic task force's FBI investigation was falling behind. And Frank Church, who was starting to look ahead to a presidential run, was growing impatient.

Throughout that autumn, Church repeatedly asked when they could hold hearings on the FBI. John Elliff, the head of the domestic task force, kept saying they needed more time to finish their investigation. In fact, the team investigating the FBI was being flooded with leads about the Bureau's past abuses, and it was struggling to keep up.

Frustrated by the slow pace of the FBI investigation, Fritz Schwarz assigned committee staffer Paul Michel to pressure Elliff and his task force to wrap up their work and prepare for public hearings. "There was a little bit of tension since the investigators wanted to keep drilling, which was good," says Michel. "But we also needed to put on some hearings."

When they finally got underway on November 18, the FBI hearings would feature some of the weirdest — and most dramatic — moments of the Church Committee.

* * *

One of the key problems that the Church Committee's investigation of the FBI uncovered was the dysfunctional nature of the Bureau's relationships with its informants. The committee's FBI hearings publicly introduced Gary Thomas Rowe Jr. as the prime example.

Rowe, an undercover informant for the FBI inside the Ku Klux Klan, became a key witness in the committee's investigation of the FBI's use of informants in connection with the civil-rights and anti-war movements of the 1960s and early 1970s. Rowe was a violent brawler in Birmingham, Alabama, when he was recruited by the FBI to infiltrate the Klan, and while he was undercover, Rowe was involved in some of the most infamous and violent attacks against the Civil Rights Movement.

The fundamental question about Rowe — as well as other FBI undercover informants — was whether they crossed the line by participating in or even instigating violence, rather than just informing the FBI about it. The FBI's ability to control the actions of its informants was a critical issue for the Church Committee.

During his appearance before the committee, Rowe inadvertently furnished a strange — and ultimately iconic — image to emerge from the committee's public hearings on the FBI.

Rowe had been placed in witness protection after identifying and testifying against other Klan members, and right before he was scheduled to appear in the committee's public hearing on December 2, Rowe balked at going public. He told staffers he didn't want to testify in front of the television cameras.

Republican staffer Andy Postal recommended that Rowe testify in a closed hearing in order to protect his identity, but Fritz Schwarz insisted that he testify in public, Postal recalled in an interview. As a compromise, Postal says, "Fritz got the idea for Rowe to wear a hood."

Schwarz said in an interview that he persuaded Rowe to testify with his face hidden, and the committee staff came up with a hokey, handmade disguise: an ill-fitting white hood that seemed fashioned from a pillowcase, with large holes cut from the fabric for the witness's eyes and mouth. It was like a dime-store version of a Ku Klux Klan hood, and it made the hulking, overweight Rowe look ridiculous. Rowe went through with it and testified in front of the network television cameras, but the image made the Church Committee look amateurish.

* * *

In sharp contrast to Rowe's clownish appearance, the FBI hearings also brought the most sobering day of the entire Church Committee. It came when Fritz Schwarz and Curt Smothers, his Republican counterpart, testified jointly before the committee in order to narrate the committee's findings about the FBI's campaign of harassment and abuse against Martin Luther King. The committee had no other witnesses that day; it was entirely given over to Schwarz and Smothers. The highest-ranking Black staffer on the Church Committee, Smothers struggled to control his emotions as he helped recount the shocking story, which had never before been so comprehensively told to the public.

"When Curt testified about the FBI targeting of Martin Luther King, that was one of the only times I ever saw him flustered," recalled Postal.

The narration of the King case by Schwarz and Smothers also deeply affected Senator Phil Hart, the man whom Mike Mansfield originally wanted to chair the committee but was now dying of cancer. Hart made a special effort to attend the hearing about the King case after being hospitalized. His remarks following the presentation of the King case created what many staffers later described as the most emotional moment of the entire Church Committee.

"Before I am going to pursue my own questions," Frank Church said after Schwarz and Smothers had finished, "I would like to recognize, after some weeks of absence, that we have Senator Phil Hart back with us...so I thought it would be entirely appropriate, Senator Hart, to turn to you first with whatever questions you would like to ask."

Hart first sought to break the tension. "I do not recommend

that others pursue the course I took in order to get this advantage, but thank you very much." Then he continued:

As I'm sure others have, I have been told for years by, among others, some of my own family, that this is exactly what the Bureau was doing all of the time, and in my great wisdom and high office I assured them that it just wasn't true. It couldn't happen. They wouldn't do it. What you have described is a series of illegal actions intended squarely to deny First Amendment rights to some Americans. That is what my children have told me was going on. Now, I did not believe it...Over the years, we have been warned about the danger of subversive organizations that would threaten our liberties, subvert our system, would encourage [their] members to take further illegal action to advance their views, organizations that would incite and promote violence, pitting one American group against another. And I think the story you have told us today shows us that there is an organization that does fit those descriptions, and it is the organization the leadership of which has been most constant in its warning to us to be on guard against such harm. The Bureau did all of those things...I am glad I got back in time to be persuaded of what my own family had not been able to persuade me of.

When Hart was finished, many committee members and staff were close to tears. His emotional speech helped them begin to understand the historic significance of the Church Committee's work.

*　*　*

Despite a year of hearings and investigations by the Rockefeller Commission, the Church Committee, and the Pike Committee into the abuses and criminal acts committed by the intelligence community, William Colby found to his relief that the CIA's ability to operate effectively around the world was largely undiminished.

In fact, despite the negative publicity, the Agency received 760 job applications from college students in the summer of 1975 — twice the number received the year before, Colby said. In an expansive interview in September 1975 with the *Chicago Daily News*,

Colby added that "the short-term [impact] on our intelligence product has been, surprisingly, not all that much...we still do some very venturesome things."

But Colby's assessment that the Church Committee had conducted its investigation without damaging national security would not stop the Ford White House and the CIA from weaponizing a Big Lie to try to discredit Frank Church in late 1975 and early 1976, just as the Church Committee finished its work and Church belatedly began gearing up to run for president.

CHAPTER 26

"One more service to render"

ON THE NIGHT of December 23, 1975, Ron Estes, the CIA's deputy station chief in Athens, was lounging on the couch in his girlfriend's apartment when the Greek driver for Richard Welch, the CIA's station chief, burst in the front door. He yelled, "A shooting, and Mr. Welch is down!!" Estes grabbed his coat and ran out with the driver, while his girlfriend yelled at him not to go.

When he got to Welch's house, Estes found the 46-year-old station chief lying on the sidewalk on his back, with his wife, Kika, kneeling beside him. Blood covered Welch's face, and Estes could see immediately that his boss was dead. "I didn't need to feel for a pulse," recalled Estes.

A police car arrived, and Estes asked the officer to call for an ambulance. When no ambulance arrived, they piled the body into Welch's car, and the police officer, with his siren blaring and lights flashing, led them through the streets of Athens to the nearest hospital. A medical team was waiting in the emergency room. They quickly placed Welch on a gurney and took him to an examining room, with Estes following. A doctor placed a stethoscope on his chest, and confirmed to Estes that Welch was dead.

Welch's driver hurriedly told Estes what had happened. He had been driving Welch and Kika home from a Christmas party at the U.S. ambassador's residence, he said, when he stopped in front of Welch's house to open the front gates of the walled compound. Just as Welch and his wife got out of the car to walk through the gates, a black car pulled up behind them, and three armed men got out.

One said in Greek to Welch, "Put your hands up!"

Replied Welch in English: "What?"

The man, armed with a .45 handgun, then fired three times.

An autopsy later showed that the first shot hit Welch in the chest, rupturing his aorta and killing him instantly. The second shot went through his coat but missed him, and the third struck him in the buttocks as he fell. The three men got back in their car and sped away. That was when Welch's driver came to get Estes.

The hospital lobby soon filled with journalists, who had most likely heard about the shooting while monitoring the police radio. Estes realized that many of them already seemed to know that Welch had been the CIA station chief. A *New York Times* reporter who covered Welch's murder wrote the next day that he had been talking with Welch at the ambassador's Christmas party just an hour before the shooting.

A press spokesman from the U.S. Embassy arrived, and Estes slipped away from the crowd of reporters. The police found the gunmen's car, which had been stolen, abandoned several blocks from Welch's home.

Once he reached the CIA station, Estes started sending cables back to CIA headquarters, and talked on a secure phone with a top CIA official. "When I finished briefing him, he said I could only hear about half of what you said. Send me a cable repeating what you said immediately, we've got to go to the President." Meanwhile, Estes had to restrain a fellow CIA officer in the station, who grabbed a pistol and said he was going to kill the KGB's Athens Rezident in revenge.

* * *

Richard Welch's murder was a direct result of the feverish political climate that gripped Greece in the mid-1970s. In July 1974, the right-wing military junta that ruled Greece backed a coup in Cyprus in order to oust the island's president and create a union between Greece and Cyprus. Making Cyprus fully Greek was a longtime objective of Greek right-wing ultranationalists, but the move immediately prompted a Turkish invasion of Cyprus.

Looking for a scapegoat, Greek junta leader Dimitrios Ioannidis bitterly blamed the United States for not stopping the Turkish invasion. That led to growing Greek hostility toward the United States. On August 19, 1974, a pro-Greek mob attacked the U.S. embassy in Nicosia, Cyprus, killing both U.S. Ambassador Rodger Davies and a local embassy employee. After a cease-fire, Cyprus was divided into Greek and Turkish zones, and the disastrous outcome of the coup in Cyprus led to the collapse of the military junta in Athens. But anger in Greece toward the United States continued unabated.

The relationship between the CIA and the KYP, the Greek intelligence service, was also poisoned, and soon the names of Richard Welch and a few other officers in the CIA's Athens station were leaked by the KYP to the Greek press. Welch's name and home address were published in an English-language newspaper and a Greek newspaper in Athens. The information about Welch and other case officers was "obviously leaked by hostile KYP officers," Estes says, "because the only names leaked were those in liaison contact with KYP." (CIA overseas stations were often divided between officers who were "in liaison contact" with the intelligence service of the local country—their identities as CIA officers thus declared to the service so they could meet with them and trade intelligence—and other officers who were not identified to the local service so they could secretly conduct operations without the knowledge of the local government.)

Welch had not been hard to find. He lived in a luxurious villa that had served as the official residence of the CIA station chief for decades. After Welch's name and home address were published in the press in November 1975, Estes talked to him about whether he should move. But Welch and Estes concluded that the threat was minimal. "We both agreed that political assassination was not part of the fabric of Greek history or culture," Estes recalled.

It was a fatal miscalculation. Welch's murder was carried out by a new, extremely violent Greek leftist guerrilla organization, called 17 November. While right-wing Greek nationalists hated the United States for betraying Greece over Cyprus, left-wing Greeks blamed the United States for helping to install the military junta in Athens in 1967. The 17 November group was named for an anti-junta student protest that had been brutally broken up by the junta on November 17, 1973.

Welch was 17 November's first target.

Almost overnight, the brutal killing of the CIA station chief upended the politics surrounding the Church Committee — and even Frank Church's presidential ambitions.

* * *

As Ron Estes and the CIA officers in Athens scrambled to deal with the traumatic aftermath of Richard Welch's murder, the Ford White House quickly realized that Welch's killing offered them a political windfall. Welch's murder came exactly a year and a day after Sy Hersh's domestic-spying story in the *New York Times* that had led to the creation of the Church Committee. After nonstop disclosures from the Church Committee about abuses and criminal acts committed by the American intelligence community, Gerald Ford and George Bush — Ford's nominee to be CIA director — were ready to launch a counterattack.

By late 1975, the CIA's public standing was at a low ebb, and the Ford White House was increasingly worried about the political impact of the Church Committee's disclosures on Ford, the first president who had never been elected either president or vice president. Ford was heading into a tough presidential-election campaign in 1976, and was not even assured of the Republican nomination. He faced a formidable challenge on the right from former California governor Ronald Reagan, and desperately needed to prove his conservative bona fides. Now, the White House and CIA had a martyred hero whose death they could lay at the feet of liberal Democrat Frank Church.

It didn't matter that Richard Welch's murder had nothing to do with the Church Committee. It didn't matter that Estes and the CIA station in Athens had reported the facts back to CIA headquarters that showed that the KYP, the Greek intelligence service, had leaked Welch's name and address to the Greek press as revenge for U.S. policy on Cyprus.

Largely through innuendo, the White House and the CIA attributed Welch's death to the Church Committee, falsely suggesting that the committee was responsible for leaking his identity and thus leaving him exposed to assassination. The disinformation campaign mounted by the Ford Administration and the CIA, with outside conservatives gleefully joining in, badly damaged public support for the Church Committee.

The White House would also use Welch's murder to get George Bush confirmed as CIA director in the Democratic-controlled Senate — where Frank Church was leading the opposition.

* * *

Richard Welch's murder occurred just days after the Senate's confirmation hearings on George Bush's nomination to be CIA director.

For Bush, the chance to be CIA director came at a critical moment in his career. Until then, his record in elected politics was not very good. He won a House seat from Texas and served two terms, but then lost a campaign for the Senate from Texas in 1970.

But after that failure, Bush started to rise in Republican ranks through a series of appointed positions. He served as chair of the Republican National Committee during Watergate, forcing him to publicly defend Nixon but earning him credit within the Republican Party for loyalty. He had also served as United Nations ambassador under Nixon, and was head of the U.S. Liaison Office in China when Ford nominated him to be CIA director.

Before long, Ford was considering Bush to be his running mate in 1976. The job as CIA director was widely seen by the Washington press corps as a stepping stone for Bush to the vice presidency. There was also already speculation that he would someday run for president himself. But Bush's political future depended on his ability to get confirmed by the Senate to the CIA post.

Standing directly in Bush's way was Frank Church, who saw Bush's nomination as an effort by Ford to install a partisan hack at the CIA — someone who would do the bidding of the White House just as Congress was seeking to curb the Agency's abuses. Church viewed the Bush nomination as a direct White House attack on his committee's investigation.

It seemed likely that Bush had enough votes in the Senate to win confirmation, but Church went all out to stop him. On December 16, Church testified as a witness against Bush during his confirmation hearings before the Senate Armed Services Committee. Church testified that Bush's confirmation was "ill-advised" because of his partisan political background, and because he had refused to rule out running as vice president in 1976. Church complained that the White House was using the CIA as a "grooming room" for Bush, "before he is brought on stage next year as a vice-presidential running mate."

But Welch's slaying quickly changed the political calculus of the confirmation fight in favor of Bush — and against Frank Church. The confirmation fight became a referendum on the Church Committee — and on whether Frank Church should be held responsible for the murder of Richard Welch.

*   *   *

The day after Welch was killed, his father, who had been living in Athens with his son, asked Ron Estes to see if his son could be buried at Arlington National Cemetery. Welch had never served in the military, so burial at Arlington would require a special exemption.

Estes says he cabled CIA headquarters about the request. Director Colby (still in place while Bush fought to be confirmed) asked President Ford, who quickly approved a waiver for Welch's burial at Arlington.

That led to a grand political moment, stage-managed by the White House. A U.S. Air Force plane flew Welch's body from Athens to Washington. Aboard the aircraft, Welch's son — a Marine Corps lieutenant wearing his dress blues — accompanied his father's body. When it arrived in the D.C. area on December 30, 1975, the plane circled Andrews Air Force Base outside Washington for 45 minutes.

Daniel Schorr, a CBS News correspondent who covered the event, wrote in his personal journal, which he published in *Rolling Stone* in 1976, that "the public relations people explain that the big cargo plane, already overhead, will stay in a holding pattern and land at 7 a.m. so that it will be available for live televising on network morning news programs. We do in fact carry it live on the CBS Morning News."

Welch's funeral service, held at Arlington a week later, was attended by President Ford, Secretary of State Henry Kissinger, CIA director William Colby, and CIA nominee George Bush. No president had ever before attended the funeral of a slain CIA officer.

After the service, Ford stood beside Welch's widow, Kika, as Welch's coffin was placed on a horse-drawn caisson. "We watch, and film...the same caisson that carried the body of President Kennedy, the folded flag given to the widow by Colby," wrote Schorr in his journal.

"It is the CIA's first public national hero," Schorr wrote. "I have a sense that Welch, dead, has one more service to render the CIA.

He will be turned into a symbol in the gathering counteroffensive against disclosure."

While Ford, Kissinger, Colby, and Bush attended Welch's funeral, the FBI was investigating a death threat against Frank Church in retaliation for Welch's murder, sent by a group calling itself "Veterans Against Communist Sympathizers."

*　*　*

The White House and CIA followed a subtle but effective strategy to use the Welch murder to poison the political climate for Frank Church and the Church Committee. Immediately after Welch's assassination, the CIA sought to blame the Fifth Estate, a left-wing group based in Washington that published *CounterSpy*, the small anti-CIA magazine that had previously published long lists of CIA officials — including Welch's name when he served a pre-Athens posting in Peru. Agency officials also blamed Philip Agee, a former CIA officer who had just published *Inside the Company*, a controversial book that had listed the names of hundreds of CIA officers and agents.

Many observers saw the CIA efforts to blame *CounterSpy* and Agee as a way to shift the blame for Welch's murder from Greek terrorists to the Agency's American critics. And if the public inferred that those American critics also included Frank Church and the Church Committee, so be it.

Conservative pundits quickly made the link explicit. In early January, right-wing columnist Smith Hempstone wrote that the blame for Welch's murder should be shared by "the congressional committees that for nearly a year have been holding the CIA up to ridicule and verbal abuse."

"It might have been nice if Sen. Frank Church and Rep. Otis Pike had managed to be on hand when Welch's 23-year-old son, a Marine lieutenant, brought his father's flag-draped coffin home to Washington's Andrews Air Force Base last week," Hempstone wrote. "But then their committees are charged with investigating the CIA, not honoring its dead."

An anonymous, pro-CIA newsletter titled *The Pink Sheet* wrote in early January that Welch's murder "is a tragic reminder of a very basic truth: There are individuals and organizations in this country whose activities are aiding the enemies of the U.S. Are we to be impotent against such fifth columnists in our midst? Please write to your congressman and senators and ask what they propose to do about this increasingly dangerous problem. Instead of harming our internal security agencies, Senator Frank Church and his colleagues should be investigating outfits like the Fifth Estate." The *Pink Sheet* diatribe was included in CIA files and was publicly released by the CIA among other files declassified in 2004. It is not clear whether it was published in the 1970s by someone affiliated with the CIA.

Meanwhile, former CIA officers began to make themselves available to the press in order to attack Church. Former CIA officer Mike Ackerman told reporters that the Church Committee shared the blame for Welch's death, adding that the committee should have conducted its investigations without publicly disclosing CIA operations.

Frank Church felt he had to respond to Ackerman. "The gentleman is misinformed, since the committee has made no disclosure of information received from any source that would possibly jeopardize the life of any CIA agent," Church told the Associated Press.

In early January, *New York Times* columnist Anthony Lewis saw through the unfolding White House-CIA strategy, accusing the administration of using "the murder of Richard Welch as a political device," exploiting his death "to arouse a public backlash against legitimate criticism."

The Washington Star's Norman Kempster agreed, writing that "only a few hours after the CIA's Athens station chief was gunned down in front of his home, the agency began a subtle campaign intended to persuade Americans that his death was the indirect result of congressional investigations and the direct result of an article in an obscure magazine. The nation's press, by and large, swallowed the bait."

The exploitation of the murder of Richard Welch by the White House and the CIA ensured George Bush's confirmation as CIA director. On January 27, 1976, Bush sailed through the Senate on a vote of 64 to 27. Ford made only one concession to the Senate before the vote, announcing that Bush would not be his running mate in 1976. (Four years later, George Bush would be elected vice president as Ronald Reagan's running mate.)

* * *

While public support for the Church Committee rapidly waned after Welch's murder, the impact was even worse for the Pike

Committee, the late-starting parallel to the Church Committee in the House of Representatives.

For months, the Pike Committee had pursued a more confrontational strategy than the Church Committee in its dealings with the Ford White House and the CIA. While Frank Church had chosen to cautiously pick his fights, compromising when necessary to avoid major legal showdowns and delays, Representative Otis Pike and his committee had waged an unrelenting war against the White House and the CIA.

The Pike Committee got a late start thanks to the prolonged battle in the House over whether Representative Lucien Nedzi was fit to serve as chairman of the new intelligence committee. Nedzi finally quit under pressure — and was replaced by Pike — after press reports revealed Nedzi's close ties to the CIA.

After the controversy over Nedzi, Pike and his committee were not in the mood to compromise with the Ford Administration. Pike refused to force his staffers to sign secrecy agreements governing the handling of classified documents; Frank Church and the Church Committee had readily agreed to the same request from the CIA.

Pike also went out of his way to taunt the Ford White House. When White House official Roderick Hills accidentally left his briefcase containing a secret document behind in the Pike Committee's office following a meeting, Pike publicly chided him for it, claiming it showed his committee was better at protecting secrets than the White House.

"Pike was very smart," Searle Field, the staff director of the Pike Committee, said in an interview. "He was absolutely independent, not willing to roll over and play dead for anybody. If anything, that may have contributed to our difficulties since he had a sharp edge to him...I liked Otis Pike, but he was a prickly character."

On the other side, CIA director William Colby thought little of Pike. Colby was willing to cooperate with Frank Church and the Church Committee, but not with the Pike Committee. Pike and Colby bickered during the Pike Committee's first public hearings in August 1975 over the committee's access to CIA budget figures, and their relationship went downhill from there.

Pike then began a months-long feud with the White House and the CIA over access to classified documents, and over whether the Pike Committee had the right to publish classified information without the president's approval. The battle ultimately turned into a face-off between Ford and Pike that overshadowed the substance of what the committee was examining.

Despite its more confrontational tone, the Pike Committee actually did only a scattershot investigation of the CIA's past abuses, leaving that largely to the Church Committee. Instead, it framed its work around two questions: how much did taxpayers spend on the CIA, and what did the nation get for the money?

"There was sort of an agreement between Church and Pike," recalls Fritz Schwarz. "We would be more focused on wrongdoing, and they would be more focused on how well or badly the intelligence community had done its job of providing intelligence on major issues."

"We knew the money end of it wasn't really headline-grabbing," added Searle Field. [But] "we thought Congress should be focused first and foremost on controlling spending. I think he [Pike] felt members of Congress would respond positively to reports of spending abuses or spending without their knowledge...[CIA officials] were very aware that they had benefited from the lack of financial oversight of their operations."

So the Pike Committee focused on the CIA's virtually nonexistent budget controls (one small CIA overseas station reported a $41,000 bill for alcohol in just one year). The committee also conducted case studies on six foreign crises during the 1960s and 1970s in which the CIA had failed to provide adequate warning to policy makers. Many of the Pike Committee's fights with the White House and CIA were over access to intelligence about those case studies, and whether the committee could publish that intelligence.

After Welch's murder, the White House felt like it no longer had to negotiate with Otis Pike, and so brought the hammer down on the Pike Committee. In January 1976, Ford wrote to Pike that he had determined that the publication of the committee's report would harm national security, and set a January 29 deadline to resolve their disputes over classified information. Ford was arguing that he could suppress the committee's report because it contained classified information that Pike had refused to redact.

Ford's ultimatum put Pike in a bind — his committee was set to expire at the end of January. Pike had to get the House to give his committee an extension so that he would have time to resolve the dispute with the White House and publish the committee's report.

But after Welch's murder, the House was in no mood to support Pike in his fight with Ford. On January 29, the House voted 246 to 124 to block the publication of the Pike Committee's report unless the president approved its contents. That effectively killed the report. "I thought going to the full House...was never going to work," said Searle Field.

Pike bitterly complained that the vote made "a complete travesty of the whole doctrine of separation of powers," and that the Pike Committee's work had been "entirely an exercise in futility."

Ford was elated, and issued a statement saying the vote showed that "a large majority of House members shares my concern that our legitimate classified national-security information be denied to our enemies and potential enemies."

Yet the White House campaign to suppress the Pike Committee's report only served to guarantee that it would be leaked to the press. One thousand copies of the report had already been printed, Searle said.

"I have the Pike Report!" CBS broadcast reporter and news analyst Daniel Schorr wrote in his private journal on January 25, days before the final House vote went against Pike. "I look for a new story that can be aired immediately."

But Schorr got frustrated when he realized that CBS News executives did not think the Pike Report was as big a deal as he did. After his initial batch of stories, Schorr was told by his producers that the Pike Report had been fully mined and there was no appetite at CBS for more stories. With interest at CBS waning, Schorr decided to give the report to the *Village Voice*.

In its February 16, 1976, issue, the *Village Voice* published the Pike Report just days after the House had voted to suppress it, igniting a political firestorm in Washington. The Ford Administration went into overdrive attacking Pike and his committee, and the leak, not the report itself, became the story. Daniel Schorr was caught in the middle.

As controversy over the leak grew, Schorr faced demands from CBS News executives to reveal whether or not he was the leaker. If he did, it would be a violation of his contract; he had obtained the report for CBS, and then leaked it to another news organization without permission.

Schorr lost his nerve and lied. He told CBS that Lesley Stahl, who was then a correspondent in the CBS News Washington bureau, had leaked it to the *Village Voice;* her boyfriend, Aaron Latham, had written the *Village Voice* story that accompanied the publication of the report. Stahl was soon warned by friends that Schorr was telling CBS officials that he believed that Stahl had rifled through his desk, copied off the Pike report, and given it to Latham.

But that was a lie; the truth was that "Schorr was raging, 'They [CBS] aren't doing it [the Pike report] big enough!'" Stahl recalled in an interview. "And so he went to [*Voice* publisher] Clay Felker" and offered him the report. "And Aaron [Latham] went to Schorr's house, and Schorr gave it to him."

"He was trying to weasel out," recalls Stahl. Schorr's behavior was "bizarre and dishonest," she adds. Stahl got a lawyer. "I knew that CBS management was talking about firing me."

Fortunately for Stahl, the *Washington Post* published a story revealing that Schorr had been the one to share the report with the *Village Voice.* Once he had been publicly identified, Schorr was forced to testify before the House Ethics Committee, which had launched an investigation into the original congressional source of the leak.

CBS suspended Schorr, publicly claiming that it had done so because the correspondent couldn't work while he was the subject of a congressional investigation. Privately, however, Stahl was informed that the suspension was because Schorr had lied about her.

After the House Ethics Committee dropped its investigation of the leak, *60 Minutes* correspondent Mike Wallace conducted a confrontational interview with Schorr, asking him why he had implicated Lesley Stahl. Schorr resigned from CBS right after the *60 Minutes* interview.

The House of Representatives never published the Pike Committee report. But the Pike Committee still had a legacy; following the leak to the *Village Voice,* the Pike Committee report was independently published, without congressional approval, in Britain in 1977 and in the United States in 1992. And, while the Pike Committee was crippled by disputes with the Ford White House, its focus on whether the CIA's intelligence assessments were valid and whether the Agency was wasting taxpayer money, while less explosive than the Church Committee's focus on major abuses, nevertheless served as a model for much of the routine, day-to-day oversight work of the permanent congressional intelligence committees that were established later.

CHAPTER 27

"I see you have a presidential haircut"

FRANK CHURCH WAS stunned by the sudden reversal of the political climate in the wake of Richard Welch's murder. In early 1976, Church had to navigate through the Pike Committee's epic flame-out and also deal with a more confrontational CIA under the leadership of its newly confirmed director, George Bush.

During one closed hearing of the Church Committee, "Bush blurted out, 'you were responsible for Welch's assassination,'" recalled Fritz Schwarz. "It pissed off everybody. We forced Bush to apologize during the hearing."

Church also privately had to convince other senators, who were wavering in their support for the Church Committee in the face of the disinformation campaign by the White House and the CIA, that the committee's investigation was not responsible for Welch's murder.

"One of the things we did was tell other senators that we didn't reveal Welch's name," recalls Loch Johnson, Church's personal designee on the committee staff. "We had to make it clear to other senators that we had nothing to do with it."

The controversy over Welch's murder hit just as Church was also trying to figure out how soon he could turn from wrapping up the committee's work to launching his presidential campaign. Carl Burke and Henry Kimelman were quietly beginning the process of setting up the campaign, and Church, still an undeclared candidate, had ramped up his travel to give speeches around the country. Church even had buttons made up for impatient supporters that said, "Wait," in big bold letters, and then in small type: "until you've heard Frank Church."

With Church's political maneuvering now out in the open, he was left more exposed to pointed barbs inside the Church Committee. "Church arrived at one meeting of the committee, and Mondale said, 'Frank, I see you have a presidential haircut,'" recalled former Church Committee staffer David Aaron. "And Church said, 'Well, I see you don't.' And Mondale said, 'People in my state like shitty haircuts.'"

Mondale's joke exposed a bigger problem. With his attention shifting to the presidential race in early 1976, Church was increasingly absent from the Church Committee in its final days, as its work was winding down. Mondale said in an interview that Church's absences meant Mondale himself had to assume a larger leadership role on the Church Committee. "Frank decided he was running for president, and that meant that he was running and he wasn't around," Mondale recalled. "It was costly to him, and probably costly to the committee, too. He had to be away so much."

But privately, Church was still torn over his competing obligations. During early 1976, the controversy surrounding Welch's murder, combined with delays in the writing and editing of the Church Committee's final report, forced Church to repeatedly put off his plans to announce his presidential campaign. "I had an investigation, Church later said. "I had taken on that responsibility. I couldn't walk away from it."

* * *

For nearly a year, while the Church Committee conducted its investigations of past abuses by the intelligence community, Bill Miller and the foreign-policy experts he had hired had largely been sidelined by Fritz Schwarz and his legion of lawyers. But when it came time to write the committee's multivolume final report, Miller's team of experts proved invaluable. One was Anne Karalekas, a young staffer hired by Miller to write a history of the CIA for the Church Committee.

Karalekas was largely left alone for nearly a year while she conducted her own historical research. She spent most of her time at CIA headquarters, digging through records. "I got no direction," Karalekas recalled. "There was so much *sturm und drang* on the committee, so I was very happily left to myself. I would take a shuttle bus out to the Agency every day."

At the CIA she was given a badge and a work space, and was free to wander the halls at the Agency's headquarters. She soon discovered that the CIA had written 75 volumes of its own internal histories of key events, and she began to interview current and former officials to provide details and context that the internal histories had missed. The result of her work was a thorough history of the Central Intelligence Agency, included in the Church Committee's final report.

By combining the historical and policy context provided by Karalekas and Miller's other experts with the investigative bombshells from Schwarz and his lawyers, the Church Committee's multivolume final report offered both a compelling narrative and a historic accounting of the sins of the intelligence community in postwar America.

The final report also included a lengthy series of recommended intelligence reforms; Frank Church considered the creation of a permanent Senate intelligence oversight committee to be the most urgent. "The intelligence community's immunity from congressional oversight had been a basic reason for the failures, inefficiencies and misdeeds of the past," Church said in a statement accompanying the release of the Church Committee's final report. He later stated that he believed that "the worth of the work done" by the Church Committee was judged by the fact that the Senate created a permanent intelligence committee in 1976, almost immediately after the Church Committee completed its work. The House of Representatives, by contrast, scarred by the experience of the Pike Committee, did not create a permanent intelligence committee until 1977.

* * *

At noon on Saturday, August 7, 1976, Charles Zatrepalek, a homicide detective with the Dade County Public Safety Department, was called to respond to a crime scene along Dumbfoundling Bay on the Intracoastal Waterway, near North Miami Beach, north of downtown Miami. The crime scene was difficult to find; it was down a dirt road, through vacant land used locally as an illegal garbage dump, and near a man-made canal that emptied into the bay. There were no homes or businesses in the area.

The body of an unknown white male had been found inside a 55-gallon drum floating in the water by three young friends who were fishing. After talking with the police officer who first responded, Zatrepalek interviewed 21-year-old Jim Blundell, who was the first of the three friends to notice the drum floating nearby and became curious because it had heavy chains wrapped around it. Blundell reached for the drum, turned it around to see its top, and looked through the holes that had been cut through its side and "saw what he thought were the remains of a body," according to Zatrepalek's police report.

Police technicians began examining the barrel, while others took photographs of the crime scene from a police helicopter and a police boat. A police diver searched the canal bed for further evidence.

Detective Julio Ojeda, Zatrepalek's partner, arrived, followed by their supervisor, Lieutenant Gary Minium, who had been working the phones. He told Zatrepalek and Ojeda that the Broward County Sheriff's office reported that a white male by the name of Johnny Rosselli, age 71, was missing from Plantation, Florida. He had left his sister's home in Plantation on July 28 at 1 p.m. and had not been heard from since. On August 3, Rosselli's car, a silver 1975 Chevrolet Impala, had been found parked at Miami International Airport. Rosselli was a known organized crime figure, Minium said, and had recently testified before the Senate about his involvement with CIA plots to kill Fidel Castro.

At 2:30 p.m., a doctor from the Medical Examiner's office arrived and directed that the entire barrel with the body still inside should be taken to the Medical Examiner's office. A tow truck, accompanied by two police technicians, transported the barrel to the Dade County Medical Examiner's office, and local television news in Miami showed footage of the tow truck, driving through brush on the dirt road near the shore, carrying the barrel covered by a sheet.

Zatrepalek and Ojeda were there when a physician with the Medical Examiner's office removed the body from the drum and began an autopsy. The examiner found that the victim had not been shot; rather, he appeared to have been strangled to death.

A police technician reported that the victim's body was severely decomposed, and the victim's mouth was gagged by a red, green, and white flowered terry washcloth, secured by adhesive tape. A length of rope was loosely knotted around the victim's neck, while the rope's other end had been sticking out of the barrel's lid. The left side of the victim's torso had been slit open. The victim's legs had been amputated at the upper thighs: the exposed bone ends indicated that a handsaw, "possibly of the hacksaw variety," had been used to fit the body into the barrel.

Zatrepalek and Ojeda then went to the FBI's Miami office to obtain the fingerprints of Johnny Rosselli. At 11:40 p.m., a police technician made a positive fingerprint match, identifying the body found in the barrel as Johnny Rosselli.

*   *   *

Johnny Rosselli's grisly murder was the horrific postscript to the Church Committee. And coming on the heels of the shocking deaths of Sam Giancana and Orlando Letelier, it sparked an immediate response from members of the Church Committee. The coincidences of the murders were piling up—and it was no longer possible to ignore the connections to the committee's investigation.

Two days after Rosselli's body was found, Senator Howard Baker called for both the FBI and CIA to provide any information they had about Rosselli's murder. "There appears to be a connection" between the Giancana and Rosselli murders, Baker told reporters. "Both agreed to testify on the same subject. Both were involved in the same assassination operation." Rosselli's murder hit Baker particularly hard; Rosselli had told Baker that he was "concerned for his safety and his life and that he was risking his well-being by testifying before the committee," according to a memo written by Church Committee Republican staffer Mike Madigan in the aftermath of Rosselli's death.

But the FBI was not interested in getting involved in the Rosselli case, any more than it had wanted to investigate Sam Giancana's murder. Immediately after Rosselli's body was found, FBI director Clarence Kelley said the Bureau did not have jurisdiction in the case.

The FBI could not stay entirely out of it, however. Under pressure from Baker and others in the Senate, Attorney General Edward Levi later announced that he was ordering the FBI to investigate

362

whether Rosselli was murdered because of his Church Committee testimony. A Justice Department spokesman said that the FBI's jurisdiction in the case would come from a federal statute that made it a crime to obstruct the proceedings of government agencies and congressional committees. Yet in spite of Levi's announcement, the FBI did little to investigate the case, and instead left it largely to the Miami police.

Gary Hart took the murder of Johnny Rosselli harder than any other member of the Church Committee. He believed that it was crucial to find out whether Rosselli had been murdered because of his Church Committee testimony, especially after Sam Giancana had also been murdered right before he was scheduled to testify. Hart was shocked that "no federal agency seemed interested in the Rosselli murder," he recalled. "Not the FBI, not the CIA — no one wanted to look into it."

"It seemed pretty obvious to me that [Rosselli] was killed because of his testimony before the committee," Hart added. "Same with Giancana. To me it set off all kinds of warning signals and red lights. I just assumed that people would jump all over it, and the FBI and CIA would send in their top people to find out who killed these guys."

Hart was frustrated that many in the press and government sought to dismiss the notion that the murders of Giancana and Rosselli were anything more than normal gangland slayings tied to internal Mafia feuds. "The Rosselli and Giancana murders have always haunted me," he later confessed.

Gary Hart and Rick Inderfurth, who was Hart's designee on the Church Committee staff, both recalled attending a closed-door meeting of key committee members, led by Frank Church, to discuss Rosselli's murder. Hart argued that the committee had to do something about the murder, that it damaged the Senate's credibility to have its witnesses killed and silenced, and Frank Church then gave his approval for Hart to meet with the Miami police investigating the case. "Church told Gary, 'go ahead, you do it,'" Inderfurth recalled. Howard Baker wanted to meet with the police too, but couldn't because of his schedule, and so he agreed to send two of his staffers instead.

On August 19, 1976, Gary Hart and Inderfurth, along with Baker staffers Mike Madigan and Howard Liebengood, flew to

Miami to meet with the detectives investigating the Rosselli murder. They registered in their hotel under assumed names to avoid press attention.

The next morning, the quartet met with the two lead detectives on the case, Zatrepalek and Ojeda, along with their boss, Lieutenant Minium, and other detectives assisting the investigation. The police showed Hart and the staffers photos of the crime scene, which were grisly and left no doubt that Rosselli's murder had been a Mafia execution. "The senator and his committee were briefed on the information that these investigators had developed to the present," a police report on the meeting states. "The senator briefed these investigators on John Rosselli's [Church Committee] testimony...At the conclusion of the meeting, these investigators, along with the other homicide investigators involved in the Rosselli case, held a meeting in which the facts that the senator had provided were discussed."

"The police seemed to be taking it seriously that Rosselli had been killed because of his Senate testimony," Inderfurth recalled in an interview.

But the police already knew that Rosselli's murder was going to be difficult to solve.

"The first problem, we all realized, we were behind at least a week since the murder," Zatrepalek recalled in an interview. "We figured probably four or five days [for Rosselli's body] to decompose, which trapped all the gas in his skin and caused him to float. It took us a couple of days to start putting all the pieces together. Most of the homicide cops helped us, which sped everything up. We did learn about John's past as we got deeper into the investigation. Which led us all over the country. The more we got into the investigation, the more names came up."

*   *   *

Zatrepalek and Ojeda plunged headlong into the film-noir world of Johnny Rosselli's life. They heard the same stories—about Rosselli, Giancana, Judith Campbell, and the CIA—that J. Edgar Hoover had discovered in 1962, and which Andy Postal and the Church Committee staff had discovered in 1975. They traveled to Washington to meet with the CIA, and to Los Angeles to interview Rosselli's old friends, lawyers, and business associates. They even subpoenaed

Meyer Lansky, the aging Mafia mastermind who had helped build the mob's casino operations in Cuba before the revolution that brought Fidel Castro to power.

But they also uncovered the grim truth about Rosselli's life since his involvement in the CIA-Mafia alliance. By 1976, Rosselli was nearly broke and living with his sister near Fort Lauderdale. He put on a suave front when he testified before the Church Committee, but his fortunes had been on a downward spiral ever since the late 1960s, when the law had caught up with him. Rosselli had been arrested in connection with a long-running scam to cheat celebrity card players at the Friars Club in Los Angeles, and he also faced immigration-related charges and deportation after the government finally unraveled his true identity as Filippo Sacco. He was convicted in the Friars Club scam and sentenced to five years in prison, and also received a short sentence on an immigration-law violation. Rosselli went to prison in 1971 and was paroled in 1973. Meanwhile, he had also been forced to testify before a federal grand jury investigating the secret ownership by the Detroit mob of the Frontier hotel and casino in Las Vegas. Maurice Friedman, another businessman involved in the Frontier deal, cooperated with prosecutors, and the leaders of the Detroit mob were convicted.

While it was clear that Rosselli had been murdered by the mob, Zatrepalek and Ojeda still struggled to determine who did it, and why. One of the main theories the detectives pursued was that Rosselli had been killed to avenge his grand-jury appearance in the Frontier case that sent the Detroit mob leaders to prison. Detroit mob boss Tony Zerilli may have blamed Rosselli, even though Rosselli had refused to talk in that case. When asked in an interview whether he thinks Zerilli, the Detroit boss, ordered the hit on Rosselli, Zatrepalek said "I would not doubt it." Federal prosecutors tried to pressure Rosselli to cooperate in the Frontier case by making it appear that he was already talking, and arranged for Rosselli to run into Tony Zerilli outside of the federal grand jury hearing in Los Angeles, according to *Handsome Johnny,* the 2018 biography of Rosselli. The scheme by the prosecutors to convince the Detroit mobsters that Rosselli was talking may have worked too well. An FBI informant later told the Bureau that Rosselli's murder was the result of the mob's belief that his testimony had led to the imprisonment of the Detroit mob leaders.

But it was possible that Rosselli's testimony to the Church Committee was also a factor in the Mafia's decision to kill him. Santo Trafficante, the mob boss of Tampa, had been involved with Rosselli and Giancana in the CIA-Mafia alliance to kill Castro, and there was plenty of evidence that Trafficante had ominous connections to Rosselli's murder.

Unlike Sam Giancana and Johnny Rosselli, Trafficante was unwilling to cooperate with the Church Committee, and he managed to avoid testifying, reportedly by leaving the country for Central America. Trafficante may have been angry that Rosselli was talking to Frank Church's committee.

Meanwhile, Miami police files show that an FBI informant told the Bureau that he had attended a meeting with mob bosses from Chicago and Cleveland where it was said that Trafficante had been given the contract to kill Rosselli. (In the same meeting, there was talk about "screwups" in the hit on Rosselli; the barrel containing Rosselli's body was supposed to have sunk in the water and never have been found.)

The Miami detectives also learned that on July 16, 1976, two weeks before he disappeared, Rosselli had dinner with Trafficante and his wife; Rosselli brought along his sister, Edith Daigle, and her husband, Joe.

In September 1976, the Miami detectives were also told by the FBI that records showed that a phone call to Santo Trafficante's home in Tampa had been made from a pay phone at 10:12 a.m. on July 28 from a pay phone at the Lauderhill Shopping Mall, just a 10-minute drive from Rosselli's sister's house. The call was made just hours before Rosselli disappeared. Zatrepalek and Ojeda collected latent fingerprints on the pay phone, but none led to any suspects.

They also subpoenaed Sam Cagnina, who was reputed to be a hitman who worked for Trafficante. There were rumors that Cagnina had bragged that he was involved in Rosselli's murder, but he didn't give them anything useful. The detectives were never able to question Trafficante himself.

"We tried to contact Trafficante a couple of times and never got a response," Zatrepalek says.

Zatrepalek and Ojeda never had enough evidence to make any arrest in the case.

Both Ojeda and Zatrepalek acknowledged in interviews that

they were caught up in an investigation into racketeering and drug trafficking within the Miami police homicide unit in the late 1970s and early 1980s. Both denied that corruption within the homicide department affected the Rosselli murder investigation.

When asked several times whether he was pressured or influenced by organized crime not to dig deeper into the murder of Johnny Rosselli, Ojeda says, "You think I was afraid of them? Nobody from our department would have been pressured by the Mafia."

Zatrepalek testified against other homicide unit officers, including Ojeda. Despite the department's corruption, he says, "nobody ever came up to us telling us stay away from the [Rosselli] investigation."

The drug kingpin who recruited the homicide officers to work for him was not Santo Trafficante, but rather Mario Escandar, whom Zatrepalek says "the Cubans got us involved with."

Escandar eventually testified against the nine Miami homicide officers who helped him traffic drugs, including Zatrepalek and Ojeda. Zatrepalek admits their cocaine use and involvement with Escandar was "absolutely a poor choice on all of us."

Johnny Rosselli's murder—like Sam Giancana's murder—has never been solved.

CHAPTER 28

"And then it was over"

EARLY ON MARCH 18, 1976, Frank and Bethine Church — along with about 100 friends, supporters, and staffers — eagerly piled into three buses in Boise and began an hour-long drive to Idaho City, a historic Old West mining town where Church planned to announce his candidacy for president of the United States.

But just as the convoy was edging out of the city, all three buses suddenly turned around and snaked back through Boise's streets. They came to a halt outside 109 West Idaho Street, a large private home near the city's downtown. Frank Church had left his glasses at his mother-in-law's house. Church ran in and got his glasses, and the buses got back on the road and started the trip all over again.

Everything about Frank Church's presidential campaign in 1976 was late.

In January 1975, Frank Church had promised Senate Majority Leader Mike Mansfield that he would not run for president until after the Church Committee's work was finished. (At least that was Frank Church's interpretation of his promise; others believed he had promised not to run at all in 1976.) The Church Committee's investigation was originally supposed to be concluded by September of 1975, but it had been extended through February of 1976, and so Church had repeatedly delayed his entry into the race.

Even then, while the investigative work was completed, the Church Committee's multivolume final report was not finished; it would not be publicly released until April 1976. But Frank Church finally and unilaterally declared in March that the committee's work was finished, and that he had fulfilled his commitment to Mansfield. "We were largely done by that time," recalls Fritz Schwarz, the committee's chief counsel.

But by mid-March, when Church finally launched his campaign, the race for the Democratic nomination was virtually over. Former Georgia governor Jimmy Carter, who had launched his own presidential campaign in December 1974, had already built a commanding lead after winning key early contests in the Midwest, the North, and the South. Carter was taking full advantage of the Democratic Party's new delegate rules, which gave a prohibitive advantage to an early front-runner.

Even Senator Joe Biden, who Frank Church had helped by lending him staff during his 1972 campaign, and then helped again after his wife and daughter were killed in a car crash just after his election to the Senate, snubbed Church and went with Carter. Biden became chairman of Jimmy Carter's national steering committee during the Democratic primary season; Biden's move to Carter was just one of many signs that influential Democrats were not waiting around for Frank Church to finally get into the race. "I think that hurt Church," when Biden endorsed Carter, recalled Susan Hunter, who worked on the Church campaign and later in his Senate office. Biden told reporters that Carter appealed to him because he was running a campaign based on his personal integrity, rather than on political issues. That was a pointed rebuke to the party's liberals, including Frank Church.

Getting into the race so late and starting so far behind meant that Church had to embrace a complicated political strategy that only offered an outside chance of success.

Ideally, Church wanted to present himself to the nation as the liberal alternative to the centrist Carter. But even that strategy wasn't possible because there were already other prominent liberals in the race, led by Representative Morris Udall of New Mexico.

So by the time he entered the race, Church figured he had one long-shot strategy that might work, and that was to pick a couple of small states where he could take on Carter one-on-one and beat him, and then turn to California, which was to hold its primary on June 8, the final day of the Democratic primary calendar.

Church was popular in California, and had worked hard to develop a network of supporters among the state's political leaders, including Leo McCarthy, the speaker of the California State Assembly. Church also had a base of financial support among wealthy California donors; he was one of Hollywood's favorite candidates. If Church could win the California primary after defeating Carter in a couple of smaller states, he and his advisers believed, he could head to the Democratic National Convention in July with a chance of turning the party against Carter and winning the nomination in a brokered convention.

But Carter was suspicious of Church's strategy, and during a secret meeting in the Idaho senator's office, he pointedly asked Church if he was part of an orchestrated "ABC" plan—an "Anybody But Carter" effort by the Democratic establishment to stop him from getting the nomination. Church denied it, insisting that he represented only himself. Yet Carter's suspicions weren't off base; Church's entire strategy was built on the idea that Carter was a weak front-runner who could be stopped at the convention once his flaws were revealed.

But even that Rube Goldberg strategy was already looking shaky by the time of Church's announcement in Idaho City. On March 12, California governor Jerry Brown announced that he was running for president. Brown was a 38-year-old political phenom who upended California politics after he was elected governor in 1974, and his entry into the presidential race meant that Frank Church had no realistic chance of winning the California primary. Most of Church's leading California supporters quickly shifted to supporting Brown.

California was so critical to Church's strategy that without a shot in the state, Church's campaign had no shot at all, recalls Mike Wetherell, Church's closest traveling aide during the campaign. "We had done a lot of work in California, talking to people, calling people," Wetherell recalled. "We talked to a lot of people who we knew would go to Brown if he announced, but would support Church if he didn't. We were fairly certain that if Brown stayed out, we could win California.

"When Brown got in, my feeling was it's over," Wetherell adds. "The end of the campaign came when Brown entered the race."

Wetherell recalls that Church knew Brown's decision spelled doom for his campaign. "I had one conversation with [Church] where he said to me that he had thought about dropping out of the race, but the fact was there were so many people who had committed to him that he didn't want to disappoint all of his supporters."

"I had to try a late, late strategy," Church recalled later. "It might have worked, but there wasn't room in it for two candidates, and there was no way to copywrite it. And along came the governor of California as another late, late candidate. And that, I think, made the race impossible."

"The strategy floundered on Brown's decision to enter the race," Church added in a 1979 interview. "Brown entered the race just before I did. But by then there was no way to stop it."

Publicly at the time he entered the race, Church insisted he wasn't too late; his campaign made up campaign pins featuring a turtle, which of course beats the hare in the end. But the truth was that by the time of Church's announcement, his presidential campaign seemed like little more than a Church family vanity project.

*   *   *

Frank and Bethine had chosen Idaho City, an old gold-rush town that had become a tourist attraction, as the site to announce the campaign because that was where Church's grandfather first lived when he came to Idaho in 1871. It was where Church's father had been born in 1889. And it was where Bethine's father had announced his bid for governor in 1940.

Church's announcement drew a crowd of about 2,500; local supporters sold $1.50 boxed lunches of baked ham, roast turkey, baked beans, rolls, and ice cream. The band from Boise High School, where Church had been student-body president, played "The Star-Spangled Banner."

With nothing to lose, Church gave an announcement address that fully expressed the radical, anti-establishment side of his personality. Despite the reduced public support for the Church Committee following Richard Welch's murder, Church centered his speech on the abuses of power that his investigation had uncovered. "Our tragedy in recent years springs from a leadership principally motivated by fear, from men of little faith," Church told the crowd.

Frank and Bethine Church in Idaho City, Idaho, at the announcement of Church's 1976 presidential campaign.

It is a leadership of weakness and fear that produces "enemy lists" of American citizens whose only offense is that of disagreeing with presidential policies. It is a leadership of weakness and fear that grants a full pardon to a former President...it is a leadership of weakness and fear which insists that we must imitate the Russians in our treatment of foreign peoples, adopting their methods of bribery, blackmail, abduction, and coercion...which permits the most powerful agencies of our government—the CIA, the FBI, and the IRS—to systematically ignore the very laws intended to protect the people.

Church then attacked the orthodoxy of American foreign policy, bringing to the campaign trail the anti-imperialist message that he had sharpened since his battles over the Cooper-Church Amendment and the Vietnam War.

I would call for a discriminating foreign policy which rec-
ognizes that the postwar period is over; that we are no longer the one rich patron of a war-wrecked world...there is
no justification any longer for us to subsidize half a hundred foreign governments scattered all over the globe...in
Africa and Asia, new societies are emerging from the grip of
19th-century colonialism. This Third World will be filled
with revolution and upheaval for the balance of this century. A volcano cannot be capped. The United States can
abide much ferment in distant places. But we cannot successfully serve as trustee for the broken empires of Europe.
The foreign policy of this country must be wrested from the
hands of that fraternity of compulsive interventionists who
have involved us in so many futile, foreign wars.

As so often happened to Frank Church, the reporters covering
his announcement largely ignored the substance of his speech,
missing the fact that he was running for president on a message
radically at odds with the cautious, Kissinger-style foreign-policy
realism that dominated Washington at the time. In fact, Church's
announcement drew more interest from the foreign press than from
American journalists; Japanese and Italian reporters dominated the
press gaggle that flew from Washington on a charter plane with
Church for the announcement. They were covering Church because
of the corporate bribery scandals in their countries triggered by the
investigations of Church's multinational subcommittee.

When Frank Church stepped down from the wooden front steps
of the county courthouse where he had delivered his speech, a
Secret Service detail took over his security—which, until that
moment, had consisted of Mike Wetherell nervously scanning the
crowd.

Bethine Church had already decided that she would be her husband's constant travel partner every day of the campaign. Along
with Wetherell, Bethine would attend every event, providing real-
time advice, coaching Church on his every move. While she was an
astute political adviser, Bethine's constant critiques sometimes exasperated Church. "During the campaign Frank once said to her,
'Bethine, have I ever satisfied you?'" recalled Wetherell. The Secret

Service gave Bethine the code name Jaws. (Frank's code was Frosty, Bethine's nickname for him.)

With Church's presidential campaign also came more intrusive questions about his health than he had ever had to face from the press before. Reporters wanted more details about Church's youthful fight with cancer in the 1940s. Church had to disclose that he had suffered testicular cancer, and that he had lost a testicle as a result of his cancer treatment.

Bill Hall, Church's press secretary, then began to get follow-up questions from reporters about whether Church could still have sex. Hall wrote in his memoir that one woman journalist seemed to be testing Church during an interview in his office, when she sat on the floor at his feet with her blouse half unbuttoned. When Church simply answered her questions about foreign policy, she seemed disappointed, Hall said. "I don't get much of a reaction from him — no man-woman reaction, if you know what I mean," the journalist told Hall over drinks later. "Off the record," she asked Hall, "can he get it on?"

She wasn't the only reporter asking. "The question persisted of whether Church was sexually functional," Hall wrote. He told Church that the questions weren't going away, so Church told him the truth. "Well, if they really have to get into that, then the answer, happily, is yes. I'd have been in a padded cell long before this if it hadn't been for the pleasures of sex." Then he added: "If it's gone that far, you'll be getting questions on this too: those radiation treatments were massive, over my entire body. I'm sterile."

*   *   *

Church traveled to Sacramento to meet with Jerry Brown days after his announcement to try to figure out how serious Brown was about his candidacy. But Church got nothing out of Brown.

In an interview, Brown described their meeting simply as "pleasant." "These things are formalities — you go and meet the press." Brown added that he "didn't really know Frank Church."

Church went ahead with a fundraiser in Los Angeles filled with celebrities, including Milton Berle and Ed Asner. After the fundraiser, Church drove to meet with Jimmy Durante, the comedy icon, at his Los Angeles home. Durante, a lifelong liberal, had traveled to Idaho to campaign for Church when he ran for reelection to the Senate, and they had become friends. Other Hollywood celebrities, notably Paul Newman, also embraced Church. But by the time he left Los Angeles, Church knew that Brown was not just a favorite-son candidate in the state; he was planning to go all out nationwide to challenge Church and Udall for the liberal vote.

With Brown in the race, California was no longer a realistic target for Church. His options narrowing, Church resolved to gamble everything on Nebraska.

The Nebraska primary was not scheduled until May 11, which gave Church time to campaign there and create a local organization. (Church did briefly contest one other state before Nebraska. He made an appearance at the South Carolina state convention on March 31, where he won precisely one delegate—his first in any state. That delegate was a rising young Black leader named Jim Clyburn, who later became one of the most influential congressional leaders in the Democratic Party in the 21st century.)

Nebraska's small size fit Church's slender campaign budget. Henry Kimelman, his chief fundraiser, later wrote that the campaign "raised and spent less than $2.2 million" during Church's entire presidential run. Desperate for cash, Church also accepted federal campaign matching funds; that led him to recuse himself by only voting "present" on legislation to amend the campaign-finance law. "I believe that casting my vote to amend the act after the fact [of receiving funding under the previous system]," said Church, "could be seen as a conflict of interest."

Forrest Church took a leave from Harvard Divinity School, where he was studying for a PhD, and moved to Nebraska to work full-time on the campaign. Former Church staffer Patrick Shea said in an interview that Forrest Church, who was then married, told him that he'd had a secret affair with a campaign worker while he was in Nebraska. The affair did not become public during the campaign.

By focusing on Nebraska, Church bypassed earlier contests in some of the biggest and most competitive states, including Wisconsin and Pennsylvania, where Carter battled Udall and Senator Henry Jackson—the conservative Democrat who had tried to sabotage Church's investigation of the CIA and Chile.

Carter's victory in the Pennsylvania primary on April 27 seemed to cement his position as the front-runner; Jackson dropped out shortly afterward. Meanwhile Hubert Humphrey—the Democratic Party warhorse who was back in the Senate after serving as vice president and losing to Richard Nixon in 1968—had been toying with entering the race. After Pennsylvania, however, Humphrey announced that he was staying out.

It seemed like Frank Church's campaign was operating on borrowed time as well.

*   *   *

But just as Jimmy Carter seemed poised to grasp the Democratic nomination, something unexpected started happening in Nebraska: Frank Church's campaign began to click. As Church barnstormed the state, he discovered that Nebraska felt very familiar. At a public forum in Idaho later in 1976, Church said that "in Nebraska, people were very much concerned about farm problems, concerned about small business, the kinds of things that would crop up here in Idaho frequently cropped up in the questions I was asked in Nebraska."

At first, Carter tried to ignore both Church and Nebraska. But Church's rise in the polls in the state began to unnerve him. Just before the primary, Carter showed up unannounced at a Democratic event in Lincoln where Church was speaking.

Carter was trying to surprise Church and steal the media spotlight, but Church's Secret Service detail warned Church and his staff that Carter was on his way. Church talked hurriedly with Ira Dorfman, his advance man, about how to handle Carter when he arrived.

Dorfman quickly scrounged up a bucket of potatoes and gave them to Church, who then presented them to Carter when he walked on stage. "Here, Governor," exclaimed Church as he handed the bucket to Carter. "Have some Idaho peanuts," prompting laughs from the audience. It was just a mild joke; Carter touted his background as a peanut farmer in Georgia, and the peanut had become a Carter campaign symbol. But Church's real message to Carter was that he had beaten him to the punch and had been ready for Carter when he arrived onstage. Carter's ambush attempt had failed.

Church stunned Carter and the political world by winning the Nebraska primary. Suddenly, Church's candidacy no longer seemed like a Church family vanity project.

Two weeks later, Church won again in both Oregon and Idaho; his victory in Oregon forced the national press to start treating his campaign seriously. On June 1, Church won in Montana, and just barely lost to Carter in Rhode Island.

But Jerry Brown had been winning too — in Maryland on May 18 and in Nevada a week later — and he was poised to sweep California on June 8. More importantly, Carter was piling up an insurmountable delegate lead.

The momentum the Church campaign had built in Nebraska and Oregon finally hit a brick wall in California.

Blocked by Brown in California, Church was uncertain what to do next. "One night Church called me up to his hotel room," recalled Ira Dorfman. "I knocked on the door, went in, and Frank and Bethine were in bed. Church asked me, 'Ira, where do you think we should go after Oregon?' I said, 'Why are you asking me?'"

In fact, there was no good answer to Church's question. "It was a checkmate situation after Oregon," Dorfman acknowledged. "We really didn't have anywhere to go."

Church's main advisers, Henry Kimelman and Carl Burke, were badly divided, but finally Church decided to campaign in Ohio, which was scheduled to hold its primary on the same day as California. It was a desperation move; Church had no organization in Ohio, and few supporters there. "We had nothing set up in Ohio," recalled Dorfman. "We just ran out of options."

Church's Ohio campaign was ill-starred from the start. He briefly had to suspend his campaign in the state to return to Idaho when a major dam broke near Idaho Falls, killing six. Church's campaign plane, chartered on the cheap, was temporarily put out of action in Cleveland when a baggage-handling truck hit one of the propellers on the aging DC-3. "We had to wait 12 hours for parts," recalls Dorfman.

Church's move into Ohio also infuriated the fading Udall, who thought he had an agreement with Church that he would leave Ohio to the New Mexico congressman in order to give him a clear shot at Carter. Udall and his supporters were suspicious that Church had come to Ohio to knock Udall out of the race and win points with Carter, thus enhancing his own chances of being named Carter's running mate. Church's late effort in Ohio was the most controversial episode of his campaign, and led to lingering, personal bitterness against Church by Udall.

On June 8, Carter won Ohio, Udall was second, and Church

third; Brown swept California. On June 14, less than three months after he began his campaign, Church dropped out of the race and endorsed Jimmy Carter.

His late success against Carter left Frank Church wondering, for the rest of his life, what would have happened if he had gotten into the race earlier.

*　*　*

In the immediate aftermath of the primary season, Jimmy Carter was inclined to choose Frank Church as his running mate. On paper, Church was the perfect choice to balance the ticket. He was a Westerner while Carter was from the South, he was a liberal, while Carter was a moderate, and Church had extensive experience in Washington and particularly in Congress, which Carter did not. Importantly for Carter, Church had also been through the presidential primary campaign, where he had been vetted by the voters and had done surprisingly well. "If an instant choice had been required at that time, it would have been Senator Frank Church of Idaho, or perhaps Senator Henry Jackson of Washington," Carter later wrote.

But many of Carter's advisers were opposed to Church. They heard from senators who didn't like him; his old reputation as a pretentious publicity hound still hung over Church like a dark cloud. "Until the very end, Frank Church of Idaho, an early critic of the Vietnam War and the CIA, was high on Carter's and Rosalynn's list (but no one else's)," Stuart E. Eizenstat, Carter's chief domestic-policy adviser, later observed.

Church himself was ambivalent about the vice presidency. He wanted Carter to offer it to him, and he would have accepted it. His office put together a talking-points memo for the press, extolling how well Church would fit on the ticket with Carter. But he wasn't willing to go all out to get it. When Carter invited him to come to his home in Plains, Georgia, for an interview about being his running mate, Church told him he couldn't make it because he was going on vacation with his family in the Caribbean. He agreed to meet with Carter later, at the start of the Democratic convention in New York instead.

Before the convention, Church did meet in Washington with Charles Kirbo, Carter's adviser in charge of vetting potential running mates, and he provided Kirbo with detailed personal information to aid in the selection process. His responses to Kirbo revealed that Frank Church had a bare bones financial profile, with little to his name other than his Senate salary of $43,025 and his house, and lived a simple personal life, unheard-of among presidential candidates and other major political figures in more recent decades.

He reported to Kirbo that his taxes had never been audited, that he had never been sued, and had never been divorced. In response to a question on Kirbo's questionnaire about whether there was "anything in your personal life which you feel, if known, may be of embarrassment in the presidential election this year in the event you should be a candidate," Church wrote, "nothing."

In addition, his doctor at Walter Reed Army Medical Center provided a letter stating that Church was in good medical condition, and that the "area of surgical absence of the left testicle showed no evidence of any active disease."

Despite Church's clean slate, his meeting with Kirbo "did not go well," recalled Church aide and family friend Peter Fenn. It seemed to Church and his aides that Kirbo "didn't like Church."

By contrast, Walter Mondale readily agreed to go to Plains to meet with Carter. As a liberal senator from the Midwest, Mondale offered the same ticket-balancing attributes as Church. But Mondale offered more; he was popular among fellow senators and he was a protégé of Hubert Humphrey, which meant that he had the full support of the Democratic Party's establishment. Mondale had also been a leading member of the Church Committee, which appealed to Carter's reformist outlook.

"I think he had seen me on a Sunday news talk show, talking about the Church Committee, and he liked how I looked and sounded," recalled Mondale in an interview. "Carter knew that I had been very active in the Church Committee, and one of the reasons I interested him was that I had that kind of knowledge of the government and what those agencies had done, and he didn't want that kind of stuff going on in his government. I think my experience on the committee was an asset to me in his decision to pick me. I don't think it was the reason, but it was something that helped.

"When I met with him about being his running mate," Mondale added, "I told him that as vice president I would like to work on implementing the recommendations of the Church Committee, and he agreed with that." Mondale offered Carter the reformist cachet of the Church Committee—without having to actually choose Frank Church.

* * *

Church soon began to hear that his chances were fading, and that Carter was focusing on other candidates, including Mondale and Senator Edmund Muskie of Maine.

Church finally met with Carter in his hotel suite at the convention in New York. The meeting started off poorly: "Church and Bethine and I were being introduced around, and I was taking pictures, and I backed up and stepped on Rosalynn Carter's foot," recalls Wetherell, still mortified decades later. "She was very gracious about it, but Bethine gave me a look that could kill." Church then talked privately with Carter, quickly realizing that it was a pro forma meeting and that he was no longer in contention. The two men had no chemistry.

"Afterward, I told Church that he [Carter] can get everything he wants from you from Walter Mondale, and Mondale is used to playing second fiddle to Humphrey," recalled Wetherell. Despite his studied ambivalence about the vice presidency, Church was upset after Carter announced that he had chosen Mondale—he had wanted the job after all. The fact that the choice was Mondale, his political rival from the Church Committee, rankled even more.

"I never talked to Frank Church about the vice presidency," Mondale said. "I know that he wanted to be selected, but Carter chose me and then it was over, and we never talked about it."

Church was suspicious that CIA officials, who despised him after the Church Committee, had worked behind the scenes to try to torpedo his selection as vice president. Just before the Democratic convention in New York, he got a call from the CIA saying the Agency had been told that the *Economist* magazine was going to publish a story revealing that the Church Committee had been infiltrated by the KGB.

"Can you imagine any rumor more certain to spook a presidential candidate than that his prospective vice president has overseen an operation which was infiltrated by the KGB?" Church told his son, Forrest, who recounted their conversation in his memoir. "This is the kind of disinformation I have been poring over ad nauseam for almost two years. I'll bet you anything that after the convention we won't hear another thing about this."

It turned out that the reporter the CIA had told Church was writing the story did not exist, and no story was ever published. "Church's feeling that he had been sandbagged by the CIA might have been an illusion," Forrest Church wrote. "One thing is certain, however. There is no member of the Senate whom the leaders of our intelligence services would have less preferred sitting a heart-beat away from the presidency."

CHAPTER 29

"I've got to do it"

AFTER JIMMY CARTER won the 1976 election and became president, it didn't take long for Frank Church to sour on Carter, and to view his support for the first Democrat in the White House since Lyndon Johnson as little more than a grim obligation.

Party loyalty meant that he sometimes had to trudge to the White House to listen in person as Carter gave his dour and interminably long addresses to the nation. Arriving at the White House for one Carter speech, Church found himself standing next to Dale Bumpers, a mordant Democratic senator from Arkansas. Both men thought Carter's speech that day was so bad that they avoided reporters so they wouldn't have to comment on it.

As they walked out of the White House, Bumpers turned to Church, shook his head, and said, "That man couldn't sell pussy on a troop train."

Frank Church couldn't hide his disdain for Carter, and gleefully recounted Bumpers's joke to Mike Wetherell, who had become his Senate chief of staff after working on his presidential campaign. Church was hardly alone; most of the leading Democrats in Congress hated the insular Carter White House, a deep anger that would be reflected in Senator Ted Kennedy's primary challenge of the incumbent Carter in 1980.

"I remember Church coming back from the White House once,

and I asked him how did it go," recalled Garry Wenske, who worked on Church's Senate staff during the Carter Administration. "And he just shook his head."

Carter and his senior aides hated Church right back. Carter's early interest in making Frank Church his running mate did not carry over into a good relationship once Carter was in the White House. For one, Zbigniew Brzezinski, Carter's national security adviser, "thought Church was a pompous blowhard," recalled David Aaron, who became Brzezinski's deputy after serving on the staff of the Church Committee. "I know that whenever Church's name came up, Brzezinski would grimace."

Yet in spite of the poisonous intraparty atmosphere, the late 1970s saw a remarkable flowering of progressive reform in Jimmy Carter's Washington, when the Democrats controlled the White House and had huge majorities in both the House and the Senate. The reformist surge that began after Carter's election in 1976 is perhaps the most underappreciated aspect of his presidency.

It was the period in which Frank Church's legacy was cemented.

*　　*　　*

Many of the most significant reforms of the intelligence community that resulted from the Church Committee—in addition to major reforms affecting corporate America stemming from Church's multinational subcommittee—came about during the Carter Administration.

The most historic legislative achievement came in 1978 with the enactment of the Foreign Intelligence Surveillance Act, which for the first time imposed significant legal limits on the ability of the CIA, the FBI, and the NSA to wiretap and spy on American citizens. The law mandated that the government had to obtain a warrant from a federal judge in a new FISA court in order to receive approval to wiretap a U.S. citizen on national-security grounds.

FISA was flawed, but it marked a revolutionary change: it brought to a close the era in the late 1960s and early 1970s when thousands of American political dissidents were subjected to secret domestic spying by the FBI, CIA, and NSA with no independent oversight.

Some of the intelligence reform measures put in place during the Carter years represented such radical reforms that new ways of governing had to be created. After FISA was signed into law by

Carter, for example, an informal group of powerful government officials gathered to try to figure out how to invent the FISA court from scratch. They had no road map.

Following his work on the Church Committee staff, Frederick Baron became a key aide to Carter's attorney general, Griffin Bell. Once FISA was passed by Congress and signed into law by Carter in October 1978, Bell brought Baron along to a secret meeting with Warren Burger, the chief justice of the Supreme Court, and Stansfield Turner, the director of the CIA. Bell and Baron joined them in Burger's Supreme Court office. "They were deciding how this new secret court was going to be set up," recalls Baron.

The details of the FISA court structure agreed upon in that secret meeting, which has never been previously disclosed, have largely remained in place for decades. It is hard to imagine decisions of such historic, long-lasting importance being made today in such an informal setting without the results being immediately leaked.

Carter also issued a wide-ranging executive order in 1978 that imposed broad new restrictions on the U.S. intelligence community, including a ban on the assassination of foreign leaders. The executive order was far stronger than a token one issued by Ford in the Church Committee's wake in 1976. The Carter Administration's Justice Department also imposed new restrictions on FBI intelligence operations, following up on work the Ford Administration started after the Church Committee.

Frank Church's multinational subcommittee investigation of U.S. corporate payoffs to foreign leaders led to the Foreign Corrupt Practices Act, which Carter signed into law in December 1977. The law for the first time made it a crime for American individuals and companies to bribe officials in foreign countries, which Church's investigation had revealed was a rampant practice by large U.S. corporations.

Church's investigations of America's decades of abusive, imperialistic policies in Latin America also helped lead to reform and new opportunities into the region. That was especially true in Panama.

Church played a leading role in the Senate passage of the Panama Canal treaties, which Jimmy Carter made a top priority early in his administration. It was an issue that Carter inherited from Gerald Ford. During the transition after the 1976 election, Ford personally warned Carter that the Panama Canal dispute should be "the number one thing" on his presidential agenda, Frank Moore, who worked on Carter's transition team, recalled in an interview. "Ford had done little on the issue," said Moore in an interview, "but he now warned Carter, 'If you don't do something, there is going to be a war down there.'" Decades of anti-American resentment in Panama, including anger about segregation in the Canal Zone that continued into the 1970s, had made the canal issue "a flash point in Central America," added Moore.

By the late 1970s, it was becoming clear that the issue of sovereignty over the canal could lead to a major crisis, and Carter concluded that U.S. control of the canal was no longer worth the risk to U.S. relations throughout Latin America. In September 1977, Carter signed treaties guaranteeing that Panama would gain control over the canal after 1999.

But the agreement sparked a firestorm of protest among conservatives, led by future presidential candidate Ronald Reagan. The right wanted to keep the canal, and saw Carter's action as a form of American surrender. Out of nowhere, the Panama Canal was suddenly a radioactive issue.

It would be up to the Senate to ratify the treaties.

After investigating the CIA's assassination plots and covert operations in Chile and Cuba, Church felt strongly that the Panama Canal treaties were critical to improving America's relationship with Central and South America. The new agreements, he hoped, would demonstrate that the United States was ready to put its jingoistic domination of Latin America in the past. He agreed to be one of two "floor managers" to navigate the treaties through the Senate, despite the political risks the controversial accords posed for Church in Idaho, where he would face reelection in 1980.

Mike Wetherell, his Senate chief of staff, advised Church not to take on a leadership role on the treaties. Wetherell knew that the Panama Canal issue would haunt Church in Idaho in 1980, and urged him to turn it over to John Glenn, the former astronaut who had become a highly popular Democratic senator from Ohio.

"I told him, Glenn has poll points to give up, and you don't," Wetherell recalled.

But Church refused to back down.

"He just said, 'no, I've got to do it,'" Wetherell said.

"Church spent months on the [Senate] floor working to get [the Panama Canal treaties] done," added Senate staffer Garry Wenske.

Just before their final passage, Church chided the conservative opponents of the treaties, arguing that they were afraid of change and were fearful of giving up obsolete symbols of America's imperial aspirations. He told the Senate that the opponents of the treaties were on a "sentimental journey back to the era of Teddy Roosevelt, the big stick, and the Great White Fleet."

Frank Church successfully shepherded the Panama Canal treaties through the Senate. They were ratified in 1978. But Mike Wetherell was right — Church's leading role would come back to haunt him when he sought reelection in 1980.

* * *

Out of the blue one August day in 1977, Frank Church was contacted by Cuba's ambassador to the United Nations, who told Church that if he came to visit Fidel Castro in Cuba, "You will find it in your interest," recalled Cleve Corlett, Church's press secretary at the time. Church's investigation of the CIA's attempts to kill Castro had prompted Castro to seek him out.

When Church told the White House about the Cuban approach, Carter and his aides were intrigued about whether it signaled that Castro wanted better relations with the United States.

"Church went to Brzezinski to talk about it, and Brzezinski said go," recalled Corlett. The White House gave Church the use of a plane from the presidential fleet, signaling to Castro that the Church visit had Carter's approval.

Castro put on a charm offensive for Church. During the four-day visit, Castro took both Frank and Bethine Church spearfishing, showed them around Ernest Hemingway's old Cuban home, and had lunch with them aboard his own yacht.

Over a dinner of fish, lobster, and limes, Castro asked Church which U.S. president he most admired. Church told him Franklin Roosevelt, and made a point of saying it was because Roosevelt had saved America from revolution during the Depression. "Castro's face darkened, and he said rather defensively, 'Well, he had the resources to do it,'" Bethine Church later recalled.

Castro also took them to the beach that had been the battleground during the Bay of Pigs invasion. "The press joined us...as

Frank and Bethine Church with Fidel Castro in Cuba, 1977.

we drove to the Bay of Pigs down a narrow country road, the only access to the beach," wrote Bethine in her memoir. "Until we drove that road and saw the spot with our own eyes, neither Frank nor I realized how badly the CIA had managed the Bay of Pigs fiasco."

As he was leaving, Church told reporters that Castro had agreed to allow the Cuban wives and children of 84 American citizens to travel overseas, including to the United States. Church had raised the issue with Castro as a gesture that could prove he was serious about improving relations with the United States.

Carter asked to see Church at the White House immediately after he landed back in Washington. Church was so exhausted from the trip that Bethine asked Susan Hunter, a staffer who had been staying in the Church's house to dog-sit Plucky, their dachshund, while they were in Cuba, to drive in a car behind Church to make sure he made it all the way to the White House.

In a report on his trip that he wrote for the Senate, Church eviscerated two decades of American efforts to isolate, overthrow, and kill Castro. "The wall the United States tried to build around Cuba has crumbled," Church wrote.

It is high time for us to discard a policy which the world community views, at best, as unworthy of a great nation and, at worst, as petulant and self-defeating. Cuba's economy did not collapse under our embargo, nor did her people rise up to welcome the American-sponsored invaders at the Bay of Pigs...Largely because of a blind and obstinate U.S. policy, Castro's stature and influence in the Third World has grown far beyond the modest size of the country he governs. There is a lesson to be learned here. A grand delusion underlaid our former policy toward Cuba.

Church's vision for a clear-eyed U.S.-Cuba relationship was far ahead of its time — so far, indeed, that as of this writing it has yet to be achieved.

*   *   *

After the Church Committee and his presidential campaign were both finished, Frank Church had one long-sought goal left in Washington: he wanted to become chairman of the Senate Foreign Relations Committee.

In 1974, Senator J. William Fulbright, Church's old nemesis, had been defeated for reelection, and Senator John Sparkman, an Alabama Democrat in his 70s, became chairman. By 1977, Sparkman was both physically and mentally unfit to be chairman; he was effectively "comatose," Frank Moore, who was then the chief of congressional relations for the Carter White House, recalled in an interview. But that didn't matter under the Senate's strict seniority rules, so that left it to Frank Church, the next in line, to act as de facto chairman until Sparkman retired following the 1978 midterm elections.

Finally, in January 1979, Frank Church became chairman in his own right, and moved quickly to put his own stamp on the committee. But as he assembled his committee staff, applicants had to get Bethine's approval. Pat Shea, who had worked on the Church Committee staff, met with Frank and Bethine Church for breakfast to discuss joining the foreign-relations staff. "Bethine told me I had to shave my beard," recalled Shea. "She said, 'I don't want anybody with a beard sitting behind my husband.'" Bethine Church's instincts for politics had still not been softened.

Now that Church was chairman of one of the Senate's most important and prestigious committees, Jimmy Carter should have worked hard to improve his personal relations with him. Instead, their relationship got worse. "We (Rosalynn and I) had lunch with Frank and Bethine Church," Carter wrote in his private diary on February 8, 1979, just after Church took over as chairman. "He's been a pain in the neck for me as chairman of Foreign Relations."

Church infuriated Carter even further in late August 1979, when he announced that intelligence showing a Soviet army brigade deployed in Cuba threatened the SALT II treaty, a new nuclear arms-limitation agreement with the Soviets that Carter had just signed. If the brigade was not removed, Church said, the Senate would not approve SALT II; Church's move helped doom one of Carter's key foreign-policy initiatives.

In 1980, during the Iranian hostage crisis, Church's relationship with Carter hit rock bottom. Just after the failure of a hostage-rescue mission ordered by Carter, the president met with the House and Senate leadership on April 25 to brief them on what went wrong. "They were quite supportive," Carter wrote in his diary, "although a couple had been acting like asses beforehand; Frank Church the worst."

The biggest problem in their relationship was that Frank Church faced reelection in 1980, and Jimmy Carter's unpopularity in Idaho

Senator Frank Church meets with President Jimmy Carter at the White House, exchanging pleasantries while masking their increasingly hostile relationship.

was killing him. By 1979, Church was already feeling politically vulnerable, and his growing alarm over Carter's low standing in Idaho helped explain his excessively hawkish response to the Soviet brigade in Cuba and his worsening rift with the White House.

Church started multitasking, hitting the campaign trail to save his job even as he ran the foreign-relations committee. "I remember one day he had lunch with [Chinese leader] Deng Xiaoping," recalled Susan Hunter, "and then later in the afternoon he had a meeting with the Idaho Swine Producers."

He also sought to soften the growing political threat he felt from the right by reminding Idaho voters about his long-standing opposition to gun control. Church agreed to write the foreword to an anti-gun control book, *Restricting Handguns: The Liberal Skeptics Speak Out*, which was published in 1979. He wrote in the book's forward that "I have always opposed all forms of federal gun control in my more than twenty years in the United States Senate. Gun controls are an anathema to the people I represent. Being born and bred in Idaho, that is a fact I know well."

But Frank Church knew that the political winds were turning against him, even as he sometimes showed signs of exhaustion, drained by the marathon he had run in 1975 and 1976 — leading the Church Committee and then running for president.

He also knew that a formidable Republican opponent was waiting for him in Idaho.

*　*　*

As the 1980 election loomed, Representative Steve Symms, a hard-right Republican who represented Idaho's first congressional district, appeared to be the most likely candidate to run for the Senate against Frank Church. Symms, whose family owned a large fruit ranch near Caldwell, Idaho, had been plotting to take on Church for years. He had even urged Bob Smith, his old friend and chief of staff in his House office, to run against Church as a stalking horse in 1974.

But just in case Symms had any last-minute doubts, James Jesus Angleton stepped in to give him a push.

The former CIA chief of counterintelligence, who had so thoroughly embarrassed himself during a public hearing of the Church Committee, was deeply embittered — and obsessed with lashing out at what he perceived to be his legion of enemies. At the top of Angleton's list of enemies was Frank Church. In the late 1970s, Angleton began meeting with Steve Symms to persuade him to run against Church. "He was from Boise, and he really despised Frank Church," recalled Symms in an interview. "He used to come over to see me in the House," he added. Angleton would recount to Symms all the damage he claimed that Church had wreaked on the CIA, and then he would say, "You should run against Church," Symms said.

"I got exposed to that [intelligence] stuff through Angleton," Symms added. "I still remember him coming over to my office and sitting on my couch, and he would smoke one cigarette after another. He would kind of put his leg up and talk to me on intelligence. He wanted Church defeated."

But at the same time, Symms was getting pressured not to run against Church by a prominent figure in Ronald Reagan's inner circle.

In the late 1970s, Nancy Clark Reynolds was in a unique position to serve as an intermediary between the rising Reagan Revolution and Frank Church. A former local television anchor in San Francisco, Reynolds served as assistant press secretary and later as a senior aide to Ronald Reagan while he was governor of California. She went on to become one of Ronald and Nancy Reagan's closest friends and confidantes.

Reagan had lost the Republican presidential nomination to Ford in 1976, but he was favored to win the nomination in 1980 — and was already shaking the party to its foundations. With Reagan in the vanguard, the GOP was undergoing a radical transformation into a right-wing party. Reagan acolytes like Steve Symms were ascending in the party's ranks all across the nation to challenge both the moderate Republican establishment and the Democratic Party's control of Congress.

In addition to being a close friend of the Reagans, Reynolds happened to be Bethine Church's cousin. Reynolds's father was D. Worth Clark, who had been a Democratic congressman from Idaho in the 1930s and 1940s and belonged to the Clark political family that dominated the state's Democratic politics for decades. (It was Virgil Clark — D. Worth Clark's wife and Nancy Clark Reynolds's mother — who had helped Bethine track down Frank when he was stationed at the secret intelligence base Camp Ritchie during World War II.)

Nancy Clark Reynolds knew Idaho politics and also understood the onrushing Reagan wave, and she saw that Steve Symms posed a real threat to Frank Church. So Reynolds called Symms and privately asked him not to run against Church.

As a Reagan disciple, Steve Symms could not ignore the call from someone as close to the Reagans as Reynolds. But Symms couldn't stand life in the House of Representatives, where Republicans were in such a small minority in the 1970s that they could get little accomplished. He was bored. The Senate would offer him much greater stature, Symms believed.

"Nancy Clark Reynolds called me and asked me not to run against Church," recalled Symms in an interview. "But I told her I'm either going to run for the Senate or I'm going back to the ranch."

* * *

Steve Symms had many flaws, but he was really good at one thing — politics. He was the first opponent to pose a real danger to Frank Church's hold on his Senate seat since he defeated Herman Welker in 1956.

Symms stuck to a conservative message that would later become Republican orthodoxy, but in the 1970s it still sounded new: small government, lower taxes, less regulation, anti-abortion, pro-gun. "My issue was, do you want more government or less government?" Symms said in an interview.

But in addition to his starkly conservative views, Symms was also very affable, like Ronald Reagan, and that made him much more of a threat to Church than any of the other right-wing candidates he had faced before.

Above all, Steve Symms was lucky in his timing.

He ran against Frank Church at the same time that Ronald Reagan was taking on Jimmy Carter, who was deeply unpopular both in Idaho and across the nation, burdened by high inflation, high unemployment, and the Iran hostage crisis, which dragged on throughout the election year. In the 1980 campaign, Carter was a deadweight around Frank Church's neck. A July 1979 survey of Idaho voters conducted by Peter Hart, the Church campaign's pollster, found that Carter had just a 19 percent positive job rating in the state. In a poll 12 months later, Hart found that Reagan was leading Carter in Idaho by 60 percent to 28 percent.

Senator Frank Church and Senator Ted Kennedy, along with Senator George
McGovern, on Capitol Hill.

Voters eager to get rid of Jimmy Carter were also starting to find
reasons to dislike Frank Church.

In 1968, Church had won despite his strong opposition to the
Vietnam War. He had patiently explained his position to voters
around the state, and most had accepted that he was following his
conscience.

But Idaho was growing even more conservative than it had
been in the 1960s, and Church's explanations of his positions no
longer resonated as widely around the state as they once had. His
prominent role in the Senate's passage of the Panama Canal treaties
and his leadership of the Church Committee's investigations of the
intelligence community stoked intense anger among Idaho conservatives. "We get just a little bit tired of hearing about your conscience,"
said one letter to the editor of the *Twin Falls Times-News* in 1978.

The darkening mood was palpable both to Church and to his staffers. "You could hear it and feel it," recalls Larry LaRocco, who served as Church's northern Idaho staffer in the late 1970s. "The complaints...what's he doing with this CIA investigation? And about the Panama Canal. It all came under the umbrella of national security."

"Frank Church was very popular with a lot of people in southern and eastern Idaho, in rural Idaho," recalled Symms. "I always thought if he hadn't gotten pulled to the left, then I wouldn't have won. He had always made it clear he would never impinge on anybody's gun rights. Frank was smart about that kind of stuff. But the CIA investigation—that didn't help him."

Meanwhile, Symms rode the Reagan wave. "To have Reagan on the ticket was a big plus," Symms said. "He came to Idaho Falls for a campaign event with me."

Symms also had plenty of help from a new trend in right-wing politics. Outside organizations based in Washington began aiding Symms by attacking Church with misleading television and print advertisements. One of the groups—the National Conservative Political Action Committee, NCPAC—targeted Church and other liberal senators in 1980, including former Democratic presidential candidate George McGovern in South Dakota, in a campaign designed to nationalize elections that had traditionally been fought on state and local issues. It was the onset of the modern slash-and-burn campaign style that has since nationalized virtually every congressional election around the country.

But Peter Hart, Church's pollster, doubts that NCPAC and related right-wing groups made much of a difference in Church's 1980 election. Those groups had blindsided Democrats in the 1978 midterm elections, but Hart said that by 1980, Democrats were learning how to blunt their impact.

"In 1980 there were so many other factors in that election that the damage from NCPAC was probably minimal," recalls Hart. "I really felt it was more about the zeitgeist and where the country was at. I worked for 10 [Democratic] senators in 1980, and five of them lost. It was the Reagan landslide that took them over."

By September 1980, Symms led Church by 49 percent to 42 percent in Hart's internal poll. And Frank Church looked dead in the water.

*   *   *

For a time, it seemed that Church wasn't up to the challenge from Symms. Just before their first debate of the campaign, "I had never seen Church so nervous," recalled Peter Fenn, who served as Church's campaign manager in 1980.

As the campaign wore on, Symms could sense that Church, who was then 56, lacked the same energy for a political fight that he had displayed in his earlier races. On the day of their second debate, Symms, who was 42, went for a 10-mile run and felt in top physical condition. "I went into the debate, and when I shook hands with Frank, he looked tired and haggard," recalled Symms. "I gripped his hand, and I told him that this is the most fun I've ever had in my life, but I could see the energy was drained from his face."

But Church recovered — and then began to fight back. Symms was in favor of granting mining and other corporate interests greater freedom to exploit Idaho's wilderness areas, and the Church campaign began to go after Symms for policies that would reduce public access for hunting, fishing, and camping. "We said they are going to lock up the places where you hunt, fish, and take the camper, and the land is going to be sold off to the California speculators and the Eastern special interests," recalls Fenn. "We hammered him."

The strategy began to pay off. By October, Hart's internal polling showed the race to be a virtual dead heat: Symms 47 percent, Church 46 percent.

Several former Church staffers said that during the campaign, they were told of allegations about Steve Symms's personal life. Frank Church refused to use any of the information against Symms — just as he had refused to use derogatory material against Herman Welker.

But Peter Fenn recalled that one former Church intern arranged for a supporter to write a letter to an Idaho newspaper raising questions about Symms and womanizing. "I was furious," said Fenn. The Church campaign disavowed it, but Fenn said that the Symms campaign believed Church was stoking the rumors about Symms.

While the race between Frank Church and Steve Symms was a toss-up, the presidential election turned into a landslide for Ronald

Reagan. On election night, November 4, 1980, Jimmy Carter, embittered and exhausted from both campaign travel and dealing with the endless Iranian hostage crisis, decided to concede defeat early in the evening, while the polls on the West Coast were still open. While Boise and southern Idaho are in the Mountain Time Zone, northern Idaho is in the Pacific Time Zone. That meant polls in the north—at that time a Democratic stronghold—were still open when Carter conceded.

Many Idaho Democrats have long believed that Carter's early concession cost Church the election by hurting northern turnout. Steve Symms won the election by just over 4,000 votes: 218,701 to 214,439.

Frank Church's political career was over.

* * *

The 1980 election was a bloodbath for the Democrats. Not only did both Church and Carter lose, but many fellow liberal icons of the Senate were defeated along with Church, including George McGovern of South Dakota, Birch Bayh of Indiana, John Culver of Iowa,

Senator Frank Church late in his career.

and Church's longtime friend Gaylord Nelson of Wisconsin. Republicans took control of the Senate for the first time since 1954.

The morning after his defeat, Church talked with reporters in the backyard of the family's house in Boise. "It's somewhat consoling, to go out in such good company," Church quipped about the wave of Democratic losses. He continued to try to project an upbeat attitude. Asked by a reporter what he and his wife planned to do next, Church said, "Bethine and I are going to stay together."

Frank Church exited politics quietly, and with relatively little apparent rancor. But Church's defeat was cause for celebration in CIA circles.

"After I won the Senate race, I was invited to a party at someone's house, and I was just about the only person there who was not former intelligence," recalled Symms. "It was quite impressive to meet all these people — and see how deeply they all despised Church."

* * *

Church stayed in Washington after he left the Senate in 1981, handling international matters for the law firm of Whitman & Ransom. He was finally making good money, yet Church and his family remained in the same house in Bethesda where they had lived since he was first elected to the Senate.

He and Bethine were able to travel widely, but Church's post-Senate life was short. In early 1984, he was diagnosed with pancreatic cancer. Unlike with his first bout with cancer, there was no experimental treatment that could save him this time.

But even as he was facing death, Church continued to sound the same alarms that had become his hallmark. In one of his last interviews, in January 1984, Church warned once again about the threat of American imperialism, now embodied by Ronald Reagan's hawkish foreign policies. "We seem unable to learn from the failure of our Vietnam policy, or the equally evident failure of our hard-line policy toward Castro in Cuba," Church told David Broder of the *Washington Post*. "It is this idea that the communist threat is everywhere that has made our government its captive and its victim.

"This country has become so conservative — so fearful — that we have come to see revolution anywhere in the world as a threat to the United States. It's nonsense. And yet that policy we have followed has cost us so many lives, so much treasure, such setbacks to our vital interests, as a great power ought not to endure.

"Until we learn to live with revolution, we will continue to blunder."

In his last few months, many senators came to visit, offering their admiration — and burying old enmities.

"Ted Kennedy came to the house three days before he died," recalled Chase Church. "I walked him out, and he was crying on the front porch, and I told my mother that's the first time I've seen a Kennedy cry."

One Republican senator who visited was Alan Simpson of Wyoming, who eagerly told Frank and Bethine Church about what he described as the loutish behavior of Steve Symms. "I was on the floor of the Senate the other day with the guy who beat you, and he started to rail and rant at me," Simpson said, Bethine recalled in her memoir. "I said to him, look, Symms, you're drunk. If you don't get off this floor right now, I will say into my microphone in what kind of situation you are in, so get off the floor! And he did." Simpson told Church that "You were beaten by a man you didn't deserve to be beaten by."

Asked about the Simpson story recounted in Bethine Church's memoir, Symms said in an interview that "Simpson exaggerated that greatly. Yeah, there is a little element of truth to that, but it is highly exaggerated." Symms said that his office had an early party that day, and that "I probably had a drink at the party, but I certainly wasn't drunk." Symms also pointed out that later that same day, he gave a two-hour floor speech that was highly regarded.

*   *   *

As Church lay dying, his achievements finally began to receive recognition. In early 1984, Congress passed legislation renaming the River of No Return Wilderness in Idaho, which Church had done so much to protect, the "Frank Church River of No Return Wilderness." Ronald Reagan signed it into law just in time for Church to be told about it.

Today, the vast wilderness area in central Idaho is best known by its nickname: "the Frank."

At dawn on April 7, 1984, Frank Church died at his home in Bethesda, Maryland. He was only 59 years old. He lay in state in the Idaho State Capitol in Boise, just as William Borah had 44 years earlier.

Forrest Church, who by then had become a prominent minister in New York, gave the eulogy for his father at the First United Methodist Church, known as the Cathedral of the Rockies, in Boise. A video of his eulogy shows that Forrest by then had the same precise diction, the same careful wordcraft, the same mannerisms as his father.

"In his life, my father was a bit like the day star, rising early to prominence, brilliant in the dusk and against the darkness, showing other stars the way." As Forrest Church spoke, Bethine Church sat in the front pew, struggling not to cry.

Frank Church was buried in Morris Hill Cemetery in Boise. Three years later, when James Jesus Angleton died, the Boise native was also buried in Morris Hill Cemetery. About one hundred feet from Frank Church.

Epilogue

"They did great damage"

FRANK CHURCH'S HISTORICAL standing has soared in the 21st century. Few American political leaders have ever enjoyed such a thorough and positive reappraisal so long after they were gone.

Ironically, Church has his nemesis, Dick Cheney, to thank for that.

In the 1980s and 1990s, Frank Church and the work of the Church Committee were largely forgotten by the press and the public. Those who did remember were often harsh in their assessments.

Sy Hersh, whose domestic-spying story had led to the committee's creation, became a severe critic of Frank Church's leadership, charging that he had too often pulled his punches. In the 1980s, the CIA's central role in the Reagan Administration's Iran-Contra arms-for-hostages scandal (several CIA officials were indicted) also raised questions over whether the reforms put in place after the Church Committee had really been strong enough to stop CIA officials from engaging in illegal activity. In her 1996 book *Challenging the Secret Government*, Kathryn Olmsted, a historian at the University of California, argued that the Church Committee had largely been a failure. Olmsted quoted former CIA director Richard Helms, who had gleefully asked, "When all is said and done, what did it achieve?" Indeed, several histories of the CIA (notably *The Man Who Kept the Secrets* by Thomas Powers and *Legacy of Ashes* by Tim Weiner) adopted a Helms-centric view of disdain toward both Frank Church and the Church Committee.

In Idaho, meanwhile, Frank Church was primarily remembered as the namesake of the state's largest wilderness area, rather than for his leadership of the Church Committee.

But the Bush Administration's draconian response to the September 11, 2001, attacks on New York and Washington permanently altered the debate over the historic importance of both Frank Church and the Church Committee.

Vice President Dick Cheney, who engineered the Bush Administration's post–9/11 "global war on terror," had never forgotten the humiliation he felt in the Ford White House as the Church Committee rummaged through the nation's dark secrets. He had tried to block the Church Committee's work, but President Ford had refused to engage in an all-out war with Frank Church so soon after Watergate.

An early glimpse of Cheney's deep and lasting resentment toward Church came in the 1980s, when Cheney—by then a Republican congressman from Wyoming—was serving on a joint congressional committee to investigate the Iran-Contra scandal. Cheney wrote a dissenting minority report in 1987 arguing that the real scandal was that Congress was trying to dictate foreign policy to the president. Cheney's report specifically blamed the Church Committee for helping to foster the modern concept of "all but unlimited Congressional power."

After the 9/11 attacks, Cheney had much greater power himself, and he had been around Washington so long that he understood better than anyone else in government the significance of the post-Church intelligence reforms. He knew they were obstacles to his objective: a post–9/11 counter-revolution in American intelligence.

In his bid to unravel the intelligence reforms put in place after the Church Committee, Cheney had the blessing of President George W. Bush, whose father, George H. W. Bush, had become Gerald Ford's very compliant CIA director after Ford fired William Colby for cooperating too much with Frank Church.

Cheney and his acolytes sought to win public support for extreme measures by loudly claiming that the Church Committee had imposed restrictions on the intelligence community that led to its failure to prevent 9/11. Dick Cheney thus enthusiastically used a deadly attack on America to refight his 30-year-old battle against Frank Church.

It was reminiscent of the Ford White House's exploitation of Richard Welch's murder to attack the Church Committee. "We also have to work, though, sort of the dark side, if you will," Cheney said on *Meet the Press* five days after 9/11. "We've got to spend time in the shadows in the intelligence world. A lot of what needs to be done here will have to be done quietly, without any discussion, using sources and methods that are available to our intelligence agencies, if we're going to be successful...We need to make certain we have not tied our [own] hands. I think one of the by-products, if you will, of this tragic set of circumstances is that we'll see a very thorough sort of reassessment of how we operate and the kinds of people we deal with."

Henry Kissinger, who had fought his own battles with Frank Church during the Ford Administration, also weighed in after 9/11, blaming Church for leaving America vulnerable. "Finding themselves in a kind of political wilderness, the intelligence services have been under assault for 30 years, ever since the floodgates were opened in the 1970s," Kissinger wrote in the *Washington Post* in 2004, following publication of *The 9/11 Commission Report*.

Kissinger and Cheney were part of a Republican chorus attacking Church after 9/11. "Mr. Secretary, I was here when Frank Church conducted long hearings about the CIA," said Senator Pete Domenici, a Republican from New Mexico, while questioning Kissinger during a Senate hearing on the 9/11 Commission's recommendations in 2004. "I was very chagrined as I watched him...I believe that [his actions] started the downfall of covert activity and clandestine activity by the CIA. I do not ask you to agree, but you seem to be half nodding."

Kissinger responded simply, "I agree."

"In any event," Domenici continued, "I do not see how CIA could attract spies. Clandestine people that you have just described, you know, they are rather peculiar. They are different. They are not just ordinary people. I do not see how they would sign up after the Church hearings. I mean, if we are going to go and disclose them in a public hearing, you have just about destroyed the clandestine activities. Is that true?"

"I think they did great damage," Kissinger responded.

* * *

But the Cheney-led attacks on the Church Committee ultimately had a surprising, unintended effect. Once the initial shock from

9/11 wore off and the war in Iraq had gone horribly wrong, American skepticism began to return. The press uncovered the Bush-Cheney post-9/11 depredations — torture, secret prisons, targeted killings, domestic spying — and it became clear why Cheney had been so intent on persuading Americans to get rid of the intelligence reforms put in place after the Church Committee. Cheney's growing legion of critics charged that he wanted the United States to abandon its morals and the rule of law in the service of his endless war.

But by trying to erase Church Committee reforms in order to engage in illicit and immoral activities, Cheney reminded the country of the importance of those reforms. Cheney's constant harping against the Church Committee's reforms eventually convinced many Americans that if Cheney hated them so much, maybe they weren't so bad. Dick Cheney became an unlikely salesman for the Church Committee.

Journalists and scholars also began to realize that the reason the Church Committee and its reforms had gone largely unnoticed in the 1980s and 1990s was that they were generally working to rein in the intelligence community. There were still scandals during that period, such as Iran-Contra, but they were scandals precisely because they violated the new compact between the executive and legislative branches that imposed greater congressional oversight and new limits on the power of the intelligence community. The importance of the Church Committee's reforms became clear only when Cheney tried to get rid of them after 9/11.

Soon, calls came from Congress and among journalists, pundits, and activists that the nation needed another Church Committee to investigate the Bush-Cheney abuses of power. The fact that the Church Committee had conducted a sweeping investigation of decades of abuses by the entire intelligence community — including the Central Intelligence Agency, the Federal Bureau of Investigation, and the National Security Agency — made it seem like the right model to investigate the equally sweeping abuses of the Bush-Cheney era. "Now, following the September 11, 2001 terrorist attacks in the United States, Senator Church is back," wrote Russell Miller, a constitutional legal scholar at Washington and Lee University School of Law, in 2008.

Church's prominence has only continued to grow in the years

since Bush and Cheney left office. Calls for a new Church Committee continued during the Obama Administration as well, after mass leaks of U.S. military and diplomatic documents by Wikileaks, followed by another mass leak of NSA documents by Edward Snowden, underscored the degree to which Obama had endorsed and extended the Bush-Cheney global war on terror. Donald Trump, meanwhile, was a walking advertisement for the need for limits on presidential power; calls for another Church Committee grew louder as Trump's illegal behavior grew more brazen.

The Church Committee has now achieved a permanent place in the American political lexicon. Its name is widely used whenever there is a new public outcry for accountability for deep governmental misdeeds. "We need another Church Committee" has become a frequent refrain in Washington. The Church Committee is now broadly defined as an American-style Truth and Reconciliation Commission. Today, both Democrats and Republicans in Congress recognize the Church Committee's iconic status and now regularly seek to assume its historic mantle. The widely praised House January 6th Committee investigation into the January 6, 2021, insurrection and Donald Trump's efforts to overturn the 2020 election was seen by political analysts as a model for how to conduct a Church Committee–style investigation in the 21st century. Later, when Republicans gained control of the House in 2023, they created a special new panel to launch wide-ranging investigations into what they alleged were the ways in which the supposed Deep State abused the rights of Donald Trump and other conservatives. In the face of widespread criticism that the panel was baldly partisan and trafficking in right-wing conspiracy theories about the existence of a so-called Deep State, Republicans sought to improve its image by referring to it as a new version of the Church Committee. Of course, anyone who remembered the Cheney-led Republican attacks on the Church Committee after 9/11 would be surprised by the more recent Republican efforts to coopt the Church Committee's name. But the Republican effort nonetheless served as a testament to the Church Committee's historic resonance.

"Of greater consequence than the resulting intelligence oversight and reform, the Church Committee's investigation stands as an historic monument to faith in constitutional governance," wrote

Russell Miller. "As a congressional body investigating the most secret realm of the presidential empire, the Church Committee represented a stubborn commitment to the Founding Fathers' vision of limited government as secured by checks and balances, even in the face of America's most vexing national trials."

The Church Committee has thus taken on a meaning that goes far beyond the committee's 1975 investigations. The old criticisms in the press at the time of the committee — that Frank Church protected the Kennedy brothers, that Church's comparison of the CIA to a "rogue elephant" ignored the fact that the Agency followed presidential orders, that Church got distracted by running for president, that the committee got sidetracked by focusing on CIA assassination plots — have long since fallen away. What is left is the core truth: Frank Church and his committee took on the CIA, the FBI, and the NSA, and succeeded in bringing them under the rule of law for the first time.

It was a massive undertaking, and in historic terms, the work of the Church Committee now arguably overshadows that of Sam Ervin's Senate Watergate Committee, which loomed so much larger at the time.

In fact, Paul Light, a widely respected analyst on government reform, has called the Church Committee possibly the greatest congressional investigation in modern American history. "It is impossible to single out one investigation...as the best of the best, but I often return to the Church Committee's 1975 investigation of intelligence agency abuses as a model of the high-impact investigation," wrote Light in *Government by Investigation*, his 2014 book ranking the most important congressional investigations in modern history. "By my reading, the investigation not only met all of the attributes of the good investigation, but also generated durable results. It did both good and well...the investigation was unquestionably long, broad, complex, visible, serious, thorough, high leverage, influential and bipartisan. It also produced lasting impact...[the committee] examined a staggering inventory of scandals...the investigation achieved its heavy footprint and high impact through a mix of fact finding, bipartisanship, and strong leadership...facts were at the heart of [its] eventual success."

"Of all the things that I did in public service," Walter Mondale said in an interview for this book near the end of his life, "there is nothing I am more proud of than my involvement with the Church Committee."

The irony, and the tragedy, is that Frank Church himself never foresaw that the Church Committee would be his greatest and most lasting legacy. On a personal level, he had never resolved the central conflict of his life: he was a radical who feared the American republic was in danger of sliding into militarism and imperialism, yet at the same time he was a Washington insider who yearned for acceptance by the nation's political elite. Ambition burned inside him to succeed in the nation's political system, even as he believed that system was abusive and corrupt and leading the United States down the same path that had destroyed Rome.

Thus running the Church Committee had not been enough. He wanted conventional political affirmation; to become president, or at least to chair the Senate Foreign Relations Committee. The failure of his presidential campaign almost certainly left both Frank and Bethine feeling as if Frank's career had not been completely fulfilled. Because he didn't think it was enough, Church didn't fully understand during his life how unique and historic the Church Committee had really been.

*　*　*

Frank Church's early death left an enormous void for his family. Bethine Church wrote in her memoir that as Frank Church lay dying, she briefly considered suicide so that she could die alongside her husband.

Instead, she went on to live another three decades as the keeper of Frank Church's legacy. She almost ran for Frank Church's old Senate seat in 1986, when Steve Symms was seeking reelection. "She was very serious," recalled Dan Williams, who helped Bethine write her memoir. She talked about the race with John Evans, Idaho's Democratic governor at the time. "She had a line she was going to use—'I'm Bethine, not Frank,'"—recalls Williams. She ultimately deferred to Evans, who ran against Symms in 1986 and lost. Idaho has not elected a Democratic senator since Frank Church, just as Church once predicted. The state has become one of the most conservative in the nation.

Bethine Church died in 2013 at the age of 90.

Forrest Church, who in college had been estranged from his father by the Vietnam War, grew to become a nationally known minister, author, and speaker — a leading liberal voice in an American religious culture dominated by harsh right-wing evangelicals.

As the senior minister of the Unitarian Church of All Souls in Manhattan, and through more than 20 books and countless public appearances, Forrest Church used his platform to advance the values of personal compassion and social justice. In the process, he gained a fame that was independent of his father.

Forrest faced a public scandal in 1991, when the All Souls congregation held a high-profile vote on whether to force him to resign after he acknowledged to the church board that he had been having an extramarital affair with Carolyn Buck Luce, a member of the congregation who was also married. Months earlier, he had announced to the church that he and his wife, Amy, were getting divorced, but at the time he had not told the church or his wife that he was having an affair. The tale got even more complicated when it was revealed that, before Luce's husband discovered the affair, Church had sent him a letter as the couple's minister offering marital counseling. The scandal made it into the pages of the *New York Times*.

Church won the vote of the congregation, remained at All Souls, and married Luce. But years later he acknowledged that he also suffered from alcoholism, and began attending meetings of Alcoholics Anonymous.

Forrest Church got sober in time for perhaps his greatest moment, when he helped minister to New Yorkers in the wake of 9/11. "He preached with the authority of a man freshly delivered from the grip of alcoholism, a man in touch as never before with the depths of his being," wrote Dan Cryer in his 2011 biography of Forrest Church.

Forrest Church died of esophageal cancer in 2009 at age 61, only slightly older than his father had been when he died.

Acknowledgments

THE FRANK CHURCH Papers, a collection housed at the Albertsons Library at Boise State University, is a critical resource for anyone seeking to understand the life of Frank Church.

A special thanks to Cheryl Oestreicher, head, Special Collections and Archives/Associate Professor, Albertsons Library, Boise State University and Alessandro Meregaglia, Archivist/Librarian & Assistant Professor, Albertsons Library, Boise State University, for their crucial help in navigating the Frank Church Papers.

Dean Hagerman provided critical research assistance at Boise State, particularly during the pandemic.

Katherine Scott, an associate historian at the U.S. Senate Historical Office, conducted a valuable oral history of the Church Committee, and also helped with related research assistance.

Liza Talbot, digital archivist at the LBJ Presidential Library, and Stacy Davis, archivist at the Gerald R. Ford Presidential Library, were also extraordinarily helpful.

Bruce Nichols, publisher of Little, Brown, is a longtime friend and mentor. Alexander Littlefield, executive editor at Little, Brown, wisely edited the book and provided invaluable guidance. As always, Tina Bennett, the best literary agent in America, is a patient friend. Allan Fallow was steadfast as the book's copyeditor.

Illustration Credits

Page	Image Credits
4	*Frank Church with a CIA dart gun.*
	AP Photo/hlg
9	*Headshot of Frank Church.*
	LBJ Library photo by Yoichi Okamo
20	*Young Frank Church with his mother and brother.*
	Frank Church Papers, Special Collections and Archives, Boise State University
33	*Frank and Richard Church in the ROTC.*
	Frank Church Papers, Special Collections and Archives, Boise State University
39	*Frank and Bethine Church at their wedding.*
	Frank Church Papers, Special Collections and Archives, Boise State University
42	*Frank Church speaks on behalf of the Crusade for Freedom.*
	Frank Church Papers, Special Collections and Archives, Boise State University

44   *Frank and Bethine Church with Bethine's mother.*

Frank Church Papers, Special Collections and Archives, Boise State University

59   *The Church family at a birthday celebration.*

Frank Church Papers, Special Collections and Archives, Boise State University

71   *Frank Church and John F. Kennedy.*

Frank Church Papers, Special Collections and Archives, Boise State University

77   *Frank Church with Lyndon B. Johnson.*

LBJ Library photo by Yoichi Okamoto

82   *Frank Church with Senator J. William Fulbright.*

U.S. Senate Historical Office

101   *Frank Church with Cecil D. Andrus.*

Frank Church Papers, Special Collections and Archives, Boise State University

132   *CIA director Richard Helms.*

LBJ Library photo by Yoichi Okamoto

150   *Senator Mike Mansfield.*

LBJ Library photo by Yoichi Okamoto

174   *Meeting of the Church Committee.*

AP Photo/Henry Griffin

179   *Frank Church, Gerald R. Ford, and others in the Oval Office.*

Gerald R. Ford Presidential Library

181   *Loch Johnson.*

Photo by Leena S. Johnson

183   Fritz Schwarz.

Photo courtesy of Frederica Perera

193   Dick Cheney.

Gerald R. Ford Presidential Library

198   Nelson Rockefeller and Gerald R. Ford.

Gerald R. Ford Presidential Library

208   John Rosselli.

Bettmann/Bettmann via Getty Images

210   Sam Giancana.

Bettmann/Bettmann via Getty Images

232   Judith Campbell Exner.

Bettmann/Bettmann via Getty Images

249   Patrice Lumumba.

Bettmann/Bettmann via Getty Images

275   James Jesus Angleton.

Bettmann/Bettmann via Getty Images

291   Gerald R. Ford with Alice Olson.

Gerald R. Ford Presidential Library

293   Sidney Gottlieb.

Bride Lane Library/Popperfoto via Getty Images

321   Frank Hampton speaks to reporters.

Chicago History Museum/Premium Archive via Getty Images

322   Frank Hampton's bedroom after a raid.

Paul Sequeira/Premium Archive via Getty Images

330   *Fritz Schwarz with William Colby.*

      U.S. Senate Photographic Studio image, courtesy U.S. Senate Historical Office

331   *Members of the Church Committee.*

      U.S. Senate Photographic Studio image, courtesy U.S. Senate Historical Office

372   *Frank Church presidential campaign announcement ceremony.*

      Frank Church Papers, Special Collections and Archives, Boise State University

387   *Frank and Bethine Church with Fidel Castro.*

      Frank Church Papers, Special Collections and Archives, Boise State University

389   *Jimmy Carter and Frank Church.*

      Frank Church Papers, Special Collections and Archives, Boise State University

393   *Edward Kennedy and Frank Church.*

      Frank Church Papers, Special Collections and Archives, Boise State University

396   *Portrait of Frank Church later in his career.*

      Frank Church Papers, Special Collections and Archives, Boise State University

Bibliography

Books

Albarelli Jr., H. P. *A Terrible Mistake*. Walterville, Oregon: Trine Day LLC, 2009.

Alter, Jonathan. *His Very Best: Jimmy Carter, A Life*. New York: Simon and Schuster, 2020.

Ambrose, Stephen E. *Eisenhower: Soldier and President*. New York: Simon and Schuster Paperbacks, 1990.

Anderson, Jack, with George Clifford. *The Anderson Papers*. New York: Random House, 1973.

Ashby, LeRoy, and Rod Gramer. *Fighting the Odds: The Life of Frank Church*. Pullman, Washington: Washington State University Press, 1994.

Bissell Jr., Richard M., with Jonathan E. Lewis and Frances T. Pudlo. *Reflections of a Cold Warrior: From Yalta to the Bay of Pigs*. New Haven, Connecticut: Yale University Press, 1996.

Blum, William. *Killing Hope: U.S. Military and CIA Interventions Since World War II*. London: Zed Books, 2014.

Boulton, David. *The Grease Machine: The Inside Story of Lockheed's Dollar Diplomacy*. New York: Harper & Row, 1978.

Brennan, John E. *Intelligence Oversight Reconsidered: Assessing the 1975–1976 Intelligence Oversight Reforms*. Virginia: Song Bird Hill Media, 2017.

Brock, G. J. *The Doves Have Won: Senator Frank Church and the Vietnam War*. Lincoln, Nebraska: Master's Thesis, The University of Nebraska, 1989.

Burns, Ken, and Geoffrey C. Ward. *The Vietnam War: An Intimate History*. New York: Knopf, 2017.

Cabell, General Charles P. *A Man of Intelligence: Memoirs of War, Peace, and the CIA*. Colorado Springs, Colorado: Impavide Publications, 1997.

Carlson, Chris. *Hells Heroes: How an Unlikely Alliance Saved Idaho's Hells Canyon*. Caldwell, Idaho: Caxton Press, 2018.

Caro, Robert A. *Master of the Senate: The Years of Lyndon Johnson.* New York: Alfred A. Knopf, Random House, 2002.

Carter, Jimmy. *Keeping Faith: Memoirs of a President.* New York: Bantam Books, 1982.

———. *White House Diary.* New York: Farrar, Straus and Giroux, 2010.

Cheney, Dick, with Liz Cheney. *In My Time: A Personal and Political Memoir.* New York: Threshold Editions, Simon & Schuster, 2011.

Church, Bethine. *A Lifelong Affair: My Passion for People and Politics.* Washington, D.C.: The Francis Press, 2003.

Church, Forrest. *Father & Son: A Personal Biography of Senator Frank Church of Idaho by His Son F. Forrester Church.* Boston: Faber and Faber, 1985.

———. *The American Creed: A Spiritual and Patriotic Primer.* New York: St. Martin's Press, 2002.

Colby, William, and Peter Forbath. *Honorable Men: My Life in the CIA.* New York: Simon & Schuster, 1978.

Cryer, Dan. *Being Alive and Having to Die: The Spiritual Odyssey of Forrest Church.* New York: St. Martin's Press, 2011.

DeBenedetti, Charles, with Charles Chatfield. *An American Ordeal: The Antiwar Movement of the Vietnam Era.* Syracuse, New York: Syracuse University Press, 1990.

Deitche, Scott M. *The Silent Don: The Criminal Underworld of Santo Trafficante, Jr.* Fort Lee, N.J.: Barricade Books, 2007.

Demaris, Ovid. *The Last Mafioso* — "biographical novel" based on interviews with Jimmy Fratianno. New York: Crown Publishing, 1980.

Devlin, Larry. *Chief of Station, Congo.* New York: Public Affairs, 2007.

De Witte, Ludo. *The Assassination of Lumumba.* London: Verso, 2001.

Dinges, John. *Our Man in Panama: The Shrewd Rise and Brutal Fall of Manuel Noriega.* New York: Times Books, 1990.

Douglas, Paul H. *In the Fullness of Time: The Memoirs of Paul H. Douglas.* New York: Harcourt Brace Jovanovich, 1971, 1972.

Eizenstat, Stuart E. *President Carter: The White House Years.* New York: Thomas Dunne Books, St. Martin's Press, 2018.

Elliff, John T. *The Reform of FBI Intelligence Operations.* Princeton, N.J.: Princeton University Press, 1979.

Ewert, Sara Dant. *The Conversion of Senator Frank Church: Evolution of an Environmentalist.* Pullman, Washington: Washington State University Press, 2000.

Exner, Judith. *My Story.* New York: Grove Press, 1977.

Feldstein, Mark. *Poisoning the Press: Richard Nixon, Jack Anderson, and the Rise of Washington's Scandal Culture.* New York: Picador, 2010.

Ferguson, Harvey. *The Last Cavalryman: The Life of General Lucian K. Truscott, Jr.* Norman, Oklahoma: The University of Oklahoma Press, 2015.

Fonzi, Gaeton. *The Last Investigation: What Insiders Know About the Assassination of JFK.* New York: Skyhorse Publishing, 2013.

Ford, Gerald R. *A Time to Heal: The Autobiography of Gerald R. Ford.* New York: Harper & Row, 1979.

Gentry, Curt. *J. Edgar Hoover: The Man and the Secrets.* New York: W. W. Norton, 1991.

Giancana, Antoinette, and Thomas C. Renner. *Mafia Princess: Growing Up in Sam Giancana's Family.* New York: William Morrow and Company, 1984.

Gibbs, David N. *The Political Economy of Third World Intervention: Mines, Money, and U.S. Policy in the Congo Crisis.* Chicago: The University of Chicago Press, 1991.

Goldwater, Barry M. *With No Apologies.* New York: William Morrow, 1979.

Gustafson, Kristian. *Hostile Intent: U.S. Covert Operations in Chile, 1964–1974.* Washington, D.C.: Potomac Books, 2007.

Hall, Bill. *Frank Church, D.C., & Me.* Pullman, Washington: Washington State University Press, 1995.

Hart, Gary. *The Thunder and the Sunshine: Four Seasons in a Burnished Life.* Golden, Colorado: Fulcrum, 2010.

Hayes, Stephen F. *Cheney: The Untold Story of America's Most Powerful and Controversial Vice President.* New York: Harper Collins, 2007.

Helms, Cynthia. *An Intriguing Life.* Lanham, Maryland: Rowman & Littlefield, 2013.

Helms, Richard, with William Hood. *A Look Over My Shoulder: A Life in the Central Intelligence Agency.* New York: A Presidio Press Book, Random House, 2003.

Hersh, Seymour M. *Reporter: A Memoir.* New York: Alfred A. Knopf, 2018.

Hitchcock, William I. *The Age of Eisenhower: America and the World in the 1950s.* New York: Simon & Schuster, 2018.

Hochschild, Adam. *King Leopold's Ghost: A Story of Greed, Terror, and Heroism in Colonial Africa.* Boston: Mariner Books, Houghton Mifflin Harcourt, 1999.

Johnson, Loch K. *A Season of Inquiry Revisited: The Church Committee Confronts America's Spy Agencies.* Lawrence, Kansas: University Press of Kansas, 2015 (originally published in 1985 by the University Press of Kentucky).

———. With James J. Wirtz. *Intelligence: The Secret World of Spies.* New York: Oxford University Press, 2015.

———. *Spy Watching: Intelligence Accountability in the United States.* New York: Oxford University Press, 2018.

———. "Operational Codes and the Prediction of Leadership Behavior: Senator Frank Church at Midcareer" (chapter in *A Psychological Examination of Political Leaders.* New York: The Free Press, 1977).

Johnson, Marc C. *Tuesday Night Massacre: Four Senate Elections and the Radicalization of the Republican Party.* Norman, Oklahoma: University of Oklahoma Press, 2021.

Johnston, James H. *Murder, Inc.: The CIA Under John F. Kennedy.* Lincoln, Nebraska: Potomac Books (an imprint of the University of Nebraska Press), 2019.

Kalb, Madeleine G. *The Congo Cables: The Cold War in Africa, From Eisenhower to Kennedy.* New York: Macmillan Publishing, 1982.

Kimelman, Henry L. *Living the American Dream.* Hong Kong: Vincent Lee Publishing, 1980.

King Jr., Martin Luther. *Why We Can't Wait.* New York: Signet Classics, Berkley Penguin Random House, 1963, 1964.

Kinzer, Stephen. *The Brothers: John Foster Dulles, Allen Dulles, and Their Secret World War.* New York: St. Martin's Press, 2013.

———. *Poisoner in Chief: Sidney Gottlieb and the CIA Search for Mind Control.* New York: Henry Holt and Company, 2019.

Kornbluh, Peter. *The Pinochet File: A Declassified Dossier on Atrocity and Account-ability.* New York: The New Press, 2003.

Lane, Frederick S. *American Privacy: The 400-Year History of Our Most Contested Right.* Boston: Beacon Press, 2009.

Laytner, Ron. *Up Against Howard Hughes: The Maheu Story.* New York: Manor Books, 1972.

Lee, Martin A. *Acid Dreams: The Complete Social History of LSD: The CIA, the Six-ties, and Beyond.* New York: Grove Press, 1985.

Lenzner, Terry. *The Investigator: Fifty Years of Uncovering the Truth.* New York: Plume, published by the Penguin Group, 2014 (first published by Blue Rider Press, Penguin Group, 2013).

Light, Paul C. *Government by Investigation: Congress, Presidents, and the Search for Answers, 1945–2012.* Washington, D.C.: The Brookings Institution, 2014.

Lukas, J. Anthony. *Big Trouble: Murder in a Small Western Town Sets Off a Struggle for the Soul of America.* New York: A Touchstone Book, Simon & Schuster, 1997.

MacPherson, Myra. *The Power Lovers: An Intimate Look at Politicians and Their Marriages.* New York: G. P. Putnam's Sons, 1975.

Maheu, Robert, and Richard Hack. *Next to Hughes.* New York: Harper Collins, 1992.

Maier, Thomas. *Mafia Spies: The Inside Story of the CIA, Gangsters, JFK, and Castro.* New York: Skyhorse Publishing, 2019.

Mailer, Norman. *Harlot's Ghost.* New York: Random House, 1991.

Mangold, Tom. *Cold Warrior: James Jesus Angleton: The CIA's Master Spy Hunter.* New York: A Touchstone Book, Simon & Schuster, 1991.

Mann, Robert. *A Grand Delusion: America's Descent into Vietnam.* New York: Basic Books, 2001.

Marks, John. *The Search for the Manchurian Candidate: The CIA and Mind Control.* New York: W. W. Norton, 1979.

May, Gary. *The Informant: The FBI, the Ku Klux Klan, and the Murder of Viola Liuzzo.* New Haven, Connecticut: Yale University Press, 2005.

McCullough, David. *Truman.* New York: Touchstone, 1992.

McDaniel, Rodger. *Dying for Joe McCarthy's Sins: The Suicide of Wyoming Senator Lester Hunt.* Cody, Wyoming: WordsWorth, 2013.

Medsger, Betty. *The Burglary: The Discovery of J. Edgar Hoover's Secret FBI.* New York: Alfred A. Knopf, a division of Random House, 2014.

Miller, Merle. *Lyndon: An Oral Biography.* New York: Ballantine Books, 1980.

Miller, Russell A. (editor). *U.S. National Security, Intelligence and Democracy: From the Church Committee to the War on Terror.* Milton Park, Abingdon, United Kingdom: Routledge, 2008.

Mondale, Walter F., with David Hage. *The Good Fight: A Life in Liberal Politics.* New York: Scribner, 2010.

Morley, Jefferson. *The Ghost: The Secret Life of CIA Spymaster James Jesus Angleton.* New York: St. Martin's Griffin, 2017.

Nguyen, Lien-Hang T. *Hanoi's War.* Chapel Hill, North Carolina: The University of North Carolina Press, 2012.

Oberdorfer, Don. *Senator Mansfield: The Extraordinary Life of a Great American Statesman and Diplomat.* Washington, D.C.: Smithsonian Books, 2003.

Olmsted, Kathryn S. *Challenging the Secret Government: The Post-Watergate Investigations of the CIA and FBI.* Chapel Hill, North Carolina: The University of North Carolina Press, 1996.

Pearson, Drew. *Washington Merry-Go-Round: The Drew Pearson Diaries, 1960–1969.* Lincoln, Nebraska: Potomac Books (an imprint of the University of Nebraska Press), 2015.

Perlstein, Rick. *Nixonland: The Rise of a President and the Fracturing of America.* New York: Scribner, 2008.

———. *The Invisible Bridge: The Fall of Nixon and the Rise of Reagan.* New York: Simon & Schuster, 2014.

———. *Reaganland: America's Right Turn, 1976–1980.* New York: Simon & Schuster, 2020.

Powers, Thomas. *The Man Who Kept the Secrets: Richard Helms and the CIA.* New York: Pocket Books, Simon & Schuster, 1979.

Prados, John. *The Family Jewels: The CIA, Secrecy, and Presidential Power.* Austin, Texas: The University of Texas Press, 2013.

———. *William Colby and the CIA: The Secret Wars of a Controversial Spymaster.* Lawrence, Kansas: The University Press of Kansas, 2009 (originally published by Oxford University Press in 2003).

Rappleye, Charles, and Ed Becker. *All-American Mafioso: The Johnny Rosselli Story.* New York: Doubleday, 1991.

Roemer Jr., William F. *Man Against the Mob.* New York: Donald I. Fine, Inc., 1989.

Rowe Jr., Gary Thomas. *My Undercover Years with the Ku Klux Klan.* New York: Bantam Books, 1976.

Rumsfeld, Donald. *When the Center Held: Gerald Ford and the Rescue of the American Presidency.* New York: Free Press, 2018.

Sampson, Anthony. *The Sovereign State of ITT.* Greenwich, Connecticut: Fawcett Publications, 1973, 1974 (a Fawcett Crest Book, reprinted by arrangement with Stein and Day Publishers).

Savage, Charlie. *Takeover: The Return of the Imperial Presidency and the Subversion of American Democracy.* New York: Little, Brown and Company, 2007.

Schulman, Robert. *John Sherman Cooper: The Global Kentuckian.* Lexington, Kentucky: The University Press of Kentucky, 1976.

Schwarz Jr., Frederick A. O. *Democracy in the Dark: The Seduction of Government Secrecy.* New York: The New Press, 2015.

———. With Aziz Z. Huq. *Unchecked and Unbalanced: Presidential Power in a Time of Terror.* New York: The New Press, 2007.

Senators of the United States: A Historical Bibliography. Compiled by Jo Anne McCormick Quatannens, Diane B. Boyle, editorial assistant; Prepared under the direction of Kelly D. Johnston, Secretary of the Senate. Washington, D.C.: Government Printing Office, 1995.

Server, Lee. *Handsome Johnny: The Life and Death of Johnny Rosselli: Gentleman Gangster, Hollywood Producer, CIA Assassin.* New York: St. Martin's Press, 2018.

Shackley, Ted, with Richard A. Finney. *Spymaster: My Life in the CIA.* Lincoln, Nebraska: Potomac Books (an imprint of the University of Nebraska Press), 2005.

Shapiro, Ira. *The Last Great Senate: Courage and Statesmanship in Times of Crisis.* Lanham, Maryland: Rowman & Littlefield, 2012.

Shenon, Philip. *A Cruel and Shocking Act: The Secret History of the Kennedy Assassination*. New York: Henry Holt and Company, 2013.

Smist Jr., Frank J. *Congress Oversees the United States Intelligence Community: Second Edition, 1947–1994*. Knoxville, Tennessee: The University of Tennessee Press, 1994.

Snider, L. Britt. *The Agency and the Hill: CIA's Relationship with Congress, 1946–2004*. Washington, D.C. Center for the Study of Intelligence, Central Intelligence Agency, 2008.

Stacy, Susan M., editor. *An Eye for Injustice: Robert C. Sims and Minidoka*. Pullman, Washington: Washington State University Press, 2020.

Stahl, Lesley. *Reporting Live*. New York: Simon & Schuster, 1999.

Stapilus, Randy. *Paradox Politics: People and Power in Idaho*. Carlton, Oregon: Ridenbaugh Press, 2009 (revised edition).

Stevenson, Jonathan. *A Drop of Treason: Philip Agee and His Exposure of the CIA*. Chicago: The University of Chicago Press, 2021.

Stockton, Bayard. *Flawed Patriot: The Rise and Fall of CIA Legend Bill Harvey*. Washington, D.C.: Potomac Books, 2006.

Stuart, Douglas T. *Creating the National Security State: A History of the Law that Transformed America*. Princeton, N.J.: Princeton University Press, 2008.

Sullivan, William C., with Bill Brown. *The Bureau: My Thirty Years in Hoover's FBI*. New York: Ishi Press, 1979.

Summers, Anthony. *Official and Confidential: The Secret Life of J. Edgar Hoover*. New York: Open Road, 1993.

Talbot, David. *The Devil's Chessboard: Allen Dulles, the CIA and the Rise of America's Secret Government*. New York: Harper Collins, 2015.

Taylor, Senator Glen H. *The Way It Was with Me*. Secaucus, N.J.: Lyle Stuart Inc., 1979.

Theoharis, Athan. *From the Secret Files of J. Edgar Hoover*. Chicago: Ivan R. Dee, Inc., 1991.

Thomas, Evan. *Robert Kennedy: His Life*. New York: Simon & Schuster, 2000.

Thompson, Douglas. *The Dark Heart of Hollywood*. Edinburgh: Mainstream Publishing, 2012.

Tomes, Robert R. *Apocalypse Then: American Intellectuals and the Vietnam War, 1954–1975*. New York: New York University Press, 1998.

Tower, John G. *Consequences: A Personal and Political Memoir*. Boston: Little, Brown, 1991.

Van Reybrouck, David. *Congo: The Epic History of a People*. New York: Ecco, an imprint of Harper Collins (English translation), 2014.

Vieth, George. *Black April: The Fall of South Vietnam, 1973–1975*. New York: Encounter Books, 2012.

Weatherby, James B., and Randy Stapilus. *Governing Idaho: Politics, People and Power*. Caldwell, Idaho: Caxton Press, 2005.

Weiner, Tim. *Legacy of Ashes: The History of the CIA*. New York: Anchor Books, 2008 (originally published in hardcover by Doubleday, 2007).

———. *Enemies: A History of the FBI*. New York: Random House, 2012.

Wicker, Tom. *On Press: A Top Reporter's Life in, and Reflections on, American Journalism*. New York: The Viking Press, 1978.

Willertz, John Richard. *The Prince of the Senate: A Biography of U.S. Senator Philip A. Hart, Jr.* Parker, Colorado: BookCrafters, 2012.

Witcover, Jules. *Marathon: The Pursuit of the Presidency, 1972–1976.* New York: Viking Press, 1977.

Woods, Randall B., editor. *Vietnam and the American Political Tradition: The Politics of Dissent.* Cambridge, United Kingdom: Cambridge University Press, 2003.

———. *Shadow Warrior: William Egan Colby and the CIA.* New York: Basic Books, 2013.

Zeilig, Leo. *Lumumba: Africa's Lost Leader.* London: Haus Publishing, 2008.

Special Collections

The Frank Church Papers, Boise State University

Interim and Final Reports of the Church Committee (Select Committee to Study Governmental Operations with respect to Intelligence Activities), Washington, D.C.: U.S. Government Printing Office, 1975 and 1976

Declassified Interviews conducted by the Church Committee, National Archives, College Park, Maryland

Transcripts of the Hearings of the Church Committee (Select Committee to Study Governmental Operations with respect to Intelligence Activities), U.S. Government Printing Office, 1976

Oral History of the Church Committee Members and Staff Interviews, U.S. Senate Historical Office, 2013–2015

Central Intelligence Agency Declassified Files, The Family Jewels Report—declassified 2007

Ford, Harold P., William E. Colby as Director of Central Intelligence (CIA internal history of William Colby's tenure as CIA director). Central Intelligence Agency: CIA History Staff, 1993 (declassified 2011)

Louie B. Nunn Center for Oral History, The University of Kentucky, Senator Walter (Dee) Huddleston Oral History Project, 2001–2002

Senate Historical Office Oral History interviews of George Tames, Washington Photographer for the New York Times, by Donald Ritchie, January 13 to May 16, 1988

Senate Historical Office Oral History interview of Carl M. Marcy, October 19, 1983

Senate Historical Office, Oral History Interview of Pat M. Holt, November 19, 1980

The Nelson Rockefeller Report to the President By the Commission on CIA Activities, June 1975 (New York: Manor Books, 1975)

The Unexpurgated Pike Report Forward by Philip Agee (McGraw Hill, 1992)

The Vietnam Hearings: Transcripts of Hearings of the Senate Foreign Relations Committee's 1966 hearings on the Vietnam War, With an introduction by J. William Fulbright (New York: Vintage Books, 1966)

Declassified Justice Department Inquiry into CIA-related Electronic Surveillance Activities, 1976

BIBLIOGRAPHY

Foreign Relations of the United States (State Department multivolume historical series on American foreign policy), Office of the Historian, U.S. State Department (Washington, D.C.: Government Printing Office)

Senate Floor Speeches by Frank Church, Congressional Record

Transcripts — Frank Church appearances on Meet the Press, NBC News

Transcripts — Frank Church appearances on Issues and Answers, ABC News

The White House, the CIA, and the Pike Committee (electronic briefing book, edited by John Prados and Arturo Jimenez-Bacardi), National Security Archive (George Washington University, 2017)

Disreputable If Not Outright Illegal: The National Security Agency versus Martin Luther King, Muhammad Ali, Art Buchwald, Frank Church, et al. (electronic briefing book, edited by Matthew M. Aid and William Burr), National Security Archive (George Washington University, 2013)

Ford Administration Stratagem of Withholding Sensitive Intelligence, Spearheaded by Dick Cheney, Set Tone for Future Clashes between Claims of Secrecy and Public's Right to Know (Electronic briefing book Edited by John Prados and Arturo Jimenez-Bacardi), National Security Archive (George Washington University, 2015)

Miami-Dade Police Files in the murder of Johnny Rosselli: Files of the Public Safety Department, Dade County, Florida Case #191-088-V Homicide: Rosselli, John (Investigation launched when body discovered on August 7, 1976)

Oak Park Police Department case files in the murder of Sam Giancana, obtained directly from the Oak Park Police Department. Files include: Incident Report, Complaint Number 75-7161, June 19, 1975

Private Papers of Gary Hart

Private Papers of Jerry Levinson

Private Papers of Patrick Shea

Private Papers of Mike Wetherell

The Gerald R. Ford Presidential Library Collections

The Lyndon Baines Johnson Presidential Library Collections

The John F. Kennedy Presidential Library Collections

Johnny Rosselli–related FBI files, collected in large-format paperback

Transcript of Johnny Rosselli's testimony before the Senate Special Committee to Investigate Organized Crime in Interstate Commerce, October 7, 1950, Chicago, Illinois (Kefauver Committee)

Testimony of Santo Trafficante, Jr. before the Senate Select Committee on Intelligence (permanent intelligence committee that succeeded the Church Committee), October 1976

United States of America v. John Rosselli; Maurice Friedman; Benjamin Teitelbaum; Manuel Jacobs (US Court of Appeals for the Ninth Circuit, 1970)

U.S. v Louis Campagna et al., 1943 (Johnny Rosselli Hollywood labor-racketeering case)

Links to FBI files about Mafia informant Dominic Blasi http://mafiahistory.us /rattrap/infblasi.html

Mafia: The Government's Secret File on Organized Crime, United States Treasury Department, Bureau of Narcotics (Government files on Mafia figures from the early 1960s), Forward by Sam Giancana, Jr. (New York: Harper Collins, 2007)

Dissertations, Journals, and Periodicals

Andrews, Cheri L. *The Victory in Vietnam Committee's Manichean Rhetoric: An Analysis of the Campaign to Recall Idaho Senator Frank Church.* Master's Thesis, Oregon State University, 1992.

Branch, Taylor. "The Trial of the CIA." *The New York Times Magazine,* September 12, 1976.

Brock, Gustaf J. "Congress Must Draw the Line: Senator Frank Church and the Cooper-Church Amendment of 1970." *Idaho Yesterdays* 35.2 (1991): 29.

Burns, Ken, and Lynn Novick. "How the Vietnam War Broke the American Presidency." *The Atlantic,* October 2017.

Church, Frank. "We are too deep in Asia and Africa." *New York Times Magazine,* February 14, 1965.

———. "How Many Dominican Republics and Vietnams Can We Take On?" *New York Times Magazine,* November 28, 1965.

———. "Of Presidents and Caesars: The Decline of Constitutional Government in the Conduct of American Foreign Policy." *Idaho Law Review,* Fall 1969.

———. "My Victory over Cancer." *Good Housekeeping,* January 1976.

———. "The Global Crunch." *Playboy,* August 1969.

Dant, Sara. "Making Wilderness Work: Frank Church and the American Wilderness Movement." *Pacific Historical Review* 77, no. 2 (May 2008): 237–272.

Erwin, Marshall Curtis. "Covert Action: Legislative Background and Possible Policy Questions." Congressional Research Service, 2013.

Eszterhas, Joe. "Rolling Stone Interview: Seymour Hersh, Toughest Reporter in America." *Rolling Stone,* April 10, 1975.

———. "Seymour Hersh Interview, Part Two." *Rolling Stone,* April 24, 1975.

Furlong, William Barry. "A Dove Versus a Dogcatcher." *New York Times Magazine,* June 25, 1967: 6–7, 49–53.

Hatzenbuehler, Ronald L. "Dissent among Mormons in the 1980 Senatorial Election in Idaho." *International Journal of Religion* 1, no. 1 (2020): 9–22.

Hatzenbuehler, Ronald L., and Bert W. Marley. "Why Church Lost: A Preliminary Analysis of the Church-Symms Election of 1980." *Pacific Historical Review* 1987.

Johnson, Loch K. "James Angleton and the Church Committee." *Journal of Cold War Studies* 15, no. 4 (Fall 2013).

Jones, Matthew. "Journalism, Intelligence and The New York Times: Cyrus L. Sulzberger, Harrison E. Salisbury and the CIA." *History* 100, no. 2 (April 2015).

Katsky, Clay Silver. *Open Secrets: Congressional Oversight of the CIA in the Early Cold War.* Master's Thesis, George Washington University, 2015.

Langston, Marc B. "Rediscovering Congressional Intelligence Oversight: Is Another Church Committee Possible Without Frank Church?" *Texas A&M Law Review,* 2015.

Moran, Christopher R. "The Last Assignment: David Atlee Phillips and the Birth of CIA Public Relations." *The International History Review* 35, no. 2 (2013).

Phillips, Eugene. "The Central Intelligence Agency's Surveillance of the New Left." *Review of History and Political Science,* 2017.

Ramparts magazine. "Vietnam Primer: An Interview with Senator Frank Church." *Ramparts*, 1966.

Schorr, Daniel. "A Backstage Journal: My 17 months on the CIA Watch." *Rolling Stone*, April 8, 1976.

Schmitz, David F. "Senator Frank Church, The Ford Administration, and the Challenges of Post-Vietnam Foreign Policy." *Peace & Change* 21, no. 4 (October 1996).

Schmitz, David F., and Natalie Fousekis. "Frank Church, the Senate, and the Emergence of Dissent on the Vietnam War." *Pacific Historical Review* 63, no. 4 (November 1994): 561–581.

Schwarz Jr., Frederick A. O. "Intelligence Activities and the Rights of Americans." *The Record of the Association of the Bar of the City of New York*, January/February 1977.

Snider, L. Britt. "Recollections of the Church Committee." *Studies in Intelligence*, Winter 1999–2000.

Tilove, Jonathan. "The New Map of American Politics." *The American Prospect*, December 19, 2001.

Trenta, Luca. "'An Act of Insanity and National Humiliation': The Ford Administration, Congressional Inquiries, and the Ban on Assassination." *Journal of Intelligence History* 17:2 (2018): 121–140.

The Village Voice. "The CIA Report the President Doesn't Want You To Read: The Pike Papers: Highlights from the Suppressed House Intelligence Committee Report." *The Village Voice*, February 16, 1976.

Zelizer, Julian E. "Frank Church and Vietnam: How Congress Helped End the Vietnam War." *The American Prospect*, 2007.

Notes

Prologue: "Senator Cathedral"

3   *killing people?:* Church Committee hearing, September 16, 1975. https://www.youtube.com/watch?v=fomOeIhEWDg.

3   *wearing sunglasses:* Church Committee hearing, September 16, 1975. https://www.youtube.com/watch?v=fomOeIhEWDg.

5   *addiction to war:* Church's remarks to the Women's National Democratic Club, September 8, 1975, Frank Church Papers.

6   *a bit of drama:* Interview of Loch Johnson.

6   *we wanted the dart gun:* Interview of Paul Michel.

6   *credited Rogovin:* Colby and Forbath, *Honorable Men,* 442.

Chapter 1: "Happier times"

17   *a 14-year-old?:* LeRoy Ashby and Rod Gramer. *Fighting the Odds: The Life of Frank Church,* 8. Published nearly 30 years ago, *Fighting the Odds,* the first biography of Frank Church, is an important resource and reference, particularly about Church's early life. The book's footnotes are an important resource as well. In addition, the Frank Church Papers at Boise State University contain an invaluable collection of the full transcripts of interviews of Frank Church and his family, friends, staff, and others, which were conducted mainly in the late 1970s and throughout the 1980s by Rod Gramer, LeRoy Ashby, and Marc C. Johnson. Many of the people interviewed in the collection, including Frank Church, have long since died, and in some cases these are the only extended interviews the subjects ever gave concerning Frank Church. Gramer and Johnson first began conducting the interviews in the late 1970s, when they were planning to jointly write a book

about Frank Church. After Johnson dropped out of the project, Gramer partnered with Ashby, and they continued to conduct additional interviews. Their book became *Fighting the Odds*. Quotes and information cited from the interviews conducted by Ashby, Gramer, and Johnson in the Frank Church Papers will be collectively cited as "Interviews of [person interviewed], A-G-J Interview Collection, Frank Church Papers."
Interview with Carl Burke, A-G-J Interview Collection, Frank Church Papers, May 23, 1979.
Interview with Bethine Church, A-G-J Interview Collection, Frank Church Papers, August 3, 1984.

17 *I remember my father reading it:* Interview with Frank Church, A-G-J Interview Collection, Frank Church Papers, January 10, 1979.

21 *Frank's father was not much of a hunter:* Interview with Stan Burns, A-G-J Interview Collection, Frank Church Papers, April 24, 1984.

21 *He was not a great hiker or camper:* Interview with Chase Church.

21 *He seemed to be a star:* Interview with LeRoy Ashby.

21 *Frank took after her:* Interview with Stan Burns.

22 *His father hated Roosevelt:* Interview with Carl Burke, A-G-J Interview Collection, Frank Church Papers, January 6, 1979.

23 *made a good campaign announcement:* Interview with Stan Burns, A-G-J Interview Collection, Frank Church Papers, April 24, 1984.

23 *Borah had been corrupt:* Interview with Bryce Nelson.

25 *During the past year, the American people:* "The American Way of Life," Frank Church, 1941 American Legion speech. Speech available online at "50 years of Winning Orations in the American Legion National High School Oratorical Contest," The American Legion. https://archive.legion.org/handle/20.500.12203/5997

27 *I knew he was going to get into politics:* Interview with Carl Burke, A-G-J Interview Collection, Frank Church Papers, January 6, 1979.

27 *Church also had a mischievous side:* Interview with Carl Burke, A-G-J Interview Collection, Frank Church Papers, January 6, 1979; Interview of Stan Burns, A-G-J Interview Collection, Frank Church Papers, April 24, 1984.

28 *Frank was the only high school student:* Church, *Lifelong Affair*, 28 (footnote).

28 *He was the first person:* Interview with Bethine Church, A-G-J Interview Collection, Frank Church Papers, August 3, 1984.

28 *To an Athlete Dying Young:* Church, *Lifelong Affair*, 31.

28 *This was depressing stuff:* Church, *Lifelong Affair*, 33.

28 *both affectionate and distant:* Church, *Lifelong Affair*, 31.

Chapter 2: "The finest diction in the Army"

29 *the feverish first days after Pearl Harbor:* The details that appear in the footnote on this page about Bethine Clark's father, Chase Clark, are from Stacy, *Eye for Injustice*, 10–14, 23–36.

32 *Young lady:* Church, *Lifelong Affair*, 40.

32 *His Selective Service card:* The National Personnel Records Center, which houses U.S. military personnel records, was unable to locate Frank Church's military records in its files. In a letter responding to a request for a copy of his files, the center said that millions of its files were destroyed in a fire in July 1973, and that the records stored in the area that suffered the most fire damage were those of Army veterans discharged or deceased from November 1, 1912 to December 31, 1959. That time period would cover Frank Church's military records. The Frank Church Papers at Boise State contain the military records that Church kept personally.

32 *He just wasn't a good strong kid:* Interview of Carl Burke, A-G-J Interview Collection, Frank Church Papers, January 6, 1979.

33 *I didn't come to Michigan:* Frank Church letter to Bethine Clark, April 6, 1945, Frank Church Papers.

34 *He wrote that he envied:* Letter from Frank Church to Bethine Clark, June 7, 1945, Frank Church Papers.

34 *the West Point scourge has gone:* Letter from Bethine Clark to Frank Church, June 10, 1945, Frank Church Papers.

35 *McLure's "court jester":* Letter from Frank Church to Bethine Clark, September 22, 1945, Frank Church Papers.

35 *If I make no mark elsewhere:* Letter from Frank Church to Bethine Clark, September 9, 1945, Frank Church Papers.

35 *McLure also made sure:* Citation for the Bronze Star awarded to Frank Church, Chinese Combat Command, Frank Church Papers.

36 *With few exceptions:* Letter from Frank Church to Bethine Clark, September 6, 1945, Frank Church Papers.

36 *Church wrote a letter back:* Letter from Frank Church to the Headquarters Commandant, USF, January 15, 1946, Frank Church Papers.

37 *the flame was still flickering:* Interview with Stan Burns, A-G-J Interview Collection, Frank Church Papers, April 24, 1984.

37 *Yesterday Bay, Carl and I managed to get seats:* Letter from Frank Church to Bethine Clark, May 21, 1947, Frank Church Papers.

37 *I have been anxious to strike out at Chiang's China:* Letter from Frank Church to Bethine Clark, November 2, 1946, Frank Church Papers.

38 *During a Stanford debate:* Letter from Frank Church to Bethine Clark, January 18, 1947, Frank Church Papers.

38 *When I was wheeled into the recovery room:* Frank Church, "My Victory over Cancer," *Good Housekeeping,* January 1976: 26–30.

40 *It was the lowest I'd ever been in my life:* Frank Church, "My Victory over Cancer," *Good Housekeeping,* January 1976: 28.

Chapter 3: "If you don't run you will never get there"

42 *That was the beginning of my disillusionment:* Interview of Frank Church, A-G-J Interview Collection, Frank Church Papers, January 10, 1979.

43 *87 Communists in Idaho:* "Welker Raps Taylor as Fellow Traveler," Associated Press, July 5, 1950, published in *Idaho State Journal.*

43 *I'm not so sure that there was that much thought given to it:* Interview of Carl Burke, A-G-J Interview Collection, Frank Church Papers, January 6, 1979.

45 *The Clark political dynasty had run out of blood-line relatives:* Taylor, *The Way It Was with Me,* 379.

45 *Glen Taylor will be nominated by the Democrats:* "Opponents in Senate Race Name 'Man to Beat' Tuesday," Associated Press, published in *Spokane Spokesman-Review,* August 9, 1956.

46 *Taylor went door-to-door in Mountain Home:* Taylor, *The Way It Was with Me,* 383–385.

47 *"The Shameful Record of Herman Welker!":* A surviving copy of "The Shameful Record of Herman Welker!" pamphlet is in the Frank Church Papers.

47 *I looked at it in horror:* Interview of Frank Church, A-G-J Interview Collection, Frank Church Papers, January 10, 1979.

47 *stand by the incinerator:* Church, *Father & Son,* 37.

47 *I always had a feeling of relief:* Interview of Frank Church, A-G-J Interview Collection, Frank Church Papers, January 10, 1979.

48 *a .22 caliber rifle:* McDaniel, *Dying for Joe McCarthy's Sins,* 1–10; "The Suicide of Wyoming Senator Lester Hunt," Drew Pearson column, June 23, 1954, published in *Prescott [Arizona] Evening Courier;* "Suicide Bullet Ends Life of Sen. Hunt," Associated Press, June 19, 1954; "Hunt Takes Life in Senate Office," *New York Times,* June 20, 1954.

49 *unless the law was changed:* McDaniel, *Dying for Joe McCarthy's Sins,* 238–243; "Curbing Congress on Slander Urged," *New York Times,* December 22, 1950.

50 *He called Glenn "Red" Jacoby:* McDaniel, *Dying for Joe McCarthy's Sins,* 287.

50 *a much more sensitive soul:* "The Suicide of Wyoming Senator Lester Hunt," Drew Pearson column, June 23, 1954, published in *Prescott [Arizona] Evening Courier.*

51 *come out and fight:* "Church Claims Foe Is Avoiding Debate," *Twin Falls Times-News,* October 29, 1956.

51 *Church noted wryly:* "Church Claims Foe Is Avoiding Debate," *Twin Falls Times-News,* October 29, 1956.

52 *Eisenhower was not an enthusiastic Welker supporter:* "Eisenhower Letter Backs Sen. Welker," *Idaho Sunday Statesman,* October 28, 1956.

52 *McCarthyite and a front man for a corrupt machine to choose between:* The *Idaho Statesman,* October 17, 1956.

52 *unholy alliance:* "Taylor to Launch Write-In Bid Monday," *Spokane Daily Chronicle,* October 20, 1956.

52 *Taylor's write-in campaign was bankrolled by Welker:* Taylor, *The Way It Was with Me,* 399–403.

Chapter 4: "Persona non grata"

54 *I had no sooner taken the oath:* The account of Frank Church's introduction to the hard politics of Lyndon Johnson comes from a wide range of sources, including: Oral history transcript, Frank Church, interview May 1, 1969, Lyndon B. Johnson Presidential Library; Interview with Frank

Church, A-G-J Interview Collection, Frank Church Papers, January 10, 1979; Caro, *Master of the Senate*, 859–861; Miller, *Lyndon: An Oral Biography*, 255–256; Bethine Church, *Lifelong Affair*, 100–101; and Ashby and Gramer, *Fighting the Odds*, 76–78.

56 *I had a Cold War perspective:* Frank Church interview, A-G-J Interview Collection, Frank Church Papers, June 12, 1979.

57 *maneuver in mystifying ways:* Caro, *Master of the Senate*, 861–866.

57 *only intellectual, not a visceral thing:* Caro, *Master of the Senate*, 971.

58 *He had to give up wearing blue suits:* Church, *Father & Son*, 48.

58 *He installed his grandfather's brass name plate:* "Senator Nails Plate of 1890s on Office Door," *Spokane Spokesman-Review*, January 15, 1957.

58 *Baker, doing Johnson's bidding:* Church, *Lifelong Affair*, 96.

58 *Church and his family lived in the same home:* Interview of Chase Church. Bethine Church kept the Bethesda house after Frank Church died in 1984; she finally sold it when she moved back to Boise in 1989.

59 *When they bought the house, for $43,500:* Church financial disclosure press release, June 22, 1976, Frank Church Papers.

59 *Church felt uncomfortable:* Interview of Peter Fenn.

59 *Marlon Brando sent me a book:* Interview of Chase Church.

60 *there are always fights:* Interview of Carl Burke, A-G-J Interview Collection, Frank Church Papers, January 6, 1979.

60 *took her out to lunch to warn her:* Church, *Lifelong Affair*, 98–99.

61 *Bethine was kind of born at the wrong time:* Interview with Monica Church.

61 *There was some friction:* Interview with Chase Church.

61 *Once in a while I just blow sky high:* Interview of Bethine Church, A-G-J Interview Collection, Frank Church Papers, June 13, 1979.

63 *nearly cost her the job:* Church, *Lifelong Affair*, 121–122.

63 *Verda Barnes had a long-term affair:* Interview with Carolyn Taylor.

63 *Everyone knew about it:* Interview with Carolyn Taylor.

63 *In Frank Church:* "Frank Church Another Borah? Critical Capital Tips Its Hat," *The Salt Lake Tribune*, January 6, 1957.

63 *A slightly embarrassing but humorous incident:* Wicker, *On Press*, 40.

Chapter 5: "A betrayal"

65 *Church broke with the Northern liberals:* Caro, *Master of the Senate*, 970–979.

66 *Johnson was warmly and massively grateful:* Frank Church oral history interview, Lyndon B. Johnson Presidential Library, May 1, 1969.

67 *has now received his reward:* Drew Pearson column, published in *Quad City Times* [Davenport, Iowa], August 17, 1957.

67 *historians later concluded the same thing:* Evans and Novak, *Lyndon Johnson;* Caro, *Master of the Senate*, 895–909. Caro devotes an entire chapter of *Master of the Senate* to the Hells Canyon episode.

67 *There was never any quid pro quo at all:* Oral history interview of Frank Church, LBJ Presidential Library, May 1, 1969.

69 *Frank, I am afraid:* Douglas, *In the Fullness of Time*, 287.

69 *he lost to Idaho Power:* Dant, "Making Wilderness Work," 237–272.

69 *study of Church's conservation record:* Dant, "Making Wilderness Work," 237–272.

70 *we should not keep a business in these mountains:* "Sen. Church sells land in Sawtooth," Associated Press, published in *South Idaho Press,* January 6, 1971.

70 *the Sagebrush rebels were sharpening their swords:* Interview of Larry LaRocco.

70 *He made it pretty clear:* John Carver oral history interview, Kennedy Presidential Library, August 19, 1968.

71 *it was definitely helpful:* Frank Church oral history interview, Kennedy Presidential Library, November 5, 1981.

72 *distasteful:* Oral history interview of John Carver for the Kennedy Presidential Library, August 19, 1968.

72 *I was a senator who was even younger:* Frank Church oral history interview, Kennedy Presidential Library, November 5, 1981.

72 *he did not want the teleprompter:* Church, *Father & Son,* 49.

72 *in content, if not in form:* the text of Church's July 11, 1960 keynote address at the 1960 Democratic National Convention is available online from the John F. Kennedy Presidential Library. https://www.jfklibrary.org/asset-viewer /archives/JFKCAMP1960/1034/ JFKCAMP1960-1034-002

73 *lousy speech:* John Carver oral history interview, Kennedy Presidential Library, August 19, 1968.

74 *Bethine, where's your fellow?:* Church, *Lifelong Affair,* 137.

75 *I came away with my first strong misgivings:* Frank Church, oral history interview, Kennedy Presidential Library, November 5, 1981.

76 *I like to believe:* Frank Church, oral history interview, Kennedy Presidential Library, November 5, 1981.

77 *a continuation of the revolution:* Schmitz and Fousekis, "Frank Church, the Senate, Etc.," 561–581.

78 *he regretted that vote:* Church, *Father & Son,* 59.

79 *there is no way for us to win their war: Ramparts* magazine, "Vietnam Primer," 1966.

79 *No sooner had he become president:* Frank Church oral history interview, Lyndon B. Johnson Presidential Library, May 1, 1969.

80 *Bethine early on told him:* Interview with Peter Fenn.

80 *He said this looking straight at me:* Frank Church oral history interview, Lyndon B. Johnson Presidential Library, May 1, 1969.

80 *ate up stories:* Pearson, Drew, *Washington Merry-Go-Round,* 291.

80 *the next time you want a dam:* Frank Church oral history interview, Lyndon B. Johnson Presidential Library, May 1, 1969.

81 *whirled around in his chair:* Schmitz and Fousekis, "Frank Church, the Senate, Etc.," 561–581.

81 *the whole philosophical argument:* Schmitz and Fousekis, "Frank Church, the Senate, Etc.," 561–581.

81 *But Church kept pushing:* Frank Church, "How Many Dominican Republics?": 44–45, 177–178.

81 *I've never been so disillusioned:* The 1966 letter, with the name and other identifying information about the soldier blacked out, is included in the Frank Church Papers.

83 *when I went to school, that was a civil war:* The Vietnam Hearings, 38.

83 *we failed to take into account:* The Vietnam Hearings, 136.

83 *more than 20,000 letters and telegrams:* The Vietnam Hearings, Introduction by Senator J. William Fulbright, ix.

83 *Once it became apparent:* Frank Church oral history interview, Lyndon B. Johnson Presidential Library, May 1, 1969.

Chapter 6: "War prolonged and unending"

86 *his father's opposition:* The account of the rift between Frank Church and Forrest Church is based on a range of sources, including interviews with Peter Fenn and Chase Church, as well as on several books, among them Church, *Father & Son;* Cryer, *Being Alive and Having to Die;* and Church, *Lifelong Affair.*

87 *loved to read Nabokov:* Interview with Peter Fenn.

87 *Much of our estrangement:* Church, *Father & Son,* 76.

87 *an angry ideologue:* The account of Ron Rankin's life and the 1967 recall campaign relies on a wide range of sources, including Furlong, "Dove Versus a Dogcatcher"; Andrews, *Manichean Rhetoric;* Stapilus, *Paradox Politics;* Weatherby and Stapilus, *Governing Idaho;* Tilove, "The New Map of American Politics"; "Coast Millionaire Finances Drive Against Idaho Senator," *Des Moines Tribune,* July 26, 1967; "Financing Viewed in Church Recall," *Idaho Statesman,* May 26, 1967; "Should Idaho Wear Far Right Label?", *Idaho Sunday Statesman,* May 21, 1967; and "Gem Aides Score Try for Recall," *Idaho Statesman,* May 10, 1967.

90 *engineered a political disaster:* Stapilus, *Paradox Politics,* 130–131.

90 *which terrified many Democrats:* Stapilus, *Paradox Politics,* 130.

90 *the campaign wounds are still bleeding:* Stapilus, *Paradox Politics,* 134.

90 *the darling of the doves:* Andrews, *Manichean Rhetoric,* 34.

91 *we'll get Senator Church:* "Recall Move Against Senator Church Opens a Right-Wing Drive to Punish Critics of Vietnam War," *New York Times,* May 25, 1967.

91 *you've got to do it yourself:* Furlong, "Dove Versus a Dogcatcher."

92 *go to the county courthouses:* Interview with Jerry Brady.

92 *typically formal language:* "Recall Move Against Senator Church Opens a Right-Wing Drive to Punish Critics of Vietnam War," *New York Times,* May 25, 1967.

92 *I went up to him:* Interview with Jerry Brady.

92 *was a godsend:* "Proposed Recall Aids Sen. Church," Associated Press, published in *Pensacola News,* September 30, 1967; "The Inquiring Reporter: What is your opinion of the filing of a petition to recall Sen. Frank Church because of his views on the Vietnam situation?," *Idaho Sunday Statesman,* May 14, 1967.

93 *quietly died:* "Attempt to Recall Sen. Church Fails," Associated Press, published in *Grand Junction Daily Sentinel,* July 27, 1967. After the recall effort failed, Ron Rankin remained a political gadfly in Idaho for decades, until the state finally moved so far to the right that his extremism was mainstream. He ran for governor and other offices 10 times in 30 years, losing every time, but in 1996 he was finally elected to the Kootenai County

Commission in Coeur d'Alene. Rankin died in 2004. William Penn Patrick died in 1973 in the crash of a World War II–era fighter plane that he was piloting, just as his business had come under investigation for being nothing more than a complex pyramid scheme.

94 *in the morning:* Church, *Lifelong Affair,* 198.

94 *The Torment in the Land: Congressional Record,* February 21, 1968.

97 *one of the great: Congressional Record,* February 21, 1968; LeRoy Ashby, "Church and Borah: Idaho's Premier Statesmen Had Nothing, And Yet, Everything in Common," *Lewiston Tribune,* July 3, 1990.

98 *a loud and imposing figure: Paradox Politics* by Randy Stapilus provides a good account of George Hansen and his political career.

98 *I advised against it:* Stapilus, *Paradox Politics,* 135.

98 *a blustery big guy:* Interview with Jerry Brady.

99 *baby killer:* Church, *Lifelong Affair,* 183.

99 *No, George:* Church, *Lifelong Affair,* 183. Hansen gave up his House seat when he ran against Frank Church for the Senate, but returned to the House in the 1970s. In 1974, Hansen was convicted of campaign-finance violations. In 1984, he went to prison for violating the Ethics in Government Act. Hansen was jailed once again in 1992 after being convicted of fraud in a multimillion-dollar investment scheme.

99 *ticking time bomb:* Cryer, *Being Alive,* 48.

99 *made things worse:* Cryer, *Being Alive,* 49.

99 *regarding him as a sellout:* The author of a biography of Forrest Church summarizes an interview with Stan Zuckerman, who worked on Church's 1968 campaign. Cryer, *Being Alive,* 49.

100 *almost completely estranged:* Church, *Father & Son,* 75.

100 *walking on eggshells:* Stapilus, *Paradox Politics,* 135.

100 *Church relied very heavily:* Interview with Cleve Corlett.

102 *later sealed:* Interviews with Chase Church and his daughter, Monica Church.

Chapter 7: "We stand up now"

103 *He desperately wanted:* Interview with Jerry Levinson.

104 *He became angrier:* Interview with Tom Dine.

104 *electoral genius:* Interview with Tom Dine.

104 *During his temptation:* Bethine, *Lifelong Affair.*

105 *So many turned up:* "Tacit Help by Officials in Government," *The Guardian,* October 16, 1969.

105 *a policy for continued engagement in Vietnam:* "Senator Frank Church Criticizes Nixon's Vietnamization Policy," *Idaho State Journal,* November 16, 1969.

105 *now so confident:* Frank Church, "The Global Crunch," *Playboy,* August 1969: 80–81, 86, 200–204.

107 *the brow of Zeus:* Frank Church, "Of Presidents and Caesars: The Decline of Constitutional Government in the Conduct of American Foreign Policy," *Idaho Law Review* 6, no. 1 (1969).

108 *They forged:* Schulman, *John Sherman Cooper,* 101–102; "John Sherman Cooper Dies at 89," *New York Times,* February 23, 1991.

109 *going to the [Senate] floor:* Interview with Tom Dine.

110 *he really believed:* Interview with Bill Miller, A-G-J Interview Collection, Frank Church Papers, July 27, 1984. Miller was also interviewed for this book before his death in 2019.

110 *By right of seniority:* Church, *Lifelong Affair.*

110 *a national figure:* Interview with Tom Dine.

111 *Liberace came:* Interview with Chase Church.

111 *He thrived on it:* Interview with Bill Miller, A-G-J Interview Collection, Frank Church Papers, July 27, 1984.

111 *Dole is so unctuous:* Interview with Tom Dine.

111 *Fulbright had a book:* Interview with Tom Dine.

112 *Bethine was aghast:* Church, *Lifelong Affair,* 193.

112 *a small cabin:* Interviews with Chase Church and Peter Fenn.

113 *a barbecue at Church's cabin:* Henry Kimelman, *Living the American Dream,* 314.

113 *met with Kissinger:* Interview with Tom Dine; interview with Bill Miller, A-G-J Interview Collection, Frank Church Papers, July 27, 1984.

114 *the doves have won:* Frank Church, "The Doves Have Won" (speech at Mills College of Education), September 11, 1970. Church had used the same phrase five days earlier on television: Frank Church, "The Doves Have Won and Don't Know It," CBS, September 6, 1970.

116 *During the final negotiations:* Zelizer, "Frank Church and Vietnam," 2007.

116 *there are literally:* Letter from Mike Wetherell to Frank Church, January 11, 1984. Private papers of Mike Wetherell.

117 *Dine helped develop:* Interview with Tom Dine.

117 *It was Frank Church:* https://www.youtube.com/watch?v=WmFFLBHniCE.

117 *"saved my sanity,":* Video of Joe Biden's remarks in Boise, the *Idaho Statesman,* August 6, 2019. https://www.youtube.com/watch?v=WmFFLBHniCE.

Chapter 8: "An enormous hue and cry"

120 *You can't count:* Carl Marcy, oral history interview, Senate Historical Office, October 19, 1983.

121 *a rising star:* Interview with Dave Schmitz.

121 *They were pissed:* Interview with Tom Dine.

122 *promised Ellsberg:* Interview with Daniel Ellsberg.

122 *McGovern ultimately refused:* Interview with Daniel Ellsberg.

123 *into the committee's possession:* Pat Holt, oral history interview, Senate Historical Office, November 19, 1980.

123 *a reporter with PBS:* Warren Unna, who died in 2017, revealed what happened in a first-person account in 1977: "Senate Guilt on CIA: Why Did It Bury Chile Documents?," *Washington Post,* November 13, 1977.

124 *"Unna explained":* Unna, "Senate Guilt on CIA."

124 *had in his possession:* Pat Holt, oral history interview.

124 *Instead of going public:* Pat Holt, oral history interview.

125 *drop some documents off:* Interview with Jeff Brindle. See also Mark Feldstein, *Poisoning the Press.*

125 *and lo and behold:* Pat Holt, oral history interview.

126 *for about eighteen months:* Pat Holt, oral history interview.

127 *a lot of guts:* Jerry Levinson's unpublished memoir, private papers of Jerry Levinson.

127 *Jerry Levinson would drive:* Interviews with Jerry Levinson and Cathy Levinson.

127 *out on a limb:* Interview with Jerry Levinson.

128 *my friends in St. Louis:* Interview with Jerry Levinson.

128 *the perfect target:* Sampson, *The Sovereign State of ITT.* Anthony Sampson's 1973 examination of ITT relied in part on the work of Jerry Levinson and Frank Church's Senate multinational subcommittee.

129 *then I understood:* Jerry Levinson's unpublished memoir, private papers of Jerry Levinson.

Chapter 9: "As long as the KGB does it"

130 *operationally nasty:* Jefferson Morely, "The Gentlemanly Planner of Assassinations," *Slate,* November 1, 2002.

132 *prepared for a showdown:* Interview with Jerry Levinson.

132 *a series of questions:* A partial transcript of the closed hearing was obtained for this book.

134 *Symington stepped in:* Interview with Jerry Levinson.

134 *Church got a call:* Jerry Levinson's unpublished memoir, private papers of Jerry Levinson.

135 *committed perjury:* Jerry Levinson's memo is quoted in Jerry Levinson's unpublished memoir, included in Levinson's private papers and obtained for this book.

136 *Church told me:* Jerry Levinson's unpublished memoir, private papers of Jerry Levinson.

136 *was exactly the opposite:* Interview with Jerry Levinson.

136 Richard Helms cut a plea deal.

136 *I wanted to talk about the CIA:* "Memorandum of Conversation, November 11, 1974, President Gerald Ford, former CIA director John McCone, Lt. General Brent Scowcroft, deputy national security advisor." *Foreign Relations of the United States, 1969–1976,* Volume XXXVII, Part 2: "Organization and Management of Foreign Policy; Public Diplomacy, 1973–1976."

137 *SEC officials were surprised:* Interview with Jerry Levinson.

137 *began to share:* Interview with Jerry Levinson.

138 *shot himself in the head:* "Suicide Note Left by Lockheed Officer," *New York Times,* August 27, 1975.

138 *a sordid tale:* The Church quote is used as an epigraph in the front of the book. Boulton, *The Grease Machine.*

138 *a pattern of crookedness:* David Montero, Longreads excerpt of his book *Kickback: Exposing the Global Corporate Bribery Network* (Viking, 2018).

139 *open to dishonorable favors and offers:* "Dutch Prince Quits Posts As Inquiry Board Assails His Links With Lockheed," *New York Times,* August 27, 1976.

140 *lasting political impact:* "Lockheed: Corporation or Political Actor?" (speech by Frank Church, October 26, 1976). Frank Church took a special, personal interest in the Lockheed-related investigations in foreign countries, particularly Japan.

140 *a strange figure:* "A Japanese Dives Plane Into House of Lockheed Agent," *New York Times,* March 23, 1976; "Japan: Kamikaze Over Tokyo," *Time* magazine, April 5, 1976.

140 *We had better make up our minds:* "Japan Rightist Got $7 million from Lockheed," *New York Times,* February 5, 1976.

141 *special attack corps is alive in Japan:* Jerry Levinson's unpublished memoir.

142 *a show horse:* Jerry Levinson's unpublished memoir.

Chapter 10: "We have stood watch"

144 *like your job?:* Interview with Tom Dine.

144 *pro-gun:* Interview with Chase Church.

144 *without a Disneyland:* "Senator Church Fields Varied Questions," *South Idaho Press,* March 15, 1974.

145 *where is Church?:* "Election 74 — comments on the campaign" (Mike Wetherell memo to Frank Church), November 14, 1974, private papers of Mike Wetherell.

145 *showing signs of discontent:* "Church Shouldn't Expect a Cakewalk," *South Idaho Press,* March 4, 1974.

146 *We stand in this year: Congressional Record,* October 29, 1971.

147 *Church erased:* Interview with Tom Dine.

148 *stalked out:* "Great Senate Debate Was One Giant Yawn," Associated Press story published in the *Des Moines Register,* September 20, 1974.

148 *Vietnam did radicalize:* Interview with Jerry Levinson.

148 *archive of documents:* Interview with Jerry Levinson.

149 *an avowed hawk:* Ford, "William E. Colby as Director of Central Intelligence," 1993.

149 *recalled overhearing:* Interview with Jerry Levinson.

150 *confines of complacency:* Speech by Senator Mike Mansfield, Boise Idaho, October 20, 1973. From the collection of Mike Mansfield speeches in the Mike Mansfield Papers, University of Montana.

150 *father figure:* Interview with Bill Miller, A-G-J Interview Collection, Frank Church Papers, July 27, 1984.

151 *Democratic formula:* Interview with John Greenfield.

152 *old friends:* Interviews with Bob Smith and Steve Symms.

152 *gave a speech:* Interview with Bob Smith.

153 *had to go back:* Interview with Bill Bader, A-G-J Interview Collection, Frank Church Papers, May 18, 1987.

153 *he did defend:* In 1979 Church wrote a letter to the Attorney General, asking him to release the FBI files on Verda Barnes so she could dispel the lingering accusations that she had Communist ties.

154 *there were problems:* Interview with Mike Wetherell.

154 *I was flabbergasted:* Interview with Bob Smith.

155 *a very bad campaign:* Interview with Frank Church, A-G-J Interview Collection, Frank Church Papers, February 13, 1979.

155 *was a prelude:* Interview with Cleve Corlett.

155 *last Democrat:* Interview with Mike Wetherell.

155 *time to gamble:* Interview with Jerry Levinson.

Chapter 11: "This will cost you the presidency"

157 *Schlesinger was shocked:* There is a wide range of source material about the Family Jewels. In 2007, the CIA released a declassified version: *Central Intelligence Agency Declassified Files: The Family Jewels Report.*

158 *a hurricane of a man:* Eszterhas, "Rolling Stone Interview," 48–52, 73–74, 77–78, 80–81.

158 *he feverishly:* Hersh's memoir, *Reporter,* provides a fascinating look at Hersh's reporting career.

159 *cardinal bureaucratic sin:* Interview with Seymour Hersh; Hersh, *Reporter.*

159 *Hersh's story dominated:* "Huge C.I.A. Operation Reported in U.S. Against Antiwar Forces, Other Dissidents in Nixon Years," *New York Times,* December 22, 1974.

160 *produced evidence:* "Huge C.I.A. Operation Reported in U.S.," *New York Times,* December 22, 1974.

160 *Baker had bombarded:* Ford, "William E. Colby as Director of Central Intelligence," 1993.

161 *Colby assured him:* "Ford Forbids C.I.A. to Act Illegally in Domestic Field," *New York Times,* December 23, 1974.

161 *had resigned:* "President Tells Colby to Speed Report on C.I.A.," *New York Times,* December 24, 1974.

162 *to write a report:* "President Tells Colby to Speed Report on C.I.A.," *New York Times,* December 24, 1974.

162 *invited Hersh:* Interview of Seymour Hersh; Hersh, *Reporter,* 220.

162 *been frustrated:* Oberdorfer, *Senator Mansfield,* 144–145.

162 *serious congressional oversight:* Oberdorfer, *Senator Mansfield* 144.

162 *invites abuse:* Oberdorfer, *Senator Mansfield,* 145.

163 *politically responsible leadership:* Oberdorfer, *Senator Mansfield,* 145.

163 *Hughes-Ryan Act:* Marshall Curtis Erwin, "Covert Action: Legislative Background and Possible Policy Questions," Congressional Research Service, 2013.

164 *formally known as:* "C.I.A.- F.B.I. Inquiry Voted by Senate," *New York Times,* January 28, 1975.

165 *Church walked up:* George Thames, oral history interview, Senate Historical Office, January 13–May 16, 1988.

165 *if these people:* Interview with Frank Church, A-G-J Interview Collection, Frank Church Papers, June 14, 1979.

166 *When Church met:* Interview with Frank Church, A-G-J Interview Collection, Frank Church Papers, June 14, 1979.

166 *A westerner:* Interview with Tom Dine.

166 *I would be chairman:* Interview with Frank Church, A-G-J Interview Collection, Frank Church Papers, June 14, 1979.

167 *implicit or explicit:* Interview with Frank Church, A-G-J Interview Collection, Frank Church Papers, June 14, 1979.

Chapter 12: "A delicate balance"

171 *who fool around:* Interview with Bryce Nelson.

171 *to be shy:* Interview with Fritz Schwarz.

173 *Tower was there:* Interview with Bill Miller, A-G-J Interview Collection, Frank Church Papers, July 27, 1984.

173 *damage control officer:* Tower, *Consequences,* 132.

173 *walked up to me:* Interview with Gary Hart.

173 *at the Remagen Bridge:* Senator Walter (Dee) Huddleston Oral History Project, 2001–2002, Louie B. Nunn Center for Oral History, University of Kentucky.

174 *without a doubt:* Tower, *Consequences,* 105.

175 *He knew the personalities:* Interview with Walter Mondale.

175 *That's the way:* Interview with Walter Mondale.

176 *meet QJWIN:* Interview with Gary Hart.

177 *I asked Angleton:* Interview with Gary Hart.

178 *Tower and I:* White House memorandum on March 5, 1975, White House meeting of Ford, Church and Tower, Gerald R. Ford Presidential Library.

179 *I had been shaken:* Mondale, *Good Fight,* 139.

Chapter 13: "The dirty facts"

180 *going to dinner:* Interview with Loch Johnson; Johnson, *Season of Inquiry Revisited,* 11–12.

181 *Kimelman wondered:* Kimelman, *Living the American Dream,* 314–315.

182 *hovering nearby:* "Head of C.I.A. Inquiry," *New York Times,* January 30, 1975.

182 *the toy store:* Interview with Fritz Schwarz.

183 *Toys:* Interview with Mary DeOreo.

184 *I had never met:* Interview with Fritz Schwarz.

184 *he didn't strike me as dynamic:* Interview with Richard Betts.

185 *You had to work:* Interview with Bill Miller, A-G-J Interview Collection, Frank Church Papers, July 27, 1984.

186 *I was amazed:* Johnson, *Season of Inquiry Revisited,* 63.

186 *the dirty facts:* Interview with Fritz Schwarz.

187 *without digging around in the sewer for facts:* Mondale, *Good Fight,* 140.

188 *these accusations:* Interviews with Fritz Schwarz and other Church Committee staffers; Johnson, *Season of Inquiry Revisited,* 63.

188 *sided with Schwarz:* Interview with Fritz Schwarz.

188 *we took that argument to Church:* Interview with Fritz Schwarz.

188 *took some drama:* Interview with Loch Johnson.

189 *I was seriously opposed:* Interview with Bill Bader, A-G-J Interview Collection, Frank Church Papers, May 18, 1987.

189 *more antagonistic:* Interview with David Aaron.

189 *kind of sat back:* Interview with Frederick Baron.

190 *You could hear everybody:* Interview with Paul Michel.

190 *To complicate matters:* Ford, "William E. Colby as Director of Central Intelligence," 1993.

191 *he is going back:* Ford, "William E. Colby as Director of Central Intelligence," 1993.

191 *But Nedzi's:* "Democrats Seeking to Oust Head of House C.I.A. Unit," *New York Times,* June 6, 1975.

192 *In personal notes:* Cheney notes, March 24, 1975, Gerald R. Ford Presidential Library.

194 *Goldwater said:* Interview with Gary Hart.

Chapter 14: "Like what?" "Like assassinations."

195 *It's such a large mandate:* "CIA unit weighs focus of inquiry" (UPI story published in *New York Times*), April 22, 1975.

195–196 *Rosenthal asked Ford:* Hersh, *Reporter,* 224.

196 *Hersh went:* Hersh, *Reporter,* 226.

197 *Buchen wrote:* Trenta, "An act of insanity," 121–140.

198 *Allegations that the CIA:* The Nelson Rockefeller Report to the President, preface.

199 *At last the staff knew:* Johnson, *Season of Inquiry,* 39.

199 *half-baked findings:* Schwarz, *Democracy in the Dark,* 177.

200 *Under your instructions:* Memo from Marsh to Ford, October 29, 1975, Gerald R. Ford Presidential Library.

200 *it was astounding:* Interview with Frederick Baron.

201 *a key player:* Interview with Frank Church, A-G-J Interview Collection, Frank Church Papers, June 24, 1979.

201 *was so disgusted:* "David Atlee Phillips Dead at 65: Ex-Agent was advocate of CIA," *New York Times,* July 10, 1988; Moran, "Last Assignment."

202 *We would find:* Interview with Frederick Baron.

202 *so importantly mis-served:* Interview with Bill Bader, A-G-J Interview Collection, Frank Church Papers, May 18, 1987.

Chapter 15: "I had been asked by my government to solicit his cooperation"

204 *a very bureaucratic meeting:* "Alleged Assassination Plots Involving Foreign Leaders," III B: Cuba, Church Committee Interim Report, 1975.

204 *instead set up shop:* Maheu and Hack, *Next to Hughes,* 46.

205 *He recruited Bing Crosby:* Maheu and Hack, *Next to Hughes,* 87–88.

207 *Chicago in 1905:* Johnny Rosselli testimony before the Senate Special Committee to Investigate Organized Crime in Interstate Commerce, October 7, 1950, Chicago, Illinois.

207 *The truth was:* Server, *Handsome Johnny,* 11; Rappleye and Becker, *All American Mafioso,* p. 12.

208 *rest of his life.:* Server, Lee, *Handsome Johnny;* Rappleye and Becker, *All American Mafioso.*

209 *In some manner:* Johnny Rosselli testimony before the Senate Special Committee to Investigate Organized Crime in Interstate Commerce, October 7, 1950, Chicago, Illinois.

209 *Maheu later told:* "Alleged Assassination Plots Involving Foreign Leaders," III B: Cuba, Church Committee Interim Report, 1975.

211 *Maheu and Rosselli:* "Alleged Assassination Plots Involving Foreign Leaders," III B: Cuba, Church Committee Interim Report, 1975.

212 *Sam Giancana was:* Maheu and Hack, *Next to Hughes,* 145–147; "Alleged Assassination Plots Involving Foreign Leaders," III B: Cuba, Church Committee Interim Report, 1975.

214 *William Harvey, an overweight:* Stockton, Bayard, *Flawed Patriot,* 143; "Alleged Assassination Plots Involving Foreign Leaders," III B: Cuba, Church Committee Interim Report, 1975.

215 *most ominous effort:* "Alleged Assassination Plots Involving Foreign Leaders," III B: Cuba, Church Committee Interim Report, 1975.

216 *We cannot overemphasize:* Declassified CIA Inspector General Memorandum for the Record: Report on Plots to Assassinate Fidel Castro, May 23, 1967.

216 *not be just Nixon:* Interview with Walter Mondale.

217 *Then I got a call:* Interview with Patrick Shea.

Chapter 16: "Who will rid me of this man?"

218 *mobster Sam Giancana:* The narrative of the Oak Park, Illinois, police investigation of Sam Giancana's murder comes from Oak Park Police Department case files, obtained directly from the Oak Park Police Department. Files include: Incident Report, Complaint Number 75-7161, June 19, 1975.

218 *The next morning:* "Andrus Salutes Dam Project," *Spokane Spokesman-Review,* June 20, 1975.

219 *a big deal in Lewiston:* Interview with Mike Wetherell.

219 *no credence:* Associated Press, published in the *Indianapolis Star* and other papers, June 21, 1975; follow-up story, Associated Press, June 22, published in the *Pensacola News-Journal.*

220 *I remember thinking:* Interview with Frederick Baron.

221 *different off camera:* "Sen. Church: Orator in Wings?" Christian Science Monitor News Service, published in the *Jackson [Tennessee] Sun* and other newspapers, July 10, 1975.

222 *not a significant factor:* Oak Park Police files in the murder of Sam Giancana.

222 *according to Oak Park police records:* Oak Park Police files in the murder of Sam Giancana.

223 *wrote a letter to Church:* Johnson, *Season of Inquiry,* 200.
223 *In the immediate aftermath:* Interviews with Patrick Shea and Michael Madigan.
224 *absolutely captivating:* Interview with Frederick Baron.
224 *wrapped himself in the flag:* Interview with Gary Hart.
224 *moment of glory:* Interview with Pat Shea.
225 *I believe at some stage:* "Alleged Assassination Plots," Church Committee Interim Report.
225 *Smathers:* The accounts of testimony before the Church Committee concerning the Kennedy Administration and the CIA's attempts to assassinate Fidel Castro are drawn from "Alleged Assassination Plots Involving Foreign Leaders," III B: Cuba, Church Committee Interim Report, 1975.
226 *who will rid me:* "Alleged Assassination Plots," Church Committee Interim Report.
227 *I do not believe:* "Alleged Assassination Plots," Church Committee Interim Report.
227 *never heard:* "Alleged Assassination Plots," Church Committee Interim Report.
228 *no one:* "Alleged Assassination Plots," Church Committee Interim Report.

Chapter 17: "The White House, can I help you?"

229 *Andy Postal:* Interview with Andy Postal.
231 *I think Frank:* Interview with Gary Hart.
231 *Church's office once:* Interview with Fritz Schwarz.
231 *we subpoenaed:* Interview with Andy Postal.
232 *Miller told Shea:* Interview with Patrick Shea.
232 *became clear:* Judith Campbell interview by the Church Committee, declassified Church Committee interviews, National Archives.
233 *Two days after:* Johnny Rosselli interview by the Church Committee, declassified Church Committee interviews, National Archives.
234 *a dead-end street:* Kenneth O'Donnell interview by the Church Committee, declassified Church Committee interviews, National Archives.
234 *the next 40 seconds:* Interview with Andy Postal.
234 *on his way to work:* Interview with David Bushong.
235 *I went out:* Interview with Burt Wides.
235 *a close friend:* "Alleged Assassination Plots," Church Committee Interim Report.
236 *confirming her earlier testimony:* Exner, *My Story.*
236 *Frank said we've got to talk to Senator Kennedy:* Interview with Gary Hart.
237 *When Hart:* Interview with Gary Hart.
237 *That was not:* Interview with Walter Mondale.
237 *wrote in her memoir:* Exner, *My Story,* 87–89.
237 *We took testimony:* Interview with Frederick Baron.
237 *I may have gone:* Interview with Fritz Schwarz.
238 *a rogue elephant:* "Church Doubts Plot Links to Presidents," *New York Times,* July 19, 1975.

239 *I'm very much afraid:* "Kennedy Name Being Protected, Says Goldwater," Associated Press, published by the *Salem [Oregon] Statesman Journal*, August 13, 1975; "JFK knew of plots to kill Cuban chief—Goldwater," the *Arizona Republic*, August 13, 1975.

239 *I have said before:* Transcript, *Meet the Press*, August 17, 1975.

240 *calmed Barry down:* Interview with Gary Hart.

241 *The dead body:* William Safire, "Murder Most Foul," *New York Times*, December 22, 1975.

241 *had to insist:* Interview with Andy Postal.

241 *Church was furious:* Interview with Patrick Shea.

241 *One by one:* Interview with Patrick Shea.

242 *I inadvertently:* Interview with Daniel O'Flaherty.

242 *didn't want to be scooped:* Interview with Patrick Shea.

242 *I got upset:* Interview with Gary Hart.

243 *He got a call:* Interview with David Aaron.

244 *Of his aides:* Memo on July 30, 1975, meeting from Mike Wetherell to Frank Church, private papers of Mike Wetherell.

244 *the consensus of the group:* Memo on July 30, 1975, meeting from Mike Wetherell to Frank Church, private papers of Mike Wetherell.

245 *an eastern state:* Interview with Mike Wetherell.

246 *It may explode:* "Washington Comments," *Indianapolis Star*, June 29, 1975.

Chapter 18: "We met your man in the Congo."

248 *go to Africa:* Interview with Edward M. Kennedy, Edward M. Kennedy Oral History Project, May 30, 2007, Miller Center, University of Virginia.

248 *in office:* The narrative of Congo and CIA plots to assassinate Patrice Lumumba relies on a wide variety of sources, including: "Alleged Assassination Plots Involving Foreign Leaders," III A: Congo, Church Committee Interim Report, 1975; Devlin, *Chief of Station, Congo*; De Witte, *Assassination of Lumumba*; Kalb, *Congo Cables*; Van Reybrouck, *Congo*; and Zeilig, *Lumumba: Africa's Lost Leader.*

248 *a destructive hurricane:* "Alleged Assassination Plots," Church Committee Interim Report.

250 *didn't know anything:* Church, *Lifelong Affair*, 132–133.

251 *stayed in touch:* Telegrams and letters from Bank Anthony to Frank Church, December 1960 to March 1961, Frank Church Papers, Boise State University.

251 *Donna Allen wrote:* Letters between Frank Church and Donna Allen, February 1961, Frank Church Papers, Boise State University.

251 *legitimate government:* Letters between Frank Church and Donna Allen, February 1961, Frank Church Papers, Boise State University.

252 *archive of secret cables:* The chronology of the CIA's attempts to assassinate Lumumba is laid out in "Alleged Assassination Plots Involving Foreign Leaders," III A: Congo, Church Committee Interim Report, 1975.

254 *my mind was racing:* Devlin, *Chief of Station, Congo*, 96.

254 *a series of cables:* "Alleged Assassination Plots," Church Committee Interim Report.

255 *I had no assurance:* Interview with Frederick Baron.

255 *severely criticized:* Devlin, *Chief of Station, Congo,* 130–131.

257 *moral responsibility:* "Report Reproves Belgium in Lumumba's Death," *New York Times,* November 17, 2001.

260 *found records:* "Alleged Assassination Plots Involving Foreign Leaders," III F: Schneider, Church Committee Interim Report, 1975.

261 *Nixon denied:* Church Committee Final Report, Book IV: Supplementary Detailed Staff Reports on Foreign and Military Intelligence, Section A: "Interrogatory Responses of Richard M. Nixon," 1976.

261 *to promote a military coup in Chile:* Church Committee Final Report, Book IV.

262 *interviewed Orlando Letelier:* Interview of Rick Inderfurth.

263 *he singled out:* Kornbluh, *Pinochet File.*

Chapter 19: "What the president wanted to happen"

266 *committee has endeavored:* Church Committee Interim Report: Alleged Assassination Plots Involving Foreign Leaders.

266 *my thinking:* Interview with Fritz Schwarz.

268 *I flipped through:* Interview with Frederick Baron.

268 *a transcript:* A transcript of the Senate's November 20, 1975, closed session was later published in the *Congressional Record.*

Chapter 20: "The abyss from which there is no return"

271 *Johnson was told:* The account of Loch Johnson's meetings with James Angleton is based on: Interview with Loch Johnson; Loch K. Johnson, "James Angleton and the Church Committee," *Journal of Cold War Studies* 15, no. 4 (Fall 2013): 128–147.

271 *His father:* Morley, *The Ghost,* 4–5.

272 *Angleton was stunned:* William Colby describes the process of firing Angleton in his *Honorable Men,* 387–388, 396, 454.

272 *Surprisingly, Angleton:* Interview with Loch Johnson.

273 *Angleton was drinking:* Interview with Loch Johnson.

274 *inconceivable:* Interview with Loch Johnson; Senator Frank Church's questioning of Angleton during Angleton's public testimony before the Church Committee, September 24, 1975.

274 *Church jumped:* Testimony of James Angleton before the Church Committee, September 24, 1975.

275 *Angleton walked down:* Church, *Lifelong Affair,* 223.

275 *got sidetracked:* Interview with Alton Quanbeck.

276 *shooting in the dark:* Interview with Britt Snider.

277 *raised a lot of issues:* Interview with Eric Richard.

278 *go find Dr. Tordella:* Interview with Britt Snider; Snider, "Recollections of the Church Committee."

279 *Tordella walked Snider:* Interview with Britt Snider.

280 *secretly launch:* Declassified Justice Department Inquiry into CIA-related Electronic Surveillance Activities, 1976.

281 *a Navy reservist:* Interview with James Bamford.

281 *keeping me very secret:* Interview with James Bamford.

282 *asked by the government:* Interview with Britt Snider.

282 *Snider met:* Interview with Britt Snider.

Chapter 21: "Under a double shadow"

284 *DeOreo, when:* Interview with Mary DeOreo.

284 *pain in the ass:* Interview with Fritz Schwarz.

289 *on one occasion:* The Nelson Rockefeller Report to the President.

290 *In a July 9 interview:* "Family Plans to Sue C.I.A. Over Suicide in Drug Test," *New York Times,* July 10, 1975.

291 *the Olsons went:* Interview with Eric Olson.

292 *Protect his guy:* Interview with Elliot Maxwell.

292 *When Maxwell:* Interview with Elliot Maxwell.

293 *He told Lenzner:* Lenzner, *The Investigator,* 198–200.

294 *failure of the CIA's leadership:* Church Committee, Book I: Foreign and Military Intelligence (Section O: "Chemical and Biological Agents and the Intelligence Community").

295 *not tellable by an American:* Interview with Eric Olson.

Chapter 22: "The man who made a police state out of America"

297 *FBI's holy grail:* Interview with Mark Gitenstein.

298 *We got nothing:* Interview with Mary DeOreo.

299 *Hoover's lair:* Interview with Bryce Nelson; Bryce Nelson, "Church: a Man Who Took Great Risks for America," *Los Angeles Times,* April 16, 1984.

299 *his feelings about Hoover:* Interview with Bryce Nelson.

300 *In his letter:* Letter from Frank Church to J. Edgar Hoover, October 26, 1961; letter from J. Edgar Hoover to Frank Church, November 9, 1961; Frank Church Papers, Boise State University.

300 *FBI internal memo:* FBI notes, June 6, 1972; Frank Church Papers, Boise State University.

301 *Despite Hoover's:* Hoover's opposition to the creation of the CIA is documented in a wide range of sources, including "Emergence of the Intelligence Establishment of the United States," *Foreign Relations of the United States Series,* 1996.

302 *spied on Kennedy:* Gentry, *J. Edgar Hoover,* 467–470.

304 *for Bradlee:* Interview with Betty Medsger.

304 *the lengthened shadow of a man:* Warren Burger eulogy for J. Edgar Hoover, May 3, 1972, in the rotunda of the U.S. Capitol. The text of Burger's eulogy is included in "Memorial Tributes to J. Edgar Hoover in the Congress of the United States," U.S. Government Printing Office, 1974.

305 *with Mondale:* Interview with Mark Gitenstein.
305 *almost no contact:* Interview with Barbara Banoff.

Chapter 23: "No holds were barred"

306 *'neutralize' him:* The chronology of the FBI's harassment of King, along with quotes from related testimony, is based on the Church Committee's "Dr. Martin Luther King Jr., Case Study," Final Report, Book III—Supplementary Detailed Staff Reports on Intelligence Activities and the Rights of Americans, 1976.
307 *Epstein was determined:* Interview with Mark Gitenstein; interview with John Elliff for the Oral History of the Church Committee, Senate Historical Office, February 21, 2014.
307 *He was already doing that:* Interview with John Elliff for the Oral History of the Church Committee, Senate Historical Office, February 21, 2014.
308 *One of the great problems:* "Dr. King Says F.B.I. in Albany, Ga., Favors Segregationists," *New York Times,* November 19, 1962.
308 *his memoir:* Sullivan, *The Bureau,* 135.
309 *March 20 memo:* The memo is reprinted in Theoharis, *From the Secret Files of J. Edgar Hoover,* 40.
309 *A review of telephone toll calls:* The Courtney Evans memo is reprinted in *From the Secret Files of J. Edgar Hoover,* 40.
310 *the suspicion was:* Interview with Mary DeOreo.
311 *Letter from Birmingham Jail:* Reprinted in *Why We Can't Wait,* chapter 5.
312 *came together:* King Jr., Martin Luther, *Why We Can't Wait,* 17.
312 *more dangerous:* "Dr. Martin Luther King Jr., Case Study," Church Committee.
312 *we must mark him now:* ibid.
313 *what he wanted to hear:* Sullivan, *The Bureau,* 138.
313 *that the FBI contended:* "Dr. Martin Luther King Jr., Case Study," Church Committee.
314 *all kinds of information:* ibid.
314 *became twisted:* Report of the Department of Justice Task Force to Review the FBI Martin Luther King, Jr. Security and Assassination Investigations, 1977.
315 *take him off his pedestal:* "Dr. Martin Luther King Jr., Case Study," Church Committee.
315 *later named Pierce:* Sullivan, *The Bureau,* 144.
315 *remove all doubt:* "Dr. Martin Luther King Jr., Case Study," Church Committee.
316 *bordered on paranoia:* ibid.
316 *most notorious liar:* "Dr. King Rebuts Hoover Charges," *New York Times,* November 20, 1964.
316 *one way out:* "Dr. Martin Luther King Jr., Case Study," Church Committee.
317 *the disturbing thing:* ibid.
317 *the political bloodstream:* ibid.
318 *to the Lorraine:* ibid.
319 *So Deke DeLoach:* Pearson, *Washington Merry-Go-Round,* 578.
319 *I suspect Deke:* ibid.

320 *Whitson asked:* Declassified FBI memo, April 1975.

320 *was eager to launch:* Interviews with Jim Dick and Barbara Banoff.

320 *chief of security:* "The Last Hours of William O'Neal," *Chicago Reader,* January 25, 1990. Many public sources of information are available about Fred Hampton's murder, the FBI, and William O'Neal's role as an FBI informant. For example: "The police raid that killed two Black Panthers, shook Chicago and changed the nation," *The Washington Post,* December 4, 2019.

320 *Fred's bed:* The story of Fred Hampton and his betrayal by William O'Neal gained reintensifying public awareness as a result of the 2021 film, *Judas and the Black Messiah.*

321 *he was very interested:* Interview with Jim Dick.

323 *On April 30th, 1976:* Declassified FBI memo from April 30, 1976, available from the National Archives, https://www.archives.gov/files/research/jfk/releases/docid-32989593.pdf

324 *Jefferson is testifying:* FBI Los Angeles field office report to headquarters, available from the National Archives, https://www.archives.gov/files/research/jfk/releases/docid-32989593.pdf

324 *If fault is to be found:* Church Committee Hearing on the FBI, November 18, 1975.

Chapter 24: "Vindicated and pleased"

328 *the handling of the prickly Kennedy issue.*

328 *this century:* "CIA's Work Unimpeded by Inquiries and Reports, Officials of Agency Assert," *New York Times,* November 10, 1975.

329 *vindicated and pleased:* Interview with Fritz Schwarz.

330 *a fat orange:* Public television coverage of first Church Committee hearing, September 16, 1975, https://www.youtube.com/watch?v=03d8-hBNvGA.

331 *no long lines: ibid.*

332 *this ghastly day:* Colby and Forbath, *Honorable Men,* 442.

333 *together or apart:* Private papers of Patrick Shea.

333 *the President's appointment:* "An Imperative for the CIA: Professionalism Free of Politics and Partisanship" (Frank Church speech), November 11, 1975.

334 *self-serving hypocrisy:* Helms, *A Look Over My Shoulder,* 437.

Chapter 25: "As dangerous as any stimulant"

336 *the impression:* Testimony of Tom Huston before the Church Committee, September 23, 1975.

337 *quite correct:* Testimony of Gordon Stewart before the Church Committee, October 21, 1975.

338 *a dangerous secret:* Aid and Burr, "Disreputable If Not Outright Illegal," 2013.

339 *most wanted to protect:* The *New York Times* published a harsh critique of the Church Committee a year after its hearings began in Taylor Branch, "The Trial of the CIA," *New York Times Magazine,* Sept. 12, 1976.

340 *the committee discovered:* Interview with Joe DiGenova.

340 *George Meany would:* ibid.

341 *as dangerous as any stimulant:* Testimony of David Phillips before the Church Committee, December 5, 1975.

341 *the record shows:* Church Committee hearing on covert action, December 5, 1975.

341 *struggling to keep up:* Interviews of Paul Michel and Loch Johnson.

342 *a little bit of tension:* Interview with Paul Michel.

343 *ever saw him flustered:* Interview with Andy Postal.

343 *The narration:* Interview with Burt Wides.

343 *I do not recommend:* Church Committee hearing on the FBI, November 18, 1975.

344 *what my own family:* ibid.

344 *Colby found to his relief:* Colby interview with *Chicago Daily News,* published in *Twin Falls Times-News,* September 9, 1975.

345 *not all that much:* ibid.

Chapter 26: "One more service to render"

346 *Mr. Welch is down!!:* Interview with Ron Estes, and private memo written by Ron Estes.

347 *wrote the next day:* "C.I.A. Station Chief Slain Near Athens by Gunmen," *New York Times,* December 24, 1975.

348 *in liaison contact with KYP:* Interview with Ron Estes.

350 *grooming room:* "Jackson Suggests Ford Veto Bush for No. 2 Spot," *New York Times,* December 17, 1975.

351 *his father:* Interview with Ron Estes.

351 *the public relations people:* Schorr, "Backstage Journal."

352 *a death threat:* "F.B.I. Studies Threats," UPI, published in *New York Times,* December 31, 1975.

352 *It might have been nice:* Smith Hempstone, "Many people helped to kill CIA agent Welch," *Rochester Democrat and Chronicle,* January 9, 1976.

352 *pro-CIA newsletter: The Pink Sheet* was included in a cache of documents declassified by the CIA in 2004.

353 *Former CIA officer Mike Ackerman:* "Ex-CIA Man Irate: Congressmen Blamed," Associated Press, published in *Spokane Chronicle,* December 29, 1975.

353 *political device:* "Death and Secrecy," *New York Times,* January 8, 1976.

353 *swallowed the bait:* "One CIA Effort That Worked," *The Washington Star,* January 11, 1976.

354 *left his briefcase:* Prados and Jimenez-Bacardi, "The White House, the CIA and the Pike Committee," 2017.

354 *Pike was very smart:* Interview with Searle Field.

355 *sort of an agreement:* Interview with Fritz Schwarz.

355 *we knew the money end:* Interview with Searle Field.

356 *going to the full House:* Interview with Searle Field.

356 *Pike bitterly complained:* "House Prevents Releasing Report on Intelligence," *New York Times,* January 30, 1976.

356 *a large majority:* ibid.

356 *I have the Pike Report!:* Schorr, "Backstage Journal."

356 *published the Pike Report:* "The Report on the CIA That President Ford Doesn't Want You To Read," *The Village Voice,* February 16, 1976.

357 *Schorr was raging:* Interview with Lesley Stahl.

357 *Schorr was suspended:* Interview with Lesley Stahl; Stahl, *Reporting Live,* 52.

Chapter 27: "I see you have a presidential haircut"

358 *It pissed off:* Interview with Fritz Schwarz.

358 *we didn't reveal:* Interview with Loch Johnson.

359 *presidential haircut:* Interview with David Aaron.

359 *costly to him:* Interview with Walter Mondale.

359 *I had an investigation:* Interview with Senator Frank Church at North Idaho College Forum, November 1976, https://www.youtube.com/watch?v=3bt2 j8n3qsA

360 *no direction:* Interview with Anne Karalekas.

360 *immunity from congressional oversight:* "To Create a Senate Select Committee on Intelligence, A Legislative History of Senate Resolution 400," Congressional Research Service, August 12, 1976.

360 *At noon:* Miami-Dade Police Files in the murder of Johnny Rosselli.

362 *his safety and his life:* Memorandum for the Record, Mike Madigan, August 13, 1976. Miscellaneous Records of the Church Committee.

363 *Hart was shocked:* Interview with Gary Hart.

363 *haunted me:* Interview with Gary Hart.

363 *Church told Gary:* Interview with Rick Inderfurth.

364 *the senator briefed these investigators:* Miami-Dade Police Files in the murder of Johnny Rosselli.

364 *the police seemed:* Interview with Rick Inderfurth.

364 *The first problem:* Interview with Charles Zatrepalek.

365 *a long-running scam:* Server, *Handsome Johnny,* 466–477; Rappleye, *All American Mafioso,* 286–292.

366 *Santo Trafficante:* Server, *Handsome Johnny,* 482; Rappleye, *All American Mafioso,* 309.

Chapter 28: "And then it was over"

368 *had forgotten his glasses:* Interview with Mike Wetherell.

369 *that hurt Church:* Interview with Susan Hunter.

370 *was so suspicious:* Kimelman, Henry L., *Living the American Dream,* 324; Interview of Frank Church, A-G-J Interview Collection, Frank Church Papers, June 14, 1979.

370 *a lot of work:* Interview with Mike Wetherell.

371 *A late, late strategy:* Interview of Senator Frank Church at North Idaho College Forum, November 1976, https://www.youtube.com/watch?v=3bt2j8n 3qsA.

371 *"Brown's decision":* Interview with Frank Church, A-G-J Interview Collection, Frank Church Papers, June 14, 1979.
371 *The band:* Church campaign schedule for March 18, 1976 announcement, Frank Church Papers.
371 *With nothing to lose:* Text of Frank Church's presidential campaign announcement speech, March 18, 1975, Frank Church Papers.
373 *the Secret Service:* Interview with Mike Wetherell.
374 *get it on?:* Hall, *Frank Church, D.C., & Me,* 91.
374 *a pleasant meeting:* Interview with Jerry Brown.
375 *a conflict of interest:* Church statement to the Senate on recusal on campaign finance legislation, Frank Church Papers.
375 *secretly had an affair:* Interview with Pat Shea. In his 2011 biography of Forrest Church, Dan Cryer also reported that Forrest had an affair while campaigning in Nebraska in 1976.
376 *In Nebraska:* Interview with Senator Frank Church at North Idaho College Forum, November 1976, https://www.youtube.com/watch?v=3bt2j8n3qsA.
376 *talked hurriedly:* Interview with Ira Dorfman.
378 *If an instant choice:* Carter, *Keeping Faith,* 38.
378 *Until the very end:* Eizenstat, *President Carter,* 90.
379 *he provided Kirbo:* A copy of Frank Church's responses on the Carter campaign's confidential questionnaire is contained in the Frank Church Papers. Church listed that in 1975, in addition to his Senate salary, he had also received $14,975 in speaking fees, while Bethine Church had received $10,000 in interest and principal payments from the earlier sale of the Clark family Idaho ranch. The couple also earned $3,656.32 in interest on municipal bonds. In addition, Church reported that Bethine owned her mother's house in Boise, where the Churches stayed when they were in Idaho. They also owned a 1965 Ford Mustang and a 1972 Chevrolet station wagon. Church reported that in 1975 he had paid $14,932 in federal income taxes.
379 *didn't like Church:* Interview with Peter Fenn.
379 *he had seen me:* Interview with Walter Mondale.
380 *stepped on:* Interview with Mike Wetherell.
380 *never talked:* Interview with Walter Mondale.
380 *Can you imagine any rumor:* Church, *Father & Son,* 122.

Chapter 29: "I've got to do it"

382 *gleefully recounted:* Interview with Mike Wetherell.
383 *shook his head:* Interview with Garry Wenske.
383 *pompous blowhard:* Interview with David Aaron.
384 *They were deciding:* Interview with Frederick Baron.
385 *there is going to be a war:* Interview with Frank Moore.
385 *Glenn has poll points to give up:* Interview with Mike Wetherell.
386 *Church spent months:* Interview with Garry Wenske.
387 *as we drove to the Bay of Pigs:* Church, *Lifelong Affair,* 251.
387 *Church told reporters:* "Cuba Agrees to Let 84 Americans Leave With Their Families," *New York Times,* August 12, 1977.

387 *Bethine asked Susan Hunter:* Interview with Susan Hunter.

387 *Church eviscerated:* "Delusions and Reality: The Future of U.S.-Cuba Relations," Report by Senator Frank Church on a Trip to Cuba, August 8–11, 1977, 95th Congress, U.S. Government Printing Office.

388 *comatose:* Interview with Frank Moore.

388 *shave my beard:* Interview with Pat Shea.

389 *He's been a pain in the neck:* Carter, *White House Diary*, 290.

390 *Idaho Swine Producers:* Interview with Susan Hunter.

390 *always opposed: Restricting Handguns: The Liberal Skeptics Speak Out,* Foreword by Senator Frank Church.

390 *Angleton stepped:* Interview with Steve Symms.

391 *he really despised Frank Church:* Interview with Steve Symms.

392 *Reynolds called me:* Interview with Steve Symms.

392 *rating in Idaho:* Internal polls of the Church campaign, Frank Church Papers, Boise State University.

394 *you could hear it and feel it:* Interview with Larry LaRocco.

394 *that didn't help him:* Interview with Steve Symms.

394 *NCPAC, targeted Church:* Johnson, *Tuesday Night Massacre*, 43–60.

394 *so many other factors:* Interview with Peter Hart.

395 *drained from his face:* Interview with Steve Symms.

395 *we hammered him:* Interview with Peter Fenn.

395 *told of allegations:* Interviews with Peter Fenn and other former Church staffers.

397 *somewhat consoling:* "Church, Chief of Senate Foreign Relations Panel, Defeated," *New York Times*, November 6, 1980.

397 *stay together:* Church, *Lifelong Affair*, 267.

397 *I was invited to a party:* Interview with Steve Symms.

397 *we seem unable to learn:* "Frank Church's Challenge," *Washington Post*, January 22, 1984.

398 *a Kennedy cry:* Interview with Chase Church.

398 *who eagerly told:* Church, *Lifelong Affair*, 278–279.

398 *highly exaggerated:* Interview with Steve Symms.

399 *stars the way:* Video of Frank Church Funeral, Frank Church Papers, Boise State University.

Epilogue: "They did great damage"

400 *gleefully asked:* Olmsted, *Challenging the Secret Government*, 3.

401 *specifically blamed:* Minority Report of the House and Senate Select Committees on Secret Military Assistance to Iran and the Nicaraguan Opposition, November 18, 1987.

401–402 *We also have to work:* Transcript of Cheney's appearance on *Meet the Press* on the Bush White House website, September 16, 2001.

402 *also weighed in:* Kissinger, Henry, "Better Intelligence Reform," *Washington Post*, August 16, 2004; Kissinger testimony before the Senate Committee on Appropriations, September 21, 2004.

403 *Senator Church is back:* Miller, *U.S. National Security, Intelligence and Democracy*, 2.

405 *greatest congressional investigation:* Light, *Government by Investigation*, 193.

405 *Of all the things:* Interview with Walter Mondale.

406 *very serious:* Interview with Dan Williams.

406 *in 1991:* "Pastor's Conduct Divides East Side Congregation," *New York Times*, October 7, 1991; Cryer, *Being Alive*, 182–207.

Index

Page numbers in *italics* indicate illustrations.

Aaron, David, 189, 243, 244, 359, 383
ABC, 129
abortion, 99
Abramson, Harold, 288
Accardo, Tony, 221, 223
Ackerman, Mike, 353
Advise and Consent (Drury), 52–53
AFL-CIO, 340
Agee, Philip, 352
Ali, Muhammad, 338
Allen, Donna, 251
Allen, Lew, Jr., 280, 338
Allende, Salvador, 123–25, 129, 133, 135, 257–58, 260–61, 262–63
American Indian Movement, 243
American Legion, 24, 94, 113
Anderson, Clinton, 55
Anderson, Jack, 124–26, 128, 153, 319, 340
Andrus, Cecil, 89–90, 100, *101*, 101–2
Angleton, James Hugh, 271
Angleton, James Jesus, 161, 177, 270–75, *275*, 278, 286, 390–91, 399
Angola, 339
Anthony, Bank, 251

anti-war activists, American
    CIA's spying on, 85–86, 273, 277, 335–36
    FBI's targeting of, 299, 303, 305, 342
    at Kent State University, 109–10
    Nixon and, 105, 273
    NSA's spying on, 280
Arab-Israeli war, 148
Arendt, Hannah, 293
Argo, 205
Army, 276, 287–88
Artichoke project, 286
Arvad, Inga, 302–3
Ashby, LeRoy, 21, 425n
Asner, Ed, 374
Assassination of Lumumba, The (De Witte), 257
Associated Press, 148, 158, 353
atomic bombs, 10, 36, 238
AT&T, 123

Bader, William, 153, 189, 202, 339
Baker, Bobby, 58, 59
Baker, Howard, 160, 172, *174*, 189, *331*, 338, 362, 363

Balletti, Arthur, 212

Bamford, James, 281

Banoff, Barbara, 187, 305, 321–22

Barnes, Jack, 62, 62n

Barnes, Verda
 accusations against, of having
  Communist ties, 154, 436n
 assisting Andrus for Democratic
  nomination, 89, 90
 assisting Biden set up Senate office, 117
 background of, 62–63, 62n
 in Church's 1968 campaign, 100
 strategy session about 1976
  presidential campaign, 244, 245

Barnett, Ross, 310

Baron, Frederick
 Bell and, 384
 on Church Committee's
  assassination report, 267, 268
 on CIA documents, 200–201, 202
 on Devlin, 255
 on Giancana's murder, 220
 interview with Hunt, 243
 on Rosselli, 224
 on tension between Miller and
  Schwarz, 187
 on testimony about NSC meetings, 237

Barthlemes, Wes, 111

Bay of Pigs, 13, 197, 213–14, 387

Bayh, Birch, 165, 396

Beale, Betty, 245–46

Beckel, Theodore, 59

Becket, Thomas, 226

Belgium, 248, 249–50, 256, 257

Belin, David, 197, 198, 199

Bell, Griffin, 384

Belmont, Alan, 309

Berle, Milton, 374

Bernhard, Prince, 139–40

Bernstein, Carl, 158–59

Betts, Richard, 184

Biden, Joseph R., Jr., 116, 117, 305, 369

Biden, Naomi, 117

Biden, Neilia, 117

Biemiller, Andrew J., 63

Bilderback, Laura. *See* Church, Laura

Birmingham, Alabama, nonviolent
 protest campaign in, 311

Bissell, Richard, 204, 207, 214, 224–25,
 253, 255

Black Chamber, 30

Black Panther Party, 320–24

Bluebird project, 286

Blundell, Jim, 361

Boggs, J. Caleb, 116–17

Boise, Tom, 89

Boise Capital News, 17, 22

Bolten, Joshua, 201

Bolten, Seymour, 201

Borah, Mary McConnell, 23, 38

Borah, William, 17, 22–24, 25, 38, 80,
 93, 155, 182, 399

Boynton, Fred, 92

Bradlee, Ben, 304

Brady, Jerry, 92, 98

Brando, Marlon, 59–60, 243

Bridges, Styles, 48, 50–51

Brindle, Jeff, 125

Broder, David, 397

Broe, William, 134, 135

Brown, Jerry, 370–71, 374, 375, 377,
 378

Brown v. Board of Education, 57

Brownell, Herbert, 301

Brzezinski, Zbigniew, 383, 386

Buchen, Philip, 197

Buchwald, Art, 338

Bumpers, Dale, 382

Bundy, McGeorge, 75, 227–28, 237, 239

Bundy, William P., 162

Burger, Warren, 304, 384

Burke, Carl, 22, 27, 29, 32, 37, 60
 as Frank's campaign manager, 43, 90,
  166, 181, 358, 377
 and Kennedy's presidential
  campaign, 73

Burns, Stan, 21, 23, 36–37

Bush, George H. W., 333, 349–51, 352,
 353, 358, 401

Bush, George W., 201, 401, 403, 404

Bush (George W.) Administration, 401

Bushong, David, 231, 233–35, 241

Cabell, Charles, 214
Cagnina, Sam, 366
Cain, Richard, 221
Cambodia, 109, 110, 113, 114, 122,
    185, 335
Camp Ritchie, 30, 31, 32, 44, 391
Campbell, Judith, 213, 229–34, *232*,
    235–37, 241, 244, 303, 309
Carter, Jimmy, 102
    Church and, 175, 378–79, 380,
        382–83, 386, 387, *389*, 389–90
    intelligence reform measures and,
        383–84
    Iranian hostage crisis and, 389, 396
    Panama Canal and, 384–85
    in 1976 presidential election, 165,
        369, 370, 375–80, 382
    in 1980 presidential election, 382,
        392–93, 396
    Salt II treaty and, 389
Carter, Rosalynn, 378, 380, 389
Carter Administration, 382–83, 384
Carver, John, 70, 73
Case, Clifford, 115, 133, 134
Case-Church Amendment, 115
Castro, Fidel, 312
    Church and, 312, 386–87, *387*
    Church Committee's investigation of
        CIA's assassination plots against,
        209–10, 215, 216, 221, 224–28,
        238, 239, 240, 247, 306, 327
    CIA's assassination plots against, 176,
        196, 200–201, 203, 204, 206–7,
        209–12, 213, 214–16, 221,
        222, 224–28, 229–34, 235–36,
        238–39, 247, 268, 303, 306, 327,
        339, 366
Castro, Raul, 214
CBS, 129, 242, 356–57
Challenging the Secret Government
    (Olmsted), 400
Chamberlain, Milt, 36
Chambers, Whittaker, 302
Chappaquiddick scandal, 165
Chavez, Cesar, 154
Cheney, Dick, 162, 400

Church Committee and, 192–94,
    193, 200, 265, 401
    in post–9/11 "global war on terror,"
        401–2, 403, 404
    Rockefeller Commission and, 192,
        197, 198, 199
Chiang Kai-shek, 10, 32, 37, 75
Chicago Daily News, 344
Child, Julia, 31
Chile
    CIA's covert activities in, 123–25,
        128–35, 147–48, 149, 247,
        257–63, 334, 338, 339
    Pinochet and, 262, 263, 264
China, 10, 32, 35, 37, 75, 147
Christian Science Monitor, 147, 221
Church, Amy Furth, 112, 406
Church, Bethine
    after Frank's death, 399, 406, 429n
    after Frank's exit from politics, 397,
        398, 406
    Angleton and, 275
    Bethesda home of, 58–59, 429n
    Biden and, 117
    campaigning during 1976
        presidential race, 368, 371, *372*,
        373–74, 377
    campaigning during 1956 Senate
        races, 43, *44*, 99
    Carters and, 380, 389
    death of, 406
    early relationship with Frank, 27, 28,
        30, 32, 33–34, 36–37, 44, 391
    education of, 30, 32
    engagement to Chamberlain, 36
    family background of, 10, 27–28,
        371, 391
    finances of, 448n
    on Frank's rehearsing of speeches, 94
    friction between Frank's staff and,
        61, 388
    at Gettysburg cabin, 112–13
    hosting parties for eclectic mix, 59,
        103
    Kennedy and, 66, 74, 76
    on Levinson, 126

Church, Bethine (*Cont.*)
  marriage to Frank, 38, 39, *39*, 40,
    61–62
  photographs of, *39, 44, 59, 372, 387*
  relationship with sons, 86, 87, 112,
    248
  Robinson Bar Ranch and, 70, 100
  role in Frank's political career, 38,
    54, 60–61, 62, 67, 80, 86, 87,
    104, 110, 149, 182, 248, 250,
    386–87, *387*, 388, 406
  temper of, 61–62
Church, Chase, 21, 61, 112, 144, 398
  childhood of, 58, *59*, 59–60
  on Liberace, 111
  marriage of, 102
Church, Frank Forrester (grandfather),
    19, 58, 371
Church, Frank Forrester, III, 5–12
  abortion and, 99
  Andrus and, 89–90, *101*, 101–2
  Angleton and, 271, 390–91
  as Army intelligence officer during
    World War II, 10, 11, 30, 31, 32,
    33, 34–36, 37, 75, 174
  Barnes and, 62, 63, 100
  Bethesda home of, 58–59
  Bethine's role in political career of,
    38, 54, 60–61, 62, 67, 80, 86,
    87, 104, 110, 149, 182, 248, 250,
    386–87, *387*, 388, 406
  Biden and, 116, 117, 369
  Borah and, 17, 22, 23, 24
  Bush confirmation hearings and,
    349–51
  Carter and, 175, 378–79, 380,
    382–83, 386, 387, *389*, 389–90
  Castro and, 386–88, *387*
  childhood of, 17–18, 19–22, *20*, 60
  as Church Committee chairman,
    7–8, *174*, 179, 180, 181–82, 188,
    195, 200, 245–46, 393
    appointment of, 165, 166–67, 172
    in CIA investigation, 175, 178, *179*,
      194, 199, 201–3, 225, 230–31,
      236, 238–41, 251–52, 256, 260,
    265–66, 267n, 268–69, 291, 292,
      327, 333, 354, 404
    in FBI investigation, 299, 305, 324,
      341, 343
    final report and, 360
    Giancana's murder and, 219, 220,
      221, 222–23
    hiring of staff for, 182–84, 186
    media coverage of, 238–40,
      242–43, 267
    meeting on Rosselli's murder, 363
    in NSA investigation, 281, 282–83
    during public hearings, 3–5, *4*, 6,
      271, 274, 329–30, *331*, 331–32,
      335, 336–37, 343
    Welch murder and, 349–51, 352,
      353, 358
  civil rights legislation and, 54–55,
    57–58, 65–66
  Colby and, 201, 262, 331–32, 354
  Congo crisis and, 248, 250–51
  conservation efforts of, 69–70, 153,
    219
  death of, 398–99, 406
  death threats against, 141, 352
  depression and, 40, 103
  desire for acceptance in Washington,
    5, 6, 103, 147, 184, 405
  early political career of, 41, *42*
  early relationship with Bethine, 27,
    28, 30, 32, *33*–34, 36–37, 44,
    391
  education of, 20, 21, 27, 29–30,
    37–38
  as emergency-powers committee
    chairman, 185
  fame and, 7, 110–11, 112–13, 118,
    220
  family background of, 17, 18, 19–22,
    371
  fears about America's imperial
    overreach, 5–6, 7, 10–11, 36, 37,
    56, 86, 93, 95, 146, 155
  finances of, 448n
  formal speaking style of, 8, 24,
    93–94, 103

friendships with other senators,
  111–12, 171
Fulbright and, 79, *82*, 83, 120–21,
  122, 127
in Fulbright hearings on Vietnam,
  81, *82*, 82–84, 85
at Gettysburg cabin, 112–13
Gulf of Tonkin Resolution and, 78
on gun control, 143–44, 390, 394
health of, 10, 20, 38–40, 58, 374,
  379, 397
Hells Canyon Dam and, 57, 67–69
Helms and, 130–31, 334
in high school, 23, 24, 25–27, 29, 371
historical standing of, 400–401,
  403–5, 406
Hoover and, 299–301
Johnson and, 10, 54–55, 58, 59, 64,
  65, 66–67, 71, 73, 76–77, 77, 79,
  80–81, 85, 89, 101, 104, 231
Kennedys and, 10, 66, *71*, 71–74,
  75–76, 230, 231, 236, 237–38,
  248, 251, 327, *393*, 398, 404
Kissinger and, 104, 113, 147–48, 339,
  402
Levinson and, 126, 127, 136, 155, 244
Mansfield and, 150, 165, 166, 172,
  190, 220, 244, 245, 257, 369
marriage to Bethine, 38, *39*, 61–62
on McClellan Committee, 120
as Multinational subcommittee
  chairman, 126, 128, 129,
  130–31, 132–36, 137–39, 140,
  141–42, 147–48, 149, 151, 257,
  383
nickname of "Senator Cathedral,"
  8, 93
Nixon and, 104, 105, 115, 118
NSA's spying on, 338
opposition to Vietnam War, 7, 10–11,
  74–77, 78–85, 87, 88–89, 90,
  91, 92, 93, 94, 95–97, 100, 101,
  103–4, 105, 106–9, 110, 111,
  113–15, 116, 300, 393
Panama Canal treaties and, 385–86,
  393, 394

photographs of, *4, 9, 20, 33, 39, 42,
  44, 59, 71, 82, 101, 174, 179, 331,
  372, 387, 389, 393, 396*
Pike Committee and, 355
political ambition of, 8, 70–71,
  72–73, 129, 167, 405
post-Senate life of, 397–98
in presidential election in 1976, 155,
  165–67, 180, 181–82, 220, 241,
  244–46, 339, 345, 358–59, 368,
  369–79, 372, 380–81, 404, 405–6
publicity-seeking side of, 5, 6, 8, 63,
  110–11, 129, 150, 166, 242
radicalization of, 11, 75, 85, 86, 95,
  103, 106, 119, 121, 146, 148, 153
recall campaign in 1967 against,
  88–89, 90–93, 100, 104, 151
relationship with sons, 86, 87,
  99–100, 112, 248, 406
in Senate elections
  in 1956, 10, 42, 43–46, *44*, 47–48,
    51–52, 53, 64, 71
  in 1980, 70
  in 1962, 74
  in 1968, 89, 90, 93, 97–99,
    100–101, 104, 151, 393
  in 1974, 143–45, 151–55, 390
  in 1980, 385, 389–95, 396
Senate Foreign Relations Committee
  Church as chairman, 388–89
shyness of, 171–72
speeches of, 25–27, 68, 72–73, 79,
  80, 92, 93–97, 105, 146, 147
Church, Frank Forrester, Jr. (father), 17,
  19, 20–22, 371
Church, Frank Forrester "Forrest," IV
  (son), 72, 78
  alcoholism and, 407
  campaigning in father's political
    races, 151, 375, 380–81
  childhood of, 38, 58, *59*, 60, 86, 87
  death of, 407
  education of, 86–87
  eulogy for father, 399
  extramarital affairs of, 375, 406–7
  marriages of, 112, 407

Church, Frank Forrester *(Cont.)*
  memoir of, 47, 72, 78, 87, 100
  opposition to Vietnam War, 86, 87, 99
  as part of Church Committee staff, 277
  public scandal as minister, 406–7
  reconciliation with father, 112
  rift with father, 86, 87, 99–100, 406
Church, Laura, 19, *20*, 21
Church, Monica, 61
Church, Richard, 19, 20, *20*, *33*
Church Committee, 119
  bipartisanship of, 172–73, 178, 185,
    199–200
  budget of, 5
  chairman of. *See* Church, Frank
    Forrester, III: as Church
    Committee chairman
  CIA investigation of, 3–5, 6–7, 8,
    11–12, 202, 241–42, 270–74,
    328, 329, 333–34, 337, 339–40,
    344–45
    assassination plots, 199–203,
      209–10, 215, 216, 221, 224–40,
      241, 247–48, 251–61, 265–69,
      267n, 270, 276, 291, 306, 327
    CIA's cooperation with, 176, 177,
      201–2
    covert action in Chile, 257–63, 338
    domestic-spying programs, 270,
      273, 277, 329, 335–37
    Family Jewels report and, 277, 279,
      280, 298
    mind-control programs, 270, 285,
      287, 289, 291–95
  creation of, 160, 164–65, 172–75,
    174, 182, 190, 276, 298, 349
  FBI investigation of, 5, 6–7, 8, 11–12,
    175, 297–99, 305–8, 313–14,
    317–23, 329, 341–44
  Ford Administration and, 178, 192–94,
    199–200, 238, 265, 267, 332, 338,
    340, 345, 349–52, 353, 358
  Giancana's murder and, 217–18,
    219–20, 221–22, 223, 362, 363
  historical prominence of, 400–401,
    402–5

  intelligence community reforms
    resulting from, 383, 400, 401, 403
  media coverage of, 6, 167, 242–43, 267
  multivolume final report of, 359–60,
    368–69
  NSA investigation of, 5, 6–7, 8,
    11–12, 178, 276–83, 338
  public hearings of, 3–5, *4*, 6–7, 270,
    274–75, *275*, 281–82, 327–32,
    330, *331*, 335, 336–38, 340–42–
    344
  public support for, 354, 371
  Rosselli and, *208*, 210, 223–24,
    232–35, 236, 268, 361–64, 365,
    366
  staff workspace of, 189–90
  tensions between committee
    members of, 184, 186–89,
    238–40, 242, 305
  Welch murder used against, 349–53,
    358
  *See also specific Church Committee
    members*
CIA
  AFL-CIO and, 340
  in Angola, 339
  assassination plots of, 196–201, 202–3
    against Castro, 176, 196, 200–201,
      203, 204, 206–7, 209–12, 213,
      214–16, 221, 222, 224–28,
      229–34, 235–36, 238–39, 247,
      268, 303, 306, 327, 339, 366
    against Diem, 247, 267n
    against Lumumba, 176, 247–48,
      250, 251–57, 268, 285
    Rockefeller Commission and, 289
    against Schneider, 247, 257–62, 276
  Bay of Pigs and, 213–14
  Bush's confirmation as director of,
    349–51, 353, 401
  in Chile, 123–26, 128–29, 131–35,
    147–48, 149, 257–63, 338, 339
  Church Committee's investigation of,
    3–5, 6–7, 8, 11–12, 202, 241–42,
    270–74, 328, 329, 333–34, 337,
    339–40, 344–45

assassination plots, 199–203,
209–10, 215, 216, 221, 224–40,
241, 247–48, 251–61, 265–69,
267n, 270, 276, 291, 306, 327
cooperation with, 176, 177, 201–2
covert action in Chile, 257–63, 338
domestic-spying programs, 270,
273, 277, 329, 335–37
Family Jewels report and, 277, 279,
280, 298
mind-control programs, 270, 285,
287, 289, 291–95
Welch murder and, 347–50
creation of, 301
domestic-spying programs of, 85–86,
270, 273, 277, 289, 329, 335–37
Eisenhower and, 12–13, 215–16, 239,
240, 248, 252–53
Family Jewels report of, 157–58, 191,
277, 279, 280, 298
FBI and, 301–2, 335–36
Ford and, 136–37, 192, 195–99
Foreign Intelligence Surveillance Act
and, 383
founding of, 12, 36
on Giancana's murder, 222
Hersh's story on domestic abuses of,
159–61, 162, 163, 164, 190–91,
192, 195, 196, 270, 272, 289, 400
Hughes-Ryan Act and, 163
human drug-testing program of, 295
Iran-Contra scandal and, 400
Kennedy and, 13, 214, 215, 216,
224–25, 226, 239
lack of oversight of, 11–13, 86,
162–63, 195, 203, 270, 337, 338
Mafia and, 203, 204, 206–7, 208,
209–12, 213, 214–15, 221, 222,
224–25, 229–34, 235–36, 268,
303, 366
Maheu and, 204–5, 206–7
mail-opening program of, 273, 289,
337
mind-control programs of, 13, 285,
286–96
Mossadeq and, 148

Nixon and, 13, 128, 129, 131, 239,
329
NSA and, 277, 279
Phoenix Program in Vietnam, 176
Pike Committee's investigation of,
190–92, 354–55
Radio Free Europe and, 42
Rockefeller Commission's
investigation of, 192, 195–99,
200
Soviet Union and, 161, 163, 227, 238
Sukarno and, 205–6
use of Welch murder against Church
Committee, 349–53, 358
Watergate scandal and, 156–57, 160
CIA and the Cult of Intelligence, The
(Marchetti and Marks), 295
Citizen's Commission to Investigate
the FBI, 303
Civil Rights Act of 1957, 66
Civil Rights Act of 1964, 316
civil-rights activists
FBI and, 305, 342
NSA's spying on, 280
See also King, Martin Luther, Jr.
civil rights legislation, 54–56, 57–58,
65–66, 67, 68, 311, 316
Civil War, 185
Clark, Bethine. *See* Church, Bethine
Clark, Chase, 27, 28, 29n, 37, 45, *59*,
63, 371, 391
Clark, D. Worth, 32, 44, 391
Clark, Jean, 44, *59*
Clark, Mark, 320
Clark, Virgil, 32, 44, 391
Clark family, 28, 38, 45, 70. *See also*
specific Clark family members
Cleveland, Grover, 19
Clyburn, Jim, 375
COINTELPRO, 305, 323
Colby, William, 162, 344–45
background of, 31, 176
Church and, 201, 262, 331–32, 354
Church Committee and, 3–4, 6,
176, 177, 201, 268, 329–30, *330*,
331–33, 338, 354, 401

Colby, William, *(Cont.)*
  on CIA's mind-control programs, 289
  Family Jewels report and, 158
  firing of Angleton, 161, 272
  Ford and, 161, 332, 333, 401
  on Giancana's murder, 222
  Hersh's interviewing of, 159
  Nedzi and, 190–91
  Olson family and, 291
  Pike Committee and, 354–55
  Rockefeller Commission and, 197, 289
  testimony to Subcommittee on
      Multinational Corporations, 135
  at Welch's funeral service, 351, 352
Cold War, 12, 56, 149, 238, 248
Congo, 12, 248, 249, 251
Connor, Eugene "Bull," 311
Consequences (Tower), 173
Cooper, John Sherman, 108–9, 110,
    111, 113, 114, 115
Cooper-Church Amendments, 108–9,
    110, 111, 112, 113–15, 172, 184
Corlett, Cleve, 100, 155, 386
Council on Foreign Relations, 106
CounterSpy, 340, 352
Cranston, Alan, 162
Cronkite, Walter, 97
Crosby, Bing, 205
Crosby, Larry, 205
Crosby, Stills, Nash and Young, 110
Crusade for Freedom, 41–42
Cryer, Dan, 407
Cuba
  Bay of Pigs and, 13, 197, 213–14, 387
  Church and, 386–88, *387*
  Eisenhower and, 12–13, 248
  See also Castro, Fidel
Cuban Missile Crisis, 74
Culver, John, 396
Cushman, Robert, 157
Cyprus, 347, 348
Czechoslovakia, 106

Daigle, Edith, 366
Dant, Sara, 69

Darrow, Clarence, 22
Davies, Rodger, 348
De Witte, Ludo, 257
Deep State, 12
DeLoach, Deke, 319
Democracy in the Dark (Schwarz), 199
Democratic Party convention in 1968,
    98, 101
Deng Xiaoping, 390
DeOreo, Mary, 284, 298, 310, 313
Devlin, Larry, 252, 253, 254–55, 257,
    268
Dewey, Thomas, 301
Dick, Jim, 321
Diem, Ngo Dinh, 75, 247, 267n
Dietrich, Marlene, 243–44
DiGenova, Joe, 340
Dillon, Douglas, 197
Dine, Tom, 104, 109, 110, 111, 117, 121,
    144, 147, 166
Dole, Bob, 111
Domenici, Pete, 402
domestic spying programs
  of CIA, 85–86, 270, 273, 277, 289,
      329, 335–37
  of NSA, 277–81, 282–83, 338, 339
Donovan, William "Wild Bill," 31
Dorfman, Ira, 376, 377
Douglas, Paul, 68–69
Dragna, Jack, 207
Drury, Allen, 52–53
DuBois, Ed, 212
Duke, Paul, 330, 331
Dulles, Allen, 13, 31, 162, 251
  CIA assassination plots and, 225,
      227, 248, 250, 252, 253
  Kennedy and, 214
  MK-ULTRA and, 285–86
Dulles, John Foster, 227, 248, 251
Durante, Jimmy, 374–75

Eagle, The, 90
Eastland, James, 164
Edwards, Sheffield, 204, 205, 206, 207,
    212, 213, 214

Eichmann, Adolf, 293
Eisenhower, Dwight D., 56, 251
    Church Committee and, 238–39
    CIA and, 12–13, 215–16, 225, 227,
        238, 239, 240, 248, 250, 252–53
    civil rights legislation and, 66
    Congo crisis and, 248, 250, 252–53
    in presidential elections, 41, 43, 52
    Welker's criticism of, 46, 51–52
Eisenhower, John, 238
Eisenhower Administration, 56, 257
    Church Committee and, 227, 236, 247
    civil rights legislation and, 57
    Idaho Power Company and, 68
    oil industry and, 148
    Sukarno and, 206
Eizenstat, Stuart E., 378
Elliff, John, 307, 323, 341
Ellsberg, Daniel, 122–23, 157, 267n, 303
Enemies (Weiner), 400
Epstein, Mike, 307–8, 319–20
Ervin, Sam, 119, 165, 276, 405
Escandar, Mario, 367
Estes, Ron, 346–47, 348, 349, 351
Evans, Courtney, 309
Evans, John, 406
Exner, Judith. *See* Campbell, Judith

Face the Nation, 179
Family Jewels report, 157–58, 191, 277,
    279, 280, 298
FBI (Federal Bureau of Investigation),
    242, 342
    Black Panther Party and, 320–24, *322*
    Church Committee's investigation
        of, 5, 6–7, 8, 11–12, 175, 297–99,
        305–8, 313–14, 317–23, 329,
        341–44
    CIA and, 301–2, 335–36
    COINTELPRO program of, 305, 323
    discovery of Campbell's affair with
        Kennedy, 213, 309
    discovery of CIA-Mafia alliance, 213
    Foreign Intelligence Surveillance Act
        and, 383

Giancana and, 221–22
    Hoover's secret files at headquarters
        of, 297–98
    Johnson and, 315–16
    Justice Department's restrictions on
        intelligence operations of, 384
    lack of oversight of, 299
    on Letelier assassination, 263–64
    Levinson and, 126
    Rosselli's murder and, 362–63, 365
    spying on and harassment of King,
        66, 305, 306, 308–9, 310,
        312–15, 316–20, 343
    spying on Kennedy, 302–3
    stolen documents of, revealing
        domestic abuses, 303–4
    targeting anti-war movement, 299, 303
    Watergate and, 156, 304–5
Felker, Clay, 357
Fellini, Federico, 171
Felt, Mark, 304
Fenn, Peter, 59, 61, 80, 86–87, 100, 277,
    280–81, 379, 395
Field, Searle, 354, 355, 356
Fifth Estate, 352, 353
FISA (Foreign Intelligence Surveillance
    Act), 383–84
Fleming, Ian, 139
Fleming, Robert, 250–51
Ford, Gerald, 164, *193*
    assassination attempts on, 5
    Church Committee and, 178, 192–94,
        199–200, 238, 265, 267, 332, 338,
        340, 345, 349–52, 353, 358
    CIA and, 136–37, 161–62, 195–99
    firing of Colby, 332, 333
    nomination of Bush as CIA director,
        349–50, 401
    Olson family and, 290–91, *291*, 295
    Panama Canal and, 384–85
    pardoning of Nixon, 151
    Pike and, 355–56
    in presidential election in 1976, 349,
        353
    reaction to Hersh's story, 161, 162

Ford, Gerald, *(Cont.)*
  Rockefeller Commission and, 192,
    195–99, *198*
  at Welch's funeral service, 351, 352
Ford Administration, 384, 402
  Church Committee and, 178, 192–93,
    199–200, 238, 265, 267, 332, 338,
    340, 345, 349–52, 353, 358
  Pike Committee and, 354, 355, 356
  response to CIA's past abuses, 161–62
  Rockefeller Commission and, 192
Foreign Corrupt Practices Act, 384
Foreign Intelligence Surveillance Act
    (FISA), 383–84
Foreign Relations of the United States, 136
France, 24, 74
Friedman, Maurice, 365
From the Secret Files of J. Edgar Hoover
    (Theoharis), 213
Frost, Robert, 332–33
Fulbright, J. William, 79, 81, 91, 111, 388
  Church and, 79, *82*, 83, 120–21, 122,
    127
  and CIA conspiracy in Chile, 123,
    124, 125, 126, 135, 148
  Pentagon Papers and, 122–23, 124, 125
  Vietnam War and, 79, 81, 82, *82*, 83,
    120, 121, 122
Fulbright hearings, *82*, 82–84, 85, 122
Furth, Amy. *See* Church, Amy Furth

Gabor, Zsa Zsa, 206
Gandy, Helen, 298
Gayler, Noel, 336
Germany, 24, 139
Germond, Jack, 328
Giancana, Sam
  Campbell's affair with, 213, 229,
    232–33, 235–36, 309
  Church Committee and, 216–17,
    219–20, 222, 223, 229, 235–36
  in CIA's assassination plot, 209, *210*,
    210–11, 212, 366
  FBI and, 221–22
  murder of, 217–18, 219–20, 221–23,
    263, 362, 363, 367

Gilpatric, Roswell, 227
Gitenstein, Mark, 297–98, 305, 307
Glasby, John, 52
Glenn, John, 385
Godfrey, Arthur, 211
Goldberg, Rube, 370
Goldwater, Barry, 77, 78, 88
  Church and, 238–39, 240, 244
  Church Committee and, 172, 173,
    174, 194, 216
Golitsyn, Anatoliy, 272, 273
Goodpaster, Andrew, 227
Gore, Albert, Sr., 121
Gospel Hump Wilderness, 70
Gottlieb, Sidney, 253–54, 268, 284–85,
    286–89, 290, 291–94, *293*,
    295
Government by Investigation (Light), 405
Graham, Katherine, 303–4
Gray, Gordon, 227, 253
Gray, L. Patrick, 304–5
Greece, political climate in the mid-
    1970s in, 347–48
Greenfield, John, 151
Griffin, Robert, 113
Gruening, Ernest, 97
Guardian, The, 105
Guatemala, 12, 215, 248
Guevara, Che, 214
Gulf of Tonkin Resolution, 78, 114
gun control, 143–44, 390, 394
Guthman, Edwin, 313

Haig, Alexander, 260, 261
Haldeman, H. R., 113
Hall, Bill, 374
Hampton, Fred, 320–23, *321*, *322*
Handsome Johnny (Server), 209, 365
Hansen, George, 98–99, 100, 432n
Harriman, Averell, 76
Harrington, Michael, 135
Hart, Gary, 194, 215
  appointment to Church Committee,
    173, 175
  frustration with committee
    members' publicity-seeking, 242

on Goldwater's criticism of Church
Committee, 240
investigation of CIA, 173, 176–77,
201, 202, 231, 256, 260, 268,
271
investigation of Rosselli's murder,
177, 363–64
on Rosselli's testimony, 224
warning to Ted Kennedy about
Campbell discovery, 236–37
Hart, Peter, 392, 394, 395
Hart, Philip, 164–65, 173, *174*, 235,
343–44
Harvey, William, 214–15
Haughton, Dan, 138
Hearst, Patricia, 5
Hedgman, Victor, 268
Hells Canyon Dam, 57, 67–69
Hells Canyon National Recreation
Area, 70
Helms, Richard, 336, 400
Angleton and, 161
background of, 31, 130, 176
Church and, 130–31, 257, 334
Church Committee testimony of,
226–27, 258, 260, 333–34, 338
and CIA conspiracy in Chile, 123,
124, 130–34, *132*, 135, 147, 257,
258, 261, 334
Justice Department's prosecution of,
130, 136
MK-ULTRA and, 286
Nixon and, 131, 156, 157, 287
Hemingway, Ernest, 386
Hempstone, Smith, 352
Hendricks, Richard, 98
Henry II, 226
Hersh, Sy
background of, 135
interview with Olson family, 290
reporting on CIA's domestic abuses,
159–61, 162, 163, 164, 190–91,
192, 195, 196, 270, 272, 289,
400
Watergate and, 158, 159
Hills, Roderick, 354

Hiss, Alger, 302
Hitler, Adolf, 22, 25, 271, 302
Ho Chi Minh, 74, 77
Hoffa, Jimmy, 7, 72
Hollings, Fritz, 117
Holt, Pat, 123, 124, 125, 126, 127
Hoover, J. Edgar, 278, 303, 324, 364
Black Panther Party and, 320
Church and, 299–301
death of, 298, 304
as foe of CIA, 301–2
Huston Plan and, 336
Johnson and, 315–16, 319
Kennedys and, 213, 302, 303,
309–10, 319
monitoring of King, 308–9, 312–13,
314, 316
personal life of, 303
press and, 303–4
secret files of, 297–98, 307
Truman and, 301
House Armed Services subcommittee
on intelligence. *See* Pike
Committee
House Un-American Activities
Committee (HUAC), 302
Housman, A. E., 28
Hower, Ward, 58
HT-LINGUAL, 273
Huddleston, Walter "Dee," 173, *174*
Hughes, Howard, 204, 205
Hughes-Ryan Act, 163
Humphrey, Hubert, 141–42, 149, 165,
175, 376, 379, 380
Hunt, E. Howard, 157, 243, 304–5
Hunt, Lester, 48–51, 53, 159
Hunt, Lester, Jr., 48, 49, 50, 51
Hunter, Susan, 369, 387, 390
Huston, Tom, 335–36
Huston Plan, 273, 329, 335–37

"I Have a Dream" speech (King), 311
Idaho, 18–19, 30n, 38, 69–70, 81–82,
89–90
Idaho Law Review, 107
Idaho Power Company, 68, 69

Idaho State Journal, 105
Idaho Statesman, 93
Inderfurth, Rick, 262, 263, 363, 364
Indonesia, 139
Inside the Company (Agee), 352
Internal Revenue Service, 318, 372
Ioannidis, Dimitrios, 347–48
Iran, 12, 148–49, 215, 248
Iran-Contra scandal, 400, 401, 403
Iranian hostage crisis, 389, 396
Israel, 148, 152, 271
ITT, 123–29, 131–32, 134–35, 147, 148,
    149, 257–58, 280

Jackson, Henry, 149, 375–76, 378
Jacoby, Glenn "Red," 50
Japan
    Lockheed bribery scandal in, 139,
        140–41
    World War II and, 10, 32, 35, 173
Japanese Americans, internment of, 30n
Javits, Jacob, 141–42, 149
Jefferson, Arthur, 320, 321–24
Jenkins, Walter, 315
John Birch Society, 91, 153, 154
Johnson, Leena, *181*
Johnson, Loch, 6, 180–81, *181*, 188,
    199, 239, 244, 272–74, 358
Johnson, Lyndon Baines, 88, 98, 103,
    382
    Church and, 10, 54–55, 58, 59, 64,
        65, 66–67, 71, 73, 76–77, 77, 79,
        80–81, 85, 89, 101, 104, 231
    CIA and, 239
    civil rights legislation and, 54,
        55–56, 57, 65, 66, 67, 68, 316
    Hoover and, 315–16, 319
    as vice president, 72, 76
    Vietnam War and, 76, 78, 79, 80, 81,
        82, 83, 85, 94–95, 114
Johnson, Robert, 252–53
Johnson Administration, 79, 83, 100,
    247
Jones, Tom, 138
Juliana, Queen, 139
jury-trial amendment, 65–66

Justice Department, 148, 229
    FBI and, 307, 314, 320, 363, 384
    on Giancana's murder, 222–23
    Helm and, 130, 136
    ITT-CIA conspiracy and, 124
    NSA and, 280

Karalekas, Anne, 359–60
Karamessines, Thomas, 260, 262
Katleman, Beldon, 206
Katzenbach, Nicholas, 311
Kefauver Committee, 207, 208–9
Kelley, Clarence, 362
Kempster, Norman, 353
Kennedy, John F.
    assassination of, 76, 177, 197, 215,
        236, 271, 272, 314
    Campbell's affair with, 213, 229–31,
        232–34, 235–37, 303, 309
    Castro and, 214, 215, 216, 224–26
    Church and, 10, 66, *71*, 71–73,
        75–76, 230, 231, 248, 251,
        327-28–328, 404
    CIA and, 13, 214, 215, 216, 224–25,
        226, 227, 228, 239
    civil rights legislation and, 311, 313
    Congo crisis and, 248, 251
    Cuban Missile Crisis and, 74
    Dietrich and, 243
    FBI's spying on, 302–3
    Hoover and, 213, 302, 303, 309–10,
        313
    in presidential election of 1960, 3,
        71, 72–73
    Vietnam War and, 74
Kennedy, Joseph, Sr., 243
Kennedy, Robert F., 72, 111
    assassination of, 98, 236, 319
    autopsy of, 298
    Hoover and, 213, 303, 310, 319
    King wiretaps and, 310, 313, 314,
        315, 319
    presidential campaign in 1968, 3, 319
Kennedy, Ted, 216, 295
    Campbell and, 236–37
    Carter and, 382

Chappaquiddick scandal of, 165, 236
Church and, *393*, 398, 404
Congo and, 248
1976 presidential election and, 244
Kennedy Administration, 76, 183, 313
Castro and, 216, 227–28
Church Committee and, 227–28,
236, 237, 327
Hoover and, 213, 310
Operation *Mongoose,* 227
Vietnam War and, 75
Kent State shootings, 109–10, 122, 335
KGB, 205, 272, 277, 347, 380
Kimelman, Henry, 112–13, 181–82,
358–59, 375, 377
King, Carole, 70
King, Martin Luther, Jr.
assassination of, 98, 318
civil rights campaign of, 57, 311–12
extramarital affairs of, 314, 316
FBI's campaign of spying on and
harassing, 66, 305, 306–9, 310,
312–15, 316–20, 343
"I Have a Dream" speech of, 311
"Letter from Birmingham Jail," 311
March on Washington and, 311, 317
Nobel Peace Prize awarded to,
316–17
NSA's spying on, 338
opposition to Vietnam War, 318
Kinzer, Stephen, 285
Kirbo, Charles, 378–79
Kirbow, Charles, 189
Kissinger, Henry, 147, 161–62, 196
Chile and, 258
Church and, 104, 113, 147–48, 339,
402
Church Committee and, 260–61,
338, 339
Ford and, 192
Levinson and, 136
Pinochet and, 263
Rockefeller Commission and, 197, 199
at Welch's funeral service, 351, 352
Kleindienst, Richard, 125
Kodama, Yoshio, 140–41

Korean War, 275
Kornbluh, Peter, 263
Ku Klux Klan, 342
KYP (Greek intelligence service), 348,
349

Lansky, Meyer, 365
LaRocco, Larry, 63, 70, 394
Lashbrook, Robert, 287, 288
Latham, Aaron, 357
League of Conservation Voters, 98
League of Nations, 22, 24
Legacy of Ashes (Weiner), 400
Lemnitzer, Lyman, 197
Lennon, John, 331
Lenzner, Terry, 284, 292, *293*, 293–94
Letelier, Orlando, 262–63, 362
"Letter from Birmingham Jail" (King),
311
Levi, Edward, 281–82, 291, 362–63
Levinson, Jerry, 103, 149
Church and, 126, 127, 136, 155, 244
Subcommittee on Multinational
Corporations and, 126–27, 129,
131–32, 134–36, 137, 138, 148
Levison, Stanley, 308, 310, 313
Lewis, Anthony, 353
Lewiston Tribune, 219
Liberace, 111
Liebengood, Howard, 189, 363–64
Light, Paul, 405
Lincoln, Evelyn, 309
Lindbergh, Charles, 24–25
Lippmann, Walter, 80
Lockheed, 138–39, 140, 141, 148
Longworth, Alice Roosevelt, 22–23
Lower Granite Dam, 219
LSD, 285, 286–88, 289–90, 295
Luce, Carolyn Buck, 406–7
Luciano, Lucky, 234
Lumumba, Patrice, 176, 247–48, *249,*
249–50, 251–57, 268, 285

MacLeish, Archibald, 31
Madigan, Mike, 189, 223, 362, 363–64
Maeno, Mitsuyasu, 140–41

Mafia-CIA alliance, 203, 204, 206–7, *208*, 209–12, 213, 214–15, 222, 366
  Church Committee's investigation into, 209–10, 215, 221, 224–25, 229–34, 235–36, 268
  FBI's discovery of, 303
Maheu, Robert, 204–5, 206–7, 209–10, 211–13, 231, 268
mail-opening program of CIA, 273, 289, 337
Man Who Kept the Secrets, The (Powers), 400
Manatos, Mike, 48, 162–64
Mansfield, Mike, 113, 117, *150*
  background of, 149–50
  Church and, 150, 165, 166, 172, 190, 220, 244, 245, 257, 368, 369
  Church Committee and, 164–65, 172, 173, 174–75, 190, 269, 343
  Hart and, 242
  Senate Watergate Committee and, 118–19
March on Washington (1963), 311, 317
Marchetti, Victor, 295
Marcy, Carl, 121, 127
Marks, John, 295
Marsh, Jack, 200
Marshall, Burke, 183–84, 313–14
Mathias, Charles, 122, 172, 173, 226–27
Maurice, Ronald, 48
Maxwell, Elliot, 292–93, 294–96
McCarthy, Eugene, 80
McCarthy, Joseph, 42–43, 48–49, 120, 162, 302
McCarthy, Leo, 370
McCarthyism, 42–43, 44, 46, 48
McClellan, John, 134–35
McClellan Committee, 72, 120
McClure, Robert, 34, 35–36
McCone, John, 123, 136–37
McGovern, George, 122, 165, 173, 181, 303, *393*, 394, 396
McGovern-Hatfield Amendment, 114
McGuire, Phyllis, 212

McMurray, John, 93
McNamara, Pat, 120
McNamara, Robert, 227
Meany, George, 340
Medsger, Betty, 303, 304
Meet the Press, 111, 239, 282, 402
Mellon, Paul, 31
Metternich, Klemens von, 147
Michel, Paul, 6, 190, 341–42
Mileck, Gene, 88, 91
Miller, Bill, 110, 339, 360
  background of, 182, 184–85
  on Church's as chair of Church Committee, 165, 166
  on Cooper-Church Amendments, 111, 113
  on leak of Campbell's identity, 241
  Schwarz and, 184, 186–89, 202, 275, 359
  as staff director for Church Committee, 109, 173, 182, 183, 184, 185–89, 232, 275
Miller, Russell, 403, 404
MINARET program, 280–81, 282, 338
mind-control programs, 13, 285, 286–96
Minidoka internment camp, 30n
Minium, Gary, 361, 364
Mitchell, John, 258, 336
Mitchell, Parren, 303
MK-ULTRA program, 285, 286–96
Moffitt, Ronni, 263
Mondale, Walter, 179
  as Carter's running mate, 175, 379–80
  as Church Committee member, 173, *174*, 175, 184, 187, 200, 216, 237, 242, 297, 305, 321, 341, 359, 379, 405
Montgomery bus boycott, 57
Moore, Frank, 385, 388
Morgan, Robert, 173, 225
Morgenthau, Hans, 79, 106
Morse, Wayne, 91
Mossadeq, Mohammad, 148
Moyers, Bill, 316
Mulroney, Michael, 268

Multinational Corporations, Senate
    Subcommittee on, 126–28,
    134–35, 147–48, 163
  abolishment of, 142
  Helms and, 130–34, *132*, 135, 149,
    334
  public hearings of, 137–39, 140, 141
  reforms stemming form, 383
Muskie, Edmund, 116, 380

National Conservative Political Action
    Committee (NCPAC), 394
National Security Act of 1947, 157,
    301
National Security Agency (NSA). *See*
    NSA (National Security Agency)
National Security Council, 148, 237,
    248, 252
National Wild and Scenic Rivers Act of
    1968, 69
NBC, 129
Nedzi, Lucien, 190–91, 192, 354
Nehru, Jawaharlal, 108
Nelson, Bryce, 23, 171, 299, 300
Nelson, Gaylord, 122, 171, 397
Nessen, Ron, 290
Netherlands, 139–40
New York Daily News, 47
New York Times, 8, 91, 149, 292
  on Forrest Church's scandal, 406–7
  Frank Church and, 79, 92, 182, 328
  Fulbright and, 121
  Hersh and, 158, 159–61, 163,
    190–91, 195, 289
  King's interview with, 308
  Multinational Corporations
    subcommittee and, 129
  on Nedzi, 191
  Pentagon Papers and, 122–23, 125
  on Welch's murder, 347, 353
New York Times Magazine, 81
Newman, Paul, 111, 375
Nixon, Richard, 54, 103, 147, 338, 376
  appointment of Schlesinger as CIA
    director, 156
  Church and, 104, 105, 115, 118

  Church Committee and, 216, 261, 335
  FBI and, 302, 304
  Helms and, 131, 156, 157, 287
  Huston Plan and, 335, 336
  ITT-CIA conspiracy and, 124–25,
    128–29
  in presidential elections, 72, 73, 101,
    131, 137
  resignation of, 136, 151, 159, 160
  use of CIA's covert-action arm of, 13,
    128, 129, 131, 239, 258, 260,
    261–62, 335, 336
  Vietnam War and, 11, 104–5, 109,
    113, 114, 115–16, 122
  Watergate scandal and, 128, 131, 137,
    151, 156, 158, 179, 193, 304,
    305, 331, 333, 350
Nixon Administration, 106, 116, 147
  Cambodia and, 185
  and CIA's covert activities in Chile,
    123, 124, 129, 130, 133, 135,
    247, 257, 258, 262, 263
  Huston Plan and, 273, 329
  Watergate and, 157
North Korea, 192, 275
Northrop Corporation, 137–38
Nosenko, Yuri, 272, 273
NSA (National Security Agency)
  Church Committee's investigation of,
    5, 6–7, 8, 11–12, 178, 276–83, 338
  domestic-spying operations of,
    277–81, 282–83, 338, 339
  Foreign Intelligence Surveillance Act
    and, 383
  MINARET program and, 280–81,
    282, 338
  Rockefeller Commission and,
    279–80, 289
  SHAMROCK program and, 277–79,
    280, 282
  Snowden's leaking of documents of,
    404

Obama, Barack, 404
Obama Administration, 404
Occupational Health and Safety Act, 153

O'Connell, Jim, 205, 206, 207, 209, 210, 212, 214
O'Dell, Jack, 308, 310
O'Donnell, Justin, 255–56, 257, 268
O'Donnell, Kenneth, 213, 234
Office of Strategic Services (OSS), 30–31
O'Flaherty, Daniel, 242
oil industry, 148–49, 153, 155
Ojeda, Julio, 361, 362, 364–65, 366–67
Olmsted, Kathryn, 400
Olson, Alice, 290–91, *291*
Olson, Eric, 288, 290, 295
Olson, Frank, 287–88, 289–91, 294, 295
On Press (Wicker), 64
O'Neal, William, 320, 321
Ono, Yoko, 331
Operation Chaos, 273, 289
Operation Condor, 264
Operation *Mongoose*, 227
Orta, Juan, 211, 212
Overseas Private Investment Corporation, 134
Oxbow Incident, 69

Panama Canal, 384–86, 393, 394
Paris Peace Accords in 1973, 116
Parks, Rosa, 57
Patrick, William Penn, 91, 92, 432n
Paul VI, 317–18
Pearl Harbor, 29
Pearson, Drew, 48, 50, 67, 159, 319, 340
Pentagon Papers, 122–23, 124, 125, 157, 267n, 303
Percy, Charles, 149
Peter Kornbluh, The (Kornbluh), 263
Philby, Kim, 272
Phillips, David, 201–2, 340–41
Pierce, Samuel, 315
Pike, Otis, 191–92, 352, 354–56
Pike Committee, 190–92, 242, 344, 354–56, 357, 358, 360
Pink Sheet, The, 352–53
Pinochet, Augusto, 262, 263–64
Playboy, 105–6
Poisoner in Chief (Kinzer), 285
Poorit, Orville, 27

Postal, Andy, 229–31, 233–34, 241, 342, 343, 364
Pound, Ezra, 271–72
Powers, Thomas, 400
presidential emergency orders, 185
Proxmire, William, 161
Puzzle Palace, The (Bamford), 281

QJ-WIN (European hit man), 176–77, 256
Quanbeck, Alton, 275–76

Radio Free Europe, 41–42
Ramparts, 78–79
Rankin, Ron, 87–89, 90–91, 92, 431n
Rather, Dan, 242
RCA Global, 280
Reagan, Nancy, 391
Reagan, Ronald, 70, 87, 91, 300, 397, 398
    Panama Canal and, 385
    in presidential elections, 349, 353, 391, 392, 394, 395–96
    as Rockefeller Commission member, 192, 195, 197
Reagan Administration, 400
Redford, Robert, 5
Restricting Handguns, 390
Reuther, Walter, 120
Reynolds, Nancy Clark, 391–92
Richard, Eric, 277, 280–81
Richardson, Elliot, 113
Ritchie Boys, 31–32
River of No Return Wilderness, 70, 398
Robinson Bar Ranch, 70
Rock, Chris, 243
Rockefeller, Nelson, 192, 195–96, 197–98, *198*, 289
Rockefeller Commission, 192, 195–99, 200, 277, 279–80, 289–90, 291, 344
Rogovin, Mitchell, 4, 6, *330*, 339
Rolling Stone, 158, 351
Roosevelt, Franklin, 22, 24, 25, 30n, 37, 41, 301, 386
Roosevelt, Teddy, 23
Rosenthal, Abe, 159, 195–96

Rosselli, Johnny
  background of, 207–9
  Church Committee and, *208*, 210,
    223–24, 232–35, 236, 268,
    361–64, 365, 366
  in CIA's assassination plot, 206–7,
    209–11, 212, 213, 214–15, 223,
    236, 268
  Kefauver Committee and, 208–9
  murder of, 361–67
Rostow, Walt, 146
Rowan, Dan, 212–13
Rowe, Gary Thomas, Jr., 342–43
Rumsfeld, Donald, 162, 192
Rusk, Dean, 77, 83, 227
Russell, Richard, 64, 162–63, 196
Ruwet, Vincent, 288

Sacco, Filippo. *See* Rosselli, Johnny
Safire, William, 178, 241
Sagebrush Rebellion, 68, 70, 152
Salt II treaty, 389
Salt Lake Tribune, 63
Samuelson, Don, 89
Saudi Arabia, 139, 148
Sawtooth National Recreation Area, 70
Scheider, Joseph, 268
Schlesinger, James, 134, 135, 156–58,
    160, 191, 281–82
Schmitz, Dave, 121
Schneider, Rene, 247, 258–60, 261–62,
    276
Schorr, Daniel, 196, 351–52, 356–57
Schwarz, F. A. O. "Fritz," 200, 239
  background of, 183–84, 186–87
  on Church, 171–72, 231
  as Church Committee's chief counsel,
    4, *174*, 182, *183*, 184, 186–89,
    195, 199, 201, 202, 233, 237, 266,
    271, 275, 282, 313, 329–30, *330*,
    339, 341–43, 358, 369
  Democracy in the Dark, 199
  on Lezner, 284
  Miller and, 184, 186–89, 202, 275, 359
  nickname of *Toys*, 183
  on Pike Committee, 355

Schweiker, Richard, 172, *174*, 177,
    293–94, 337
Scott, Hugh, 128, 172–73, 178
Scowcroft, Brent, 136
Search for the Manchurian Candidate, The
    (Marks), 295
Season of Inquiry, A (Johnson), 199
Secades, Rolando Cubela, 215
Securities and Exchange Commission
    (SEC), 137
segregation, 57, 66
Senate Armed Services Committee,
    162–63, 276, 350
Senate Foreign Relations Committee
  Borah as chairman of, 23
  Church as chairman of, 388–89
  Church as member of, 67, 77, 81, *82*,
    82–84, 85
  Fulbright as chairman of, 79,
    120–21, 122
  Kissinger and, 147–48
  Subcommittee on Multinational
    Corporations. *See* Multinational
    Corporations, Senate
    Subcommittee on
  Vietnam War and, 77, 81, *82*
Senate Judiciary Committee, 125
Senate Select Committee to Study
    Governmental Operations with
    Respect to Intelligence Activities.
    See Church Committee
Senate Watergate Committee, 128, 160,
    328, 405
  creation of, 118–19, 165, 172
  hearings of, 330, 331
  Huston Plan and, 335
  office of, 189, 284
September 11, 2001, attacks, 401–2, 403
17 November (Greek leftist guerrilla
    organization), 348
SHAMROCK program, 277–79, 280, 282
Shea, Patrick, 388
  Brando and, 243
  Campbell and, 232, 241
  Colby and, 332–33
  on Forrest Church's affair, 375

Shea, Patrick, *(Cont.)*
  on Giancana's murder, 216–17, 220
  Rather and, 242
  Rosselli and, 223–24
Shephard, Alan, 93
Shriver, Sarge, 165
Simpson, Alan, 398
Sinatra, Frank, 213, 237
60 Minutes, 242, 357
Smathers, George, 60, 225–26
Smathers, Rosemary, 60–61
Smith, Robert L., 152–53, 154–55, 390
Smith, Will, 243
Smothers, Curt, *174*, 189, 230, 233,
  330, *331*, 343
Snider, Britt, 276–80, 282
Snow, Herbert, 93
Snowden, Edward, 404
South Idaho Press, 145
Southern Christian Leadership
  Conference, 311, 313, 317, 318
Soviet Union, 56, 275
  CIA's efforts to spy on, 161, 163, 227,
    238
  Congo crisis and, 250, 252
  Kissinger and, 147
  Salt II treaty and, 389
Sparkman, John, 388
Spellman, Francis, 318
Spokesman-Review, 45
Sporkin, Stanley, 137
Springsteen, Bruce, 7
St. Louis Post-Dispatch, The, 114
Stahl, Lesley, 357
Stein, John, 177
Stennis, John, 165
Stern, Carl, 304
Steunenberg, Frank, 18
Stevens, Sayre, 6
Stewart, Gordon, 337–38
Stewart, Potter, 113
Stimson, Henry, 30
Sukarno, 205–6
Sullivan, William, 306, 308, 312–13,
  314–15, 316, 317, 318, 319–20, 336
Supreme Court, 57, 99, 193

Sweeney, Louise, 221
Symington, Stuart, 121, 127–28, 134
Symms, Steve, 152, 155, 390–91, 392,
  394–95, 396, 397, 398, 406

Tanaka, Kakuei, 140, 141
Taylor, Carolyn, 62n, 63
Taylor, Glen, 44–46, 47, 52, 53, 62, 63, 64
Taylor, Maxwell, 227
Taylor, Valorie, 62n
Tet Offensive, 94–95
Thames, George, 165
Theoharis, Athan, 213
Thornburgh, Richard, 222–23
Three Days of the Condor, 5
Thuermer, Angus, 222
Tierney, Jack. *See* Barnes, Jack
Timberlake, Claire, 250
Time magazine, 314
Times-News (Twin Falls), 51, 300, 393
Tolson, Clyde, 303
Tordella, Louis, 278–79, 282
"Torment in the Land, The" speech
  (Church), 94, 95–97
Tower, John, 4, 5, 172–73, *174*, 178,
  179, 189, 200, 201, 202, 238,
  242, 268, 282
Townley, Michael, 264
Trafficante, Santo, Jr., 210–11, 212, 214,
  268, 366
Trujillo, Rafael, 247
Truman, Harry, 41, 44, 301
Trump, Donald, 340, 404
"Tuft of Flowers, The" (Frost), 332–33
Turkey, 347–48
Turner, Stansfield, 384
Twin Falls Times-News, 393

Udall, Morris, 165, 369, 375, 377
United Farm Workers, 154
Unna, Warren, 123, 124

Varona, Anthony, 212, 214–15
Veterans Against Communist
  Sympathizers, 352
Viaux, Roberto, 259, 260

Victory in Vietnam Committee, 88–89
Viet Cong, 74, 82, 94
Vietnam War
  American attitudes about, 81–82,
    83–84, 178, 179
  Case-Church Amendment on, 115
  Church's opposition to, 7, 10–11,
    74–77, 78–85, 87, 88–89, 90, 91,
    92, 93, 94, 95–97, 100, 101, 103–4,
    105, 106–8, 109, 116, 300, 393
  Cooper-Church Amendments on,
    108–9, 110, 113–15
  Cronkite's report on, 97
  Fulbright hearings on, 82, 82–84, 85,
    120, 122
  Johnson and, 76, 78, 79, 80, 81, 82,
    83, 85, 94–95, 114
  Kennedy and, 74
  King's opposition to, 318
  McGovern-Hatfield Amendment on,
    114
  Nixon and, 11, 104–5, 109, 113, 114,
    115–16, 122
  Paris Peace Accords and, 116, 118
  Tet Offensive during, 94–95
  Vietnamization in, 104–5
Village Voice, 356, 357
voting rights, 66

Wachtel, Harry, 317
Wall Street Journal, 129
Wallace, George, 311
Wallace, Henry, 37, 44, 45, 56, 62
Wallace, Mike, 357
Warren Commission, 177, 197
Washington Evening Star, 77
Washington Post, 129, 303–4, 357, 402
Watergate Committee, Senate. *See*
    Senate Watergate Committee
Watergate scandal, 151, 178, 193, 243, 329
  CIA involvement in, 156–57, 160
  FBI investigation of, 304–5
  reporters' investigation of, 158–59
  Senate Watergate Committee on,
    118–19, 128, 160, 165, 172, 189,
    284, 328, 330–31, 335, 405

Waters, Robert, 138
Weiner, Tim, 400
Welch, Kika, 346, 351
Welch, Richard, 346–47, 349–50,
    351–53, 358, 359, 371, 401
Welker, Herman, 395
  blackmail scheme against Hunt, 48,
    49–51, 159
  Church and, 42, 43, 46, 47–48, 51,
    392
  death of, 52–53
  drinking and erratic behavior of,
    46–47, 53
  in Senate elections, 42, 43, 44, 45,
    46, 47–48, 51–52, 64, 392
Wenske, Garry, 383, 386
West Germany, 139
Western Union International, 280
Wetherell, Mike, 116, 155, 219
  as Church's campaign aid, 145, 154,
    244–45, 370–71, 373
  on Church's meeting with Carter,
    380
  as Church's Senate chief of staff, 382,
    385–86
White, George Hunter, 286–87
Whitson, Lish, 319–20
Wicker, Tom, 64, 196, 338
Wides, Burt, 235
Wikileaks, 404
Williams, Dan, 406
Williams, Edward Bennett, 206
WI-ROGUE, 256
Wisner, Frank, 286
Women's National Democratic Club, 6
Woodward, Bob, 158–59
World War II, 24–25, 30, 30n, 31–32, 49
World Wildlife Fund, 139

Young, Andrew, 317
Young, Whitney, 338

Zatrepalek, Charles, 360, 361, 362,
    364–65, 366–67
Zelizer, Julian, 116
Zerilli, Tony, 365

About the Authors

James Risen is a two-time Pulitzer Prize–winning journalist and author. Throughout his career, Risen's explosive investigative reporting has triggered a series of political firestorms. Among his bestselling books are *State of War: The Secret History of the CIA and the Bush Administration* and *Pay Any Price: Greed, Power, and Endless War.* He lives in the Washington, D.C., area with his wife.

Thomas Risen has spent years reporting on U.S. politics and national security, including the intelligence community, digital surveillance, and the War on Terror. He currently works as an aviation journalist and lives in the Washington, D.C., area with his wife and daughter.